Lab Lit

Lab Lit

Exploring Literary and Cultural Representations of Science

Edited by Olga A. Pilkington and Ace G. Pilkington

LEXINGTON BOOKS
Lanham • Boulder • New York • London

Published by Lexington Books
An imprint of The Rowman & Littlefield Publishing Group, Inc.
4501 Forbes Boulevard, Suite 200, Lanham, Maryland 20706
www.rowman.com

6 Tinworth Street, London SE11 5AL

British Library Cataloguing in Publication Information Available

Library of Congress Control Number: 2019913681

ISBN 978-1-4985-6598-1 (cloth)
ISBN 978-1-4985-6600-1 (pbk.)
ISBN 978-1-4985-6599-8 (electronic)

Contents

Preface   vii
Olga A. Pilkington and Ace G. Pilkington

Introduction: What's in a Name?   1
Olga A. Pilkington

1   *Frankenstein*, Scientism, and the Cultural Reception of Discovery   13
Amanda Scott

2   Female Scientists Under Strain: Transitions from Lab to Lit to Screen   29
Dean Conrad and Lynne Magowan

3   Lab Lit and Science Fiction: Similarities and Separations   51
Ace G. Pilkington

4   Lab Lit and Popular Science   63
Olga A. Pilkington

5   Where Science Meets Fiction: A History and Theory of Laboratory Production   79
Matt Hadley

6   The Use of Forensic Techniques to Uncover Social Disorder in Caleb Carr's Alienist Novels   99
Kimberley H. Idol

7   Barbara Kingsolver's *Flight Behavior*: The Sciences in a Post-Fact World   113
Theda Wrede

8 The Short Fiction of Andrea Barrett: Lab Lit as Sociology of
Science   141
Stephanie Chidester

9 The Honest Look at Science and Poetry   175
Elaine Pearce

10 Addressing the Gender Gap in STEM through Theater   185
Eileen Trauth and Suzanne Trauth

11 Using Science in Writing Mystery Novels   197
Beverly Connor

12 Lab Lit: Illuminating a Hidden World through the Medium of
Fiction   211
Jennifer L. Rohn

Conclusion: Lab Lit: Teaching Accessible Science   241
Olga A. Pilkington

Index   255

About the Contributors   261

About the Editors   265

Preface

Olga A. Pilkington and Ace G. Pilkington

Laboratory literature (lab lit) is a genre of literary fiction that has been steadily gaining popularity for the last thirty years. However, while the influences of science on literature and literature on science have been subjects of vibrant scholarly discussions, there has not yet been a comprehensive investigation of lab lit in a single volume.

As a critical look at the genre, our collection of essays covers a range of topics from the historical development of lab lit to its relationship with science fiction to representations of gender. The aim of this work is to formalize the name for the genre and to promote critical recognition. While the interest in the crossover between literature and science has increased in recent decades and manifested itself in a variety of publications ranging from journal articles to scholarly monographs, no systematic critical investigation has come from those literary studies. The social sciences have done a fine job documenting the history and the philosophical underpinnings of science and the non-fiction and fiction it inspired. Multiple monographs and edited collections will attest to that. However, literary studies have so far shied away from exploring the "intruder" in their midst.

This collection is different. The contributors are well versed in literary studies *and* sciences, thus offering unique approaches that illuminate both through the intricate interplay of the issues raised in lab lit. The essays here look at literary fictions while exploring scientific facts—they embrace the creative nature of the texts analyzed and look at science through the prism of imagination.

We discuss historical developments of lab lit (see Amanda Scott's, Kimberley Idol's, and Matt Hadley's essays) and offer literary analyses which use the elements of ecocriticism, feminism, and sociology of science (see essays by Eileen Trauth and Suzanne Trauth, Elaine Pearce, Theda Wrede, and Stephanie Chidester). We also look at the process of creating lab lit (see Beverly Connor's essay) and explore lab lit's relationships with science fiction (see Ace Pilkington's essay) and popular science (see Olga Pilkington's essay).

The book includes eleven chapters and a case study section, which introduces a new short story by Jennifer Rohn along with the author's explications.

Intended for an audience interested in new developments in literature and literary criticism as well as new directions in science, this is a collection that will also appeal to any educated reader. Social scientists will enjoy the new ways in which lab lit presents and shapes the realities of daily laboratory life. Professional scientists will have a chance to look at themselves through the mirror of the imagination and, perhaps, will discover new dimensions of their own identities. Educators will be able to use this collection as a starting point for teaching lab lit in the classroom.

If you have spent hours doing bench work or have never visited a laboratory, we invite you on a tour that will make you understand more fully what it means to dedicate a life to science.

Introduction

What's in a Name?

Olga A. Pilkington

It is, perhaps, part of human nature to think in binary—on or off, either/or, right or wrong. It is no wonder therefore that academic disciplines and, in more general terms, spheres of human inquiry are often presented in opposition to each other. One is either a scientist or a scholar; one's work is either fact or fiction, and if one writes about science, it is either popularization or science fiction. But for a long time there has existed a third, albeit less known and less critically acclaimed, option. This book is dedicated to illuminating this genre with the critical insight of experts who are familiar with both science and literature.

Up until the beginning of the twenty-first century, there was no name for a genre of literature that dealt with science in its present state, unembellished by the brilliant possibilities of the future. When Charles Sheffield, the only person ever to be president of both the Science Fiction Writers of America and the American Astronautical Society, defined science fiction, he wrote, "Science fiction consists of stories set on the shore or out in the shallow coastal water of that huge scientific land mass. Stay inland, safe above high tide, and your story will be not science fiction, but fiction about science. Stray too far, out of sight of land, and you are in danger of writing fantasy— even if you think it's science fiction."[1] His definition is insightful and in the process of explaining science fiction also explicates fantasy and that other genre—"fiction about science." Note that Sheffield is not using the phrase "fiction about science" as a name for a genre, the way he does with "science fiction" and "fantasy." However, even without giving it a proper name, he correctly identifies the purpose and the main objective of that third branch of writing connected to science. It is a genre that invites an exploration not in

1

binary terms of science or literature but in tandem—science as a subject matter and an inspiration *for* literature. This genre has been developing since the nineteenth century when professional and amateur science cultures started coming into existence and being written about. But only recently did it get a name and recognition as a separate and self-contained branch of fiction.

Lab lit (Lab Lit, lablit, or lab-lit) is short for Laboratory Literature. As the spelling variations indicate, the name is still in the process of being formalized, but in this book, we and our contributors will use "lab lit," as we attempt to settle not only the matter of the name and definition but also give this genre much-needed critical recognition. The term was coined in 2001 by Jennifer Rohn,[2] a cell biologist and novelist based at University College London, who is a contributor to this collection. Earlier attempts at defining the genre include the name "science-in-fiction" proposed by Carl Djerassi, a scientist—the inventor of the birth control pill—and a prominent novelist. In the foreword to *The Bourbaki Gambit*—a novel "that concentrates the unforgivingly bright light of contemporary life on today's scientists"—Djerassi explains, "I call my genre 'science-in-fiction' to distinguish it from science fiction."[3]

Lab lit, according to Rohn's definition, is "a small but growing genre of literary fiction (or other fiction media) in which scientific characters, activities or themes are portrayed in a realistic manner."[4] The words "realistic manner" are key to understanding this genre. As Rohn and other novelists/scientists attempt to place their works within genre definitions, they inevitably contrast what they write with science fiction. Kirk Smith explains, "Science fiction is always about the future, whereas fiction about science is often set in the present—even in the past, as in the case of fictionalized biographies."[5] Rohn agrees that lab lit "is distinct from science fiction, in which the actions take place in speculative worlds."[6] Lab lit is about current science or science that is just coming into existence, and when a lab lit author writes about, let's say, an environmental problem (as Barbara Kingsolver does in *Flight Behavior*), her setting is recognizable as the present day. In dealing with today's science, lab lit often teaches its fundamentals. Katherine Bouton, writing for the *New York Times*, notes that in Kingsolver's novel, the reader "gets some basic ecology."[7] As Theda Wrede's essay demonstrates, Kingsolver's reader also gets some idea of what it is like to be a scientist in a post-fact world, where even the most basic scientific truths are received with skepticism.

There is an obvious connection between the two genres, as many authors who are mostly known for their science fiction works also contribute to lab lit. Alan Lightman with his novel *Einstein's Dreams* is an example. It is also easy to see how hard science fiction could overlap with lab lit. Gregory

Benford's *Timescape* and *Cosm* are good examples. Ace G. Pilkington's essay explores this topic in more detail.

With the popularity, critical recognition, and the fan base that science fiction has acquired, it is not surprising that lab lit is seen and defined in connection with the mega-genre. Some might even suggest that lab lit is a more timid version of science fiction, as Charles Sheffield seems to do. However, lab lit is not a direct descendant of science fiction. It would be more accurate, perhaps, to identify it as a sibling, both of whom emerged out of the professional scientific culture that was becoming popular in eighteenth- and nineteenth-century England. Matt Hadley's essay touches on this topic.

Lab lit, in Rohn's words, strives to illuminate "a largely unknown or obscure world" of science as it might appear to some lay readers. This is why "lab lit tends to focus on the intricacies of scientific work and scientists as people."[8] This is the focus of Stephanie Chidester's essay, as she discusses Andrea Barrett's short fiction and the writer's exploration of the nature of humanity through the lens of science.

The scientific community and its culture are the core of lab lit, and one more point of departure from science fiction, "in science fiction, the major characters can be almost anything—soldiers, explorers, adventurers, colonists; the list is endless—whereas in fiction about science, the main characters are always scientists."[9] In that way, lab lit can appear mundane—it would not be uncommon to read about something "that you and I could easily encounter were we to walk into a research institute, field station or any other place where scientists are doing what they do."[10]

In fact, if we look for a close connection between lab lit and science fiction, lab lit is more closely related to early science fiction—narratives about scientists based on the real science of the day. The works of Mary Shelley or H.G. Wells are typically classified as science fiction. However, they are often based on the scientific facts of their time. As Ace G. Pilkington points out in his *Science Fiction and Futurism: Their Terms and Ideas*, H.G. Wells, in a 1934 preface to a collection of his works wrote, "In my student days we were much exercised by talk about a possible fourth dimension of space."[11] Pilkington notes further that Wells subsequently explored the idea "in his novel *The Time Machine* (serialized in *National Observer* 1894, book publication 1895)."[12] Mary Shelley gave *Frankenstein* a realistic setting and "pondered the contemporary scientific theory of galvanism (that is, the animation of dead flesh by electrical currents), which then seemed plausible."[13]

Wells's and Shelley's endeavors could be compared to Ian McEwan's explorations of the relative nature of time in his novel *The Child in Time*. Thelma, a retired physicist, gives the main character, Stephen, and the reader a rather cynical overview of modern theories of time:

> There's a whole supermarket of theories these days. . . . One offering has the
> world dividing every infinitesimal fraction of a second into an infinite number
> of possible versions, constantly branching and proliferating. . . . Then there are
> physicists who find it convenient to describe time as a kind of substance, an
> efflorescence of undetectable particles. There are dozens of other theories,
> equally potty. They set out to smooth a few wrinkles in one corner of quantum
> theory. . . . But whatever time is, the common-sense, everyday version of it as
> linear, regular, absolute, marching from left to right, from past through the
> present to the future, is either nonsense or a tiny fraction of the truth. [14]

McEwan is drawing inspiration for his story line from the untested theories
that are occupying the bright scientific minds of today. Tomorrow it might
prove all nonsense and appear to future generations of readers to be as
ludicrous as galvanism. But today, there is still the possibility of the truth for
any one of those interpretations, and this is what allows McEwan's work to
be regarded by some as presenting elements of lab lit and by other, more
skeptical, readers to be approaching science fiction.

Susan Gaines's novel *Carbon Dreams* is another example of extrapolat-
ing from the scientific knowledge available at the time of the writing. In the
"Author's Note and Selected References," Gaines opens up about the nature
of the research her main character conducts: "Tina's actual research projects
are fictional, based on sound scientific principles, but with no exact analogues in the real world. . . . They are . . . developed in a credible manner,
with results that fit plausibly into gaps in our knowledge and highlight the
real trends and upheavals apparent in the scientific literature."[15] Isn't this
similar to what Mary Shelley was doing in *Frankenstein*?

Mary Shelley with her Dr. Frankenstein is celebrated as a progenitor of
their genres by both the lab lit and science fiction camps. The claim to Mary
Shelley is not accidental; it reveals the deeper connection the two genres
have with science itself. As this book demonstrates, science and literature do
not stand in opposition to each other. They are inseparable parts of human
inquiry "because, just as an artistic creation lives in the mind of its creator, so
too does a scientific idea. We labour under the illusion that discoveries and
ideas lie somewhere out there in nature—but in truth the science is in the
discoverer's head."[16]

One of lab lit's major goals is to present the culture of science as connected with what is commonly understood as creative endeavors—literature,
music, art. This is why there is a disclaimer "literary fiction (or other fiction
media)" in Rohn's definition. Lab lit characters are not obsessed with one
subject to the exclusion of all else, but are well-rounded personalities who,
despite their scientific training, do not perceive the world in binary—as fact
not fiction, as logic not intuition, as truth not beauty. They, just like real
scientists, write and read poetry, appreciate art, and listen to rock and classical music while performing experiments. In *The Honest Look*, for example,

Rohn plays out the tension between science and literature through the personal struggles of her main character, Claire Cyrus. It is only when she lets herself be both a scientist and a poet that Claire finds her equilibrium. A.S. Byatt also makes a point of recognizing the artistic and the logical as continuations of each other. She writes of her characters in *The Virgin in the Garden*, "My heroine, brooding about seventeenth-century metaphors . . . and my mathematician, were in fact struggling with the same problem."[17] Charles Sheffield, in his science fiction novel *Cold as Ice*, which has some similarities with lab lit, has one of his artificially enhanced geniuses (initially designed as human weapons) grow up to be a classical composer. Especially interesting is the sheer enthusiasm and detailed knowledge of the scientists and other experts who come to listen to her *Galilean Suite* on Ganymede, the largest moon of Jupiter. Even Rustum Battachariya, a determined recluse, attends the concert, albeit remotely and from his own comfortable quarters.

At the same time, lab lit is clearly and unapologetically about science. It is an invitation to the interested public to come into the laboratory and to take a look. It is an invitation back into the fold. Professional science as a social category was virtually non-existent until the nineteenth-century. Before then, the sciences were accessible to lay persons and, in fact, attracted many amateurs who ended up making scientific contributions.[18] "Amateurs considered themselves to be members of the republic of science, a large international community or network of people who investigated nature and reported their results to each other."[19] Even in the early decades of the twentieth century, there were many books that glorified the contributions of amateur scientists and encouraged the readers of those books to make contributions of their own. The alienation between the public and scientists can be attributed to many causes (the increasing complexity of research procedures, the desire of the professionals to monopolize scientific knowledge, etc.) and even to a specific person—T.H. Huxley.

As Bernard Lightman explains, "Huxley and his allies . . . worked to purge scientific societies of wealthy, aristocratic amateurs, Anglican clergymen enthralled by natural theology and women with a keen interest in science."[20] Huxley's goal was to establish professional scientists as the only keepers and distributors of Natural knowledge. Now that the doors of the laboratory were tightly shut to all but the select few, Huxley and his like-minded colleagues sought to create a specialized, jargon-laden way of communicating scientific advances that only professionals would be able to handle. "Complicated experiments, perhaps in combination with model building, were described in detached language, heavily spiced with complex scientific terms, in effect excluding the participation of non-professionals."[21] In doing so, this group of self-appointed gate-keepers "dismantled the bridge between elite science and public discourse. Scientific naturalists worked to cleanse scientific thought of those elements that previously had connected public and scientific culture, including anthropomorphic, anthropocentric, teleological and ethical views of nature."[22]

Having succeeded in expunging the involvement of amateurs, Huxley and his followers (John Tyndall for example) proceeded to control how science was delivered to the lay masses. Melanie Keene calls this legacy of controlled popularization "familiar science."[23] It firmly establishes the laboratory as the domain of the professional and explains science to the masses in terms of familiar objects easily found in the home or its immediate surroundings. Keene describes "familiar science" as an educational technique. However, its effect went beyond educating the public; it cemented the privileged position of the professional scientist while firmly denying the layman the opportunity to contribute to scientific knowledge.

At the same time, many agree that the separation of the professional from the amateur is, in the words of Bensaude-Vincent, "a necessary ingredient of our [western] notion of science."[24] Djerassi attributes the relative invisibility of lab lit as a genre to this very idea: "Science is conducted within a close-knit culture whose members are generally reluctant to disclose their tribal secrets. This may be one reason why so few novels, plays, or films use ordinary scientists as main characters."[25]

Djerassi wrote those words in 1994, a time when lab lit was just emerging on the market. However, the *Economist* designates 1986 as the year when the "flowering [of the genre] began" with the publication of Hugh Whitemore's *Breaking the Code*—a play based on the life of Alan Turing, which was filmed in 1996. At that point, the *Economist* claims, "novelists and playwrights bashed down the laboratory door, put on white coats and made themselves perfectly at home among the test tubes and the bunsen burners."[26] It is worth noting that Ian McEwan wrote *The Imitation Game*, a television play for the BBC about Turing, in 1980. (The 2014 film *The Imitation Game* is based on Whitemore's work.)

The publications of lab lit works have increased since then—with 2005 seeing a record number of titles in a survey of the period from the 1930s to 2010.[27] Still, the genre is new, and Djerassi's explanation rings true even today. If the 2000s are the "golden age" of lab lit, it is due not to the welcoming scientists like Djerassi or Rohn, for example, but to authors without scientific training, like Allegra Goodman, since according to Rohn's figures, they contribute more titles than practicing scientists.[28]

A reader new to lab lit might wonder if the works written by non-scientists hold the true accounts of the experiences of the scientific community. Do authors like Goodman "demand of [themselves] a degree of accuracy and plausibility that impart to [their] storytelling a high ratio of fact to fiction"?[29] They do. Their work is grounded in research on the realities of scientific life in general and on a discipline they are writing about in particular. As David Brin points out in "The Heresy of Science Fiction," those authors who plot their stories around scientific developments are quite often "former English majors." These people, "who could not close an equation if their lives depended on it . . . seek out pioneers in any field, plying them with pizza and beer, till they explain something new and wonderful, in terms that any reader could understand."[30] Allegra Goodman, for example, had to learn from scientists "about the care and breeding of mice" in preparation for her novel *Intuition* that deals with a group of researchers working in a cancer research laboratory who come to experience the exaltation of discovery and the consequences of fraud.[31]

"Veri-fiction"—that is another name that Djerassi uses to describe his own stories about scientists, but it is a good name for any true lab lit work. In its fidelity to the realities of scientific work, lab lit is close to popular science and can introduce the reader to the basics of a particular discipline. In fact, when it comes to some aspects of laboratory processes, lab lit is better suited to address the interests of a lay reader than popular science. The general public tends to associate science with the laboratory. For example, when Dorothy Rosenthal conducted a study asking college students who majored in liberal arts what images came to their minds if they thought of scientists, most responded with descriptions of laboratory equipment.[32] Yet traditional popular science media (books, articles, blogs) give very sparse and generic descriptions of the procedures and the apparatus used in everyday laboratory work. As I note in my article published in *Science as Culture*, "Popular science tends to focus on apparatus that is in some way extraordinary or functions in unexpected ways."[33] A good example would be the Large Hadron Collider of Conseil Européen pour la Recherche Nucléaire (CERN). Here is how Brian Greene describes it in his article for the *Smithsonian*:

> Winding its way hundreds of yards under Geneva, Switzerland, crossing the French border and back again, the LHC is a nearly seventeen-mile-long circular tunnel that serves as a racetrack for smashing together particles of matter. The LHC is surrounded by about 9,000 superconducting magnets, and is home to streaming hordes of protons, cycling around the tunnel in both directions, which the magnets accelerate to just shy of the speed of light.[34]

This extraordinary apparatus, however, does not represent the daily realities of laboratory work. And popular science often fails to give the public a glimpse into how ordinary equipment operates. If anything, popular science sometimes creates an impression that the scientists are working without any apparatus at all. This is where lab lit steps in to fill in the blanks. It supplies detailed descriptions of equipment no matter its size, appearance, or importance. In fact, in "these novels apparatus is used as a means of characterization for the scientists, and it is not unusual to have apparatus itself treated as a character."[35]

Susan Gaines's novel *Carbon Dreams*, for example, uses laboratory equipment to describe the emotional state of her heroine:

> . . .when she [Tina] opened the door of the instrument lab and heard the pump, she realized that the HPLC had other plans, and her heart sank. . . . Sometimes she felt like the thing was alive, manipulating her every move. . . . She almost wished it would explode. But, of course, it would never do anything that heroic. It would just burn out, leading her on, tormenting her to the very end. [36]

At first, it appears that the author is focusing on the instrument; however, a careful reader will notice that "the scientist endows her equipment with human emotions by projecting her own. At the point when the apparatus malfunctions, it is Tina's emotions that are presented in terms of the apparatus." She might want the machine to "explode," but it is she who is ready to burst in anger and frustration. The equipment might seem "alive" to her, but she is the only living creature in the laboratory, and while she accuses her apparatus of being manipulative, "she is the one who physically manipulates the machinery. In this instance, the apparatus is both a character and a foil for the main [character]." [37]

Jennifer Rohn uses a similar technique in *The Honest Look*, but she goes one step further and assigns unmistakable human qualities to the equipment her researcher uses: "She fed the [machine] a few sips of buffered saline, then twiddled a knob to burp the air out of its labyrinth of flexible latex microtubing." [38] This apparatus proceeds to act like a human baby. It displays satisfaction when the "feeding" proceeds: the machine "emitted a self-satisfied bleep and a sprinkling of flashes on the console." [39] And it cries when something is not to its liking: the apparatus "began to ping in panic." [40] This is no longer a projection of the scientist's feelings—the heroine is not showcasing her maternal instinct—instead this is a sustained effort to treat laboratory equipment as equal to the scientist who works with it. In this regard, lab lit is ahead of popular science in recognizing the important role of the non-human contributors to scientific progress.

Lab lit brings to the forefront not only contemporary scientific ideas (as popular science does) but also the emotional issues of competitiveness among scientists, the difficulties of getting funding, the dedication to one's research goals, and the ethical dilemmas of using human or animal subjects, to name just a few. These works allow the reader to co-experience what it is like to be a scientist. Reading a lab lit novel, a play, or a collection of poems will not make us scientists, but it will change "the nature and quality of the self we pretend to become as we read." [41] That is, for the duration of the work, a reader will be immersed in the world of the scientific community and will have to ponder the same questions and make decisions about the same problems as the scientists who inhabit the fictional laboratory. Inevitably, this journey into the laboratory will create a deeper understanding and a sense of connection with the real world of science. As Peter J. Rabinowitz suggests, in lab lit "we have the use of science to create more radically imaginary persons—not in the text, but in the reader: not simply more self-confident selves or wiser selves or more forward-thinking selves, but previously unimaginable selves."[42]

The connection between imagination, fiction, and science can also be more direct. After all, the idea of fictionality—that is imaginative representation of real-world events—is not foreign to professional science even if it is commonly associated with literature. There are two ways of looking at fictionality. One (and this is perhaps the most common way) is to regard it from the point of view of literary fiction, another is from the point of view of science. Monika Fludernik supplies a good definition of the literary kind of fictionality. She calls it "the subjective experience of imaginary human beings in an imaginary human space."[43] She emphasizes "the subjective experience," saying that literary fictions "set out to represent" the human experience and create an "evocation of 'real-life' experience."[44] A work of literature must project the emotional experiences of its characters since emotional reactions are more unique and subjective than physical responses. Dramatization not only of external events but also of inner states is therefore essential to literary fiction.

An important aspect of Fludernik's definition—the qualification "imaginary" assigned to the characters and their surroundings—is taken for granted when literary fictions are discussed. However, it comes to the forefront when real-life activities like doing scientific experiments are in question. How can "imaginary human beings" or "imaginary human space" fit into the world of science?

The immediate answer is they cannot; this is, essentially, what separates reality from fiction. However, studies in the philosophy of science began advocating for a non-literary kind of fictionality as early as the beginning of the twentieth century, starting with Hans Vaihinger in 1924. More recently, Arthur Fine (1993) has revived these ideas, which inspired a number of further explorations in the twenty-first century. Fictionality, from this scientific point of view, is usually understood as "the role played by particular methods of model building such as abstractions, idealisations, and the employment of highly hypothetical entities."[45] A good example is Mauricio Suárez's 2009 collection *Fictions in Science: Philosophical Essays of Modeling and Idealization* or Adam Toon's 2012 monograph *Models as Make-Believe: Imagination, Fiction and Scientific Representation*.

This non-literary view of fictionality focuses on an important aspect of the scientific process—hypothesizing. As Brian Stableford says in *Science Fact and Science Fiction*, "Speculation plays a key role in scientific thought, which overlaps that of extrapolation but usually makes more use of imagination in proceeding far beyond matters of logical deduction. It is the process used to generate hypotheses, including specific predictions, whose subsequent testing by observation and experiment produces and refines scientific knowledge."[46] The aspects of imagination and experientiality present in Fludernik's definition are replaced with the discussion of the possibilities and probabilities. And philosophers of science have circulated the idea that fictionality in science is "analogous to literary . . . fiction."[47]

These insights demonstrate a logical path from the laboratory to the page. In the end, lab lit is written not only to promote a positive image of science and its practitioners (though it is one of the major goals) but also to tell interesting stories about people who are connected to science. Lab lit is first and foremost about people: it presents scientists not as mysterious keepers of Nature's secrets but as human beings with whom a reader can easily relate. There is humor, there is drama, there is suspense, and there is love—a life of science is a full one, as the essays in this collection demonstrate. It is, in fact, a very important part of being human.

NOTES

1. Charles Sheffield, *The Borderlands of Science: How to Think Like a Scientist and Write Science Fiction* (New York: Baen, 1999), 7.

2. Jennifer Rohn, "More Lab in the Library," *Nature* 465 (2010): 552.

3. Carl Djerassi, *The Bourbaki Gambit* (New York: Penguin Books, 1994), xiii.

4. Jennifer Rohn, "What Is Lab Lit (the genre)?," lablit.com. Jennifer Rohn. Mar. 7, 2005. Accessed Nov. 15, 2018. http://www.lablit.com/article/3.

5. Kirk Smith, "Questions About Genre," *Fiction about Science: The Blog.* Kirk Smith. Feb. 10, 2013. Accessed 17 Mar. 2016. http://fictionaboutscience.com/questions-about-genre/.

6. Jennifer Rohn, "More Lab in the Library," 552.

7. Katherine Bouton, "In Lab Lit, Fiction Meets Science of the Real World," *New York Times.* Dec. 3, 2012. Accessed Nov. 6, 2018 http://www.nytimes.com/2012/12/04/science/in-lab-lit-fiction-meets-science-of-the-real-world.html?_r=0.

8. Jennifer Rohn, "More Lab in the Library," 552.

9. Kirk Smith, "Questions About Genre," http://fictionaboutscience.com/questions-about-genre/.

10. Jennifer Rohn, "What Is Lab Lit (the genre)?" http://www.lablit.com/article/3.

11. Ace G. Pilkington, *Science Fiction and Futurism: Their Terms and Ideas* (Jefferson, NC: McFarland, 2017), iv–v.

12. Ibid., 137.

13. Julie Maxwell, "The Rise of Lab Lit," *Oxford Today* 26, no. 2 (2014): 35.

14. Ian McEwan, *The Child in Time* (New York: Anchor Books, 1999), 135–36.

15. Susan Gaines, "Author's Note and Selected References," in *Carbon Dreams* (Berkeley, CA: Creative Arts Books Company, 2001).

16. Simon Mawer, "Science in Literature," *Nature* 434 (2005): 299.

17. A.S. Byatt, "Fiction Informed by Science," *Nature* 434 (2005): 294.

18. Olga A. Pilkington, "Popular Science as a Means of Emotional Engagement with the Scientific Community," *International Journal of Science, Culture, and Sport* 4, no. 1 (March 2016): 119.

19. Bernadette Bensaude-Vincent, "A Genealogy of the Increasing Gap between Science and the Public," *Public Understanding of Science* 10 (2001): 102.

20. Bernard Lightman, "Marketing Knowledge for the General Reader: Victorian Popularizers of Science," *Endeavour* 24, no. 3 (2000): 101.

21. Ibid. 101.

22. Ibid. 101.

23. Melanie Keene, "Familiar Science in Nineteenth-Century Britain," *History of Science*, 52, no. 1 (2014): 53–71.

24. Bernadette Bensaude-Vincent, "A Genealogy of the Increasing Gap between Science and the Public," 100.

25. Carl Djerassi, *The Bourbaki Gambit*, xiii.

26. "Science in Fiction Is Not Science Fiction." *Economist*, Aug. 20, 1998. Accessed Nov. 5, 2018. http://www.economist.com/node/162287.

27. Julie Maxwell, "The Rise of Lab Lit," 35; Jennifer Rohn, "More Lab in the Library," 552.

28. Jennifer Rohn, "More Lab in the Library," 552.

29. Carl Djerassi, *The Bourbaki Gambit*, xiii.

30. David Brin, "The Heresy of Science Fiction," in *Insistence of Vision* (Lanham: The Story Plant, 2016), 18.

31. Allegra Goodman, "Acknowledgments," in *Intuition* (New York: The Dial Press, 2006).

32. Dorothy Rosenthal, "Images of Scientists: A Comparison of Biology and Liberal Studies Majors," *School Science and Mathematics* 93, no. 4 (Apr. 1993): 213.

33. Olga A. Pilkington, "Popular Science versus Lab Lit: Differently Depicting Scientific Apparatus," *Science as Culture* 26, no. 3 (2017): 286.

34. Brian Greene, "Mind over Matter," *Smithsonian*, 44, no. 4 (July 2013): https://www.smithsonianmag.com/science-nature/how-the-higgs-boson-was-found-4723520/.

35. Olga A. Pilkington, "Popular Science versus Lab Lit: Differently Depicting Scientific Apparatus," 286.

36. Susan Gaines, *Carbon Dreams*, 36.

37. Olga A. Pilkington, "Popular Science versus Lab Lit: Differently Depicting Scientific Apparatus," 301.

38. Jennifer Rohn, *The Honest Look* (Cold Spring Harbor, NY: Cold Spring Harbor Laboratory Press, 2010), 58.

39. Ibid., 64.

40. Ibid., 65.

41. Peter J. Rabinowitz, "'The Impossible Has a Way of Passing Unnoticed': Reading Science in Fiction," *Narrative* 19, no. 2 (May 2011): 208.

42. Ibid., 209.

43. Monika Fludernik, *Towards a 'Natural' Narratology* (New York: Routledge, 1996), 39.

44. Ibid., 41, 12.

45. Ann-Sophie Barwich, "Science and Fiction: Analysing the Concept in Science and Its Limits," *Journal for General Philosophy of Science* 44 (2013): 357–58.

46. Brian Stableford, *Science Fact and Science Fiction: An Encyclopedia* (New York: Routledge, 2006), 497.

47. Joseph Rouse, "Laboratory Fictions," in *Fictions in Science: Philosophical Essays on Modeling and Idealization*, ed. Mauricio Suárez (London: Routledge, 2009), 37.

BIBLIOGRAPHY

Barwich, Ann-Sophie. "Science and Fiction: Analysing the Concept in Science and Its Limits." *Journal for General Philosophy of Science* 44 (2013): 357–73.

Bensaude-Vincent, Bernadette. "A Genealogy of the Increasing Gap between Science and the Public." *Public Understanding of Science* 10 (2001): 99–113.

Bouton, Katherine. "In Lab Lit, Fiction Meets Science of the Real World." *New York Times*. Dec. 3, 2012. Accessed Jun. 5, 2017 http://www.nytimes.com/2012/12/04/science/in-lab-lit-fiction-meets-science-of-the-real-world.html?_r=0.

Brin, David. *Insistence of Vision*. Lanham: The Story Plant, 2016.

Byatt, A.S. "Fiction Informed by Science." *Nature* 434 (2005): 294–96.

Djerassi, Carl. *The Bourbaki Gambit*. New York: Penguin Books, 1994.

Fludernik, Monika. *Towards a 'Natural' Narratology*. New York: Routledge, 1996.

Gaines, Susan. *Carbon Dreams*. Berkeley, CA: Creative Arts Books Company, 2001.

Goodman, Allegra. *Intuition*. New York: The Dial Press, 2006.

Greene, Brian. "Mind over Matter." *Smithsonian*, 44, no. 4 (2013): 25–96.

Keene, Melanie. "Familiar Science in Nineteenth-Century Britain." *History of Science* 52, no. 1 (2014): 53–71.

Lightman, Bernard. "Marketing Knowledge for the General Reader: Victorian Popularizers of Science." *Endeavour* 24, no. 3 (2000): 100–06.

Maxwell, Julie. "The Rise of Lab Lit." *Oxford Today* 26, no. 2 (2014): 35.

Mawer, Simon. "Science in Literature." *Nature* 434 (2005): 297–98.

McEwan, Ian. *The Child in Time*. New York: Anchor Books, 1999.

Pilkington, Ace G. *Science Fiction and Futurism: Their Terms and Ideas*. Jefferson, NC: McFarland, 2017.

Pilkington, Olga A. "Popular Science as a Means of Emotional Engagement with the Scientific Community." *International Journal of Science, Culture, and Sport* 4, no. 1 (March 2016): 118–25.

Pilkington, Olga A. "Popular Science versus Lab Lit: Differently Depicting Scientific Apparatus." *Science as Culture* 26, no. 3 (2017): 285–306.

Rabinowitz, Peter J. "'The Impossible Has a Way of Passing Unnoticed': Reading Science in Fiction." *Narrative* 19, no. 2 (May 2011): 201–15.

Rohn, Jennifer. *The Honest Look*. Cold Spring Harbor, NY: Cold Spring Harbor Laboratory Press, 2010.

Rohn, Jennifer. "More Lab in the Library." *Nature* 465 (2010): 552.

Rohn, Jennifer. "What Is Lab Lit (the genre)?" lablit.com. Jennifer Rohn. Mar. 7, 2005. Accessed Nov. 3, 2018. http://www.lablit.com/article/3.

Rosenthal, Dorothy. "Images of Scientists: A Comparison of Biology and Liberal Studies Majors." *School Science and Mathematics* 93, no. 4 (Apr. 1993): 212–16.

Rouse, Joseph. "Laboratory Fictions." In *Fictions in Science*, edited by Mauricio Suárez. New York: Routledge, 2009.

"Science in Fiction Is Not Science Fiction." *Economist*. Aug. 20, 1998. Accessed Jan. 8, 2018. http://www.economist.com/node/162287.

Sheffield, Charles. *The Borderlands of Science: How to Think Like a Scientist and Write Science Fiction*. New York: Baen, 1999.

Sheffield, Charles. *Cold as Ice*. New York: Tom Doherty Associates, 1992.

Smith, Kirk. "Questions About Genre." *Fiction about Science: The Blog*. Kirk Smith. 10 Feb. 10, 2013. Accessed Mar. 17, 2016. http://fictionaboutscience.com/questions-about-genre/.

Stableford, Brian. *Science Fact and Science Fiction: An Encyclopedia*. New York: Routledge, 2006.

Chapter One

Frankenstein, Scientism, and the Cultural Reception of Discovery

Amanda Scott

If Mary Shelley could see our day, undoubtedly she would be amazed at how her novel has influenced our culture. Shelley wrote *Frankenstein* as a result of a ghost-story contest among friends in the rainy summer of 1816 while they stayed near Lake Geneva, Switzerland. In her party were Lord Byron, John Polidore, and Percy Bysshe Shelley. Her idea for the novel came upon her like a "waking dream," as she described it in her preface to the 1831 edition of the novel:

> I saw the pale student of unhallowed arts kneeling beside the thing he had put together. I saw the hideous phantasm of a man stretched out, and then, on the working of some powerful engine, show signs of life, and stir with an uneasy, half vital motion. Frightful must it be; for supremely frightful would be the effect of any human endeavour to mock the stupendous mechanism of the Creator of the world.[1]

This is an apt description of the infamous moment in the novel that has haunted the western world ever since.

In popular culture, the novel's monster, who is commonly dubbed "Frankenstein" himself, has come to represent an entire subgenre of gothic horror. Noting the novel's cultural prevalence, Barbara Braid called Frankenstein's creation "one of the strongest memes of modernity."[2] Shelley's novel still sells around 500,000 copies each year, and according to the Open Syllabus Project, it is the most widely taught novel in college courses.[3] Scholars concede that *Frankenstein* is perhaps the most adapted and most adaptable novel of all time. In his *The Illustrated Frankenstein Movie Guide*, Steven Jones tracks over four-hundred adaptations between 1910 and 1994, and of course, this list continues to proliferate. (See Dean Conrad and Lynne Ma-gowan's essay for a discussion of some cinematic adaptations.) It's safe to speculate, as Stuart Curran has done, that if we were to count all of the films inspired and influenced by *Frankenstein*, we would be in the thousands.[4] More importantly for my purposes here, *Frankenstein* has strongly affected public notions about science. Perhaps unique to this novel is that we not only continue to reimagine it, but we also continue to utilize it to contextualize emerging technologies. Unsurprisingly, these attitudes toward science appear in film. Peter Weingart and his colleagues surveyed 222 films with scientific themes and found that some variation of the "mad scientist" existed in about 60 percent of them. Of these mad scientists, about a third of them form creations that get outside of their control and about 60 percent of these scientists invent something that causes harm to others.[5] Isaac Asimov coined the term Frankenstein Complex in 1939 "as part of his campaign to show robots as safe and effective tools, [and] it means an irrational fear that the products of human ingenuity (especially robots, androids, or anything else with human-like intelligence) will inevitably turn on their creators as Victor Frankenstein's Monster did."[6]

As Weingart's research elucidates, there is a wide spectrum of cultural influence stemming from Frankensteinian tropes. I wholeheartedly agree with Alan Rauch, who noted, "The novel is arguably one of the most influen-tial works in the conceptual practice of science and technology and Mary Shelley one of the most influential thinkers."[7] So what exactly is *Franken-stein* saying about science and why is this "meme of modernity," as Braid calls it, still haunting us two-hundred years later? This chapter seeks to answer these questions by explicating how *Frankenstein* represents science itself, and furthermore, how language in general can taint our approach to science. In illuminating the novel in this way, we can understand it as an early example of lab lit, for it presents contemporary science in an empirical, rather than supernatural, way.

Analyzing notions of science in *Frankenstein* should begin with consider-ation for its contribution to the literary canon and early literature about sci-ence. Many have called the novel the first work of science fiction, but others insist it is primarily a gothic novel preoccupied with the occult. Another group argues, as Shelley herself suggested in her 1831 preface excerpted above, that the novel serves as a cautionary tale about creation. Some even perceive it to be anti-scientific. Noting critics' strikingly different ways of categorizing the novel, Andrew Bartlett suggests that "Frankenstein is notori-ous for seeming able to mean almost anything, depending on the inflection one's subcultural resentment takes and the ideological scalpel one has sharp-ened." He goes on to suggest that the only other literary figure whose mean-ing is as widely contested is the ghost in Shakespeare's *Hamlet*.[8] At the heart of this adaptability is Mary Shelley's philosophical upbringing and ideological complexity. She does not necessarily present truths and falsities, but rather, she presents tensions between several different ideas: morality and daringness, education and experience, life and death. David Ketterer rightly describes her style as "philosophical appreciation of sliding relationships between the Self and the Other."[9] It is precisely this intellectual talent of appreciating "sliding relationships" that makes Shelley's exploration of science so rich.

For some critics, *Frankenstein* is, first and foremost, a work of science fiction. This conclusion is quite understandable, as *Frankenstein* is one of the first novels, and one of the most influential nineteenth-century novels, to explore scientific themes. In the genre formation of science fiction, H.G. Wells and other *fin de siècle* writers were long thought of as the progenitors of the genre, but in 1973, Brian Aldiss wrote a semi-scholarly book titled *Billion Year Spree: The True History of Science Fiction* in which he considered Mary Shelley's novel as the first novel in this genre.[10] In the decades since, a consensus seems to have developed placing *Frankenstein* as the literary forebearer of science fiction. Scholars cite several characteristics of the novel to qualify their estimation of it as such. For Martin Willis, it is the monstrosity of Victor's creation "whose malign purpose is the destruction of the human race;"[11] this is an archetype that has become a staple to science fiction.[12] For Paul Alkon, *Frankenstein*'s "ability to pose challenging questions about the human condition in an age of science" is what signifies its clear status as science fiction.[13] He notes the scientific realism in the text as a supporting factor for it fitting into this genre, but he qualifies this by mentioning that realism in scientific matters is not an end unto itself, but is used rather "to afford a unique vantage point for contemplation of the human condition."[14] In spite of these arguments, Mark Rose cautions against making judgments about prototypical novels of science fiction from a modern-day perspective: "From a historical point of view it may be misleading to speak of even such relatively recent writers as Shelley [in terms of science fiction]. . . . We should understand that in labelling, say, *Frankenstein* as science fiction we are retroactively recomposing that text under the influence of a generic idea that did not come into being until well after it was written."[15] It's important, then, that we not commit a teleological fallacy in determining *Frankenstein* as straightforward science fiction, for it addresses science in a way uncommon to most literature in that genre.

Frankenstein may seem like a work of science fiction because of how it predicts our modern realities of cloning and reproductive technologies, but it is far different from H.G. Wells's novellas. Shelley does not situate her narrative in the future nor does she formulate the monster's creation as a fantastical event. Rather, if we look closely at the novel, we'll see that it actually represents the science of Mary Shelley's day, which she was apparently well-versed in. Despite the novel's gothic properties, it is not supernat-

ural or fantastical. Victor's creation of his super species is grounded in the
debates of early nineteenth-century Europe and is meant to be a serious
reflection on science. When one considers the gothic horror that the Frankenstein myth represents, it may be difficult to see Victor Frankenstein's creation as the product of late eighteenth- and early nineteenth-century science,
but many scholars have convincingly argued just that. Historicist Edith Birkhead posits that "by resting her terrors on a pseudo-scientific basis . . . Mrs.
Shelley waives her right to entire suspension of disbelief."[16] Martin Willis
reads the novel as more squarely scientific stating that "Frankenstein is completely immersed in the scientific culture of the time."[17]

Most useful to my exploration is Kathryn Harkup's recent book *Making a
Monster: The Science Behind Mary Shelley's Frankenstein*. In it she provides
in-depth historical context for the scientific trends of the eighteenth and
nineteenth centuries in Europe as well as particular contexts for all of the
scientific processes that Victor takes part in to make his creature. Harkup
illustrates how the general public became more interested in and entertained
by science at this time. Harkup explains, "There was little distinction between serious scientific research and experiments designed to entertain" in
Shelley's day.[18] In post-Enlightenment Europe, science was not only a
means of expanding human knowledge, but it was also applied to real-life
scenarios for the first time.[19] James Rieger, an editor for 1982 edition of the
text, downplays Mary Shelley's scientific knowledge,[20] but according to
Harkup's assessment of *Frankenstein*, it appears that Shelley, though not a
scientist herself, was likely well acquainted with present-day scientific experiments through hearing about them from her father, William Godwin, and
later her husband, Percy.

This was an interest that many Romantic writers shared with Shelley. In
their "Romanticism and Romantic Science," Yannis Hadzigeorgiou and Roland Schulz explore what they term "Romantic Science," namely scientific
inquiry informed by Romantic ideals. They illustrate how the Romantics
inquired about nature in sophisticated ways that could invite "mystery and
wonder" as well as transform people's perception of the natural world.[21]
Robert Mitchell also traces the intersections between Romantic art and science. He insists that while some might see the similarities of science and art/
literature as foreign, the Romantics didn't. They were preoccupied with science, especially the question of where life comes from. Romantic poets were
experimenting with their style and asking sophisticated questions about nature in a way not dissimilar to how early nineteenth-century scientists were
asking questions. It is then perfectly fitting that *Frankenstein* would be an
early example of lab lit because it was conceived in this milieu of experimentation.[22]

The realistic nature of the novel begins with its central character. Victor
Frankenstein has long been termed a Promethean figure and sometimes a

Faustian figure. While we can see significant similarities between these figures, Kathryn Harkup argues that the inspiration for Frankenstein was, at least in part, from the contemporary scientist John Hunter, a physiologist who dissected hundreds of bodies to gain knowledge about human life and anatomy.[23] Victor's drive to exhume corpses to form his creature may seem like the pure stuff of horror, but it was actually a common practice in Shelley's day. Because of the enthusiasm for the sciences, particularly anatomy and medicine, there were many young medical students who wished to learn. Because dissecting human cadavers was the primary means to accomplish this, bodies were always in high demand, and grave robbing was a lucrative business. There was a steady black market for fresh corpses, which were quickly dissected until they were too putrid to work with any longer. As a result of this huge demand and the culture of the time, parliament eventually passed a law allowing those convicted of homicide to be publicly dissected after their executions. Barbaric in the extreme, this practice supposedly deterred crime and also alleviated shortages for the anatomy schools.[24] In light of this widespread practice, particularly in London at the time, we can see how the specimen collection in *Frankenstein* drew from contemporary practice.

The hunger for knowledge so well typified in those eighteenth-century anatomy schools is also clear in *Frankenstein*, not just in Victor but also in the novel's primary narrator, Robert Walton, who expresses his passion for exploring on his voyage to the Arctic before he encounters Victor. He expresses his desire to learn "the secret of the magnet" and to find new routes for trade in that northward region. When Victor later tells Walton his story, he gives him a stern warning about his hunger for knowledge: "Learn from me, if not by my precepts, at least by my example, how dangerous is the acquirement of knowledge and how much happier that man is who believes his native town to be the world, than he who aspires to become greater than his nature will allow."[25] When we take into account the frame narrative structure of the novel, *Frankenstein* is one scientist's retelling of another scientist's pursuit and downfall. Both men experience the payoffs and consequences of voracious appetites for knowledge and notoriety, and both seem to be the product of the scientific spirit of their day.

The central action of the novel, of course, is that Frankenstein gives his creature life. When it comes to the actual animation of the creature, Shelley utilized a lot of scientific discussion about electricity as a means of reanimating the dead. This iconic passage of the creature's birth reads:

> With an anxiety that almost amounted to agony, I collected the instruments of
> life around me, that I might infuse a spark of being into the lifeless thing that
> lay at my feet. It was already one in the morning; the rain pattered dismally
> against the panes, and my candle was nearly burnt out, when, by the glimmer

> of the half-extinguished light, I saw the dull yellow eye of the creature open; it
> breathed hard, and a convulsive motion agitated its limbs.[26]

This is the moment most commonly scrutinized to discuss science in the
novel. In terms of the idea of electrocution, there is no explicit mention of it
here. But in Martin Willis's assessment, because of the phrase "spark of
being" in this passage, "There can be no question that the rhetoric of electricity informs this description."[27]

Electricity was a force that scientists and the whole of society were quite
interested in. There were documented instances of apparent death when a
person was then brought back to life with a jolt of electricity, and Luigi
Galvani (1737–1798), whose methods are mentioned in Shelley's 1831 preface, electrified animal corpses in a way that caused their limbs to twitch as if
alive.[28] Harkup traces scientific practice and links Victor's experiment to
those of his real eighteenth- and nineteenth-century counterparts at great
lengths, removing all doubt that *Frankenstein* was intentionally based on
present-day scientific discussions. It is then important, in the shadow of the
mega-genre of science fiction, to make clear that *Frankenstein*, though forward-thinking by our twenty-first-century estimation, is not projecting some
sort of dystopian future, as some popular notions of the novel might suggest.
Rather, it was musing on the philosophical implications of the scientific
explorations of its day—situating the novel in the genre of lab lit rather than
science fiction as we understand it today.

The implied presence of electricity is not only important as an example of
realistic scientific substance, but it also gets at the heart of what is most
compelling to me about *Frankenstein*. It is a novel about science, but more
importantly, society's reception of this novel serves as a model for how we
interpret and understand science through language. The serious philosophical
inquiry that the novel poses about science is another trait that makes it an
important example of early lab lit. When Victor enlivens his creature with a
"spark of being," Shelley implicitly comments on the discussions happening
about science in her day—namely the vitalist/materialist debate. In this important movement, scientists questioned whether life was the result of some
essence or spark or the result of a perfectly configured organism. Vitalists
believed that life came from a divine source that wasn't completely definable
because of its fluid and mystical nature. Materialists believed that life was
simply a result of wholeness and denied any supernatural connection to it.
The theological implications of this issue made the debate that much more
involved. Martin Willis explains that scientific experiments with electrical
power were:

> intended to legitimize one set of beliefs. For the Romantic scientists, proving
> that electricity was a universal force that had some bearing on human spiritual

existence would greatly enhance their continued insistence on the importance of natural forces as cosmic and transcendent and of science as a pragmatic tool for reading the world's mysticism. For the materialist scientists, discovering electricity to be just another natural phenomenon that offers no elucidation of cosmic principles would deal a heavy blow to the occultist tendencies of the Romantics and place materialist method and philosophies at the center of scientific authority.[29]

Noting the ideological complexity of how both the vitalists and materialists viewed electric power, we can see Shelley's affinity for complex relationships at work. Frankenstein's method of animating his monster is explicitly political to early nineteenth-century theological discussions, and both sides of this debate espouse the electrical phenomenon as support for their worldview of where life comes from. This popular debate about science in Shelley's day was the first, and far from the last, to which *Frankenstein* would contribute.

In Shelley's day, the novel received a lot of negative reactions because it was seen as blasphemous to have a scientist create life. In her important 1993 essay "*Frankenstein* and Radical Science" Marilyn Butler explains how the vitalist/materialist debate gained notoriety shortly after the novel's publication and adversely affected the critical reception of *Frankenstein.* Butler also speculates that this backlash to the novel prompted Shelley's clear remonstrance against science and our notion of "playing God" in her preface to the 1831 edition of the novel,[30] which I quoted at the beginning of this chapter.[31] She calls the monster a "hideous progeny," suggesting that "unhallowed arts" created him; in fact, she calls the whole notion of creation through science "supremely frightful."[32] At face value, then, we might take Shelley at her own word and read *Frankenstein* as cautionary and anti-scientific, but in my estimation, the novel's ethical message is much more complicated, as is the reception of the novel in our modern age.

For more recent scholars, there is some consensus that Shelley was making a statement in favor of vitalism. Maurice Hindle sees Victor's unfettered experimental practice as a turn away from the essence of vitalism to the misled agnosticism of materialism, which fails to recognize the sanctity of life.[33] Hogsette also sees *Frankenstein* as a clear critique of materialism, stating that Victor "exerts a transgressive autonomy that denies God's natural design and moral law in an attempt to create life in the absence of woman after his own filthy image. The result of such an irresponsible pursuit and application of science is emotional chaos, spiritual devastation, domestic disruption, and existential despair."[34] For these critics, then, *Frankenstein* is anti-scientific and cautionary.

However, with the famous interpretability of the novel, it is unsurprising that some scholars have also read it as being a tale that champions the materialist scientist's taking over the role of God. George Levine suggests that the Frankensteinian myth expunges Christian and pagan myths and questions mankind's limits.[35] Paul Cantor frames this Frankensteinian power to create as an empowering ideal of humanistic self-fulfillment. He muses, "Man need no longer be in awe of his creator; he need no longer even feel grateful for being created. He can turn his back on God with a good conscience and set about charting his own course, seeking out ways to remake an imperfectly created world, even to change his own nature for the better."[36] Thus, herein lies another striking example of *Frankenstein*'s chameleon-like ability to fill different roles. What's more, these critics illustrate how scientific creation in the novel can be utilized to affirm a more religious mentality about the sanctity of life or it can affirm a more agnostic view of the world as an accidental and imperfect creation.

This scientific creation has come to signify something of mythical proportions to modern critics and audiences. Critics often compare Victor to both Prometheus of Greco-Roman mythology and Faustus of German legend. One need not make an inductive leap to link the first figure to Victor. The novel's subtitle, after all, is *The Modern Prometheus*. The Faustus figure is also an understandable linkage, for the German legend is based on the itinerant alchemist and astronomer Johann Georg Faust. The resemblance to Frankenstein is clear. However, it is the discussion that surrounds these two important literary archetypes that can illuminate the novel as a symbol for our relationship with science. In short, the Promethean myth frames Frankenstein's scientific pursuits as a constructive act of daring, while the Faustian myth frames his pursuits as damning hubris.

Shelley utilizes the Promethean myth in both its Greek form and Roman form. In the Greek version of the myth, Prometheus steals fire from the Gods to share with men and is chained to a cliff as punishment, where vultures eat out his liver until it grows back. In the Roman version of the myth, often referred to as "Prometheus Plasticator," he deftly uses clay and water to sculpt man and gives animation to these forms with the fire he has stolen. James F. McGrath is one critic who believes the Promethean presence in *Frankenstein* conveys the idea that "science, with its attendant technology, gives mortals real godlike power. The challenge is, then, can human beings wield such power responsibly? Or are they doomed by their very nature to fall short and wreak destruction on themselves and others?"[37] In contrast, Paul Alkon questions the meaning of this Promethean figure in the text:

> If he is "The Modern Prometheus" as *Frankenstein*'s subtitle states, are we to take this parallel as a compliment to Frankenstein because it implies that he was attempting something as noble as Prometheus's theft of fire from the gods for humanity's benefit? Or should we take the parallel as ironic condemnation of a modern world where self-deluded scientists who regard themselves as Promethean benefactors in reality provide only dangerous monstrosities?[38]

He poses an excellent question. As we will see in the modern usurpations of *Frankenstein* that I will explore later, the "modern" designation for Victor as a Promethean figure is quite appropriate. Andrew Bartlett ruminates on Victor as a Prometheus as well. While Prometheus shares fire with humanity, Bartlett concludes, "thanks to Victor, men share . . . nothing much, except perhaps an example they have little desire to follow."[39] For some, then, Victor fails to be a valid Prometheus, perhaps because of the complications of the modern age.

In this question of whether Frankenstein is a true Promethean figure or not, without a doubt Victor himself imagines his own discovery as a positive, world-altering event. His quest is to overcome death and create a new species. He explains his fantasy:

> Life and death appeared to me ideal bounds, which I should first break through, and pour a torrent of light into our dark world. A new species would bless me as its creator and source; many happy and excellent natures would owe their being to me. No father could claim the gratitude of his child so completely as I should deserve theirs. Pursuing these reflections, I thought that if I could bestow animation upon lifeless matter, I might in process of time (although I now found it impossible) renew life where death had apparently devoted the body to corruption.[40]

We can see in this passage the motivation to provide "a torrent of light into a dark world" through his discovery. His professed aim is to overcome death, in a sense, and thereby become a benefactor to humankind. This drive, however, is also fraught with egotism, and that is what many critics focus on when comparing Frankenstein to Dr. Faustus.

When critics analyze the Faustian nature of Frankenstein's creation, they tend to focus on the effect of the creation, rather than the motivation preceding it, which is also true of Faust, who sets out to discover the secrets of the universe. The Faustian side of Victor Frankenstein is the irrevocable results of his creation. Just as Faustus loses his soul to Mephistopheles, Victor's life is irrevocably changed when his creature wakes. Paul Alkon asserts that though Frankenstein has often been considered a Faustian variant, he actually replaces the Faust figure for a modern audience. He avers, "What makes Victor Frankenstein not merely echo but displace Faust as the archetypal figure of our age is precisely the realization that what we may carelessly or poetically describe as the 'miracles' of modern science are brought about by human, not supernatural, agency."[41] In this sense, then, damnation in our modern world may not be brought about as supernatural punishment for wrongdoing, but Alkon asserts that through reckless technology, we may damn ourselves.

The scholarly views above provide another testimony of the "sliding relationships" that Shelley demonstrates in her work. Victor Frankenstein is either a Promethean benefactor or a Faustian villain, depending on one's point of view. The employment of both of these figures evokes a sort of cautionary view; Victor is either willfully "playing with fire," so to speak, or hubristically evoking creative powers unto his own damnation. So, if the novel is a cautionary tale about creation, does this make the novel anti-scientific? The simple answer is no; however, as with all matters with Shelley, the argument about science is quite nuanced or even ambiguous.

As I established earlier, *Frankenstein* does not reject science—the data-driven practice of discovery that makes up science itself. Rather, the novel draws attention to some of the problematic ways that we think and talk about science. This is a concept that Bartlett terms "scientism," or humankind's tendency to mistake anthropology for biology. This notion of scientism draws on the tradition of the French philosopher Bruno Latour, who explored the disjuncture between scientific facts and language. Latour argues that though we perceive science as infallible and language as completely malleable, it is impossible to record scientific information without language, and so science itself is implicitly subjective to a point.[42] What becomes so challenging about addressing scientism as a potential way of tainting science itself is that we cannot escape language.[43] Bartlett points out, "We cannot reduce anthropology to biology because we cannot reduce human language to anything other than itself. In other words, an anthropology founded on language must be explicit in its presuppositions about what language is and does."[44,45] One example of scientism that Bartlett explains is how we often explain science through modifiers in our language such as "*nothing but, no more than, only, just, merely, simply.*"[46] Such reduction treats scientific knowledge with an air of infallibility. But the nature of science itself only encourages more questions and further research; it does not insist on consensus and closure in inquiry like scientism. While linguistic presentation of science may suggest closure, the science itself does not.

Without espousing the specific term "scientism," Alkon recognizes Shelley's critique of the language and ideas that surround science: "For Mary Shelley it is the dream of science, not the sleep of reason, that produces monsters."[47] This "dream of science," I would suggest, is the Promethean notion of the scientist. Victor tells himself a clear narrative about his work as a means of bestowing knowledge upon the world and altering death; however, this fantasy of science infects the actual methodology of his work. The reality of his creation is much different than his idealistic notions had led him to believe. He fantasizes about the life-bringing legacy he is building: "No father could claim the gratitude of his child so completely as I should deserve theirs."[48] But, in reality, his creation brings more death and destruction than anything else. Thus, one type of scientism in the novel is the fantasy of creation, focusing on the positive attributes of a creation without considering its downsides.

Willis comes to a similar conclusion about the problematic notions surrounding science. He concludes that *Frankenstein* is indeed a cautionary tale, but not of the same sort that other scholars had hitherto suggested. He calls it "a caution against narrative, against those stories science tells of itself and that it begins to believe."[49, 50] This line of thinking from Bartlett and Willis is the most accurate way to understand Mary Shelley's complex tensions between the glorifying of and cautioning against scientific creation.[51]

What's most interesting about scientism in the novel is that while Victor is deluded with the fantasy of discovery before his monster awakes, he abandons all hope of a positive outcome once his creature shows signs of life. Many critics have pointed out that the real downfall of Frankenstein's creature is that he is not properly nurtured and cultivated. Frankenstein gives him life but fails to supervise him further. What's more, he slights his creation and lies to him later on. Victor displays another human reaction to science when he is horrified with his creation: "Now that I had finished, the beauty of the dream vanished, and breathless horror and disgust filled my heart. Unable to endure the aspect of the being I had created, I rushed out of the room and continued a long time traversing my bed-chamber, unable to compose my mind to sleep."[52] He then falls into a nervous fever. The language and the human emotion that infiltrates his scientific discovery taints the outcome significantly, and in this regard we can attribute *Frankenstein*'s failure not to having created his "monster" in the first place, but to the flawed attitude he applies to his work.

This fall from egotism to abject horror is quite Faustian, and perhaps unsurprisingly, this fear of creation is the aspect of Frankenstein that seems to dominate our present-day reception of the novel. Ronald Bailey asserts that "the meme of Frankenstein as a mad scientist who unleashed a disastrously uncontrollable creation on the world has been hijacked by anti-modernity, anti-technology ideologues to push for all manner of bans and restrictions on the development and deployment of new technologies."[53] This is where the scientism of *Frankenstein* is so interesting. We can see the way that language infects scientific inquiry in the novel, but the reception of the novel proves equally fascinating. David Hogsette notes the present-day realities in genetics and reproduction that to some are akin to Victor's creation and views *Frankenstein* as "a terrifying mirror reflecting a horrific reality we are unprepared to accept."[54] Perhaps most provocative in this scholarly conversation is when Lester Friedman and Allison Kavey basically attribute our fear to Shelley herself, soft pedaling that she "cannot be held solely, or perhaps even chiefly responsible, for the contemporary fear of scientific expertise, medical research and technical innovations."[55] To suggest that a two-hundred-year-old novel inspired our modern-day fear seems problematic, and this scholarly assertion serves as another teleological problem in the way that we read *Frankenstein*. Again, I assert that the novel serves as a mirror for our anxieties, not the origin of them.

If we survey reactions in the press to world-altering technologies, we can see how our culture has hijacked *Frankenstein* and projected modern fears onto the narrative. After the United States. dropped the atomic bomb on Hiroshima and Nagasaki, Hanson W. Baldwin warned in *Time* magazine that in doing so, the United States. and its Allies had "unleashed a Frankenstein monster."[56] In the same vein, Paul Alkon conjectured, "When Hiroshima was destroyed, *Frankenstein* irrevocably became science fiction."[57] This famous mention of the novel illustrates how retrospective the notion of science fiction really can be. Though Shelley in no way conceived it to foretell the future, many in modernity interpret it as self-fulfilling prophecy. Herein we can see a teleological fallacy associated with *Frankenstein*. Surely the monster does not have much in common with the atomic bomb, nor can we rightfully compare the handful of deaths the creature causes in the novel with the hundreds of thousands who died because of the atomic bomb. Yet, Hanson Baldwin found this Romantic figure (and, no doubt, its 1931 film adaptation) as the most apt reference to express his horror.

Ronald Bailey catalogues other moments in which journalists and scholars have evoked the Frankenstein "meme" to voice fear about progressing technologies. For example, Rachel Carson titled her 1962 anti-pesticide article, "Chemical Frankenstein: Are Pesticides the Monster That Will Destroy Us?" One could also note how *Frankenstein* is evoked as a scare tactic in the conversation about genetically modified food—"Frankenfood."[58] In this nickname we see the fear associated with *Frankenstein*, particularly the irrevocable effects of a new, unnatural creation. Journalist Douglas McCauley made a similar reference writing about the developing technology that would aim to revitalize extinct species. He called these potential creatures "Franken-species," also known as necrofauna. Paul Ehrlich suggests that these de-extinctionists "have been fooled by a cultural misrepresentation of nature and science . . . traceable perhaps to Mary Shelley's *Frankenstein*."[59]

A commonality in all these reactions to *Frankenstein* is the notion that the motivation behind a new technology might be altruistic, but the effects could be detrimental in an irrevocable way. The notion of genetically modified organisms as "Frankenfood" seems especially appropriate in this way. GMOs were created, in part, as a means of fighting world hunger and preventing food waste, but many fear that altering original organisms will have far-reaching ecological and nutritional effects. Again, Frankenstein's monster is evoked as a meme that represents uncanny unnaturalness and a force that once unleashed is impossible to contain. As these mentions in journalism illustrate, *Frankenstein*'s cultural capital in our thinking about science is unmatched.

One case in point: in Michael Moore's essay on Saddam Hussein entitled "We Finally Got Our Frankenstein," he compares the dictator to Frankenstein's monster and insists that we helped to create Hussein and then he got out of control.[60] This example from Moore is fascinating because it highlights a modern sense of ethics. For Moore, Saddam Hussein is a Frankensteinian monster because he not only was a product of evil, but a product of our own negligent creation, in his view. *Frankenstein* then, evokes scientism relating to our culpability in science. Changes to our world are no longer perceived as passive threats created by Deity; rather, we have become the overreaching Gods who are damning the world's future through our own negligence.

I would suggest that these cultural usurpations of the novel don't really tell us anything pertinent to the novel's themes; instead, this reception shows us how language is utilized to conceptualize science. *Frankenstein* is not only a serious novel about science, but it also has brilliantly reflected our changing attitudes about science over the years. Shelley's superb style and her subtle use of tension in the novel enables her audience to perceive creation and science in whatever terms they are predisposed to. In the same vein, our society frequently uses *Frankenstein* to express apprehension about a new technology. This novel serves as an important contribution to lab lit because it shows how language permeates our attitudes about science and how the way we present science through language may also create problems in the public's ability to accept new discoveries and assess their risks appropriately. The novel reflects Shelley's contemporary realities of scientific exploration and has incited philosophical conversations about science ever since. *Frankenstein* reminds us that surrounding the empiricism of science will always be the anthropological reaction to it.

NOTES

1. Mary Shelley, *Frankenstein*, Norton Critical Edition. (New York: Norton, First Printing Edition, 1996), 172.

2. Barbara Braid, "The Frankenstein Meme: Penny Dreadful and The Frankenstein Chronicles as Adaptations." *Open Cultural Studies* no. 1 (2017): 233.

3. Ronald Bailey, "Victor Frankenstein Is the Real Monster: Mary Shelley's Misunderstood Masterpiece Turns 200," *Reason* 5, (April 2018): 58.

4. Stuart Curran, "*Frankenstein* in Popular Culture," *Study Aids: In Popular Culture. Romantic Circles* (2009). http://www.re.umd.edu/editors/frakenstein/pop/pop/html.

5. Peter Weingart, Claud Muhl, and Petra Pansegrau, "Of Power Maniacs and Unethical Geniuses: Science and Scientists in Fiction Film," *Public Understanding of Science* (2003): 282–85.

6. Ace G. Pilkington, *Science Fiction and Futurism: Their Terms and Ideas* (Jefferson, NC: McFarland, 2017), 77.

7. Alan Rauch, *Useful Knowledge: The Victorians, Morality, and the March of Intellect.* (Durham: Duke UP, 2001), 96.

8. Andrew Bartlett, *Mad Scientist, Impossible Human: An Essay in Generative Anthropology* (Aurora, CO: The Davies Group Publishers, 2014), 92.

9. David Ketterer, *Frankenstein's Creation: The Book, the Monster, and Human Reality* (Victoria, B.C.: Department of English at U Victoria, 1979), 104.

10. Brian Aldiss, *Billion Year Spree: The True History of Science Fiction* (New York: Doubleday, 1973), 12.

11. It is essential to note, however, that Frankenstein does not create his monster to destroy the human race; rather, the creature is quite benign and demonstrates his altruistic nature in his assistance to the De Lacey family early in the novel. It is only after Frankenstein refuses to create him a mate that he retaliates and becomes violent. Even at his most violent, Willis's estimation of the Creature as having the desire to cause the destruction of the human race is unreasonable. The risk of this creature procreating with a mate may pose risk to the human race in some far-off time, but this is rather far removed from the scope of the narrative.

12. Martin Willis, *Mesmerists, Monsters, and Machines: Science Fiction and the Cultures of Science in the Nineteenth Century* (Kent, OH: The Kent State UP, 2013), 89.

13. Paul K. Alkon and Raymond Kuhn, *Science Fiction Before 1900: Imagination Discovers Technology* (London: Routledge, 2002), 28.

14. Ibid., 5.

15. Mark Rose, *Alien Encounters: Anatomy of Science Fiction* (Cambridge, Mass.: Harvard UP, 1981), 5.

16. Edith Birkhead, *The Tale of Terror: A Study of the Gothic Romance* (London: Constable, 1921), 164.

17. Willis, *Mesmerists, Monsters, and Machines*, 64.

18. Kathryn Harkup, *Making the Monster: The Science Behind Mary Shelley's Frankenstein* (New York: Bloomsbury Sigma, 2018), 184.

19. Ibid., 15.

20. James E. Rieger, ed., *Frankenstein; or, The Modern Prometheus, 1818 edition* (Chicago: Chicago UP, 1982), xxvii.

21. Yannis Hadzigeorgiou and Roland Schulz, "Romanticism and Romantic Science: Their Contribution to Science Education," *Science & Education 23*, no. 10 (Oct 2014): 1963–2006.

22. Robert Mitchell, *Experimental Life: Vitalism in Romantic Science & Literature* (Baltimore: The Johns Hopkins UP, 2013)

23. Harkup, *Making the Monster*, 136.

24. Harkup, *Making the Monster*, 126–31.

25. Shelley, *Frankenstein*, 31.

26. Shelley, *Frankenstein*, 34.

27. Willis, *Mesmerists, Monsters, and Machines*, 76.

28. Shelley, *Frankenstein*, 171–72.

29. Willis, *Mesmerists, Monsters, and Machines*, 67–68.

30. Marilyn Bulter, "*Frankenstein* and Radical Science," in *Frankenstein*, ed. Paul Hunter (New York: Norton, 1996), 302–13.

31. As Marilyn Butler points out, because of the severe backlash against the 1818 edition of the novel and how that must have figured into Mary Shelley's revisions to her 1831 edition, academia at large recognizes the first edition as the preferred text. This is a departure from the usual situation, where the latest edition of an author's work is definitive.

32. Shelley, *Frankenstein*, 172.

33. Maurice Hindle, "Vital Matters: Mary Shelley's Frankenstein and Romantic Science," *Critical Survey* 2, no. 1 (1990): 31–34.

34. David S. Hogsette, "Metaphysical Intersections in Frankenstein: Mary Shelley's Theistic Investigation of Scientific Materialism and Transgressive Autonomy," *Christianity and Literature* 60, no. 4 (Summer 2011): 547.

35. George Levine, "The Ambiguous Heritage of Frankenstein," in *The Endurance of Frankenstein: Essays on Mary Shelley's Novel* (Berkeley: U of California P, 1979), 6–7.

36. Paul A. Cantor, *Creature and Creator: Myth-Making and English Romanticism* (Cambridge: Cambridge UP, 1984), xiii–xiv.

37. James F. McGrath, *Religion and Science Fiction*, (Cambridge, England: The Lutterworth Press, 2012), 80–81.

38. Alkon and Kuhn, *Science Fiction Before 1900*, 28.

39. Bartlett, *Mad Scientist, Impossible Human*, 95.

40. Shelley, *Frankenstein*, 32.

41. Alkon and Kuhn, *Science Fiction Before 1900*, 30.

42. Bruno Latour, *We Have Never Been Modern*, trans. Catherine Porter (New York: Harvester Wheatsheaf, 1993), 31.

43. For more on the exploration of the relationship between language and science see Helena Calsamiglia, "Popularization Discourse." *Discourse Studies* 5 no. 2 (2003): 139–46; G. Nigel Gilbert and Michael Mulkay, *Opening Pandora's Box: A Sociological Analysis of Scientists' Discourse* (Cambridge: Cambridge UP, 1984); Michael D. Gordin, *Scientific Babel: How Science Was Done Before and After Global English* (Chicago: U of Chicago P, 2015); Wiley Souba, "The Language of Discovery," *Journal of Biomedical Discovery and Collaboration* 6 (2011): 53–69.

44. Bartlett, *Mad Scientist, Impossible Human*, 37.

45. See also Olga Pilkington, *Presented Discourse in Popular Science: Professional Voices in Books for Lay Audiences* (Leiden, Netherlands: Brill, 2018).

46. Bartlett, *Mad Scientist, Impossible Human*, 32.

47. Alkon and Kuhn, *Science Fiction Before 1900*, 5.

48. Shelley, *Frankenstein*, 32.

49. Willis, *Mesmerists, Monsters, and Machines*, 93.

50. See also Pilkington, *Presented Discourse*, 14–17, 144–49 and Randy Schekman "How Journals Like *Nature*, *Cell* and *Science* are Damaging Science," *The Guardian*, 9 December 2013, https://www.theguardian.com/commentisfree/2013/dec/09/how-journals-nature-science-cell-damage-science.

51. The problematic nature of narrative in general is worth noting here. We get the sense on reading *Frankenstein* that characters do not fully grasp the importance of each other's narratives. Robert Walton, for example, doesn't seem to sense the full gravity of Frankenstein's message. Victor Frankenstein doesn't understand the importance of the creature's story to him.

52. Shelley, *Frankenstein*, 32.

53. Bailey, "Victor Frankenstein Is the Real Monster," 58.

54. Hogsette, "Metaphysical Intersections in Frankenstein," 533.

55. Lester D. Friedman and Allison B. Kavey. *Monstrous Progeny: A History of the Frankenstein Narratives* (New Brunswick, NJ: Rutgers UP, 2016), 64.

56. Ibid., 59.

57. Alkon and Kuhn, *Science Fiction Before 1900*, 9.

58. For one such example of the usage of this term, see Steve Cerier, "Frankenfoods? A 'terrible word' that could describe more foods than you might realize," *Genetic Literacy Project*, April 13, 2018. https://geneticliteracyproject.org/2018/04/13/frankenfoods-a-terrible-word-that-could-describe-more-foods-than-you-might-realize/.

59. Qtd. in Bailey, "Victor Frankenstein Is the Real Monster," 59.

60. Michael Moore, "We Finally Got Our Frankenstein," *AlterNet*, December 14, 2003. https://www.alternet.org/story/17389/we_finally_got_our_frankenstein.

BIBLIOGRAPHY

Aldiss, Brian. *Billion Year Spree: The True History of Science Fiction.* New York: Doubleday, 1973.

Alkon, Paul K., and Raymond Kuhn. *Science Fiction Before 1900: Imagination Discovers Technology.* London: Routledge, 2002. *ProQuest Ebook Central,* http://ebookcen tral.proquest.com/lib/dixie-ebooks/detail.action?docID=1433981.

Bailey, Ronald. "Victor Frankenstein Is the Real Monster: Mary Shelley's Misunderstood Masterpiece Turns 200." *Reason* (April 2018): 57–62. https://reason.com/archives/2018/03/04/victor-frankenstein-is-the-rea.

Bartlett, Andrew. *Mad Scientist, Impossible Human: An Essay in Generative Anthropology.* Aurora, CO: The Davies Group Publishers, 2014. *ProQuest Ebook Central.*

Birkhead, Edith. *The Tale of Terror: A Study of the Gothic Romance.* London: Constable, 1921.

Braid, Barbara. "The Frankenstein Meme: Penny Dreadful and The Frankenstein Chronicles as Adaptations." *Open Cultural Studies* no. 1 (2017): 232–243.

Butler, Marilyn. "*Frankenstein* and Radical Science." *Frankenstein,* ed. Paul Hunter. New York: Norton, 1996, 302–313.

Cantor, Paul A. *Creature and Creator: Myth-Making and English Romanticism.* Cambridge: Cambridge UP, 1984.

Curran, Stuart. "*Frankenstein* in Popular Culture." *Study Aids: In Popular Culture. Romantic Circles* (2009). http://www.rc.umd.edu/editions/frankenstein/Pop/pop.html.

Friedman, Lester D. and Allison B. Kavey. *Monstrous Progeny: A History of the Frankenstein Narratives,* New Brunswick, NJ: Rutgers UP, 2016.

Hadzigeorgiou, Yannis, and Roland Schulz. "Romanticism and Romantic Science: Their Contribution to Science Education." *Science & Education* 23, no. 10 (Oct 2014): 1963–2006.

Harkup, Kathryn. *Making the Monster: The Science Behind Mary Shelley's Frankenstein.* New York: Bloomsbury Sigma, 2018.

Hindle, Maurice. "Vital Matters: Mary Shelley's Frankenstein and Romantic Science." *Critical Survey* 2, no. 1 (1990): 29–35.

Hogsette, David S. "Metaphysical Intersections in Frankenstein: Mary Shelley's Theistic Investigation of Scientific Materialism and Transgressive Autonomy." *Christianity and Literature* 60, no. 4 (Summer 2011): 531–59.

Ketterer, David. *Frankenstein's Creation: The Book, the Monster, and Human Reality.* Victoria, BC: Department of English at U Victoria, 1979. *English Literary Studies* 16.

Latour, Bruno. *We Have Never Been Modern.* Trans. Catherine Porter. New York: Harvester Wheatsheaf, 1993.

Levine, George. "The Ambiguous Heritage of Frankenstein." *The Endurance of Frankenstein: Essays on Mary Shelley's Novel.* Berkeley: U of California P, 1979: 3–30.

McGrath, James F. *Religion and Science Fiction.* Cambridge, England: The Lutterworth Press, 2012.

Mitchell, Robert. *Experimental Life: Vitalism in Romantic Science & Literature.* Baltimore, MD: The Johns Hopkins UP, 2013.

Moore, Michael. "We Finally Got Our Frankenstein." *AlterNet,* December 14, 2003. https://www.alternet.org/story/17389/we_finally_got_our_frankenstein.

Pilkington, Ace G. *Science Fiction and Futurism: Their Terms and Ideas.* Jefferson, NC: McFarland, 2017.

Rauch, Alan. *Useful Knowledge: The Victorians, Morality, and the March of Intellect.* Durham: Duke UP 2001.

Rieger, James E., ed. "Preface." In *Frankenstein; or, The Modern Prometheus, 1818 edition.* Chicago: Chicago UP, 1982.

Rose, Mark. *Alien Encounters: Anatomy of Science Fictio.* Cambridge, MA: Harvard UP, 1981.

Shelley, Mary. *Frankenstein.* Norton Critical Edition. New York: Norton, First Printing Edition, 1996.

Weingart, Peter, Claud Muhl, and Petra Pansegrau. "Of Power Maniacs and Unethical Geniuses: Science and Scientists in Fiction Film" *Public Understanding of Science* (2003): 279–87.

Willis, Martin. *Mesmerists, Monsters, and Machines: Science Fiction and the Cultures of Science in the Nineteenth Century.* Kent, OH: The Kent State UP, 2013. *ProQuest Ebook Central,* http://ebookcentral.proquest.com/lib/dixie-ebooks/detail.action?docID=3120170 .

Chapter Two

Female Scientists Under Strain

Transitions from Lab to Lit to Screen

Dean Conrad and Lynne Magowan

I keep six honest working men
(They taught me all I knew);
Their names were What and Why and When
And How and Where and Who.[1]

It has been said that the English writer Rudyard Kipling was inspired to write this poem by his daughter, Elsie, whose inquiring mind as a child earned her the family nickname "Elsie Why."[2] That might well have been reason enough to use its first stanza to open a chapter which highlights the role of a female scientist; however, the poem itself is also a useful introduction to a key difference between science fiction and laboratory literature. Namely, the application of the scientific method. As Olga Pilkington points out in her introduction to this volume, "lab lit" can be characterized as "science *in* fiction." As such, it concerns itself with the established, investigative cycle that includes observation, hypothesis, experiment, and conclusion. Science fiction is concerned less with this methodology, and more with the ramifications of its results. Stretching the Kipling link into this genre distinction, then: lab lit is in the business of explaining "how is?" leaving science fiction to imagine "what if?" The remaining variables of inquiry—"why," "when," where," and "who"—add texture to these pursuits.

Of course, genre definition is never quite that easy. Defining lab lit is made more difficult by its close relationship with science fiction. And that, as Ace Pilkington and many others have pointed out elsewhere, is already a notoriously difficult genre to pin down.[3] When non-literary media are added to the mix, the relationship between lab lit and science fiction becomes even closer—making the challenge of definition and distinction greater. This chapter examines first what happens when the "where?" is cinema, and then the effect when the "who?" is female. In doing so, it explores the rationale behind some of the "honest working women" of lab lit within the medium of film.

WHERE . . . ?

It is probably safe to assume that the majority of people who have a connection with *Frankenstein* know it primarily through screen adaptations (although this may well not be true of the majority of people who choose to read this book). It is this primary relationship with the material that will skew notions about whether the work is lab lit, science fiction or something else. While Mary Wollstonecraft Shelley's original 1818 novel, *Frankenstein; or, The Modern Prometheus*,[4] explores some early nineteenth-century questions regarding morality, the sanctity of life, Man's relationship with God, and so forth, recourse to rigorous scientific method is largely missing. It is the "what if?" not the "how is?" that draws filmmakers back to Frankenstein again and again. It enables them to tell stories of good and evil, overlaid by themes of heroism and redemption, as Robert De Niro shows in his portrayal of the tortured creature in Kenneth Brannagh's 1994 version, *Mary Shelley's Frankenstein*.[5] More important to filmmakers than both scientific method and psychological exploration, however, is *Frankenstein*'s potential for visual impact. Film is, after all, primarily a visual medium. Following tracks laid down by Boris Karloff in dramatic, prosthetic makeup, destroying Universal Pictures studio sets in James Whale's 1931 classic,[6] De Niro's creature is a grotesque. The focus in both films—and many other adaptations—is the ramifications of scientific experimentation, not the methodology used. Indeed, the creature himself has often been taken out of the context of Shelley's original story and reduced to a mere destructive force to be challenged by other characters, such as Wolf Man, Dracula, Abbott and Costello, and so on.[7] By this reckoning, *Frankenstein* is science fiction—at least when it is taken onto the screen.

In fact, it might be argued that Arthur Conan Doyle's original *Sherlock Holmes* stories are more lab lit than is *Frankenstein*; after all, Holmes applies science to his investigations and explains his method. Much of this is retained for versions of these stories produced for television, whose once-small screens made it a more receptive place for the discussion of process. The most popular Sherlock Holmes feature films, however, tend to be those adapted from tales that have more visually dramatic potential, such as *The Hound of the Baskervilles*.[8] As televisions have increased in size, visual impact has been required to add interest to Holmes's thought processes. For example, the hugely successful 2010 version, *Sherlock*,[9] uses sophisticated screen techniques, graphics, and editing to convey the detective's method as a progression of visual elements rooted in science: equations, graphs, diagrams, and so forth. Science on the screen in general (and cinema in particular) relies on visual techniques. The time-honored playwright's adage, "show, don't tell," translates screen lab lit into a progression of motifs leading to an outcome, rather than explanations leading to a conclusion.

Ironically, it is an essential lab lit element missing from Mary Shelley's original *Frankenstein* that generates some of its most memorable screen moments—namely, the "scene" when the creature comes to life. Shelley's rather understated description at the beginning of chapter 5, "I collected the instruments of life around me, that I might infuse a spark of being into the lifeless thing . . . ,"[10] is transformed by Whale's 1931 film into lightning bolts, electrical capacitors, conductors, dials, gadgets, imposing sets, and dramatic music, as well as the protagonist's ecstatic cry, "It's alive!" It has more visual impact than the original, "I saw the dull yellow eye of the creature open"; and, crucially, it turns it into screen science fiction.

However, there is danger inherent in this pursuit. Cinema's "show, don't tell" philosophy often denies the viewer her imagination, leading to the familiar cry of the film critic: "It's not as good as the book!" The 2000 film *Hollow Man*,[11] a loose adaptation of H.G. Wells's 1897 story *The Invisible Man*,[12] makes an attempt to portray the psychological deterioration of the original hero; however, more effort seems to have been spent on the impressive effects that make Kevin Bacon disappear. Cinema is littered with adaptations that follow this pattern.

The central fear for the filmmaker is that the scientific method—the mainstay of lab lit—will appear dull to the viewer. The 1950 movie *Destination Moon*[13] is credited as an adaptation of Robert Heinlein's 1947 juvenile adventure novel *Rocket Ship Galileo*; in reality, it is channeling a much earlier forensic approach, presented in what is perhaps the first lab lit tale (and perhaps the first science fiction story), *Kepler's Somnium*, a 1634 account of a trip to the moon.[14] To help turn method into motif, *Destination Moon*'s producers hired former Nazi rocket-expert Herman Oberth. While this undoubtedly brought authenticity to the production,[15] rather too much emphasis is placed on scientific and technical veracity, resulting in a film that is often more didactic than dramatic.

What seems clear is that lab lit is tricky territory for those filmmakers attempting faithfully to bring its literature to the screen. This then was the challenge facing one of the best-selling lab lit novels of all time.

WHAT . . . ?

If lab lit does indeed entail, as Jennifer Rohn asserts, "scientific characters, activities or themes . . . portrayed in a realistic manner,"[16] then Michael Crichton's 1969 novel *The Andromeda Strain* is certainly lab lit. It records, often in forensic detail, a scientific response to the arrival on Earth of a deadly pathogen—the strain of the title—that has killed all but two of the forty-eight residents of the small town of Piedmont, Arizona. Although Michael Crichton essentially wrote a Sherlock Holmes story for the Space Age, he describes his book in a filmed interview as "a howdunnit, a variation of a whodunnit, with scientists playing detective."[17] It is a combination that should point to a firm reliance on scientific methodology. Indeed, taking inspiration from Len Deighton's 1962 novel, *The IPCRESS File*,[18] Crichton augments these lab lit credentials by presenting much of his story as a *bona fide* government report—including technical diagrams, charts, data-tables, and equations, presented in computer printouts, teletype messages, and classified communique transcripts. Added to this is a credible (but entirely fictional) bibliography. Even the acknowledgments section suggests a serious research piece, with thanks offered to various (again fictional) personnel from NASA, Caltech, the U.S. Navy, the Whitehouse Press Corps, and so on.

In this front matter, Crichton also telegraphs the "science *in* fiction" style that underpins *The Andromeda Strain*; this appears as a caveat or a warning to his reader:

> This is a rather technical narrative, centering on complex issues of science. Wherever possible, I have explained the scientific questions, problems, and techniques. I have avoided the temptation to simplify both the issues and the answers, and if the reader must occasionally struggle through an arid passage of technical detail, I apologize.[19]

Of course, this "apology," with its bogus allusion to temptation avoided, is, in truth, just another "reality" technique, used to prepare the reader for the forensic, lab lit approach that Crichton has chosen to follow. This approach is, in turn, cemented by a team of four male scientists who painstakingly isolate the space pathogen in an attempt to discover what it is, how it functions, and how it might be destroyed. Crichton plays to his strengths as a medical student to imagine a convoluted biological process by which the bug has killed the people of Piedmont. As a result, his text is peppered with biology-based passages, seemingly lifted from Crichton's own medical student textbooks. The author adds to these lab lit methods by guiding the reader through various investigative procedures. Detailed explanations of electron microscopy are supported by references to research papers listed in the fictional bibliography; the workings of atomic filters and sterile chambers are described with technical terminology; and animal-based experiments are presented alongside vivid descriptions of the onerous processes of decontamination that the human scientists themselves have to undergo, as they travel down through the increasingly sterile levels of their secret underground laboratory—Wildfire.

All of this scientific exposition and technical explanation points potentially to a novel which could not easily be made into a film; or, at least, one that would feel more akin to the dry and dull *Destination Moon* than the dynamic and dramatic *Frankenstein*. And yet, *The Andromeda Strain* was taken up by experienced producer/director Robert Wise and a major Hollywood movie studio. Wise was already a successful science fiction director, having made the 1951 classic *The Day the Earth Stood Still*.[20] He could doubtless see, however, that *The Andromeda Strain*, while compelling on the page, presented a number of additional challenges to the filmmaker; this was never going to yield a standard, "cookie-cutter" science fiction movie. It required this director, whose accomplishments encompassed many film disciplines and genres, [21] to negotiate what would become new cinematic territory—one allied to lab lit.

The Day the Earth Stood Still had also been adapted from literature. It is based on the Harry Bates 1940 short story "Farewell to the Master,"[22] very little of which remains in Edmund North's screenplay. In a filmed interview, fellow screenwriter Nelson Gidding points out that Wise preferred his adapted scripts to be written by someone other than the original author, who can be "very bound to the concepts that he wrote."[23] Changes inevitably need to be made in the service of a movie. This is one reason why Gidding, an adaptation specialist and Wise's regular collaborator, was a good fit to write the screenplay for *The Andromeda Strain*.[24] It seems surprising then that, despite all of this Hollywood hedging and careful preparation, the eventual 1971 science fiction movie remains remarkably close, in plot and spirit, to the 1969 lab lit book.

Printed on the back cover of the 1993 Arrow books edition of *The Andromeda Strain* is the following quote from a *Life* magazine review:

> Science fiction, which once frightened us because it seemed so far-out, now frightens because it seems so near. *The Andromeda Strain* is as matter-of-fact as the skull-and-crossbones instructions on a bottle of poison—and just as chillingly effective.[25]

This factual nearness is crucial to the success of the movie. Ironically, it is the novel's framing as a written dossier of true events that supplies the intimacy and immediacy required by the filmmakers to translate the words into what Wise calls "much more science fact than fiction."[26] This "true story" element is reproduced on posters for the film in phrases like, "The story covers 96 of the most critical hours in man's history!" and "It could happen!"[27] The closeness of this threat lends drama to the events. The screenplay continues this by avoiding the, often expository and explanatory, flashbacks that are used throughout the novel to introduce characters and scientific ideas. It is essential to the success of the film that the story is set in the here-and-now—or, at least, the here-and-very-near-future.

This drive toward a sleek, linear script mirrors the clean, clinical, laboratory reality projected by the film. Its importance is reflected in the number of inherently filmic passages in the book that, ironically, do not actually make it to the screen. These include a graphic description of the dissection of Piedmont's Dr. Benedict;[28] the vomiting of bloody bile by Mr. Jackson, one of the two survivors at Piedmont;[29] and an underwater sequence, in which scientist Burton continues his journey down through the increasingly sterile levels of the Wildfire facility.[30] It is possible that these events were not filmed due to budget restrictions or rating requirements; however, their omission also keeps the movie free from the emotional distractions of biological mess and human viscera—allowing the focus to remain firmly on the technology and techniques of the scientific investigation.

This focus—which extends to the presentation of the mathematical structure of the pathogen itself—is part of a structured, sanitized approach that ironically moves the movie further away from science fiction, and toward lab lit. If the above observations about successful science fiction cinema are correct, this is an approach that should have ensured the failure of *The Andromeda Strain*. Instead, Wise's film has become a classic of the genre.

WHY . . . ?

Michael Crichton wrote a "techno-thriller"; that is, "a suspense novel in which the manipulation of sophisticated technology, as of aircraft or weapons systems, plays a prominent part."[31] This description is not inconsistent with lab lit, but the name itself feels altogether more dynamic and dramatic. That already offers a clue as to why *The Andromeda Strain* translated so effectively onto the screen. Of course, Mary Shelley could not have written *Frankenstein* with cinema in mind; however, Michael Crichton's primary inspiration, *The IPCRESS File*, had been turned into a successful film in 1965,[32] so he may well have harbored hopes of a screen adaptation for his own work. The most obvious nod to cinema in *The Andromeda Strain* novel is the generation of jeopardy that leads to a dramatic sequence at the end of the narrative. What amounts to the weakest lab lit element of the original story is telegraphed when Dr. Hall is given a special key. This puts him in possession of the only means to disable Wildfire's self-destruct device: an atomic bomb installed beneath the laboratory. In the event that the self-destruct sequence is activated and needs to be stopped, Hall is required to insert his key into one of the substation boxes situated around the facility. Adding to this potential threat is the fact that Wildfire is not complete. Among the few items of equipment that are yet to be installed are the crucial substations on the deepest, most impenetrable level of the underground facility. While all of the scientific equipment required to tell the logical, lab lit story is in place, the equipment required to ensure against a chaotic, science fiction finale is not. The inevitable happens: the self-destruct sequence is triggered by a breach in Wildfire's bio-security protocols, forcing Hall to race through the building looking for a functioning substation.

Dissecting differences between science fiction books and films in his seminal 1970 work *Science Fiction in the Cinema*, John Baxter suggests that the genre's literature supports "logic and order," whereas its films support "illogic and chaos."[33] If this is true, then Crichton has indeed introduced a filmic element to his novel, fabricated to set up the dramatic finale, in which Hall is forced to climb up through the central core of the facility to find a floor with a working substation. Again, this is an inherently filmic sequence, which is further augmented on screen by replacing the ligamine darts that protect the core from animal invaders in the book with (science fiction) lasers.

This notion of a fabricated jeopardy leading to a filmic action sequence is supported further by the fact that, although Hall does eventually manage to halt the self-destruct countdown at Wildfire, another atomic device is successfully dropped by the U.S. Airforce over Piedmont anyway. It has no effect at all on the pathogen. In what amounts to a *deus ex machina* ending—the "god from the machine" reveal that has its roots in Greek theater of the fifth-century BC—the Andromeda bug eventually dies spontaneously, requiring no intervention from humans. It is an anti-climax akin to the ending of H.G. Wells's 1898 novel *War of the Worlds*,[34] in which the malign Martians are eventually thwarted by Earth-based (God-created) bacteria.

This *deus ex machina* ending also betrays Crichton's patchy approach to science in the original novel. While he may not limit his forensic analysis completely to his specialist field of medicine, his descriptions of non-biological science are not as deep and detailed as his biological ones. For example, in a file describing the workings of Wildfire, a section entitled "Alterations" offers eighty-plus words outlining the theory and function of organism-trapping "Millipore Filters," whereas the hardware that controls the "Atomic Self-Destruct Device" is merely given a series of file references, including "See AEC/file 77-14-0023. SUMMARY APPENDED."[35] As was noted above, Crichton was playing to his strengths as a medical student. Indeed, he notes himself, "I was in medical school being taught all these complicated matters. I didn't do any research at all actually; I wrote it based on what I knew."[36] It is inevitable then that there would be what Baxter might regard as "illogical" gaps in the science.

These gaps in the science of the lab lit book allow space for invention and innovation on screen; this, once again, fulfills science fiction cinema's need for visual motifs. As a result, technological innovations that are outlined in Crichton's novel make it to Wise's movie in augmented form. These include a precursor to a modern A.I. assistant device, and a medical-diagnostic program, introduced by nurse/technical assistant Karen Anson, played by Paula Kelly, with: "Medcom's got one of the best minds here. It's a medical data analyzer that can diagnose as well as prescribe."[37] In addition, the film adds many other cutting-edge technologies, including moving computer graphics and a light pen used to select items on a computer screen.

Despite all of these filmic techniques and tropes adding to the film's "science-fiction-ness," it is hard to get away from the novel's potentially mundane, drawn-out, and repetitive procedures, such as the sterilization of the scientists, the dissection of the alien sample, or the discovery of the size of its killer particles using those millipore filters. Without explanation of the technical and scientific processes, however, *The Andromeda Strain* would have no plot (beyond the manufactured dramatic climax). Process is the story. In order to make this work on screen, the filmmakers, rather than shying away from Crichton's essential mechanics of scientific investigation, make a virtue of them. As noted above, Wise and his directors of art and photography do this through carefully crafted visual elements, such as the bright green, magnified, electron microscope image of the pathogen. This takes up much of the screen, amplifying its status as a clear and present threat to the scientists. It is this threat, along with many other challenges to the scientists' well-being, that is crucial to the success of *The Andromeda Strain* on film.

Wise and Gidding ensure that people are at the center of these processes. By emphasizing character reactions to events like the death of a laboratory monkey or the intrusive nature of the decontamination procedure, the movie makes them—through human, personal response, discomfort, and jeopardy—points of identification for the viewer. Through these and other techniques, *The Andromeda Strain* introduces to science fiction cinema a dramatization and humanization of experimental processes which had rarely been seen in the genre before—at least not in such concentrations. Visual motifs and scientific methods have been combined in *The Andromeda Strain* in a celebration of people-through-process; the result is a hybrid form, a subgenre that successfully presents lab lit on screen. This is "process porn."

As an experienced screenwriter, Nelson Gidding was well aware that audience identification with the characters is crucial to any drama. This, combined with the added need to humanize the scientific processes described in the original story, is what must have led him to suggest *The Andromeda Strain*'s most radical film innovation: a female scientist.

WHO . . . ?

The clinical microbiologist Peter Leavitt from Crichton's book appears in Wise's film as Ruth Leavitt, played by Kate Reid. This gender switch came at a time when there were few professional women in science fiction cinema. With the notable exception of Dr. Zira, played by Kim Hunter, in the 1968 film *Planet of the Apes*,[38] the 1950s phenomenon described by Bonnie Noonan as "the emerging woman professional, particularly in the fields of science,"[39] had largely faded by the end of the 1960s. Zira herself would be sidelined and killed off in 1971, during her second sequel, *Escape from the Planet of the Apes*.[40] Despite—or perhaps because of—the many social, sexual, political and cultural changes that were affecting women as Second Wave feminism took hold, science fiction was retreating toward the tales of male fantasy and self-discovery that have always served as the genre's default position. As a result, *The Andromeda Strain*—with its strong-willed female scientist—stands out amid films such as *THX 1138*, *A Clockwork Orange*, *The Omega Man*, *Solaris*, and *Silent Running*.[41]

Initially, Wise was skeptical about the change suggested by Gidding,[42] which seems ironic, given that an entirely invented female character had been pivotal to the director's 1951 classic, *The Day the Earth Stood Still*. The source material for that film contains no women at all. Helen Benson is introduced as voice-of-reason and mediator between Klaatu, the male alien, and the patriarchally structured human race. However, Benson is also a mother and secretary, traditional roles which filmmakers of the 1950s regularly used as a touchstone—a point of safe familiarity—for audiences of the genre's fantastic narratives. Despite Noonan's succession of female scientists, it is clear from Wise's reaction to Gidding's suggested gender switch that this particular glass ceiling was some way from being shattered. It was not an auspicious start for Ruth Leavitt.

Wise admits that his mind was changed only after seeking the opinions of real scientists, reporting their response as: "That would be fine with us, we know many great female scientists and that would not violate the film at all."[43] Once again, realism is revealed to be a preoccupation for the director and a primary arbiter when including an element in the film. It would seem that not only were previous screen scientists having some impact on perceptions, but real women in real labs were making their mark too. Science fiction cinema, however, has a habit of giving with one hand and taking with the other, especially when it comes to female characters. Despite screenwriter Gidding's success in turning Peter into Ruth, questions raised—not least by the director—clearly generated enough doubt for him to look again at the new role. Just as Helen Benson's status as mother and secretary had contributed to her "ordinary" representation, allowing the audience to accept her extraordinary actions, Ruth Leavitt would be subject to changes that would make her "acceptable" too. And some of those changes fundamentally altered the nature and function of the character as it transitioned from male to female.

Dr. Ruth Leavitt retains a doctorate, but she is not a professor of pathology with a happy family life and a Nobel Prize as Peter is in the book; nor is she famous in the academic world for formulating the "Rule of 48," [44] which sagely warns scientists not to blindly trust their data. These book-to-film omissions may seem like surface changes that merely dilute Ruth Leavitt's backstory; however, the down-grading of the character does not stop there. In fact, reducing Ruth's academic achievements is the first step in a process which denies her crucial knowledge that had been held by Peter.

In one of the novel's expository flashbacks, it is explained that Peter's "Rule of 48" had been invoked "when he and the other Wildfire planners drew up the study known as the Vector Three."[45] The technicalities of this are less important than the fact that Professor Peter Leavitt had helped to design the secret laboratory facility. Crichton duly uses him as a source of knowledge to explain the setup to other characters in the book—and, by proxy, to the reader. In one sequence, Peter is describing the importance of a nondescript dirt track to Dr. Hall, as they approach Wildfire by car: "We took great pains about it. . . . Had to get rid of the tractor treadmarks. A hell of a lot of heavy equipment has moved over these roads."[46] Once inside, Peter Leavitt continues to explain the workings of the facility to Dr. Hall and Dr. Burton. In the film, however, it is Ruth Leavitt who has the procedures explained to her by Dr. Stone. Although she does display a seemingly innate knowledge of many of the facility's technical processes throughout the film, Leavitt has had no role in the creation of Wildfire. Instead, she generally takes over the role of on-screen proxy for the ignorant audience, asking questions and receiving explanations.

This development is indicative of science fiction cinema's treatment of women throughout its history. Whatever the advances, women's roles have regularly been restricted by male creatives' notions of "reality," which are, in turn, tied closely to perceptions of what audiences at a given time would accept and expect—especially of a professional scientist. Despite this genre history, the example presented in *The Andromeda Strain* seems particularly curious because the female character who is denied knowledge is adapted from the male character that possessed this knowledge. This raises the question: Why not switch the gender of the already-ignorant Dr. Hall, and leave Prof. Peter Leavitt intact? The most obvious answer is that Hall, the key-holder, is crucial to the dramatic, physical sequence at the climax of the story. This role could not easily be given to a woman at that time. The second, rather less obvious, answer reveals a deeper misogyny: Leavitt has a fundamental weakness.

In the novel, Peter suffers from what appears to be a combination of epilepsy and narcolepsy, which causes him occasionally to lose track of his actions:

> It had happened again. And this time, for ten minutes. What had gone on? He couldn't remember. But it was ten minutes gone, disappeared, while he had dressed—an action that shouldn't have taken more than thirty seconds.[47]

A variation of this ailment is one trait that screenwriter Gidding chooses to keep when Peter Leavitt becomes Ruth Leavitt. At various points in the movie she is affected by flashing red lights. This is trivial at first, but eventually it immobilizes her, potentially jeopardizing the mission and causing her to be rescued by a male colleague. And so, the unfamiliar appearance of a smart, sassy, sarcastic female scientist in the form of Dr. Ruth Leavitt was tempered in 1971 by a fundamental weakness. It is a familiar treatment—one that has consistently diminished and undermined female professionals in science fiction cinema.

HOW . . . ?

Lisa Tuttle has described the archetypal professional female science fiction literature role as "an object lesson to girl readers that career success equals feminine failure."[48] This would appear to be the model followed by the makers of *The Andromeda Strain* when they chose to present Ruth Leavitt as an overweight, irascible, a-sexual spinster. Her image supports Tuttle's implication that pretty, young women do not do science in fiction; indeed, Ruth's presentation throughout the film essentially makes her "one of the boys." It is these characteristics that prompt Eva Flicker to feature Leavitt in the "Male Woman"[49] category for "Between Brains and Breasts," her brief 2003 sketch of female professionals across a number of film genres. As an androgynous entity, Ruth presents no threat to the science status quo, or to the men—on screen or in the cinema audience. Whether this model holds true for written lab lit will doubtless be made clear through other essays in this volume; it cannot, however, be used as a general description for female scientists (or other professionals) in science fiction film. Other dowdy, irascible female scientists do exist, including Prof. Mabel Chapel, played by Amelia Hall in *Iceman*,[50] but they are rare. Dr. Ruth Leavitt's prominent role in *The Andromeda Strain* makes her rarer still.

Indeed, as if to contradict Tuttle's "feminine failure" with regard to literature, science fiction cinema has, more often than not, emphasised the "feminine" aspects of its female scientists. This can be seen from characters in those 1950s movies, including: chemist Dr. Lisa van Horn, played by Osa Massen in *Rocketship X-M*,[51] mathematician Joyce Hendron, played by Barbara Rush in *When Worlds Collide*;[52] and Faith Domergue's two characters, physicist Dr. Ruth Adams and marine biologist Prof. Lesley Joyce, in *This Island Earth* and *It Came from Beneath the Sea*, respectively.[53] It is clear that these particular, attractive women served to reinforce the notion of "Us" in the fight against the invading "Them" in narratives that allegorize the Cold War, the rise of the military-industrial complex, and other jolts to society throughout the post-war period. "Femininity," as projected by physical appearance, was being used as a touchstone—a point of safe familiarity—for audiences; however, this is not the only method that science fiction cinema has used to fulfill its apparent need to restrict its female scientists.

As has been noted elsewhere, even Dr. Zira was diminished by the genre. Before she is eventually killed off in *Escape from the Planet of the Apes*, her rational voice of reason becomes lost to "parody and self-mockery"[54] when she is used as a spokesperson for a male notion of the Women's Liberation Movement. Zira is then replaced in her role as the primary professional primatologist by the human Dr. Stephanie Branton, played by Natalie Trundy, in a handover that highlights another of the genre's gender restrictions that has been noted elsewhere. That is, the female scientist tends to follow the "life sciences"; in so doing, "she reflects the values of Mother Nature using zoology, biology, psychology, and the like."[55]

It is another "life science" that provides a rationale for this general phenomenon:

> In psychoanalytical terms, a cinema-goer's willingness to enjoy and accept what is on the screen is a function of her imagination (the unconscious, unfettered id) and her sense of reality (the socially structured super-ego). Imagination is pleasurable; this is what brings audiences to the cinema, but too much, according to Christian Metz . . . has the potential to alienate people. This "cinematic paradox" demands a balance: enough imagination to be exciting, but grounded in enough reality to be believable. More than any other genre, science fiction relies on this id/super-ego transaction.[56]

Long before the imaginative gender switch in *The Andromeda Strain* was balanced by Ruth Leavitt's own Achilles' heels, the genre's "id/super-ego transaction" had been regularly attenuating female roles in science fiction cinema.

The women introduced to the 1920 film version[57] of Stevenson's 1886 novella *The Strange Case of Dr. Jekyll and Mr. Hyde*,[58] starring the celebrated stage actor John Barrymore, are a virgin for Jekyll and a vamp for Hyde; they are both pawns in an attempt to add visual titillation to the original lab lit story, turning it into an exploration of private fantasy and sexual repression in Victorian England. The new, female creature created by Henry Frankenstein as a mate for his monster in James Whale's 1935 *Frankenstein* sequel *Bride of Frankenstein*[59] is not the grotesque that Boris Karloff is; instead, she is the beautiful, sexual lure, played by Elsa Lanchester. By the post-war 1940s, *Daily Planet* reporter Lois Lane in the Saturday morning chapter-play series *Superman*[60] was reflecting the contemporary, "acceptable" face of the professional woman. The female journalist had been seen in the genre as early as the 1920 chapter serial *The Screaming Shadow*[61] and may well have owed the "believability" of her representation to the high profiles of real-life Hollywood columnists Hedda Hopper and Louella Parsons. It was noted above that the female scientists who appeared in the 1950s tended to be attractive; there are also many examples of their knowledge being restricted by gender preconceptions. One example of this can be seen in the 1951 movie *The Thing from Another World*.[62] When the male scientists prove unable to kill the marauding creature of the title, it is actually the female assistant Nikki Nicholson, played by Margaret Sheridan, who provides the solution; however, it does involve the application of ("feminine") domestic science: the woman suggests that they "cook it." Like *The Andromeda Strain*, Ralph Nelson's 1968 film *Charly*[63] is adapted from best-selling literature;[64] it also features a scientist who transitions from male to female for the movie version. This female scientist, Dr. Strauss, played by Lilia Skala, is given responsibility for the eponymous Charly's emotional intelligence, leaving his cognitive skills the remit of Dr. Nemur, the remaining male scientist. And so, Strauss's role has been shifted to what is essentially a surrogate mother to the male protagonist. Bringing this brief list of female roles attenuated by the id/super-ego transaction into the 1970s is *Colossus: The Forbin Project*,[65] whose female computer specialist, Dr. Cleo Markham, played by Susan Clark, is required (albeit willingly) to pose as the lover of the leading male computer specialist in order to fool the omniscient, omnipotent, rogue computer of the title.

This phenomenon is not restricted to the 1950s and 1960s. In her study of female scientists and engineers in popular films from 1991 to 2001, Jocelyn Steinke offers examples in which male professionals "downplay or question the expertise of female engineers and scientists;"[66] although, Steinke does also note an apparent trend by this time toward "female scientists and engineers as equal members of research teams."[67]

Although seemingly different in nature, and sometimes subtle in approach, each of the above female representations meets the needs of Metz's "cinematic paradox": that is, it tempers imagination with reality—or at least a notion of reality. Adding to the movie's attenuated Dr. Leavitt, *The Andromeda Strain* continues with further subtle and diverse examples of this phenomenon. Most notably, an advanced auto-vocal-response system loses credibility and significance for the male scientists when it is discovered that its sexy, female voice belongs to an elderly spinster, and the traditional nurse/technical assistant figure in both book and film is female (although it should be noted that the film, unusually for the time, features a black performer: Paula Kelly). In Crichton's book, computer assistant Karen Anson explains "the working of the computer"[68] to Dr. Hall; however, this event does not appear in the movie. Instead, Karen Anson is the name given to the nurse character. By way of contrast, much is made in the book of Dr. Burton's investigative mistake when he fails to pursue lines of inquiry. This male failure does not make it to the film.

This presentation of differences between male and female capacity in *The Andromeda Strain* becomes most overt in an example that survives intact from Crichton's book to Wise's film. It is the fictional "Odd Man Hypothesis." This deals with the ability of men and women to make critical emotion-free decisions—most notably here, the decision to abort (or not) Wildfire's countdown to atomic self-destruct, using the special substation key. Alongside this outline, Crichton presents the following results of a study into the hypothesis:

Group Index of Effectiveness
Married males .343
Married females .399
Single females .402
Single males .824 [69]

Married men are presented as being too attached to their wives to make objective life-or-death decisions; whereas single men ("odd men") are unencumbered by emotional attachment. In this study, women remain prone to subjective (and emotional) decision making whether they are married or single. This "hypothesis" is another reason why Dr. Hall (the key-holder) could not become the female character in Gidding and Wise's 1971 film.

While it is more likely in 2019 to see Hall's role played by a woman, female roles in science fiction cinema in general have continued to be dented, downplayed, or diminished by the application of gender generalizations. Perhaps, however, there are times when women actually benefit from traditional notions about divisions of labor between the sexes.

WHEN . . . ?

Despite the movie's clear shortcomings, one of the legacies of *The Andromeda Strain* is Kate Reid's capable, no-nonsense, female scientist, Dr. Ruth Leavitt. She proves perfectly capable of holding her own amid the men, and it is she who makes the central discovery that leads to the theory about how to kill the pathogen. She is also, according to Robert Wise, "the most interesting character of all,"[70] which is ironic, given the director's initial skepticism regarding her inclusion in the film. If, as Jocelyn Steinke asserts, "images of female scientists and engineers presented in popular films are symbolic models that serve as sources of information about women, gender roles, and female scientists and engineers,"[71] these legacies are important. Given cinema's wide reach and cultural impact, it is likely that roles such as Reid's will have had some effect in another direction: that is, on the representation of the female scientist in literature. And if Olga Pilkington is correct in her assertion that lab lit itself is "a particularly fertile space for the development of female writers, characters and analysts and academics,"[72] that genre too will surely have been influenced by high-profile individuals on screen. Cinema and television certainly were.

Although the 2008 *Andromeda Strain* television mini-series,[73] produced by Ridley Scott and his brother Tony, is billed on the DVD case as being "based on the novel by Michael Crichton," it owes a great deal to Wise's film. Indeed, this version presents *two* female science professionals: the black Dr. Charlene Barton and the white Dr. Angela Noyce, played by Viola Davis and Christa Miller, respectively. Its additional billing as "The Epic Television Event" betrays a further drift away from the original lab lit approach; and, true to this promise, the series manufactures tension between the scientists and conflict between male political, military, and media characters introduced in invented subplots. Crichton's original logic and methodology is duly fractured into a series of visually arresting, diluted-science set pieces. This is television science fiction, not screen lab lit. The balanced hybrid, "process porn," that carries the original film is missing.

Back in the late 1970s, Michael Crichton built on the success of *The Andromeda Strain* by writing and directing the 1978 screen adaptation of Robin Cook's 1977 lab lit novel *Coma*,[74] which follows an already female surgeon, Dr. Susan Wheeler, as she investigates the unusually high number of coma incidents at her Boston hospital. Crichton's screen version[75] replicates much of the patronizing, patriarchal environment through which Wheeler, played by Geneviève Bujold, struggles in the book. While it retains Cook's condemnation of this masculinized medical hierarchy, it also telegraphs Dr. Wheeler's femininity in a naked shower scene and a rather curious up-skirt sequence. As noted above, this was familiar territory; and it continues to be one that science fiction filmmakers seem reluctant to vacate.

In 1979, Lt. Ripley's femininity was telegraphed in her "strip" scene toward the end of Alien.[76] In 1980, Yvette Mimieux's Dr. Kate McCrae was reduced to a damsel-in-distress in The Black Hole.[77] Princess Leia swaps a thermal detonator for her infamous gold bikini in the 1983 Star Wars sequel, Return of the Jedi.[78] Mother Nature is reflected in Catherine Hicks' cetacean biologist, Dr. Gillian Taylor, in *Star Trek IV: The Voyage Home*.[79] Mathematician Trinity, played by Carrie-Anne Moss, is reduced to chasing after her male messiah Neo in The Matrix,[80] but not before she has spawned a trend for the leather-clad, kick-boxing babes who have peppered the genre for the first two decades of the twenty-first-century. And during that time, Sandra Bullock fell to Earth in the "process porn" movie *Gravity*,[81] playing the psychologically tormented mother Dr. Ryan Stone, who would not realistically have been allowed into space in the first place. Even this small sample indicates that modern science fiction cinema remains replete with examples of the id/super-ego transaction; and despite occasional characters like Letitia Wright's genius scientist-cum-engineer Shuri in *Black Panther*[82] seeming to break the mold, the genre appears set to continue placing female scientists under strain.

Perhaps, however, this outcome is not entirely negative. Back in *The Andromeda Strain* movie, one of the characteristics given to the female Dr. Ruth Leavitt is a conscience. She is the scientist who expresses horror at the discovery that the pathogen had been collected in space by "Scoop," a military project designed to discover and develop biological weapons. With her cry, "Wildfire was built for germ warfare—and you knew!"[83] Ruth becomes the film's moral compass; it is a role that is also replicated across 120 years of the genre in the form of many female mediators and voices of reason. It is a role taken in the 2016 film *Arrival*[84] by Dr. Louise Banks, whose portrayal won Amy Adams many awards and plaudits. The story's focus on the female professional's methodological approach, as she attempts to decipher the alien language, makes it an example of lab lit; the "feminine" motifs of compassion, openness, and experience as a mother help to convert it to science fiction. The combination—lab lit on screen—eventually enables Dr. Banks to reach the conclusions needed to save the day.

If science fiction cinema has tended to corral and restrict its female characters, perhaps lab lit on screen offers them a place to thrive, to question, to experiment, to be themselves—to be *female*. It is an ambition echoed in that poem by Kipling about his daughter, Elsie—a call to honest working women everywhere:

> She sends 'em abroad on her own affairs,
> From the second she opens her eyes—
> One million Hows, two million Wheres,
> And seven million Whys!

NOTES

1. Rudyard Kipling, "I Keep Six Honest Working Men," *Ladies' Home Journal* (London: n.p., 1900). [Also published as part of the "The Elephant's Child," collected in *Just So Stories*, 1902].

2. "The Elephant's Child," ed. Lisa Lewis. *The Kipling Society*. Accessed July 4, 2018. http://www.kiplingsociety.co.uk/rg_elephantschild1.htm.

3. For a clear general survey of science fiction definitions, begin with John Clute and Peter Nicholls, eds., *The Encyclopedia of Science Fiction*, 2d ed. (London: Orbit, 1993), esp. 311–14. Then cf. (in chronological order) Kingsley Amis, *New Maps of Hell: A Survey of Science Fiction* (New York: Harcourt, Brace and Co., 1960); Brian Ash, ed., *The Visual Encyclopedia of Science Fiction* (New York: Harmony, 1977); Robert Scholes and Eric S. Rabkin, *Science Fiction: History, Science, Vision* (New York: OUP, 1977); Brian W. Aldiss and David Wingrove, *Trillion Year Spree: The History of Science Fiction* (London: Victor Gollancz, 1986); Edward James, *Science Fiction in the Twentieth Century* (Oxford and New York: Oxford University Press, 1994), esp. 2–14; Adam Roberts, *The History of Science Fiction* (Basingstoke: Palgrave Macmillan, 2007), esp.1–20; and for a comprehensive examination of the genre and its themes, see: Ace G. Pilkington, *Science Fiction and Futurism: Their Terms and Ideas* (Jefferson: McFarland, 2017).

4. Mary [Wollstonecraft] Shelley, *Frankenstein; or, The Modern Prometheus* (London: Wordsworth Classics, 1993). [First published, 1818, by Hughes, Harding, Mavor & Jones].

5. Kenneth Brannagh, *Mary Shelley's Frankenstein* (USA: American Zoetrope / TriStar / Japan Satellite Broadcasting / Indieprod, 1994). Film.

6. James Whale, *Frankenstein* (USA: Universal Pictures, 1931). Film.

7. See: Roy William Neill, *Frankenstein Meets the Wolf Man* (USA: Universal, 1943); Erle C. Kenton, *House of Dracula* (USA: Universal, 1945); Charles T. Barton, *Abbott and Costello Meet Frankenstein* (USA: Universal, 1948). Films.

8. Arthur Conan Doyle, *The Hound of the Baskervilles* (London: George Newnes, 1902).

9. Mark Gatiss and Steven Moffat, creators, *Sherlock* (UK / USA: BBC Wales / Hartswood / Masterpiece, 2010–2017). Television series, fifteen episodes to date.

10. Shelley, *Frankenstein; or, The Modern Prometheus*, 45.

11. Paul Verhoeven, *Hollow Man* (USA / Germany: Columbia / Global Entertainment, 2000). Film.

12. H.G. Wells, *The Invisible Man* (London: C. Arthur Pearson, 1897).

13. Irving Pichel, *Destination Moon* (USA: George Pal Productions, 1950). Film.

14. See: John Lear, *Kepler's Dream* ["With the full text and notes of *Somnium, Sive Astronomia Lunaris, Joannis Kepleri*," 1634. Translated by Patricia Frueh Kirkwood] (Berkeley and Los Angeles: University of California Press, 1965).

15. See: Rafeeq O. McGiveron, "From Selenite Suicide to Bonestell Backdrops: Robert A. Heinlein on the Course to Desination Moon," in *The Fantastic Made Visible: Essays on the Adaptation of Science Fiction and Fantasy from Page to Screen*, ed. Matthew Wilhelm Kapell and Ace G. Pilkington (Jefferson: McFarland, 2015), 28–42, esp. 37–39.

16. Olga Pilkington, introduction in the current work.

17. Laurent Bouzereau, *A Portrait of Michael Crichton* [Included with *The Andromeda Strain*, Universal DVD 820-148-1] (USA: Universal, 2001). DVD.

18. Len Deighton, *The IPCRESS File* (London: Hodder & Stoughton, 1962).

19. Michael Crichton, *The Andromeda Strain* (London: Arrow, 1993), 5. [First published 1969].

20. Robert Wise, *The Day the Earth Stood Still* (USA: 20th Century Fox, 1951). Film.

21. Robert Wise's diverse movie portfolio includes: sound effects editor on the Fred Astaire musical *Top Hat* (Mark Sandrich, *Top Hat* [USA: RKO, 1935]); film editor on the masterpiece *Citizen Kane* (Orson Welles, *Citizen Kane* [USA: Mercury Productions / RKO, 1941]); a director of crime drama, *I Want to Live!* (Robert Wise, *I Want to Live!* [USA: Figaro / UA, 1958]) horror, *The Haunting* (Robert Wise, *The Haunting* [UK / USA: Argyll Enterprises / MGM, 1963]); and later the director/producer of *West Side Story* (Robert Wise and Jerome Robbins, *West Side Story* [USA: Mirisch / Seven Arts, 1961]); and *The Sound of Music* (Robert Wise, *The Sound of Music* [USA: 20th Century Fox, 1965]).

22. Harry Bates, "Farewell to the Master," in *Astounding Science Fiction* (October 1940).

23. Laurent Bouzereau, *The Making of The Andromeda Strain* [Included with *The Andromeda Strain*, Universal DVD 820-148-1] (USA: Universal, 2001). DVD.

24. Robert Wise, *The Andromeda Strain* (USA: Universal / Robert Wise Productions, 1971). Film.

25. Crichton, *The Andromeda Strain*, cover.

26. Bouzereau, *The Making of The Andromeda Strain*.

27. Bouzereau, *The Making of The Andromeda Strain*.

28. Crichton, *The Andromeda Strain*, 76.

29. Crichton, *The Andromeda Strain*, 84.

30. Crichton, *The Andromeda Strain*, 117–18.

31. "Techno-thriller," Dictionary.com. Accessed July 4, 2018. http://www.dictionary.com/browse/techno-thriller.

32. Stanley J. Furie, *The Ipcress File* (UK: Rank Films, 1965). Film.

33. John Baxter, *Science Fiction in the Cinema* (New York: A.S. Barnes and Co. / London: Zwemmer, 1970), 10–11.

34. H.G. Wells, *War of the Worlds* (London: William Heinemann, 1898).

35. Crichton, *The Andromeda Strain*, 109.

36. Bouzereau, *A Portrait of Michael Crichton*.

37. Wise, *The Andromeda Strain*.

38. Franklin J. Schaffner, *Planet of the Apes* (USA: APJAC Productions / 20th Century Fox, 1968). Film.

39. Bonnie Noonan, *Women Scientists in Fifties Science Fiction Films* (Jefferson: McFarland, 2005), 49.

40. Don Taylor, *Escape from the Planet of the Apes* (USA: 20th Century Fox / APJAC Productions, 1971). Film.

41. See: George Lucas, *THX 1138* (USA: American Zoetrope, 1970); Stanley Kubrick, *A Clockwork Orange* (UK: Polaris Productions / Warner Bros, 1971); Boris Sagal, *The Omega Man* (USA: Walter Seltzer Productions, 1971); Andrei Tarkovsky, *Solaris* (USSR: Mosfilm / Unit Four / Creative Unit of Writers and Cinema Workers, 1971); Douglas Trumbull, *Silent Running* (USA: Universal / Michael Gruskoff Productions / Douglas Trumbull Productions, 1971). Films.

42. See: Bouzereau, *The Making of The Andromeda Strain*.

43. Bouzereau, *The Making of The Andromeda Strain*.

44. Crichton, *The Andromeda Strain*, 131.

45. Crichton, *The Andromeda Strain*, 131.

46. Crichton, *The Andromeda Strain*, 96.

47. Crichton, *The Andromeda Strain*, 206.

48. See: Clute and Nicholls, *The Encyclopedia of Science Fiction*, 1343.

49. Eva Flicker, "Between Brains and Breasts—Women Scientists in Fiction Film: On the Marginalization and Sexualization of Scientific Competence," in *Public Understanding of Science* 12 (2003): 311.

50. Fred Schepisi, *Iceman* (USA: Universal, 1984). Film.

51. Kurt Neumann, *Rocketship X-M* (USA: Lippert, 1950). Film.

52. Rudolph Maté, *When Worlds Collide* (USA: George Pal Productions / Paramount, 1951). Film.

53. Joseph Newman, *This Island Earth* (USA: Universal, 1955); Robert Gordon, *It Came from Beneath the Sea* (USA: Clover, 1955). Films.

54. Dean Conrad and Lynne Magowan, "Damn, Dirty Dames: Dissecting Difference in *Planet of the Apes*," in *The Fantastic Made Visible: Essays on the Adaptation of Science Fiction and Fantasy from Page to Screen*, eds Matthew Wilhelm Kapell and Ace G. Pilkington (Jefferson: McFarland, 2015), 101–16, at 111.

55. Dean Conrad, *Space Sirens, Scientists and Princesses: The Portrayal of Women in Science Fiction Cinema* (Jefferson: McFarland, 2018), 83.

56. Conrad, *Space Sirens, Scientists and Princesses*, 135–36.

57. John S. Robertson, *Dr. Jekyll and Mr. Hyde* (USA: Famous Players Lasky, 1920). Film.

58. Robert Louis Stevenson, *The Strange Case of Dr. Jekyll and Mr. Hyde* (London: Longmans, Green & Co., 1886).

59. James Whale, *Bride of Frankenstein* (USA: Universal Pictures, 1931). Film.

60. Spencer Gordon Bennet and Thomas Carr, *Superman* (USA: Columbia, 1948). Chapterplay, fifteen episodes.

61. Duke Worne, *The Screaming Shadow* (USA: Hallmark Pictures, 1920). Chapter-play, fifteen episodes.

62. Christian Nyby, *The Thing from Another World!* (USA: RKO / Winchester, 1951). Film.

63. Ralph Nelson, *Charly* (USA: Selmur / Robertson Associates, 1968). Film.

64. See: Daniel Keyes, "Flowers for Algernon," in *The Magazine of Fantasy & Science Fiction* (April 1959). Print. [First book edition, Harcourt, Brace and World, 1966].

65. Joseph Sargent, *Colossus: The Forbin Project* (USA: Universal, 1970). Film.

66. Jocelyn Steinke, "Cultural Representations of Gender and Science: Portrayals of Female Scientists and Engineers in Popular Films," in *Science Communication* (September 2005): 46.

67. Steinke, 47.

68. Crichton, *The Andromeda Strain*, 148.

69. Crichton, *The Andromeda Strain*, 109–11.

70. Bouzereau, *The Making of The Andromeda Strain*.

71. Steinke, 52.

72. Olga Pilkington, introduction in the current work.

73. Mikael Salomon, *The Andromeda Strain* (USA: Universal / Scott Free / Traveler's Rest, 2008). DVD, TV mini-series, four episodes. [quotations taken from Universal DVD 8256506-11].

74. Robin Cook, *Coma* (New York: Little, Brown and Co., 1977).

75. Michael Crichton, *Coma* (USA: MGM, 1978). Film.

76. Ridley Scott, *Alien* (UK / USA: 20th Century Fox / Brandywine Productions, 1979). Film.

77. Gary Nelson, *The Black Hole* (USA: Walt Disney, 1980). Film.

78. Richard Marquand, *Star Wars: Episode VI—Return of the Jedi* (USA: Lucasfilm Ltd. / 20th Century Fox, 1983). Film.

79. Leonard Nimoy, *Star Trek IV: The Voyage Home* (USA: Paramount / ILM, 1986). Film.

80. Wachowski [Brothers], *The Matrix* (USA: Warner Bros. / Village Roadshow Pictures / Groucho II Film Partnership / Silver Pictures, 1999). Film.

81. Alfonso Cuarón, *Gravity* (USA / UK: Warner Bros. / Esperanto Filmoj / Heyday Films, 2013). Film.

82. Ryan Coogler, *Black Panther* (USA: Marvel Studios, 2018). Film.

83. Wise, *The Andromeda Strain*.

84. Denis Villeneuve, *Arrival* (USA: Paramount / FilmNation Entertainment / Lava Bear Films / 21 Laps Entertainment / Xenolinguistics, 2016). Film.

BIBLIOGRAPHY

Aldiss, Brian W., and David Wingrove. *Trillion Year Spree: The History of Science Fiction*. London: Victor Gollancz, 1986.

Amis, Kingsley. *New Maps of Hell: A Survey of Science Fiction*. New York: Harcourt, Brace and Co., 1960.

Ash, Brian, ed. *The Visual Encyclopedia of Science Fiction*. New York: Harmony, 1977.

Bates, Harry. "Farewell to the Master." First published in *Astounding Science Fiction*, October, 1940.

Baxter, John. *Science Fiction in the Cinema*. New York: A. S. Barnes and Co. London: Zwemmer, 1970.

Clute, John, and Peter Nicholls, eds. *The Encyclopedia of Science Fiction*. 2d ed. London: Orbit, 1993.

Conan Doyle, Arthur. *The Hound of the Baskervilles*. Original edition, London: George Newnes, 1902.

Conrad, Dean. *Space Sirens, Scientists and Princesses: The Portrayal of Women in Science Fiction Cinema*. Jefferson: McFarland, 2018.

Conrad, Dean, and Lynne Magowan. "Damn, Dirty Dames: Dissecting Difference in *Planet of the Apes*." In *The Fantastic Made Visible: Essays on the Adaptation of Science Fiction and*

Fantasy from Page to Screen, eds. Matthew Wilhelm Kapell and Ace G. Pilkington. 101–106, Jefferson: McFarland, 2015.

Cook, Robin. *Coma*. New York: Little, Brown and Co., 1977.

Crichton, Michael. *The Andromeda Strain*. London: Arrow, 1993. [First published 1969].

Deighton, Len. *The IPCRESS File*. London: Hodder & Stoughton, 1962.

Flicker, Eva. "Between Brains and Breasts—Women Scientists in Fiction Film: On the Marginalization and Sexualization of Scientific Competence," *Public Understanding of Science* 12 (2003): 307–18.

James, Edward. *Science Fiction in the Twentieth Century*. Oxford and New York: Oxford University Press, 1994.

Keyes, Daniel. "Flowers for Algernon." First published in *The Magazine of Fantasy & Science Fiction*, April 1959. [Book edition, Harcourt, Brace and World, 1966].

Kipling, Rudyard. "I Keep Six Honest Working Men." First published in *Ladies' Home Journal*, 1900. [Also published as part of the "The Elephant's Child." Collected in *Just So Stories*, 1902].

Lear, John. *Kepler's Dream* ["With the full text and notes of *Somnium, Sive Astronomia Lunaris*, Joannis Kepleri." 1634. Translated by Patricia Frueh Kirkwood]. Berkeley and Los Angeles: University of California Press, 1965.

Lewis, Lisa, ed. "The Elephant's Child." *The Kipling Society*. Accessed July 4, 2018. http://www.kiplingsociety.co.uk/rg_elephantschild1.htm.

McGiveron, Rafeeq O. "From Selenite Suicide to Bonestell Backdrops: Robert A. Heinlein on the Course to *Desination Moon*." In *The Fantastic Made Visible: Essays on the Adaptation of Science Fiction and Fantasy from Page to Screen*, ed. Matthew Wilhelm Kapell and Ace G. Pilkington, 28–42. Jefferson: McFarland, 2015.

Noonan, Bonnie. *Women Scientists in Fifties Science Fiction Films*. Jefferson: McFarland, 2005.

Pilkington, Ace G. *Science Fiction and Futurism: Their Terms and Ideas*. Jefferson: McFarland, 2017.

Roberts, Adam. *The History of Science Fiction*. Basingstoke: Palgrave Macmillan, 2007. [Palgrave Histories of Literature series. First published, 2005].

Scholes, Robert, and Eric S. Rabkin. *Science Fiction: History, Science, Vision*. New York: OUP, 1977.

Shelley, Mary [Wollstonecraft]. *Frankenstein; or, The Modern Prometheus*. London: Wordsworth Classics, 1993. [First published, 1818, by Hughes, Harding, Mavor & Jones].

Steinke, Jocelyn. "Cultural Representations of Gender and Science: Portrayals of Female Scientists and Engineers in Popular Films." *Science Communication* (September 2005): 27–63.

Stevenson, Robert Louis. *The Strange Case of Dr. Jekyll and Mr. Hyde*. Original edition, London: Longmans, Green & Co., 1886.

"Techno-thriller." Dictionary.com. Accessed July 4, 2018. http://www.dictionary.com/browse/techno-thriller.

Wells, H.G.. *The Invisible Man*. Original edition, London: C. Arthur Pearson, 1897.

Wells, H.G.. *War of the Worlds*. Original edition, London: William Heinemann, 1898.

FILMOGRAPHY

Barton, Charles T. *Abbott and Costello Meet Frankenstein*. USA: Universal, 1948. Film.

Bennet, Spencer Gordon, and Thomas Carr. *Superman*. USA: Columbia, 1948. Chapter-play, fifteen episodes.

Bouzereau, Laurent. *A Portrait of Michael Crichton* [Included with *The Andromeda Strain*, Universal DVD 820-148-1]. USA: Universal, 2001. DVD.

Bouzereau, Laurent. *The Making of The Andromeda Strain* [Included with *The Andromeda Strain*, Universal DVD 820-148-1]. USA: Universal, 2001. DVD.

Brannagh, Kenneth. *Mary Shelley's Frankenstein*. USA: American Zoetrope / TriStar / Japan Satelite Broadcasting / Indieprod, 1994. Film.

Coogler, Ryan. *Black Panther*. USA: Marvel Studios, 2018. Film.

Crichton, Michael. *Coma*. 1978. USA: MGM, 1978. Film.

Cuarón, Alfonso. *Gravity*. USA / UK: Warner Bros. / Esperanto Filmoj / Heyday Films, 2013. Film.

Furie, Stanley J. *The Ipcress File*. UK: Rank Films, 1965. Film.

Gatiss, Mark, and Steven Moffat, creators. *Sherlock*. UK / USA: BBC Wales / Hartswood / Masterpiece, 2010–2017. Television series, fifteen episodes to date.

Gordon, Robert. *It Came from Beneath the Sea*. USA: Clover, 1955. Film.

Kenton, Erle C. *House of Dracula*. USA: Universal, 1945. Film.

Kubrick, Stanley. *A Clockwork Orange*. UK: Polaris Productions / Warner Bros, 1971. Film.

Lucas, George. *THX 1138*. USA: American Zoetrope, 1970. Film.

Lucas, George. 1977. *Star Wars: Episode IV—A New Hope*. USA: Lucasfilm / 20th Century Fox, 1977. Film.

Marquand, Richard. *Star Wars: Episode VI—Return of the Jedi*. USA: Lucasfilm Ltd. / 20th Century Fox, 1983. Film.

Maté, Rudolph. *When Worlds Collide*. USA: George Pal Productions / Paramount, 1951. Film.

Neill, Roy William. *Frankenstein Meets the Wolf Man*. USA: Universal, 1943. Film.

Nelson, Gary. *The Black Hole*. USA: Walt Disney, 1980. Film.

Nelson, Ralph. *Charly*. USA: Selmur / Robertson Associates, 1968. Film.

Neumann, Kurt. *Rocketship X-M*. USA: Lippert, 1950. Film.

Newman, Joseph. *This Island Earth*. USA: Universal, 1955. Film.

Nimoy, Leonard. *Star Trek IV: The Voyage Home*. USA: Paramount / ILM, 1986. Film.

Nyby, Christian. *The Thing from Another World!* USA: RKO / Winchester, 1951. Film.

Pichel, Irving. *Destination Moon*. USA: George Pal Productions, 1950. Film.

Robertson, John S. *Dr. Jekyll and Mr. Hyde*. USA: Famous Players Lasky, 1920. Film.

Sagal, Boris. *The Omega Man*. USA: Walter Seltzer Productions, 1971. Film.

Salomon, Mikael. *The Andromeda Strain*. USA: Universal / Scott Free / Traveler's Rest, 2008. DVD, TV mini-series, four episodes. [quotations taken from Universal DVD 8256506-11].

Sandrich, Mark. *Top Hat*. USA: RKO, 1935. Film.

Sargent, Joseph. *Colossus: The Forbin Project*. USA: Universal, 1970. Film.

Schaffner, Franklin J. *Planet of the Apes*. USA: APJAC Productions / 20th Century Fox, 1968. Film.

Schepisi, Fred. *Iceman*. USA: Universal, 1984. Film.

Scott, Ridley. *Alien*. UK / USA: 20th Century Fox / Brandywine Productions, 1979. Film.

Tarkovsky, Andrei. *Solaris*. USSR: Mosfilm / Unit Four / Creative Unit of Writers and Cinema Workers, 1971. Film.

Taylor, Don. *Escape from the Planet of the Apes*. USA: 20th Century Fox / APJAC Productions, 1971. Film.

Trumbull, Douglas. *Silent Running*. USA: Universal / Michael Gruskoff Productions / Douglas Trumbull Productions, 1971. Film.

Verhoeven, Paul. *Hollow Man*. USA / Germany: Columbia / Global Entertainment, 2000. Film.

Villeneuve, Denis. *Arrival*. USA: Paramount / FilmNation Entertainment / Lava Bear Films / 21 Laps Entertainment / Xenolinguistics, 2016. Film.

Wachowskis [Brothers]. *The Matrix*. USA: Warner Bros. / Village Roadshow Pictures / Groucho II Film Partnership / Silver Pictures, 1999. Film.

Whale, James. *Frankenstein*. USA: Universal Pictures, 1931. Film.

Whale, James. *Bride of Frankenstein*. USA: Universal Pictures, 1931. Film.

Welles, Orson. *Citizen Kane*. USA: Mercury Productions / RKO, 1941. Film.

Wise, Robert. *The Day the Earth Stood Still*. USA: 20th Century Fox, 1951. Film.

Wise, Robert. *I Want to Live!*. USA: Figaro / UA, 1958. Film.

Wise, Robert. *The Haunting*. UK / USA: Argyll Enterprises / MGM, 1963. Film.

Wise, Robert. *The Sound of Music*. USA: 20th Century Fox, 1965. Film.

Wise, Robert. *The Andromeda Strain*. USA: Universal / Robert Wise Productions, 1971. Film.

Wise, Robert, and Jerome Robbins. *West Side Story*. USA: Mirisch / Seven Arts, 1961. Film.

Worne, Duke. *The Screaming Shadow*. USA: Hallmark Pictures, 1920. Chapter-play, fifteen episodes.

Chapter Three

Lab Lit and Science Fiction

Similarities and Separations

Ace G. Pilkington

Science (with the technological innovations it makes possible) is the most powerful force in history. To misquote Andrew Marvell (and after him Ursula K. Le Guin[1]) it is vaster than empires and far more rapid. It has made change the one constant in human society, and we have begun to discuss not whether or not everything will be transformed into something else but how fast it will happen. Marvell's image of "time's wingèd chariot"[2] is specially appropriate if we imagine it being constantly modified to increase its speed. In a sense, by this point in the twenty-first century most forms of literary expression are about science and its various disciplines and effects, either explicitly or implicitly. Even histories and historical novels are structured to some extent by the technologies and scientific principles their subjects lived among. As I write this, I'm looking at a book cover which reads *Mr. Lincoln's High-Tech War*.

Isaac Newton was one of the first scientific celebrities, and both Alexander Pope and Voltaire wrote about him. "Tsar Peter of Russia traveled to England in 1698 eager to see several phenomena: shipbuilding, the Greenwich Observatory, the Mint, and Isaac Newton."[3] Gale E. Christianson says "he specifically requested a meeting with the author of the *Principia*. It took place in the Tower of London, where Newton talked science with the czar and gave him a tour of the mint."[4] Voltaire points out one of the advantages of such fame and those who responded to it, gravitation, "now so evidently demonstrated, and before the time of the great Newton so little known, by which all the planets gravitate towards each other, and which retain them in their orbits, was already become familiar to a sovereign of Russia, while other countries amused themselves with imaginary vertices, and, in Galileo's nation, one set of ignorant persons ordered others, as ignorant, to believe the earth to be immoveable."[5] According to Albert Einstein, Newton's work "determined the course of Western thought, research, and practice to an extent that nobody before or since his time can touch."[6] However, in spite of his brilliance, Newton was only one in a rising tide of scientists who were washing away the ignorance of what was about to become an old and vanished world. The number and impact of scientists has done nothing but increase since then. In 1985 in *Triumph of the West*, J. M. Roberts said, "There are more scientists alive and working in the world today than have lived, worked, and died in the whole of human history hitherto."[7] And there are more scientific celebrities than ever before. People like Michio Kaku, Neil deGrasse Tyson, the late Stephen Hawking, and Brian Greene (to stick to physicists of one kind or another) write best-selling books, speak as experts in science programs, and appear or have appeared as themselves in sitcoms and science fiction series.

In the midst of this explosion, there are three genres for which science and scientists are central, popular science, science fiction, and lab lit. For popular science, the main emphasis is science itself, and the scientists are ever-successful facilitators of new discoveries. The focus on scientific concepts, however, does not allow popular science to develop fully fledged characters (though there are clear traces of characterization) and a reader quite often walks away from these books with an inaccurate impression of the scientists' infallibility. On some level, popular science, in its promotional attempts, is closer to research literature than it is to lab lit. A popular account, just like a professional research article, will highlight some aspects of the research process and deliberately obscure other, less flattering details. It is, in many respects, an alternative dissemination outlet for the scientific community, and as such, it is constrained by similar demands to appear objective and unbiased. At the same time, popular science authors employ a variety of techniques that link their prose to fiction rather than to professional publications. Olga Pilkington's essay in this volume explores some of them.

One way genres can be defined is by how they connect with and differ from related genres, comparing suspense with mystery, for example. Lab lit is often paired with science fiction, with some critics wondering if they are, in fact, different things or if lab lit is just one room in the large and drafty mansion (located no doubt somewhere on an alien planet with a green sky) that is science fiction. Olga Pilkington has explicated lab lit in detail in the introduction to this book, giving as her starting point Jennifer Rohn's definition that it is "a small but growing genre of literary fiction (or other fiction media) in which scientific characters, activities or themes are portrayed in a realistic manner."[8] She also uses Charles Sheffield's metaphorical placement of the genre as "safe above high tide," instead of "out in the shallow coastal water," where science fiction is located or "out of sight of land," where fantasy can be found.[9]

There are many answers to the question of what science fiction is. Isaac Asimov's version seems to me to be as sensible as any (and far more sensible than most).

> He says (in *Asimov on Science Fiction*) that SF is about "events played against social backgrounds that do not exist today" but "could, conceivably, be derived from our own by appropriate changes in the level of science and technology." (17). . . . Asimov also says "that the field can scarcely have existed in its true sense until the time came when the concept of social change through alterations in the level of science and technology had been evolved in the first place" (18). He sets that time at the point when "the rate of change . . . becomes great enough to be detected in . . . an individual lifetime" (18). He cites the Industrial Revolution as the watershed event and declares, "Science fiction had to be born sometime after 1800" (80).

[10] That is also pretty much when lab lit began. (See, for instance, Amanda Scott's essay on *Frankenstein*.)

Perhaps it would be easier to see their differences if we first look at what brings them closest together, and for that, we need to examine a subgenre of science fiction called hard science fiction. Despite Charles Sheffield's very careful geographical separation of science fiction and fantasy, the two things are not always so far apart. Asimov suggests that the process of writing science fiction involves straightforward extrapolation from a simpler present to a "scientifically more complex future, and quite often for him it did. But look at the novel *Childhood's End* by Arthur C. Clarke, the author Asimov said was "most like me."[11] *Childhood's End* tells the story of what looks like a takeover of Earth by space aliens designated the Overlords. However, it turns out that the Overlords have come to oversee the inevitable transformation of humans into a new and telepathic species which will become part of the Overmind, the incomprehensible controlling force that spans the galaxy. The new, transformed generation of human children joins the Overmind at the end of the story, crushing Earth to obtain the energy for their journey. In the words of David N. Samuelson, "The Overmind clearly parallels the Oversoul, the Great Spirit, and various formulations of God, while the children's metamorphosis neatly ties in with mystical beliefs in Nirvana, 'cosmic consciousness,' and 'becoming as little children to enter the Kingdom of God.'"[12] This is mythology, not science, and yet it is also science fiction. John Huntington refers to "that 'classic' status it now enjoys."[13] Samuelson says "it does illustrate certain aspects of SF at its best."[14]

And perhaps it does, but it has nothing to do with lab lit, any more than *Star Wars* does or the planetary romances of Edgar Rice Burroughs or most of the works of Ray Bradbury. In *A Princess of Mars* by Edgar Rice Burroughs, John Carter looked up at the red planet from a desert in Arizona, and, as he says, "closed my eyes, stretched out my arms . . . and felt myself drawn with the suddenness of thought through the trackless immensity of space."[15] It is a trip to Mars that is pure fantasy. Hard science fiction, on the other hand, is what Asimov had in mind when he described the entire genre. In my definition from *Science Fiction and Futurism: Their Terms and Ideas*, it is "science fiction that extrapolates from science and provides rational (and often detailed) technical explanations for its wonders."[16] Obviously, this territory is very close to lab lit. However, scientific explanations are not the same as actual scientists working at science. In fact, hard science fiction frequently has more to do with the future impact of science than with its present practice. Hard science fiction makes predictions (many of which have turned out to be correct) and in some cases sets out to hasten the advent of or even to create the changes it describes.

Take for example, the impact of Asimov's robot stories and novels. He wanted to change the way people looked at "robots," to move them away from the sort of Frankenstein creatures who were to be found in so many early SF stories. As a result, "The idea behind 'robot' (at least the idea as interpreted by Isaac Asimov and similar techno-optimists) and the word itself began—as so often happens—to change the real world."[17] Whether Asimov wanted to change more than science fiction or not, he succeeded in doing so.

> In 1950, Isaac Asimov's first collection of stories about good robots, *I, Robot*, was published. Asimov said, "As a machine, a robot will surely be designed for safety as far as possible. If robots are so advanced that they can mimic the thought processes of human beings, then surely the nature of those thought processes will be designed by human engineers and built-in safeguards will be added" (*The Rest of the Robots* xiii). "Joseph Engelberger, who built the first industrial robot, called Unimate, in 1958, attributes his long-standing fascination with robots to his reading of *I, Robot* when he was a teenager" (Asimov, Warrick, Greenberg 69). That is one of history's fastest turnarounds from inspiration to implementation. "In 1959, General Motors was the first to install a test model Unimate in its Turnstead die-casting plant. But orders for more Unimates did not come until 1961" (Asimov and Frenkel 33). Few people were more committed to the use of the word "robot" than Joseph Engelberger, Over and over, the advice was "Don't call it a robot. Call it a programmable manipulator. Call it a production terminal or a universal transfer device." The word is *robot* and it should be *robot*. I was building a robot, damn it, and I wasn't going to have any fun in Asimov terms, unless it was *robot*. So I stuck to my guns (Asimov and Frenkel 25).[18]

At least a small part of Asimov's fiction had been turned, very deliberately, into reality, in the same way that later on Captain Kirk's communicator would be turned into a cell phone by Martin Cooper.[19]

However, neither Asimov's "positronic brain" nor the long social experiment he recounted in his fictional lives of robots over many years approached scientific accuracy, described what it was like to work in labs, or consistently rose to the highest level of hard science fiction. Over the years, Asimov recounted his "invention" of the positronic brain often. He said, "Since I began writing my robot stories in 1939, I did not mention computerization. . . . The electronic computer had not yet been invented and I did not foresee it. I did foresee, however, that the brain had to be electronic in some fashion." He felt, though, that what he had to have was something more "futuristic." Luckily, "the positron—a subatomic particle exactly like the electron but of opposite electric charge—had been discovered only four years before. . . . It sounded very science fictional indeed, so I gave my robots 'positronic brains' and imagined their thoughts to consist of flashing streams of positrons, coming into existence, then going out of existence almost immediately."[20]

As a result, Asimov's stories about robots had far more to do with what might be possible than with what was currently happening in labs or factories. It is perhaps the nature of truly inspired science fiction to provide the thought bridge of extrapolation from something seemingly far off to something that leaps into existence surprisingly quickly. Usually, of course, that leap is made possible only by the hard work of scientists and engineers, but there is still a clear gap between the two and an equally clear difference between the kinds of fiction. It is one of the glories of SF that it has frequently inspired that hard work even when it had far more to do with imagination than implementation.

The hardest of hard science fiction, on the other hand, tries to stay closer to current science, and it is not infrequently written by people who are scientists themselves. In those circumstances, the fact that hard science fiction and lab lit have intermingled shouldn't surprise anyone, and it certainly doesn't suggest that they are only slightly different manifestations of the same thing. After all, it is not uncommon for genres to mix and overlap even when they are relatively alien to each other, as with Joss Whedon's combination of science fiction and the western in his short-lived television series *Firefly* or with Beverly Connor's mysteries that are also obviously and intentionally lab lit. (See her essay in this volume.)

Gregory Benford's *Timescape* is a clear example of a crossover between lab lit and hard science fiction. Benford is a physicist, and he says of the novel, "The underpinning of it all was a scientific paper on tachyons, particles which can travel faster than light, which I wrote with William Newcomb and David Book."[21] He started with writing a story about an English laboratory and went on eventually to the novel. The science fiction element is, of course, time travel, but it does not catapult humans back to the time of the dinosaurs or forward to Earth's final days. Instead, it is particles that make possible a very limited communication with the recent past in stuttering Morse code in order to warn of an impending ecological disaster. There are the usual science fiction (and physics) questions of time paradoxes and alternate timelines, but the novel also contains elements that are standard in lab lit, in-depth characterizations of scientists and clear descriptions of their work. As Benford put it in "Time and *Timescape*," "Rather than the convenient Wellsian traveler, I used scientists as I knew them, warts and all, doing what they would—trying to use the new discovery to communicate something they cared about."[22]

There are, for instance, at least seventy-eight references to "lab" in the book. More importantly, there is a sense of comfort in scientific environments and a pleasure in the details, "Renfrew went down the catwalk to the floor of the laboratory and stepped nimbly over the wires and cables. . . . Renfrew greeted each of the technicians as he came to them, asked questions about the running of the ion focusers, and gave his instructions. . . . The liquid nitrogen went *tick* and burbled in its flask. Powered units hummed in spots where there was a slight voltage mismatch. The oscilloscopes' green faces danced and rippled with smooth yellow curves. He felt at home."[23] In a similar way we are told, "When Isaac Lakin came into the nuclear resonance laboratory anyone, even a casual visitor, could tell it was his."[24]

It is not hard to see Gregory Benford's own experiences behind those of his imagined scientists. In his words, "I simply let go, pouring in detail about scientists, the way they think, how they live and that hardest of subjects, the way it feels to *do* science, the oddly incommunicable sensation of discovering something true and strange and new."[25] David G. Hartwell, Benford's long-time editor and friend, writes of *Timescape*, "It is . . . the story of scientists doing science, in the world yet removed from it, wedded to ideas and methodology and technical language for specialized communication, yet fully human. *Timescape* is the most realistic depiction of working people yet achieved in an SF novel, a standard against which other works are now measured."[26] And a standard that places it squarely in lab lit territory, a term that Hartford and Benford might well have used if they had been familiar with it. Clearly, Benford did not quite understand how important that picture of scientists would be to other people. He writes, "I published the novel and was astonished at its success. I thought it was quirky, somewhat self-indulgent and, in its fascination with how it feels to do science, obviously destined for a small audience. Yet this rather private novel has been my most successful."[27]

In spite of Hartwell's well-deserved praise of *Timescape*, it is far from being the only work of science fiction that can be identified as lab lit. There are a number of others, including two we've included in this book, *Frankenstein* and *The Andromeda Strain*. However, I want to discuss an example that fits into three categories, lab lit, hard science fiction, and the technothriller (see Dean Conrad and Lynne Magowan's essay on *The Andromeda Strain*). "A technothriller is a story set in the very near future (or even the present) with technological elements that may or may not be science fiction; it is often difficult (and often deliberately made to be difficult) to tell. A good example . . . is *Jurassic Park*" and its sequels (again in film and print). "At least a part of the appeal of such novels and movies is the rapidly shifting line between fiction and fact created by the speed of technological change."[28] "Not only do technothrillers explore the cutting edge of scientific transformation, they also, in the nature of dramatic presentations, go over that edge, and frequently criticize its possibly painful outcomes. Like the sci-fi movies of the 1950s, which were haunted by radioactive monsters and alien invasions, technothrillers simultaneously explore the present, extrapolate the future, and compartmentalize the actual and hypothetical dangers, placing them neatly in a format that allows for their neutralization in the time it takes to watch a movie or read a book."[29]

Michael Crichton's *Jurassic Park* is science fiction, a technothriller, and lab lit. The three genres are adjacent to each other, but they do not necessarily overlap; a technothriller may be cutting-edge technology without tipping over into science fiction, and just as clearly, science fiction or technothrillers may deal in highly technical details without attempting to show what it is like to work in a lab or be a scientist. *Jurassic Park*, however, manages all three (as does *The Andromeda Strain*, one of Crichton's other novels and films), and in the process helps to clarify the differences in the genres.

The 1995 James Bond film *GoldenEye*, for example, is a technothriller with science fiction elements swirling around the two satellites, but the comparatively brief and largely stereotypical inclusion of computer programmers does not come close to making it lab lit. Early in Crichton's novel of *Jurassic Park*, on the other hand, we are introduced to a paleontological dig in the badlands outside Snakewater, Montana, with Alan Grant, Ellie Sattler, and the students who make up the rest of their team. Grant is excavating a small fossil in the burning hot sun. "Working patiently with a dental pick and an artist's camel brush, he exposed the tiny L-shaped fragment of jawbone. It was only an inch long and no thicker than his little finger. The teeth were a row of small points, and had the characteristic medial angling. Bits of bone flaked away as he dug. Grant paused for a moment to paint the bone with rubber cement before continuing to expose it. There was no question that this was the jawbone from an infant carnivorous dinosaur."[30] Grant hopes to find the complete skeleton, which would be the first of its kind. Ellie Sattler, in response to a question about what she does, says, "Paleobotany. . . . And I also do the standard field preps." The trailer where such things happen has "a series of long wooden tables, with tiny bone specimens neatly laid out, tagged and labeled. Farther along were ceramic dishes and crocks. There was a strong odor of vinegar."[31]

In the words of Ryan Britt, "Jurassic Park is a novel founded in science and explanations of science. Crichton often digresses to discuss what was in 1990, cutting-edge paleontology. The evolutionary link between birds and dinosaurs wasn't common knowledge, and public perception of dinosaurs as slow and dumb was still, partially, the norm. So, through Grant, Crichton geeks out about the newish dinosaur theories. On the technical front, he'll even give the reader a few pages of computer code to realistically convey what kind of hacker-conflicts John Arnold is facing at the hands of Nedry."[32] Indeed, Crichton, through Dr. Wu, lays out some of the dinosaur DNA patterns as well.[33]

Michael Crichton was trained as a medical doctor, and his books and screenplays were heavily researched, sometimes for very long periods. He said in an interview about the *Jurassic Park* novels and films, "Ordinarily, my working method is to do years of research. In the first book, it was probably about 10 years from start to finish of which maybe three years were really writing and the other period of time was accumulating. Of course, I wasn't only doing that during that time. But, I allowed myself a very long gestation period in that sense."[34] As one would expect from a writer of technothrillers that sometimes overlap with lab lit, Crichton's work is tied closely to reality. He said, "In general, I prefer to take what is already true, if I can. I don't know how you would get the reality without taking the reality. So, in *Jurassic Park*, I think it's true that all the characters are based even loosely on real people. The most obvious and best known is Alan Grant, who is Jack Horner, who was an advisor on the film, eventually."[35]

Crichton cowrote the screenplay, and in her *New York Times* review, Janet Maslin called the film "a gripping, seductively scientific account of a top-secret theme park."[36] It's hard to overstate the combined impact of Crichton's story and the movie's special effects. Paleontologist John Long wrote, "When the first *Jurassic Park* movie hit the silver screens in 1993, I cried."[37] Elizabeth Jones, whose doctoral degree included a study of the impact of *Jurassic Park* on research into DNA, says, "To some extent, *Jurassic Park* did actually drive and develop the science and technology of ancient DNA research."[38] That included Jack Horner proposing "a project to investigate DNA from dinosaurs to the National Science Foundation. The grant was funded the same year the film was released."[39] Nothing like the resurrected dinosaurs of Crichton's imagination has emerged, but "research over the last decade has suggested that proteins may be preserved in some fossils, which could revolutionize paleontology."[40] Though there is a good deal of controversy, there are finds as old as 80 million and even 195 million years. More important than *Jurassic Park*'s influence on DNA research is its influence on the study of paleontology itself. "A whole generation of paleontologists can describe just where they were when they first saw *Jurassic Park* and just what it meant to them."[41] And beyond that there are those who were not old enough to be scientists yet "Paleontology is experiencing a golden age, with a new dinosaur species discovered every 10 days on average. Those inspired by the film *Jurassic Park* as children are now exiting Ph.D. programs and injecting the field with new talent."[42] They're called, not surprisingly "the *Jurassic Park* Generation."[43]

The distinction between lab lit and science fiction is clear even though they can happily coexist in some films and novels. It is possible to write science fiction, even the very hardest of hard science fiction, without scientists being in it, but the same is not true for lab lit. It is possible to write science fiction with scientists included but without exploring their lives, though the same is not true for lab lit. It is possible to write science fiction without caring about the nature of scientific discovery and what it feels like to make a life inside such a world, but the same is not true for lab lit. At the same time, there is a great curiosity about science and scientists, about their thoughts and lives, their successes and frustrations that drives much of science fiction, many technothrillers, and all of lab lit. It is this meeting ground that makes their mixing and overlap possible and that can sometimes suggest that they are the same. However, though they may start from a very similar place, the paths they follow go, more often than not, to very different destinations, to a world turned upside down by dangerous science in the case of technothrillers, to a world transformed into something new and nearly unrecognizable in the case of science fiction, or to a world where scientists live human lives in the midst of explorations which are at once extraordinary and comfortable in the case of lab lit.

NOTES

1. Ursula K. Le Guin, "Vaster than Empires and More Slow," in *The Wind's Twelve Quarters* (New York: Harper & Row, 1975), 181–218.

2. Andrew Marvell, "To His Coy Mistress," in *The Complete Poems* (New York: Alfred A. Knopf, 1984), 23.

3. James Gleick, *Isaac Newton* (New York: Pantheon, 2003), 156.

4. Gale E. Christianson, *Isaac Newton and the Scientific Revolution* (Oxford: Oxford University Press, 1996), 112.

5. Voltaire, *The History of Peter the Great, Emperor of Russia* (@AnnieRoseBooks, 2015), Kindle locations 1276–1280, Kindle Edition.

6. Original source unidentified, quoted in Robert K. Massie, *Peter the Great: His Life and World* (New York: History Book Club, 1980), 164.

7. J.M. Roberts, *Triumph of the West* (London, UK: British Broadcasting Corporation, 1985), film.

8. Jennifer Rohn, "What Is Lab Lit (the genre)?", lablit.com. Jennifer Rohn. Mar. 7, 2005. Accessed Nov. 15, 2018. http://www.lablit.com/article/3.

9. Charles Sheffield, *The Borderlands of Science: How to Think Like a Scientist and Write Science Fiction* (New York: Baen, 1999), 7.

10. Ace G. Pilkington, "Introduction: Science Fiction and Fantasy Conquer the World," in *The Fantastic Made Visible*, ed. Matthew Wilhelm Kapell and Ace G. Pilkington (Jefferson, NC: McFarland, 2015), 8.

11. Isaac Asimov, "Preface," in *Tales from Planet Earth*, Arthur C. Clarke (New York: ibooks, 2001), vii.

12. David N. Samuelson, *"Childhood's End*: A Median Stage of Adolescence?," *Science Fiction Studies* 1, no.1 (Spring 1973): https://www.depauw.edu/sfs/backissues/1/samuelson1art.htm.

13. John Huntington, "From Man to Overmind: Arthur C. Clarke's Myth of Progress," in *Arthur C. Clarke*, ed. Joseph D. Olander and Martin Harry Greenberg (Edinburgh: Paul Harris Publishing, 1977), 211.

14. David N. Samuelson, *"Childhood's End*: A Median Stage of Adolescence?," https://www.depauw.edu/sfs/backissues/1/samuelson1art.htm.

15. Edgar Rice Burroughs, *A Princess of Mars* (New York: Ballantine Books, 1963), 20.

16. Ace G. Pilkington, *Science Fiction and Futurism: Their Terms and Ideas* (Jefferson, NC: McFarland, 2017), 170.

17. Ibid., 120.

18. Ibid., 120–21.

19. Ibid., 18.

20. Isaac Asimov, "My Robots," in *Robot Visions* (New York: Roc, 1991), 454.

21. Original source unidentified, quoted in David G. Hartwell, "Introduction," in *Timescape*, Gregory Benford (Norwalk, CT: The Easton Press, 1980), 9.

22. Gregory Benford, "Time and *Timescape*," *Science Fiction Studies* 60, no. 20 (July 1993): https://www.depauw.edu/sfs/backissues/60/benford60art.htm.

23. Gregory Benford, *Timescape* (Norwalk, CT: The Easton Press, 1980), 17.

24. Ibid., 57.

25. Original source unidentified, quoted in David G. Hartwell, "Introduction," 9.

26. David G. Hartwell, "Introduction," 9–10.

27. Gregory Benford, "Time and *Timescape*," *Science Fiction Studies* 60, no. 20 (July 1993): https://www.depauw.edu/sfs/backissues/60/benford60art.htm.

28. Ace G. Pilkington, "Introduction: Science Fiction and Fantasy Conquer the World," 2.

29. Ace G. Pilkington, *Science Fiction and Futurism: Their Terms and Ideas*, 190–91.

30. Michael Crichton, *Jurassic Park* (New York: Alfred A. Knopf, 1990), 33.

31. Ibid., 35

32. Ryan Britt, "Revisiting Jurassic Park's Tangled Bookish Roots," electricliterature.com, Jun. 10, 2015. Accessed Oct. 5, 2018. https://electricliterature.com/revisiting-jurassic-parks-tangled-bookish-roots-6e3dddda8e.

33. Michael Crichton, *Jurassic Park*, 101–05.

34. "Beyond Jurassic Park Interview," jurassicpark.wikia.com. Accessed Nov. 20, 2018. http://jurassicpark.wikia.com/wiki/Beyond_Jurassic_Park_interview.

35. Ibid.

36. Janet Maslin, "Review/Film; Screen Stars with Teeth to Spare," *New York Times*, Jun. 11, 1993. Accessed Oct. 14, 2018. https://www.nytimes.com/1993/06/11/movies/review-film-screen-stars-with-teeth-to-spare.html.

37. John Long, "Creating Dinosaurs: Why Jurassic World Could Never Work," *The Conversation*, Apr. 13, 2015. Accessed, Aug. 20, 2018. https://theconversation.com/creating-dinosaurs-why-jurassic-world-could-never-work-35484.

38. Elizabeth Jones, "Sci-fi and Jurassic Park Have Driven Research, Scientists Say," *The Conversation*. Jun. 201, 2015. Accessed Aug. 15, 2018. https://theconversation.com/sci-fi-and-jurassic-park-have-driven-research-scientists-say-42864.

39. Ibid.

40. Eva Botkin-Kowacki, "How a 195-Million-Year-Old Dinosaur Bone Could Still Have Soft Tissue in It," csmonitor.com, Jan. 31, 2017. Accessed Nov. 5, 2018. https://www.csmonitor.com/Science/2017/0131/How-a-195-million-year-old-dinosaur-bone-could-still-have-soft-tissue-in-it.

41. Andrew Whalen, "Dinosaurs After 'Jurassic Park': Paleontologists on What's Changed, 25 Years Later," *Newsweek*, Jun. 17, 2018. Accessed Nov. 5, 2018. https://www.newsweek.com/jurassic-park-25-year-anniversary-dinosaurs-feathers-paleontology-979605.

42. Alisa Chang and Ari Shapiro, "Many Paleontologists Today Are Part Of The 'Jurassic Park' Generation," *All Things Considered*, NPR, Jul. 10, 2018. Accessed, Sep. 5, 2018. https://www.npr.org/2018/07/10/627782777/many-paleontologists-today-are-part-of-the-jurassic-park-generation.

43. Ibid.

BIBLIOGRAPHY

Asimov, Isaac. "My Robots." In *Robot Visions*. New York: Roc, 1991.
———. "Preface." In *Tales from Planet Earth*, by Arthur C. Clarke. New York: ibooks, 2001.
Benford, Gregory. "Time and *Timescape*." *Science Fiction Studies* 60, no. 20 (July 1993): https://www.depauw.edu/sfs/backissues/60/benford60art.htm.
———. *Timescape*. Norwalk, CT: The Easton Press, 1980.
"Beyond Jurassic Park Interview." jurassicpark.wikia.com. Accessed Nov. 20, 2018. http://jurassicpark.wikia.com/wiki/Beyond_Jurassic_Park_interview.
Botkin-Kowacki, Eva. "How a 195-Million-Year-Old Dinosaur Bone Could Still Have Soft Tissue in It." csmonitor.com. Jan. 31, 2017. Accessed Nov. 5, 2018. https://www.csmonitor.com/Science/2017/0131/How-a-195-million-year-old-dinosaur-bone-could-still-have-soft-tissue-in-it.
Britt, Ryan. "Revisiting Jurassic Park's Tangled Bookish Roots." electricliterature.com. Jun. 10, 2015. Accessed Oct. 5, 2018. https://electricliterature.com/revisiting-jurassic-parks-tangled-bookish-roots-6e3dddda8e.
Burroughs, Edgar Rice. *A Princess of Mars*. New York: Ballantine Books, 1963.
Chang, Alisa, and Ari Shapiro. "Many Paleontologists Today Are Part of the 'Jurassic Park' Generation." *All Things Considered*, NPR, Jul. 10, 2018. Accessed, Sep. 5, 2018. https://www.npr.org/2018/07/10/627782777/many-paleontologists-today-are-part-of-the-jurassic-park-generation.
Crichton, Michael. *Jurassic Park*. New York: Alfred A. Knopf, 1990.
Christianson, Gale E. *Isaac Newton and the Scientific Revolution*. Oxford: Oxford University Press, 1996.
Gleick, James. *Isaac Newton*. New York: Pantheon, 2003.
Jones, Elizabeth. "Sci-fi and Jurassic Park Have Driven Research, Scientists Say." *The Conversation*. Jun. 201, 2015. Accessed Aug. 15, 2018. https://theconversation.com/sci-fi-and-jurassic-park-have-driven-research-scientists-say-42864.
Hartwell, David G. "Introduction." In *Timescape*, by Gregory Benford. Norwalk, CT: The Easton Press, 1980.
Huntington, John. "From Man to Overmind: Arthur C. Clarke's Myth of Progress." In *Arthur C. Clarke*, edited by Joseph D. Olander and Martin Harry Greenberg. Edinburgh: Paul Harris Publishing, 1977.
Le Guin, Ursula K. "Vaster than Empires and More Slow." In *The Wind's Twelve Quarters*. New York: Harper & Row, 1975.
Long, John. "Creating Dinosaurs: Why Jurassic World Could Never Work." *The Conversation*. Apr. 13, 2015. Accessed, Aug. 20, 2018. https://theconversation.com/creating-dinosaurs-why-jurassic-world-could-never-work-35484.
Marvell, Andrew. "To His Coy Mistress." In *The Complete Poems*. New York: Alfred A. Knopf, 1984.
Maslin, Janet. "Review/Film; Screen Stars with Teeth to Spare." *New York Times*, Jun. 11, 1993. Accessed Oct. 14, 2018. https://www.nytimes.com/1993/06/11/movies/review-film-screen-stars-with-teeth-to-spare.html.
Massie, Robert K. *Peter the Great: His Life and World*. New York: History Book Club, 1980.
Pilkington, Ace G. "Introduction: Science Fiction and Fantasy Conquer the World." In *The Fantastic Made Visible*, edited by Matthew Wilhelm Kapell and Ace G. Pilkington. Jefferson, NC: McFarland, 2015.
———. *Science Fiction and Futurism: Their Terms and Ideas*. Jefferson, NC: McFarland, 2017.

Roberts, J.M. *Triumph of the West*. London, UK: British Broadcasting Corporation, 1985.

Rohn, Jennifer. "What Is Lab Lit (the genre)?" lablit.com. Jennifer Rohn. Mar. 7, 2005. Accessed Nov. 15, 2018. http://www.lablit.com/article/3.

Samuelson, David N. "*Childhood's End*: A Median Stage of Adolescence?" *Science Fiction Studies* 1, no. 1 (Spring 1973): https://www.depauw.edu/sfs/backissues/1/samuelson1art.htm.

Sheffield, Charles. *The Borderlands of Science: How to Think Like a Scientist and Write Science Fiction*. New York: Baen, 1999.

Voltaire. *The History of Peter the Great, Emperor of Russia*. @AnnieRoseBooks, 2015, Kindle Edition.

Whalen, Andrew. "Dinosaurs After 'Jurassic Park': Paleontologists on What's Changed, 25 Years Later." *Newsweek*. Jun. 17, 2018. Accessed Nov. 5, 2018.https://www.newsweek.com/jurassic-park-25-year-anniversary-dinosaurs-feathers-paleontology-979605.

Chapter Four

Lab Lit and Popular Science

Olga A. Pilkington

It is a truth universally acknowledged that an individual in possession of an interest in science but lacking professional expertise must be reading popularizations. A quick survey of studies devoted to examining readers who want to learn about various sciences suggests that popular science books, magazine articles, and blogs are the only options for such individuals.[1] Ken Hyland neatly divides these readers into "an elite educated audience" and "the public." The first group consumes "popular science books . . . written by scientists"; the second "gets most of its information about science from specialised magazines like *New Scientist* and *Scientific American*."[2] Lab lit does not figure into the equation. At the same time, novels about scientists are better equipped to respond to certain demands of lay audiences than popular science is.

One of the points often made about the influence of popular science is its ability to demystify the scientific community and its activities.[3] Popular science is supposed to humanize science: to show scientists as relatable and fallible human beings, as personalities. However, there are limited ways and spaces in which popular science can develop characterizations. One way to project the personalities of scientists and to portray them as relatable is through the use of presented discourse: speech and thought of scientists introduced to the readers as direct quotes or paraphrases. This is an excellent means to dramatize events and to inject emotionality into a popular scientific narrative.[4]

Employing this technique is not easy since the conventions of non-fiction writing do not allow for extensive use of Direct Speech to present dialogues—the most common and commonly recognized marker of dramatization. Popular science authors have to resort to using the resources available to create the same effects as a literary text would. This means using indirect discourse (most often Narrator's Presentation of Speech Acts—paraphrases that indicate that someone spoke without introducing many details) to produce dialogic exchanges.[5]

A typical dialogue a reader of popular science is likely to come across will look like this:

> By that May, when Wheeler visited Bohr in Copenhagen and discussed Everett's ideas, the reception was icy.[6]

or

> In the pressroom afterward, reporters tried to get more comments from him [Peter Higgs], but he demurred.[7]

To an untrained eye these exchanges do not look like dialogue, yet there are two speakers in each case, and they are communicating with each other. In the first sentence, John Wheeler is conversing with Niels Bohr. The subject of their conversation is Hugh Everett's ideas about the multiverse. We also know from this interaction that Bohr did not appreciate the new "interpretation of quantum mechanics"[8] that Everett offered. As a result of this information, readers can deduce that Bohr was not open to new ideas and was not interested in anyone else interfering in his field of study. In other words, he does not come through as a likable person.

In the second sentence, the dialogue is between Peter Higgs and the press. The journalists are asking questions, and the scientist is avoiding answering them. Through this exchange, Peter Higgs emerges as cautious—the journalists want to know more about the newly discovered boson named after him. It is also clear that, earlier, Higgs was more talkative on the subject.

Such presentations of communication would not be normally considered conversations—there are too few details. Readers have to fill in what the authors left out. They will, inevitably, do this because readers expect to learn about scientists as personalities and not only as researchers.[9] However, the power of such dialogues to create characters is limited. Lab lit affords much better opportunities for expressing personalities. As David Herman points out, in fiction, "a rich context of felt experience emerges" as a result of a "character's conversation."[10] Here is how Allegra Goodman uses dialogue to illustrate her characters' emotions:

> "So there's nothing wrong with my work, but it's not good enough for you," she challenged Cliff.
> "No, I didn't say that."
> "That's what you were thinking."
> "Look, if I ever thought that, I'm sorry. Just, please . . ."
> Gravely, she turned on him. "But you aren't sorry."

"Stop!"
"I just thought . . ." she began.
"Don't think anything. Just leave me alone." [11]

There is a combination of the author's report of character conversation ("she challenged Cliff" and "Gravely, she turned on him") and the actual utterances that illustrate these reports. Thus, the reader knows not only what happened, but how exactly it was phrased. The emotions of this short exchange would be recognizable to many readers who very likely had heard or used these very words themselves to express frustration and anger. Such a level of familiarity between scientists and the public would be hard to achieve using the dialogic means available to popular science.

Granted, the subject of this exchange is more personal than what one usually finds in popular science. However, it is a mistake to assume that there is no illustration of the scientists' personal lives in popularizations. Voices of spouses and friends are frequently used to show members of the scientific community outside their professional domains. In many instances, there is humor involved in such interactions.

Parkinson and Adendorff mention humor as one of the mechanisms by which popular science makes its human subjects more interesting, less intimidating, and ultimately familiar to the readers. Not everyone will be able to relate to a scientist discussing her latest results with colleagues, but many would feel more at ease with a conversation that involves a spouse, especially if that spouse points out certain areas where a particular scientist is lacking. For example, Bill Bryson in his popular science bestseller *A Short History of Nearly Everything* uses Direct Speech to juxtapose Bob Evans's extraordinary talent for spotting supernovae with his lack of other, more practical, skills, thus showing the scientist in a more personal light:

"I just seem to have a knack for memorizing star fields," he told me, "I'm not particularly good at other things," he added. "I don't remember names well."
"Or where he's put things," called Elaine [Evans's wife] from the kitchen. [12]

Such exchanges are common as lead-ins to more serious scientific topics since they are usually used to introduce the scientists whose works and contributions will now be addressed in detail.

By contrast, in lab lit even when matters of science are discussed, dialogue can be used to showcase emotion and to make the readers privy to the types of conversations that might happen in a real lab. Thus, in lab lit, dialogic exchanges are more than just attempts at humor or passages of intense emotion; they play a vital role in re-creating the world of the scientific community for the readers. Here is an example of a laboratory conversation found in Allegra Goodman's *Intuition*:

"Marion," Feng said.
"What is this?" He was turning a mouse slowly in his hand. "Is this mouse correct?"
"What do you mean?"
"Is this from the protocol?" Feng asked.
"I've already checked that. This is the correct mouse. This is number three hundred sixty-three," she said, pointing to the metal tag on the mouse's translucent ear.
"Then where is it?" Feng asked.
"Where is what?"
"The tumor," he said. [13]

Without the larger context of the novel, this conversation, even though it uses everyday vocabulary and almost no scientific terminology, might seem a bit odd. The researchers are dissecting mice infected with cancer to see how effective certain treatments are. A complete absence of a tumor is of great significance. This kind of reader exposure to laboratory activities is what Jennifer Rohn suggests quintessential lab lit does; it recreates for the reader "a scene that you and I could easily encounter were we to walk into a research institute." [14]

There are examples of laboratory conversations in popular science as well; however, their goal is to display the personalities of the scientists, not necessarily to recreate a laboratory experience for the readers:

> Still unaware of what caused the noise, Wilson and Penzias phoned Dicke at Princeton and described their problem to him in the hope that he might suggest a solution. Dicke realized at once what the two young men had found. "Well, boys, we've just been scooped," he told his colleagues as he hung up the phone. [15]

First of all, because most of this exchange is introduced as a paraphrase, the effect is not the same. A short instance of Direct Speech is designed not so much to let the readers eavesdrop on the scientists, but to expose them to Dicke's ways of speaking around his colleagues—the readers are to believe that Dicke referred to his fellow researchers as "boys" and used the verb "scooped" to indicate that Penzias and Wilson had beaten them to the discovery of the cosmic microwave background radiation.

This very short comparison of one particular feature of both genres makes it clear that lab lit offers more authentic representations of laboratory activities [16] and more access to the personalities of scientists. With this in mind, should we still consider popular science the prime means of introducing the members of the scientific community to non-professionals? If readers want to know scientists as people, lab lit is a much more fertile ground to support that interest. Works of lab lit offer not only fully fledged conversations among scientists but also employ other means of characterization such as telling the readers what a particular scientist is thinking:

> Joshua slouched in the corner of his seat as the train swept through dark farmlands. . . . The topic of Alan Fallengale was still lodged in his mind. Joshua was thinking back to when they had first met, when Alan had been almost likable. He'd still been a womanizer, conceited about his appearance and fond of those vile colours of clothing he still favoured, but at least he knew how to have a laugh and wasn't so obsessed about being the best.[17]

Presentation of thought is a common feature of popular science as well. However, there it plays a very different role. In the example above, Joshua's thoughts give readers access to his inner world, and through it, the readers are able to see what the character thinks about his colleague. One of the quickest ways to find out what a person is like is to ask someone who knows him or her. The same effect is achieved here. Thought presentation allows for a simultaneous characterization of both Joshua and Alan. Joshua's perception is intimate—otherwise the same information would have been given in a conversation not as a thought. Non-fiction, and therefore popular science, cannot deliver this level of intimacy.

Thought presentation is a common way to allow the readers to co-experience what Monika Fludernik calls "an imaginary human space,"[18] which is inhabited by characters. Because it is only in fiction that a reader *knows* what other people are thinking and because it is only in fiction that thoughts are presented as well-constructed linguistic units, scholars are able to suggest that this form of presented discourse immediately signals fictionality.[19] This leaves popular science—a non-fiction genre—with very constricted resources for the characterization of scientists using presented thought.

It does not mean that popular science never shows scientists as thinking. It does that often. The subject matter of their thoughts, however, is very different from what a reader is likely to find in a lab lit novel or short story. It turns out that in popular science books scientists are shown as thinking almost exclusively about science.[20] There are no detours into the brilliant minds' inner worlds, no access to intimate details, no elaborate reflections on relationships. In fact, thought presentation in popular science has generic overtones and is used most often to showcase scientific hypotheses and announce discoveries.

> Many scientists at the time were skeptical, but Shope wondered if rabbit "horns" were also tumors, somehow triggered by an unknown virus.[21]

This is what a typical instance of thought presentation looks like in popular science. The verbs usually used to signal thought processes are quite limited, with "wonder," "come up with an idea," "think," and "assume" used most often. It is also possible to determine by the choice of the verb if a hypothesis will find proof (a positive hypothesis), or if it will fail (a negative hypothesis). The preference for certain verbs and the patterns associated with them suggest that, in popular science, presentation of thought is used not so much as a method of characterization but functions as "a mitigating strategy which helps the speaker disclaim any ultimate knowledge or access to . . . other people's minds."[22] That is, thoughts of scientists are presented to readers as generic ideas rather than as personal insights.

If the characterization of scientists is not popularizations' forte (even though the authors do try to employ multiple strategies to shape scientists into characters[23]), that leaves the explanation of actual science as a prominent domain of popular science and, perhaps, not lab lit. But even in this area lab lit presents competition. Granted, the science found in lab lit may be fictional (though plausible) or experimental (not yet approved as fact by the scientific community). At the same time, this is what popular science does as well. In the words of Jean Parkinson and Ralph Adendorff, "Popular texts function as narratives of research, reporting on new knowledge claims not yet endorsed as fact by the research community."[24] Popular science plays on the readers' desire to glimpse the future and to reap the benefits of tomorrow's experiments today. A good example of this is Michio Kaku's story about the discovery of resveratrol—a chemical first detected in red wine that could potentially increase life span. The search for the chemical began with a theory of caloric restriction—as Kaku explains, "that is, lowering the calories we eat by 30 percent or more" might increase the life span by 30 percent.[25] To date, this is untested in humans. However, animal trials show promising results, and the "Holy Grail of aging research is to somehow preserve the benefits of caloric restriction without the downside (starving yourself)."[26] This might be achieved by stimulating certain genes "called SIRT genes, which produce proteins called sirtuins." In 1991 an MIT research team "looked for chemicals that activate the sirtuins, and found the chemical resveratrol."[27] However, resveratrol's benefits hinge on an untested theory about the causes of aging and the role sirtuins play in it.[28] In other words, there are no proven facts beyond the animal studies, which include the 2009 "University of Wisconsin study . . . that [demonstrated that] after twenty years of caloric restriction, monkeys on the restricted diet suffered less disease across the board."[29] That does not stop popularizers from presenting resveratrol as a possible miracle cure available right now.

A reader of Kaku's *Physics of the Future* will no doubt be optimistic about the potential of sirtuin-activating chemicals, having been bombarded with all the theories about the benefits of resveratrol. He will likely not pay much attention to the lack of actual facts and to the references to exclusively animal studies. Just like fictional literature, popular science is in the business of creating a certain mood for its readers—the mood of optimism and complete and unwavering confidence in science.[30]

In this respect, lab lit is more honest, as it shows the fallibilities of science (as the mistakes and weaknesses of its individual practitioners) as well as its triumphs. Academic dishonesty and its devastating effects are important themes in lab lit. They are in some way vital to the realism of the genre. While the promotion of science and scientists is the number one goal of lab lit, the realistic representation of laboratory life and of scientists as people is a close second. Human error (deliberate falsification of results especially) is something that professional science and, by extension, popular science do not want to bring to light. This does not equal the absence of such occurrences. In popular science this translates into a focus on narratives where mistakes (deliberate or otherwise) end in legitimate discoveries and in nearly complete omission of stories where a scientist falsifies experimental results.

In popular science, the stories of fortuitous mistakes can be labeled serendipity narratives and usually include the discovery of the wave-like properties of electrons by Davisson and Germer[31] or Poincaré's chaos theory.[32] Even benign chance and serendipity are regarded with caution in professional and popular science. In professional science, they are associated not with blind luck or anything else out of human control but with preparedness. As Robert K. Merton and Elinor Barber note, "To preparedness may be linked such qualities as alertness, flexibility, courage, and assiduity."[33] That is, human effort and application of the scientific method are behind even the most unlikely discoveries.

When it comes to falsified results, popular science authors, if including such stories, which rarely happens, use these narratives to emphasize the scientific community's ability to self-regulate: to distinguish and to discredit the offenders, who are always individuals and not laboratories or research institutions. The most famous examples include Ronald Richter's cold fusion reactor "thermotron" and Pons and Fleischmann's "discovery" of cold fusion.[34,35]

What popular science essentially dismisses is explored fully in lab lit. Allegra Goodman's novel *Intuition* and Jennifer Rohn's *The Honest Look* are but two examples that investigate fraud and its consequences in the world of science. In both cases, the good guys emerge victorious, yet the stories are not that simple. They are human dramas that explain to the public the immense pressure scientists feel to come up with amazing results fast and the incredible desire they have to improve the human condition. These are quite often the motivations for less than pristine ethics. For the most part, there are no innately evil or mad scientists in lab lit; however, some may argue that Richard Rouyle in Jennifer Rohn's *Experimental Heart* seems to be innately evil and possibly mad, and the same could be argued about Eugene Mallabar in William Boyd's *Brazzaville Beach*. However, lab lit is too multifaceted for simplistic labels even for its minor characters—the "mad scientist" trope oftentimes serves to introduce the issues of mental health in the world of science.

One of the important points of the genre is to dispel the stereotype of a scientist as "crazed, reclusive and up to no good."[36] It is not news that "real-life scientists have been perceived as secretive, obfuscatory, unable to communicate outside their discipline, having different allegiances from other people, suppressing human affections and ruthless in their idealism, prepared to sacrifice humans, animals and safety in their reckless pursuit of knowledge."[37] However, as Jennifer Rohn aptly points out, "Geeks, the aloof and the obsessive can be found in every walk of life."[38] Lab lit sets out to counter not only individual perceptions and presentation but to invalidate the myth of the mad scientist. Roslynn Haynes suggests that "the mad, evil scientist is almost invariably a semiotic figure. He (the gender specificity is factual) is rarely intended to refer to any particular scientist, or even to appear realistic."[39] She argues that the stereotype is a reaction to the persistent presentation of scientists as omniscient and omnipotent that originated in the early nineteenth century at the advent of the professionalization of science, and that remained unchallenged until the middle of the twentieth century.[40] Haynes sees the stereotypical mad scientist as "the prototypical scientist of counter-culture."[41] Today, however, she optimistically declares, "this entrenched stereotype of the mad, bad scientist has been progressively eroded."[42] This is, in no small part, the effect of lab lit.[43] Haynes notes that "the diversity of setting and research areas in . . . recent novels about scientists indicates the marked change from the stereotypical mad, evil scientist or the foolish inventor. These scientists are credible, modern people working in the real world, engaging with issues in science, society and relationships."[44]

Despite the apparent victory of the good scientist over the evil counterpart, the problem of stereotyping remains, and the image of a socially inept, awkward, and sick person as a representative of a scientific genius can still be found in the pages of popular science books. Here is what Bill Bryson has to say about Isaac Newton:

> Newton was a decidedly odd figure—brilliant beyond measure, but solitary, joyless, prickly to the point of paranoia, famously distracted (upon swinging his feet out of bed in the morning he would reportedly sometimes sit for hours, immobilized by the sudden rush of thoughts to his head), and capable of the most riveting strangeness.[45]

To be fair, this is not all Bryson has to say about the great scientist, but the highlighting of the oddities is telling.[46] In the case of Darwin, Bryson mentions the scientific accomplishments of the man but also draws attention to the fact that he:

fell prey to strange disorders that left him chronically listless, faint, and "flur-
ried," as he put it. The symptoms nearly always included a terrible nausea and
generally also incorporated palpitations, migraines, exhaustion, trembling,
spots before the eyes, shortness of breath, "swimming of the head," and, not
surprisingly, depression.
The cause of the illness has never been established, but the most romantic and
perhaps likely of the suggested possibilities is that he suffered from Chaga's
disease, a lingering tropical malady that he could have acquired from the bite
of a Benchuga bug in South America. A more prosaic explanation is that his
condition was psychosomatic. [47]

It would take quite a bit of room and a separate essay to examine such
presentations of scientists in popularizations. Suffice it to say that Bryson is
not the only one to bring to his readers' attention the mental and physical
challenges of intellectuals. [48] Haynes also notes the trend, but she is not
limiting it to popular science but looks at biographic accounts as well. She
writes, "There has been increasing interest in exploring the human turmoil of
historical figures in science as subjects for novels. While some of these
characters may seem to revert to the stereotype of the inhuman, obsessive
scientist, unable to form enduring relationships, they are depicted with a new
level of understanding and empathy." [49] Such accounts play into the public's
perception of genius as socially awkward, emotionally stunned, and generally flawed; they are designed to comfort an average person. In doing so, these
representations of scientists, be they rooted in biographical accounts or pure
fictions, do not support the message of lab lit.

According to Rohn's definition of lab lit, such novels would not qualify
and do not represent the genre. [50] Lab lit celebrates the normality of science
without hiding its problems; therefore, there is a healthy mixture of various
characters, but the emphasis is on natural diversity, not on the sickliness or
the odd habits of some individuals.

The difference in presenting scientists between popularizations and lab lit
can be attributed to the slightly different solidarity dynamic in the two genres. Popular science, according to Parkinson and Adendorff, "show[s] solidarity with the reader . . . by distancing the reader and writer from scientists
as a group." [51] The focus on the unusual in the presentation of scientists
further establishes this kind of solidarity as the scientists become perceived
as "the other." Lab lit, by contrast, strives to showcase the ordinariness of the
members of the scientific community and their similarity with the reader.
The connection is often initiated through references to the arts and the humanities. In *The Honest Look*, for instance, Rohn makes casual, passing
references to music and design in such a way that it does not make these
mentions stand out in a science-themed novel. Art becomes the background,
part of the context in which she places her characters: "On Tuesday evening,
Alan and Claire were listening to Mahler and . . . she was leaning against him

on the Corbusier,"[52] or "On hearing her news, Rachel was more worried than Claire had expected, her eyes shadowed like a charcoal sketch."[53] These light touches complement one of the major tensions in the novel—the main heroine's internal struggles between following her heart down the path of poetry and pursuing her scientific goals. (For more on the relationship of the arts and the humanities with the sciences, see Elaine Pearce's essay.)

When references to mythology, literature, or history come up in lab lit works, they are always introduced on their own merits. They do not appear as mechanisms that ease the reader into the science of the novels. (For more on how lab lit handles scientific explanations, see Beverly Connor's essay.) Popular science does things differently. Literature, especially the classics, is a common go-to representative of the arts in popular science. However, literature is always juxtaposed against the sciences. Used often in explanations, literary references are stripped of their own significance and showcased only as lesser adjuncts to scientific content. For example, here is how William Bynum uses a quote from Shakespeare:

> Shakespeare had Mercutio, in *Romeo and Juliet*, say, "A plague on both your houses!" . . . His audiences would have understood what he meant. Most doctors thought that plague was a new disease, or at least one that Galen had not written about.[54]

The type of understanding that Bynum attributes to the Bard's original audiences is a scientific understanding (that of plague as a disease) not a metaphorical understanding (plague as a curse, a symbol of horrible things to come), which he assigns to the reader and modern Shakespearean audiences. The truth is in a combination of both meanings, yet the popularizer discards the metaphorical value of Mercutio's statement and seemingly devalues it in favor of a more scientific interpretation.

Deconstruction of literary texts and deliberate misquoting are also strategies that popular science uses to explain its concepts. For instance, Sam Kean writes that "some scientists misquote Tolstoy . . . perhaps all healthy bodies resemble each other, while each unhealthy body is unhealthy in its own way," to illustrate medical cases where "large-scale symptoms are identical" while "the underlying genetic causes . . . might be different."[55] Kean also uses the same opening lines of *Anna Karenina* to demonstrate a process of chromosome sequencing:

> As observers have noted, the process was analogous to dividing a novel into chapters, then each chapter into sentences. They'd photocopy each sentence and shotgun all the copies into random phrases—"Happy families are all," "are all alike; every unhappy," "every unhappy family is unhappy," and "unhappy in its own way."[56]

What's interesting about both examples from Kean is that he is not directly taking credit for having produced these allusions to literature. In each case, he refers to the people who are involved with the concepts and technologies he is writing about (either "scientists" or "observers") as those who came up with these mentions of Tolstoy's work.

One more example of literature serving science can be found in Enrico Coen's book *Cells to Civilization*:

> As well as responding to individual events, animal nervous systems can also respond to sequences of events over time. If you repeatedly stimulate the slug's siphon, the gill-withdrawal reflex progressively weakens. . . . It is a case of what Marcel Proust called *the anaesthetizing effect of habit.* [57]

It is a more clever reference than the example immediately preceding it because it draws a parallel rather than simply utilizing the lines from a novel. In this case, the literary reference adds an additional layer of deeper meaning and promotes a metaphorical understanding as a supplement to the scientific fact.

Another way for the humanities to appear in popular science is through a comparison of imagination and reality. For instance, Michio Kaku in *Physics of the Future*, refers to Greek and Roman mythology quite often. For example, "Today, we are like Vulcan, forging in our laboratories machines that breathe life not into clay but into steel and silicon."[58] This comparison is prefaced by a full paragraph explaining and summarizing to the readers various mythological accounts of creation, including the story of Vulcan. The contrast between this presentation and that of Rohn's references to music and design is striking. The lab lit author trusts the reader to know, while the popularizer assumes total ignorance. There is a juxtaposition of the two worlds in Kaku: one of science and the other of the arts/humanities. There is also an assumption that a person interested in one lacks the knowledge of the other.

Ultimately, the messages about science and scientists that lab lit and popular science send out are different. As an outlet of the scientific community,[59] popular science is still adjusting its attitude toward the public and learning to present science in a balanced way.[60] Simply put, popular science wants to convince its readers that the members of the scientific community are infallible geniuses and science is the only way to inquire about the world, whereas lab lit wants to show scientists as ordinary and commonplace people with a variety of interests—not that much different from the reader herself. Lab lit, it could be argued, strives to project "a scientist-next-door" type of character.

The difference in the messages comes from (in addition to a difference in solidarity) a slight discrepancy in the target audiences. When it comes to the communication of science, lab lit and popular science do not always attract the same readership. Popular science is written for non-professionals, but this does not mean non-scientists. As Greg Myers points out, "There is no single public for science."[61] That is, science, especially the popular variety, targets a very broad audience which includes scientists themselves. "Even a well-educated scientist cannot be a specialist in all fields and branches even of her own discipline let alone the multitude of areas of knowledge that today's science covers."[62] Myers gives the following example, "When I go to the doctor, I treat her as an expert in medicine, but her relation to current medical research will generally be as a continuing student, not as a participant, and the medical journals have to perform a kind of popularizing function for her."[63]

Lab lit is not targeting fellow scientists in the same way popularizations do. One of the goals of these novels is to show the reader what it is like to be a scientist—what a laboratory might look like, what kinds of conversations a person might have with colleagues, what questions and dilemmas will arise, and so on. Someone who is already a member of the scientific community knows this full well. On some level, popularizations communicate science, while lab lit communicates scientists and their experiences.

Which aspect of science communication is more valuable? There is research that suggests it is the communication of personal experiences.[64] However, knowledge of science is also extremely important in a world that is becoming more scientifically and technologically advanced by the minute. Ultimately, these two modes of science writing complement each other, and as lab lit receives more recognition as a literary genre and a genre in the spectrum of scientific writing, it will undoubtedly be used alongside popular science to introduce lay audiences to science and the people who make it possible.

NOTES

1. See, for example, Esther Laslo, Ayelet Baram-Tsabari, and Bruce V. Lewenstein, "A Growth Medium for the Message: Online Science Journalism Affordances for Exploring Public Discourse of Science and Ethics," *Journalism* 12, no. 7 (2011): 847–70; María José Luzón, "Public Communication of Science in Blogs: Recontextualizing Scientific Discourse for a Diversified Audience," *Written Communication* 30, no. 4 (2013): 428–57; Sophie Moirand, "Communicative and Cognitive Dimensions of Discourse on Science in the French Mass Media," *Discourse Studies* 5, no. 2 (2003): 175–206; Greg Myers, *Writing Biology: Texts in the Social Construction of Scientific Knowledge* (Madison, WI: The University of Wisconsin Press, 1990); Greg Myers, "Fictions for Facts: The Form and Authority of the Scientific Dialogue," *History of Science* 30 (1992): 221–47; Jon Turney, "Accounting for Explanation in Popular Science Texts—an Analysis of Popularized Accounts of Superstring Theory," *Public Understanding of Science* 13 (2004): 331–46; Jon Turney, "Boom and Bust in Popular Science" *Journal of Science Communication* 6 no. 1 (2007): 1–3.

2. Ken Hyland, "Constructing Proximity: Relating to Readers in Popular and Professional Science," *Journal of English for Academic Purposes* 9 (2010): 118.

3. See for example, Hyland, "Constructing Proximity"; Olga A. Pilkington, *Presented Discourse in Popular Science: Professional Voices in Books for Lay Audiences* (Leiden: Brill, 2018); Olga A. Pilkington, "Structural Complexity of Popular Science Narratives of Discovery as an Indicator of Reader Awareness: A Labov-Inspired Approach," *Linguistic and Philosophical Investigations* 16 (2017): 7–28; Rom Harré, "Some Narrative Conventions of Scientific Discourse," in *Narrative in Culture: The Uses of Storytelling in Sciences, Philosophy, and Literature*, ed. Christopher Nash (London: Routledge, 1994), 81–100.

4. Pilkington, *Presented Discourse in Popular Science*; Olga A. Pilkington, "Presented Discourse in Popular Science Narratives of Discovery: Communicative Side of Thought Presentation," *Linguistic and Philosophical Investigations* 17 (2018): 7–28.

5. Pilkington, *Presented Discourse in Popular Science*, 18–31, 71–83.

6. Brian Greene, *The Hidden Reality: Parallel Universes and the Deep Laws of the Cosmos* (New York: Alfred A. Knopf, 2011), 190.

7. Sean Carroll, *The Particle at the End of the Universe: How the Hunt for the Higgs Boson Leads Us to the Edge of a New World* (New York: Plume, 2012), 185.

8. Greene, *The Hidden Reality*, 190.

9. Jean Parkinson and Ralph Adendorff, "The Use of Popular Science Articles in Teaching Scientific Literacy," *English for Specific Purposes* 23 (2004): 389.

10. David Herman, *Basic Elements of Narrative* (Hoboken, NJ: Wiley-Blackwell, 2009), 147.

11. Allegra Goodman, *Intuition* (New York: The Dial Press, 2006), 8.

12. Bill Bryson, *A Short History of Nearly Everything* (New York: Broadway Books, 2003), 30.

13. Goodman, *Intuition*, 20.

14. Jennifer Rohn, "What Is Lab Lit (the Genre)?" *LabLit.com*. 2005. http://www.lablit.com/article/3.

15. Bryson, *A Short History*, 12.

16. See also Olga Pilkington, "Popular Science versus Lab Lit: Differently Depicting Scientific Apparatus," *Science as Culture* 26, no. 3 (2017): 285–306.

17. Jennifer Rohn, *The Honest Look* (Cold Spring Harbor, NY: Cold Spring Harbor Laboratory Press, 2010), 117.

18. Monika Fludernik, *Towards a 'Natural' Narratology* (New York: Routledge, 1996), 39.

19. Dorrit Cohn, "Signposts of Fictionality: A Narratological Perspective," *Poetics Today* 11, no. 4 (1990): 775–804; Paul Dawson, "Ten Theses against Fictionality," *Narrative* 23, no. 1 (2015): 74–100; Mick Short, "Thought Presentation Twenty-Five Years On," *Style* 41, no. 2 (2007): 225–41.

20. Pilkington, *Presented Discourse in Popular Science*, 94–104.

21. Carl Zimmer, *A Planet of Viruses* (Chicago: University of Chicago Press, 2011), 24.

22. Jarmila Mildorf, "Thought Presentation and Constructed Dialogue in Oral Stories: Limits and Possibilities of a Cross-disciplinary Narratology," *Partial Answers: Journal of Literature and the History of Ideas* 6, no. 2 (2008): 288.

23. Pilkington, *Presented Discourse in Popular Science*, 67–141.

24. Parkinson and Adendorff, "The Use of Popular Science Articles," 388.

25. Michio Kaku, *Physics of the Future: How Science Will Shape Human Destiny and Our Daily Lives by the Year 2100* (New York: Doubleday, 2011), 147.

26. Ibid.

27. Ibid., 148.

28. Ibid., 148–49.

29. Ibid., 147.

30. Pilkington, *Presented Discourse in Popular Science*, 14–18, 141–51.

31. Greene, *The Hidden Reality*, 193.

32. Marcus du Sautoy, *The Number Mysteries: A Mathematical Odyssey through Everyday Life* (New York: Palgrave Macmillan, 2011), 229–30.

33. Robert K. Merton and Elinor Barber, *The Travels and Adventures of Serendipity: A Study in Sociological Semantics and the Sociology of Science* (Princeton, NJ: Princeton University Press, 2004), 171.

34. Kaku, *Physics of the Future*, 236–37.

35. For more on narratives of failed discovery, their structure and ideology, see Olga A. Pilkington, *The Language of Popular Science* (Jefferson, NC: McFarland, forthcoming), chapter 4.

36. Rohn, "What Is Lab Lit?"

37. Roslynn D. Haynes, "Whatever Happened to the 'Mad, Bad' Scientist? Overturning the Stereotype," *Public Understanding of Science* 25, no. 1 (2015): 4.

38. Rohn, "What Is Lab Lit?"

39. Haynes, "Whatever Happened," 2.

40. Ibid., 2–3.

41. Ibid., 3.

42. Ibid., 5.

43. Ibid., 5–8. Haynes acknowledges lab lit among other influences (such as the general familiarity of science, accessibility of popularization, and science education).

44. Ibid., 7.

45. Bryson, *A Short History*, 46.

46. This is an unfair characterization of Newton. See, for example, Thomas Levenson, *Newton and the Counterfeiter: The Unknown Detective Career of the World's Greatest Scientist* (New York: Mariner Books, 2010).

47. Bryson, *A Short History*, 385.

48. See also Timothy Ferris, *Coming of Age in the Milky Way* (New York: William Morrow and Company, 1988), 149–50 (description of Lambert); Sam Kean, *The Violinist's Thumb and Other Lost Tales of Love, War, and Genius, as Written by Our Genetic Code* (New York: Little, Brown and Company, 2012), 204–205 (description of Buckland), 240–41 (discussion of Kim Peek, a savant).

49. Haynes, "Whatever Happened," 7.

50. In "What Is Lab Lit?" Rohn writes, "Other approved variations of the stereotypical scientist, as seen especially in films, include the affable geek who has problems getting laid (such as the protagonists of the Eighties movie classic *Weird Science*) and the clever ice princess (with beauty also typically disguised by spectacles and constrained hair) who just needs to get laid—preferably by the swashbuckling, non-scientific hero—to allow her cold, analytical nature to thaw into warm humanity (as seen in the recent film *I, Robot*). This is not to say that there are no scientists like this today—many stereotypes crystallize around a kernel of truth—but I would argue that they are rare."

51. Parkinson and Adendorff, "The Use of Popular Science Articles," 389. However, Massimiano Bucchi, *Science and the Media: Alternative Routes in Scientific Communication* (London: Routledge, 1998), 2, and Greg Myers, "Discourse Studies of Scientific Popularization: Questioning the Boundaries," *Discourse Studies* 5, no. 2 (2003): 265–79, demonstrate that professional scientists also read popularizations when they need to familiarize themselves with research outside their immediate spheres of expertise. In such cases, distancing of the reader from the scientific community in general does not apply; though distancing of scientists that belong to a certain discipline from those who belong to other disciplines is possible.

52. Rohn, *The Honest Look*, 265.

53. Ibid., 133.

54. William Bynum, *A Little History of Science* (London: Yale University Press, 2012), 42.

55. Kean, *The Violinist's Thumb*, 312.

56. Ibid., 300–301.

57. Enrico Coen, *Cells to Civilization: The Principles of Change That Shape Life* (Princeton: Princeton University Press, 2012), 141.

58. Kaku, *Physics of the Future*, 65.

59. See Pilkington, *Presented Discourse in Popular Science*, 1–4.

60. Significant developments have been made, and modern popular science no longer sees the public as completely ignorant. However, the legacy of negative attitudes toward the public is slow to recede.

61. Greg Myers, "Fictionality, Demonstration, and a Forum for Popular Science: Jane Marcet's *Conversations on Chemistry*," in *Natural Eloquence: Women Reinscribe Science*, ed. Barbara Gates and Ann B. Shteir (Madison: University of Wisconsin Press, 1997), 43.

62. Pilkington, *The Language of Popular Science*, introduction.

63. Myers, "Discourse Studies of Scientific Popularization," 268.

64. Susan T. Fiske, Amy J. C. Cuddy, Peter Glick, and Jun Xu, "A Model of (Often Mixed) Stereotype Content: Competence and Warmth Respectively Follow from Perceived Status and Competition," *Journal of Personal and Social Psychology* 82, no. 6 (2002): 878–902; Arthur M. Sackler, ed., *Science of Science Communication II: Summary of a Colloquium* (Washington, DC: The National Academies Press, 2014).

BIBLIOGRAPHY

Bryson, Bill. *A Short History of Nearly Everything*. New York: Broadway Books, 2003.

Bynum, William. *A Little History of Science*. London: Yale University Press, 2012.

Carroll, Sean. *The Particle at the End of the Universe: How the Hunt for the Higgs Boson Leads Us to the Edge of a New World*. New York: Plume, 2012.

Coen, Enrico. *Cells to Civilization: The Principles of Change That Shape Life*. Princeton: Princeton University Press, 2012.

du Sautoy, Marcus. *The Number Mysteries: A Mathematical Odyssey through Everyday Life*. New York: Palgrave Macmillan, 2011.

Fludernik, Monika. *Towards a 'Natural' Narratology*. New York: Routledge, 1996.

Goodman, Allegra. *Intuition*. New York: The Dial Press, 2006.

Greene, Brian. *The Hidden Reality: Parallel Universes and the Deep Laws of the Cosmos*. New York: Alfred A. Knopf, 2011.

Haynes, Roslynn D. "Whatever Happened to the 'Mad, Bad' Scientist? Overturning the Stereotype." *Public Understanding of Science* 25, no. 1 (2015): 1–14.

Herman, David. *Basic Elements of Narrative*. Hoboken, NJ: Wiley-Blackwell, 2009.

Hyland, Ken. "Constructing Proximity: Relating to Readers in Popular and Professional Science." *Journal of English for Academic Purposes* 9 (2010): 116–27.

Kaku, Michio. *Physics of the Future: How Science Will Shape Human Destiny and Our Daily Lives by the Year 2100*. New York: Doubleday, 2011.

Kean, Sam. *The Violinist's Thumb and Other Lost Tales of Love, War, and Genius, as Written by Our Genetic Code*. New York: Little, Brown and Company, 2012.

Merton, Robert K., and Elinor Barber. *The Travels and Adventures of Serendipity: A Study in Sociological Semantics and the Sociology of Science*. Princeton, NJ: Princeton University Press, 2004.

Mildorf, Jarmila. "Thought Presentation and Constructed Dialogue in Oral Stories: Limits and Possibilities of a Cross-disciplinary Narratology." *Partial Answers: Journal of Literature and the History of Ideas* 6, no. 2 (2008): 279–300.

Myers, Greg. "Discourse Studies of Scientific Popularization: Questioning the Boundaries." *Discourse Studies* 5, no. 2 (2003): 265–79.

———. "Fictionality, Demonstration, and a Forum for Popular Science: Jane Marcet's *Conversations on Chemistry*." In *Natural Eloquence: Women Reinscribe Science*, edited by Barbara Gates and Ann B. Shteir, 43–60. Madison: University of Wisconsin Press, 1997.

Parkinson, Jean, and Ralph Adendorff. "The Use of Popular Science Articles in Teaching Scientific Literacy. *English for Specific Purposes* 23 (2004): 379–96.

Pilkington, Olga A. *Presented Discourse in Popular Science: Professional Voices in Books for Lay Audiences*. Leiden, Netherlands: Brill, 2018.

———. "Presented Discourse in Popular Science Narratives of Discovery: Communicative Side of Thought Presentation." *Linguistic and Philosophical Investigations* 17 (2018): 7–28.

———. "Popular Science versus Lab Lit: Differently Depicting Scientific Apparatus." *Science as Culture* 26, no. 3 (2017): 285–306.

————. "Structural Complexity of Popular Science Narratives of Discovery as an Indicator of Reader Awareness: A Labov-Inspired Approach." *Linguistic and Philosophical Investigations* 16 (2017): 7–28.

————. *The Language of Popular Science*. Jefferson, NC: McFarland, forthcoming.

Rohn, Jennifer. *The Honest Look.* Cold Spring Harbor, NY: Cold Spring Harbor Laboratory Press, 2010.

————. "What Is Lab Lit (the Genre)?" *LabLit.com*. 2005. http://www.lablit.com/article/3.

Zimmer, Carl. *A Planet of Viruses*. Chicago: University of Chicago Press, 2011.

Chapter Five

Where Science Meets Fiction

A History and Theory of Laboratory Production

Matt Hadley

It was, as the famous story has it, a dreary night near Geneva in 1816 when the hideous creature that would become Frankenstein's monster leapt into the imagination of Mary Shelley and sparked to life her literary masterpiece. [1] During this same historical moment, another figure was stirring to life whose origin would prove much more difficult to pin down, but whose importance would be no less monumental for the future: the modern scientific laboratory. Though a literary work, *Frankenstein* is one of the first historical accounts of the true power and ethical implications of the modern space of scientific experimentation and practice. In fact, Shelley's novel is as good a text as any to question the conditions of possibility for the scientific laboratory; as a historical document, it prefigures the inchoate science of biology and its driving question, What is life? Frankenstein has since become an adjective synonymous today with the results of scientific experimentation whose consequences and implications exceed the reasoned expectations or assumed outcomes of scientific and technological advances. Thus, the novel was also prescient for how it made the social, political, and ethical inextricable aspects of scientific practice, carried forward today by those working in science and technology fields. (For more on this, see Amanda Scott's essay.)

Beyond the novel's foresight for a world to come, calling to a future science yet to be determined, I am most intrigued by how *Frankenstein* forces the reader to recognize the god-like power made possible by the laboratory (brought further to spectacular life in Whale's 1931 film), at a moment in time when the laboratory, while not yet fully established, was soon to emerge as the hegemonic space for legitimate scientific practice. With the rise of the laboratory as a point of connection and departure, I would like to understand the ways in which Shelley's literary account of the laboratory and the materialization of the laboratory as a space of scientific labor feed into one another, bridging the perceived chasm between fiction and science.

To this end, I begin my essay with a brief history of the modern scientific laboratory in order to show the points of contact between laboratory and scientific practice with its representation in fiction. From there I sketch out moments of contact between theories of the laboratory in science studies with promising analogues in literary discourse. The laboratory is an artificially constructed world in and through which living or non-living "actors," to follow the language of science and technology studies scholar Bruno Latour, show their mettle through experimental trials that provide the material inscriptions or traces of objects or artifacts, thus grounding moments that lead to their transposition into knowledge and to asserting their material reality.[2] Of course, the literary laboratory at first glance has a much different ontological status than the scientific laboratory. The former, one might claim, is immaterial, and exists only within the minds of the author and the audience, whereas the latter has a real, material, factual, or concrete existence. One can physically step into the scientific laboratory in a markedly different way than one might metaphorically "step into" a fictional space. I take this point, though I would argue that even fiction has a bearing on material reality, especially if we consider the fact that production of fiction, as with the production of science, involves writing, which is itself a material process of inscription.[3] I admit that there's a gambit here I'm making in claiming a common denominator for such distinct social practices, but if anything, I hope at least to advance the work already done on the production and function of literature that a focus on the laboratory makes possible.

As Latour notes in the epigraph above, the world must first become a laboratory for it to be knowable. It is beyond my scope here to extend this claim to its logical conclusion, but I will offer that if it can be accepted that literature offers its readership a certain form of knowledge about the world, then we would have to grapple with the presence of the laboratory in this particular type of knowledge production. In this sense, figurations of the laboratory in literature are something like second-order reflections on the labor and processes of production, of the inscriptive practices and their ramification for the material historical world, of literature itself. Thus, my essay will turn from a more concrete consideration of the history of the laboratory and the rise of its representation in literature, to a consideration of the function and temporality of lab lit as itself a laboratory for socio-cultural experimentation.

LABORATORY SPACE: A BRIEF HISTORY

One need not go farther than the *Oxford English Dictionary* to glimpse the figurative range of the term laboratory. The *OED* records the first use of the English word laboratory in 1592. It was first considered a "room or building for the practice of alchemy and the preparation of medicines," and later became "one equipped for carrying out scientific experiments or procedures, esp. for the purposes of research, teaching, or analysis; (also) one in which chemicals or drugs are manufactured." As a subset of the primary definition, which registers the term's origin in the Latin for workplace, or *laboratorium*, is the figurative definition: "In extended and fig. use. Something likened to a scientific laboratory, esp. in being a site or centre of development, production, or experimentation."[4] Below, one can see that the first record of the figurative use of the term in English appears in 1654, with subsequent entries up through 2006, making rather clear the figurative and conceptual potential the concept of laboratory has already amassed:

1654 W. CHARLETON *Physiologia Epicuro-Gassendo-Charltoniana* III. xv. 342 Some more worthy Explorator . . . shall wholly withdrawe that thick Curtain of obscurity, which yet hangs betwixt Natures Laboratory and Us.

1664 H. POWER *Exper. Philos.* I. 65 The Soul (like an excellent Chymist) in this internal Laboratory of Man, by a fermentation of our nourishment in the Stomach [etc.].

1709 J. REYNOLDS *Death's Vision* x. 68 The House and Laboratory of the Soul, With all its Vital Furniture's Destroy'd.

1794 R. J. SULIVAN *View of Nature* I. 461 Fissures and caverns of rocks are the laboratories, where such operations are carried on.

1814 H. DAVY *Agric. Chem.* 15 The soil is the laboratory in which the food is prepared.

1860 M. F. MAURY *Physical Geogr. Sea* xviii. §740 Like the atmosphere it [*sc.* the sea] is a laboratory in which wonders by processes the most exquisite are continually going on.

1870 J. H. NEWMAN *Ess. Gram. Assent* II. viii. 260 A notion neatly turned out of the laboratory of the mind.

1901 *Ann. Amer. Acad. Polit. & Social Sci.* 18 149 Switzerland . . . is so often called the political laboratory of Europe.

1956 C. WILSON *Outsider* iii. 51 The *Bildungsroman* is a sort of laboratory in which the hero conducts an experiment in living.

2006 *N.Y. Rev. Bks.* 13 July 8/1 New Prospect, a place where the Great Depression never lifted, supplies Updike with an ideal laboratory in which to
cultivate the germ of militant Islamism.[5]

Not only is "Nature" conceived as a laboratory, but "man," or more precisely
in the analogy, the human body, is conceived as the laboratory of the "soul"
(which I would argue is a much more forgiving conceptualization of the body
than, for example, Plato's notion of body as prison). From the ten quotations
listed above, spanning almost four centuries, the figurative use of the laboratory designates variously the soil, the atmosphere, the sea—all particular
laboratories within the larger laboratory of nature—the nation as a political
laboratory, as well as the everyday space of the city as a lab. The laboratory
as a figure seems to extend to any structure that might be conceived as a
delimited space, something that contains, that provides walls indicating the
boundaries that regulate flows, interactions, and behaviors. In this sense, the
figurative use of the laboratory is seen in cases where what is being figured
must already take on the characteristics of an enclosure, a site or center, a
clearing that gives way to a type of interior space, or an organized configura-
tion that provides the conditions that make possible production in a broad
sense.

Of particular interest to literary practice is the notion that the mind becomes a kind of laboratory for the production of ideas inscribed within a
paper would as the literary text. Added to this is the recognition of the
Bildungsroman, a novel in which a protagonist develops through the clashes
with an external world, as itself a laboratory construct. I began with the
definition of the laboratory to show that many of the spaces associated with
fictional works—minds, settings, literary texts themselves—have already
been deemed metaphors for the lab. I would like to carry this somewhat
farther, however, and take these metaphorical valences into something more
like analogues and to propose that literary works themselves are not merely
like laboratories, but truly are laboratories in a very material sense.

A more concrete history of the scientific laboratory, as most historical
accounts of the space will attest, is difficult, if not impossible. There are, of
course, histories of specific laboratories ascribed to the efforts of individuals,
though nothing that would definitively mark an origin for the space in general. The practices of the modern laboratory are so dispersed throughout the
entire social landscape that we can only think of the gradual sedimentation of
the space of the laboratory over time—a slow historical process of repeated
practices that led to the necessary existence of the laboratory for the sciences.
Another way to say this, then, is that the historical space of the laboratory
must be thought of in terms of a process of individuation that involved not
only the practices of scientists, but also the entire historical milieu that gave

rise to the consolidation of the lab, including the literary representations of these spaces of experimentation.

Labs have most likely always existed, even if not recognized as such, though historians have attempted to date an important historical shift to a more recognizably modern lab. Lord Kelvin, then Sir William Thomson, published a history of the laboratory in an 1885 issue of the journal *Nature*, wherein he credits the first two decades of the nineteenth century with fostering the emergence of the first modern laboratory. This is in line with the introduction to Frank James's *The Development of the Laboratory: Essays on the Place of Experiment in Industrial Civilization*, where he states unambiguously that "laboratories did not exist in the pre-industrial age."[6] Indeed, scientific laboratories as we know them today clearly require the advances in machinery and technology which made the laboratory apparatus possible, such as key instruments of measure and imaging. Even so, the attempt to locate the historical shift is often confounded by the inability for historians of science to imagine something akin to scientific work happening in the absence of a laboratory. As Lord Kelvin quips when considering the pre-modern history of the laboratory, "No doubt Aristotle had his."[7] This very same sentiment is again echoed in an entry in the 1895 Smithsonian Institute annual report: "Doubtless Aristotle had his laboratory."[8] One of the first recorded public laboratories, aside from that of the Ptolemies in Alexandria during the third century BC that "gradually sank into a place for metaphysical discussions," was developed by King Frederick II for anatomy.[9] This space, which Lord Kelvin dubs "the first laboratory," suggests a connection between the laboratory and the human form, one echoed in the figurative definitions above. Since then, there seems to have been a designated space for the study of anatomy, though it won't be until the sixteenth century that this type of space will have a lasting and important public role. While anatomy was an important precursor, it was the alchemical sciences that stand as the clear catalyst for modern science and its space of labor. Key here is the fact that alchemy required a space of *experimentation*, one that could be regulated and controlled. Of course, it would take a redirection of the more metaphysical aspirations of alchemy—the philosopher's stone, the transmutation of metals, or the search for eternal life, and so on—before the practices of alchemy would be taken into the modern discipline of chemistry, one of the first modern disciplines to use the lab systematically.

One can't overemphasize the importance of the laboratory for the founding and continued practice of science in its modern guise. In their book *Order Out of Chaos*, Nobel laureate and physical chemist Ilya Prigogine and science and technology philosopher and historian Isabella Stengers evoke French philosopher of science Alexandre Koyré, who "defined the innovation brought about by modern science in terms of 'experimentation.'"[10] Modern science was intimately tied to the increasing importance of experimentation through laboratory practices. So much so that one could say that the labor associated with the practice of science is unthinkable (i.e., Aristotle *must* have had his) without a proper space for experimentation, without a production of space whose dimensions and relations allow for the unfurling of living processes as well as for the repetitions and recreations necessary for the solidification of scientific truth.

Turning now to the literary connections with the rise of the lab, it seems fair to say that these spaces of scientific labor co-originated with literature that sought to represent laboratory practices. I would argue that Shelley's knowledge of the scientific discourse of her contemporaries allows her to play out, through the character of Victor, many of the monumental shifts in the sciences, transitions that required the use of the laboratory. Franken-stein's space of labor does not belong to one particular science; the figure draws from all of the various isolated and solitary spaces of study and inven-tion—from the alchemist's lab, to the medical room, to the philosopher's library, to the chemical laboratory. Chemistry was of course well established by the time of Shelley's writing. It was considered one of the most prestig-ious of the natural sciences, perhaps on par with, if not exceeding physics as the cutting-edge field, lending its discoveries of and experimental practices on the microscopic structure of nature to practically all other fields of scien-tific study. Victor's transition from an interest in alchemy to legitimate scien-tific work begins, therefore, with chemistry after an inspiring lecture by the professor M. Waldman. When Frankenstein met this lecturer face to face, Waldman explains to him that "chemistry is that branch of natural philoso-phy in which the greatest improvements have been and may be made; it is on that account that I have made it my peculiar study." He then impresses upon Frankenstein the need to know all branches of natural philosophy, a state-ment that will lead Victor to acquire a breadth of expertise in a wide range of scientific pursuits. Waldman continues: "But at the same time I have not neglected the other branches of science. A man would make but a very sorry chemist, if he attended to that department of human knowledge alone. If your wish is to become really a man of science, and not merely a petty experimen-talist, I should advise you to apply to every branch of natural philosophy, including mathematics."[11]

Victor was shown Waldman's laboratory and given instruction as to what he should procure for his own. We never know precisely with what Franken-stein fills his laboratory, other than the flesh and bones of human and animal bodies. He does, however, describe the use of his "instruments of life," perhaps first encountered in Waldman's laboratory, though now turned to-ward a subject of study that more approached anatomy, physiology, or medi-cine, and predates anything like a biological laboratory by at least half a century. In fact, if the distinction between a "naturalist" and a "biologist" turns on the use of the laboratory, Victor Frankenstein would be one of the earliest literary figures of the modern biological scientist.

The encounter between Victor and Waldman resonates with the fact that *Frankenstein* was first published at roughly the historical moment when the alchemist's cave gave way to the chemistry lab as a valued and institutional-ized space for pedagogy. As Shelley wrote, the image of the laboratory still would have straddled the line between its alchemical heritage and chemistry as a modern discipline. While some of the major players in the push for laboratory spaces may not have been explicitly referenced in the novel, Shel-ley's journal mentions having read, for example, Sir Humphrey Davy's *Ele-ments of Chemical Philosophy* in 1816 with Percy Shelley. This is no small point, considering that Humphrey Davy, one of the most vocal chemists in England at the time, was noted for making appeals to the general public for laboratory funding and was instrumental in the establishment and legitimiza-tion of the use of the laboratory for the practice and teaching of chemistry.[12] In fact, one of the major shifts in the prominence of the lab comes precisely through the further and more intense public investment in these labs as spaces of instruction.

By the end of the 1800s, scientists working in chemistry, physics, and the life sciences (anatomy, medicine, physiology, biology, etc.) found their workshops transplanted from private dwellings to public universities. It was the housing of the laboratory in publicly funded spaces of education that solidified the laboratory as the most important site for experiment, discovery, and invention. The pedagogical use of the lab not only standardized laborato-ry practices, it also secured funding for the further outfitting and develop-ment of these spaces. It wasn't until 1825, just seven years after the publica-tion of *Frankenstein*, that Justus von Liebig would establish the first teaching laboratory soon after his appointment at the University of Giessen, thus establishing a model space for scientific work and definitively connecting laboratory work to research, invention, experimentation, and instruction.[13] Without the rigid disciplinary distinctions between the various natural sci-ences and with significant overlap and relevance of, for example, chemistry to anatomy or physics, Liebig's chemistry lab gave way to the establishment of laboratories for research and instruction in practically all other scientific disciplines such as physics, physiology, pathology, and finally, toward the end of the nineteenth century, biology.

Before considering the constitution of the biological laboratory, it would be useful to consider the literary critical discussion of the treatment of sci-ence in *Frankenstein*, which commonly leads to the conclusion that Shelley draws from the full range of popular discussions of science at the time in her novel. Not only was Shelley influenced by the debates and controversies of her contemporaries over materialism, galvanism, and vitalism, to name a few, she was also known to have attended lectures of notable scientific intellectuals in British society. Marilyn Butler confirms the influences of the sciences for Shelley by deciphering early reviews of the novel that claim *Frankenstein* to "covertly promote . . . favourite projects and passions of the times." Butler continues to explain that the "novel's network of allusions to contemporary science [was] not science as formally taught, but current scientific activity as represented to the British public in the 1810s by lectures, newspapers, a few accessible books, above all the serious Reviews."[14] The point here is not to elucidate the serious science to be found in the novel, as some seem to want to do, as if to disregard or forget the fact that we are dealing with a figurative text, but rather to show how the novel is intimately tied to the sciences as represented within the public imagination of the time.

Recognizing this allows for a more complicated reading of the scant description given of the lab itself: "In a solitary chamber, or rather cell, at the top of the house, and separated from all the other apartments by a gallery and a staircase, I kept my workshop of filthy creation."[15] Rather than a focus on exhaustive physical description, as one might expect from a Realist novel, the novel reverberates with the impact of the lab as a space of wonder, fear, and fascination. For example, the cellular space of the lab, where the unspeakable and unimaginable possibilities of nature occur in tight quarters and behind closed doors, generates a feeling of the sublime that resonates with other settings and experiences, such as the encounters between Victor and his sublime creature amid the awe-inspiring backdrop of the Alps. Furthermore, the illicit and morally questionable nature of the alchemist's labors, their unbridled, otherworldly aspirations and passions, imbue Victor's entire character and feed his drive to conquer the natural world by discovering the principle of life.

And finally, there may be no clearer indication for the impact of the public conceptions of the lab on the novel than the fact that the description of the laboratory itself says more about Frankenstein than it does about his lab. Through a kind of pathetic fallacy frequently used in the novel wherein the external world reflects the internal conditions of a character, the description inadvertently builds upon the moral and psychological character of Victor as "solitary," "separated," and "filthy." Granted, Shelley most likely wouldn't have seen a laboratory firsthand, so her description would have drawn from public lectures and written accounts. Yet, what might at first be seen as a failure of representation could also be seen as a profoundly important characterization of the labor that occurs in the scientific laboratory, a characterization that would counter the notion of the lab as a space free from subjective or cultural bias. If the description of the laboratory describes Victor more than the space itself, then it's possible to say that the scientific laboratory is also and importantly constituted through Frankenstein's character, morality, and cultural perspectives. In other words, scientific spaces of labor, following out this point, should be seen as indelibly marked by the cultural, political, economic, and affective forces moving through them and operating as part of their composition.

If the chemistry laboratory, central to the form and narrative of *Franken-stein*, was the dominant space of scientific labor at the beginning of the nineteenth-century, the biological laboratory is dominant at the turn of the twentieth century. To illustrate the importance of this shift to literary history, H.G. Wells, whose "scientific romances" are among the first instances of science fiction, would have been among those quite familiar with the increasing importance of this new space of experimentation and learning. In their essay "Constructing South Kensington: The Buildings and Politics of T. H. Huxley's Working Environments," Sophie Forgan and Graeme Gooday show how Huxley, Wells's most beloved and influential teacher, was a central figure in the introduction of the laboratory into the normal practice of the biological sciences. It was due to Huxley that the laboratory became a central feature in the pedagogy of the life sciences. As they explain:

> For Huxley the laboratory was far more central to biology teaching than for any of his predecessors. He often proclaimed that only a carefully managed programme of experimental work would give teachers the essential authority of having had 'direct' contact with the inner workings of 'Nature'. But establishing the laboratory, rather than the 'field' or the museum, as the definitive site for learning life science in the early 1870s, was by no means a straightforward task. [16]

The coming to prominence of the laboratory, indeed, was not easily managed, for it involved the costly construction of spaces specific to the training of teachers and students. Huxley was, however, determined and ultimately succeeded in making the laboratory a formalized part of his instruction by 1872. [17] Wells, then, was among the first generation of students who would have experienced the laboratory as the preeminent space for scientific research. For this reason, I would argue that Wells's literary representations of the space of the laboratory warrant our critical attention as key texts in laboratory literature.

The Laboratory as "Utopian Enclave"

Building spaces for experimenting with social change becomes urgent in the contemporary world when we face the threats of climate change, the ascendant forms of authoritarian political systems, as well as the near-universal hold of neoliberalist policies and governance over the economic and social spheres giving rise to greater vulnerabilities in already marginalized and oppressed groups. The questions of an ontology of the future are deeply imbued with the urgency to experiment with alternative worlds tied to new ways of living. Fredric Jameson begins his 2005 book on utopian and speculative fictions, *Archaeologies of the Future*, with a recognition that the global universality of capitalism and its naturalization as an economic system led to the crippling of any attempt to imagine an alternative. This, then, becomes his case for the utmost significance of utopian thought today, a belief that had been shared by H.G. Wells in his day. As Jameson explains, "The Utopians not only offer to conceive of such alternate systems; Utopian form is itself a representational meditation on radical difference, radical otherness, and on the systemic nature of the social totality, to the point where one cannot imagine any fundamental change in our social existence which has not first thrown off Utopian visions like so many sparks from a comet."[18] While *Archaeologies* is Jameson's book on the (dys/u)topian genres of science fiction, I argue that it also offers useful concepts and insights for an understanding of the formal aspects and potential function of lab lit. One of the more useful ways to think about the role of the laboratory for literature grows out of what Jameson calls the "utopian enclave," a formal aspect of the speculative text that bears at times, as I hope to show, a striking resemblance to philosopher and historian of science Robert Kohler's theory and history of the scientific lab.

Kohler locates the emergence of the biological laboratory in the distinction between the field and the lab. In *Landscapes and Labscapes: Exploring the Lab-Field Border in Biology*, Kohler discusses how the laboratory's hegemonic status for scientific research involved the positing of "field work" as outmoded labor for the biological scientist at some point between 1840 and 1870, a period he refers to as the "laboratory revolution" for the sciences.[19] However, in agreement with the above discussion of Huxley, he claims that it won't be until the late 1890s that this particular work environment will be the commonly accepted zone for legitimate scientific experimentation and observation.

One of the most notable characteristics of the space of a laboratory, according to Kohler, is its homogeneity. It is unrooted to any locality or element of place, whereas the field as a space is indissociable from its particular location. This manipulation of space/place is one of the very components of the work of a laboratory scientist. As Kohler explains, "Laboratory workers eliminate the element of place from their experiments. Field biologists use places actively in their work as tools; they do not just work *in* a place, as lab biologists do, but *on* it. Places are as much the object of their work as the creatures that live in them."[20] While I find this conception of the lab-field border compelling, I would take slight issue with the notion that lab biologists "just work *in* a place." The very labor of producing a space as universal or homogenous requires the lab worker to maintain constantly a certain kind of spatialization of the lab such that the scientist is not merely working *in* a space, but very much *with* and *through* and *on* a space precisely to make it placeless. As Lefebvre will show in *The Production of Space*, spaces are not mere geometric containers separate from the activity within, they are rather emergent products of and participants in the very actions and practices of the space itself.[21] With that qualification aside, I do take Kohler's point that laboratories, as distinct from the very rooted place of the field, are spaces constructed as devoid of place. They are walled off from the surrounding environment, and flows in and out of the laboratory must be highly regulated in order to maintain the integrity of its universal validity, which is in marked contrast to the field. In Kohler's words:

> Laboratories . . . are socially homogeneous; access is restricted to those who are qualified and have legitimate business there. Socially as well as physically and biologically, the field is a more ambiguous and unstable place than any lab. Labs are separate, a world apart from the world; nature connects field biologists to other social worlds.[22]

A "world apart from the world," an autonomous world within another surrounding world: in other words, the lab is an "enclave" of sorts within a larger social world. This points to a peculiar quality of the laboratory's relationship to that which exists beyond its walls. The field is permeable; it is in a varied and multi-directional relationship with the social world, never really under control though easily reinscribed as a place for work, recreation, conservation, and so on. The relationship of the lab to the surrounding world moves only in one direction: from the lab out to the rest of the world. Though there is research out of social sciences that challenges this notion.[23] Its communication with the outside is regulated and controlled; it is always a decision made from within the laboratory to see what is happening in the wider world. As Kohler explains, "It is precisely the stripped-down simplicity and invariability of labs—their placelessness—that gives them credibility." This is crucial for the truth claims of the lab in that "generic places sustain the illusion that their inhabitants' beliefs and practices are everyone's beliefs and practices."[24]

Building on Kohler's characterization, I understand the laboratory to be a network of various forces and materials that form an autopoietic, autonomous space, or as Bruno Latour calls it, an "alternate world," that tracks the existence and behavior of organic or inorganic entities through their traces and opens the potential for the reconfiguration of social structures, for challenging dominant presuppositions, and for producing the conditions of possibility for the emergence of new forms. I realize that this claim seems at odds with the homogeneous and conservative nature of the lab as described above, so I would like to expand upon Kohler's conceptualization by insisting on the ambiguity of laboratory practice. Even while Kohler's take elaborates the laboratory's crucial role in the validation and universal grounding of truth claims by the sciences, it skirts over the use of the laboratory as a space in and through which life is encouraged to assume previously unknown or unimaginable forms. This is, in fact, precisely what Kohler himself makes visible in his earlier monograph *Lords of the Flies: Drosophila Genetics and the Experimental Life*, in which he considers the history of genetics that relied so heavily on laboratory conditions to encourage the rapid genetic mutations of fruit flies as a means to map the genetic constitution of living creatures.[25] This is all to say, then, that the scientific laboratory (as is true of lab lit) may feed into the interests and wishes of hegemonic or dominant groups just as easily as it may give rise to possible lines of flight, a fact to which Kuhn's concept of paradigms can attest.

To return once again to H.G. Wells, I offer a passage from his *Experiment in Autobiography*, a literary laboratory experimentation in its own right, which echoes in many ways the characterization of the laboratory, yet is attuned toward the spaces of potential for radical, worldwide social transformation:

> Mankind is realizing more and more surely that to escape from individual immediacies into the less personal activities now increasing in human society is not, like games, reverie, intoxication or suicide, a suspension or abandonment of the primary life; on the contrary it is the way to power over that primary life which, though subordinated, remains intact. Essentially it is an imposition upon the primary life of a participation in the greater life of the race as a whole. In studies and studios and laboratories, administrative bureaus and exploring expeditions, a new world is germinated and develops. . . . We originative intellectual workers are reconditioning human life.[26]

The desire heard in such a rally-cry is clearly one of utopian aspiration for a reconditioned life made possible through a world state, for which Wells explicitly advocated. While Wells may perhaps overestimate the role of the "intellectual worker" here, there is a clear recognition of the universal implications of the spaces of labor, connecting the individual to the larger global community, as well as a stated will that these seeds of labor will be further cultivated to bring forth a new world. Shelley and Wells use the figure of the laboratory as a way to experiment with the dominant modes of life of their times.

Today, the laboratory is still a dominant figure for the production of resources and knowledge, tied to the massive biomedical and biotechnical industries. It is through the function of the laboratory that nature and culture become irrecuperably blurred, as was understood so well by those early biometricians and eugenicists. It is through the productions of the laboratory that living forms or chemical structures biologically tied to organic life become profitable. The laboratory is a site that is readily funded—indeed, it seems to be the privileged space to which the allocations of grants and resources are directed. It is, in other words, today the most effective and successful tool of economic development, though also a site in which the human species itself might find powerful resources to redefine itself. And so while keeping with my insistence on the fundamental ambivalence of the laboratory, I would argue that if there is a figure for the utopian enclave in the contemporary world, it would have to be found in the laboratory.

INSCRIBING TRACES OF THE FUTURE

The literary laboratory as a space for the cultivation of utopian dreams and aspirations, beyond the also important mimetic function of representing scientists at work in their trade, implants the traces of a possible future within the present, and therefore opens the space for the experimentation with social systems, human relations, relations between humans and non-humans, or relations between the organic and inorganic, and constructed and natural worlds. The alternative world of the literary laboratory allows for the unforeseen to come into focus while also allowing for these elements of political life to develop, alter, mutate, or perhaps at times to dissolve. It would seem, then, that the laboratory of and within literature is at odds with the concrete space and practices of the scientific laboratory that authorizes and draws out the material realities of the world as they truly exist here and now. I would, however, like to push back on this notion to show that while the literary laboratory may trade in that which does not yet exist, or in what is given to the reader as explicitly fictional, it may have much more in common with the practices of the scientific laboratory than one might think. In this sense, it's not enough to say that the scientific laboratory provides merely a metaphor or figuration for the function of lab lit. It would be more accurate, as I will try to show below, to say that the laboratory of science and literature both partake in one and the same process, namely the production of inscriptions within the world, which is to say the production of a collective sense of reality—the fate or ontological consistency of which remains entirely open.

A dominant conception of scientific fact, one in line with a platonic metaphysics, understands truth as that which materializes through a process that involves the articulation of a substance that preexisted its representation in scientific figures and discourses. In this Platonic sense, the production of new knowledge deals less with a possible future, but rather seeks to return to the stability of an original and preexisting truth. One point of contact between literary, poststructuralist, and scientific theorists has been to refute this very position, showing how the material inscriptions and traces that constitute both the production of science and literature are not merely copies of an eternal, preexisting reality, but rather should be seen as the grounds for the development of reality itself—the traces constituting the material foundations for what is, and for what is to come. The laboratory inscriptions are not references to a forgotten knowledge to be regained by seeing through the degraded copies of the material world, they are rather traces of the future material world in the making.

In *Science in Action*, Latour patiently and meticulously demonstrates this point by showing how scientific facts assume the status of a stable and resistant truth from out of the chaos of open-ended experimentation and dissent. And here I think it's important to preempt the charges against science studies or continental philosophies of science as somehow refuting reality or the possibility for an objective world. Latour himself attempts to clear up this misunderstanding in the first chapter of *Pandora's Hope* by stating clearly that his point is emphatically *not* to say that reality is pure fabrication or social construction. Refusing to believe in gravity will not save you from a fifteen-story fall. Rather, Latour is attempting to move beyond the impasses of realism and relativism, to show how when we follow science as it is produced, we can see much more clearly the role of that which is often ignored in the production of scientific fact, namely the social, rhetorical, economic, and political forces at play. Returning then to Latour's discussion of the production of truth, scientific facts become robust not through their apotheosis from the complexity and mess of society into a transcendent realm of eternal truths, that resplendent realm of unworldly forms, but rather through the connections made to the surrounding world—the proliferation of associations and alliances made when a particular truth claim stabilizes its status as fact or as reality. He describes this process as the mobilization of allies, which involves the number of citations to a particular claim, the use made of a claim by subsequent claims, the deployment of rhetorical strategies to win over possible dissenters, and so on. Latour explains that "the number of external friends the text comes with is a good indication of its strength, but there is a sure sign: references to other documents. The presence or the absence of references, quotations and footnotes is so much a sign that a document is serious or not that you can transform a fact into fiction or a fiction into fact just by adding or subtracting references."[27] He recognizes, of course, the stabilization of truth also has to do with prestige, institutional support, access to funds, and so on. In other words, references and allies may be a crucial aspect of our sense of reality, but it does matter whom one references and befriends.

Up to this point in his book, Latour is speaking only of scientific writing, the world of paper, and the rhetorical strategies employed in the production of scientific truth. To truly understand the production of science, however, Latour shows that one must turn back from the textbook facts and the world of paper to the laboratory, that is, to the spaces in which scientists can be found in action, experimenting with the world, producing the very data in question in scientific debate. For Latour, the laboratory is defined simply as a space in which various media, instruments, and apparatus inscribe the behaviors and qualities of what he calls the "actors" under investigation.[28] While the path to a recognizable and stable truth is long, the laboratory is that space in which material inscriptions of experiments in process become the crucial building blocks for scientific knowledge. The laboratory apparatus, itself as an array of instruments and human and non-human, living and non-living actors, gives form to the inscriptions of a real material history that becomes further enmeshed within the larger networks and connections that add stability to the scientific facts or truths. Refuting the outcome of a laboratory becomes much harder than refuting a claim made in an article. In order to disprove the evidence of a laboratory, one must either have access to the lab, in order to perform the experiments himself, or build a laboratory of his own.

To understand how I see Latour's work as relevant to a discussion of the literary laboratory, or of literature as lab, I want to turn to Timothy Lenoir's introduction to his edited collection *Inscribing Science,* which helps me show how these studies of the scientific laboratory become useful for theorizing the production of literature and its purchase on the surrounding historical, material world. Written at a key moment for the debate surrounding C. P. Show's "two cultures," Lenoir's book pushes back on the Alan Sokal–led attack on the poststructuralist use of the sciences and their (misperceived) attack on objective truth, showing how the philosophy of Derrida (one of Sokal's main antagonists), and specifically the concept of the trace, is actually much more aligned with the laboratory studies of Latour, among others, that focus on the inscription practices by instruments and apparatus within the laboratory.[29] Lenior claims that the collection of essays offers "reasons for seeing a common thread linking Derrida's philosophical concerns with the interests of scholars of scientific practice and cultural studies of science."[30] The overall thrust of this work, he claims, is the "proposal that while these different approaches from poststructuralist semiotics and literature studies may seem strange companions for science studies, when brought together under what [he is] calling studies of the materialities of communication, this new synthesis offers a fruitful orientation for moving beyond the impasse currently represented by the 'culture wars.'"[31] Lenoir continues to solidify his claims by showing just how the deconstructive work of Derrida's concept of the trace shares a good deal with the treatment of the processes of inscription found in laboratory studies. The point of contact for Lenoir, in part, is found through a recognition by both Derrida and science studies scholars of the constitutive power of inscription made possible through media and instruments of the laboratory.

I am in a position now to return to Jameson's *Archaeologies of the Future,* and to discuss this somewhat elliptical and seemingly paradoxical title for his work. Jameson allows me to recognize the ways in which the laboratory and its products, whether scientific or literary, both share in the processes of producing our material reality. An archeology, as a study of history, points to a speculative text's relationship to the past, in the sense that all imaginative texts are pieced together from what he calls the "raw materials" of the history of an author.[32] The title also suggests that the tools and methods used to study the traces of the past might be equally useful for a study of what is to come. More fundamentally, Jameson explains that what he is attempting to theorize, in and through utopian and speculative fiction, is an adequate conception of one often overlooked or unrecognized aspect of the temporality of being:

> The presumption is that Utopia, whose business is the future, or not-being, exists only in the present, where it leads the relatively feeble life of desire and fantasy. But this is to reckon without the amphibiousness of being and its temporality: in respect of which Utopia is philosophically analogous to the trace, only from the other end of time. The aporia of the trace is to belong to past and present all at once, and thus to constitute a mixture of being and not-being quite different from the traditional category of Becoming and thereby mildly scandalous for analytical Reason. Utopia, which combines the not-yet-being of the future with a textual existence in the present is no less worthy of the archaeologies we are willing to grant to the trace.[33]

Appropriating the tools of archaeology, Jameson orients his excavating instruments to "the other end of time" so as to further solidify the traces of a possible, though not yet materialized, future. I suggest, carrying out Jameson's own claim, that we think of the future traces of laboratory literature in analogous terms to the processes through which a scientific fact achieves its robustness by enlisting allies and points of reference, defending its outcomes, and inserting itself into larger networks of connection to the surrounding world. In this sense, the material inscriptions of lab lit as traces of the future are open to their potential actualization or concretization via a similar process, yet from "the other end of time." Think, for example, of the technologies, concepts, and social configurations that began life as cognitive novum—such as Gibson's cyberspace, Verne's submarine, self-driving cars, *Star Trek*'s touchscreens, tablets, and cell phones, or video calls, and the list goes on—that attain a more robust truth through their integrations into the larger surrounding world. Lab lit, then, inscribes the traces of a future whose status is similar to those traces in the scientific laboratory, the ontological status of both relying on the further investments in, and motivations for further assuring their status as truth. Of course, the implications here for new technologies is one thing, but when it comes to the question of society, of our organizations with and relationships to the other actors in the world, the argument takes on a much more urgent ethical and political tone.

Returning science and fiction to their processes of production, turning back to the laboratory, it is possible to say now that fiction as much as science can be understood to play into the processes of production of reality itself. While the apparatus or machinery of the novel has been constructed in a specific way (the writing that builds the worlds, characters, affects, and social relations), the reader enters and observes as one might observe the processes of inscription within the scientific laboratory. Yet, just as scientific truth is a product of collective negotiation, and the results of a laboratory can always be retested and contested, the reader is not merely a passive consumer of the fictional text, but rather experiments with what they find, actively drawing out the affects and perspectives the work makes possible. Working with and on their own preconceptions and the "raw materials" of history, the reader might affirm at times what they expected to be true of the world, or conversely might find the sparks of an altogether new world. Through the utopian enclaves of literature, and the reality-building capabilities of inscription considered in this essay, it is now possible to claim that, like the laboratory for the sciences (a space of inscription in which nature or reality is experimented upon, tested, and heatedly contested), literature works become themselves laboratories in which the controversy over what constitutes reality can be reopened and relived. Lab lit is an especially fruitful ground for such explorations since it unites the scientific and the social.

NOTES

1. Mary Shelley, "Introduction to *Frankenstein*, Third Edition (1831)," in *Frankenstein*, ed. J. Paul Hunter (New York: Norton, 1996), 165–68.

2. For more on the role of the laboratory and instruments in the production of scientific knowledge, see Bruno Latour, *Science in Action*: *How to Follow Scientists and Engineers Through Society* (Cambridge: Harvard University Press, 1987), specifically chapter 2, "Laboratories."

3. When speaking of the processes of production, or the conditions of possibility for literature, I am indebted in part to Pierre Macherey's *A Theory of Literary Production*, trans. Geoffrey Wall (London: Routledge, 1978), even while I take issue with the clear distinctions he sets up between the literary object and the science of its analysis.

4. "Laboratory." *OED Online*. August 2018. Oxford University Press. http://www.oed.com.ezp2.lib.umn.edu/view/Entry/104723?redirectedFrom=laboratory#eid (accessed August 31, 2018).

5. "Laboratory," *OED*.

6. Frank James, *The Development of the Laboratory: Essays on the Place of Experiment in Industrial Civilization* (London: Macmillan, 1989), 1.

7. Sir William Thomas, "Scientific Laboratories," *Nature* 31 (1885): 409.

8. William Welch, "The Evolution of Modern Scientific Laboratories," in Smithsonian Institution. Board of Regents., et al., *Annual Report of the Board of Regents of the Smithsonian Institution* 1895. Smithsonian Institution, 1846: 495. https://library.si.edu/digital-library/book/annualreportofb1895smit.

9. Welch, "The Evolution of Modern Scientific Laboratories," 495.

10. Ilya Prigogine and Isabelle Stengers, *Order Out of Chaos: Man's New Dialogue with Nature* (Toronto: Bantam, 1984), 5.

11. Mary Shelley, *Frankenstein* (New York: Norton, 1996), 28.

12. Sir Humphrey Davy, *Elements of Chemical Philosophy* (Philadelphia: Bradford and Inskeep, 1812). This is most notable in his introduction, "Historical View of the Progress of

Chemistry," where he elaborates the essential link between the science in question and alchemy.

13. H.G. Good, "On the Early History of Liebig's Laboratory," *Journal of Chemical Education* 13, no. 12 (December 1936): 557. DOI: 10.1021/ed013p55.

14. Marilyn Butler, "*Frankenstein* and Radical Science," in *Frankenstein*, ed. J. Paul Hunter. (London: Norton, 1996), 302.

15. Mary Shelley, *Frankenstein* (New York: Norton, 1996), 33.

16. Sophie Forgan and Graeme Gooday, "Constructing South Kensington: The Buildings and Politics of T. H. Huxley's Working Environments," *The British Journal for the History of Science* 29, no. 4 (December 1996): 449. DOI: 10.1017/S0007087400034737.

17. Sophie Forgan and Graeme Gooday, "Constructing South Kensington: The Buildings and Politics of T. H. Huxley's Working Environments," 449.

18. Fredric Jameson, *Archaeologies of the Future: The Desire Called Utopia and Other Science Fictions* (London: Verso, 2005), xii.

19. Robert E. Kohler, *Landscapes and Labscapes: Exploring the Lab-Field Border in Biology* (Chicago: University of Chicago Press, 2002), 3.

20. Kohler, *Landscapes and Labscapes*, 6.

21. See Henri Lefebvre, *The Production of Space,* trans. Donald Nicholson-Smith (Cambridge: Blackwell, 1991).

22. Kohler, *Landscapes and Labscapes*, 7.

23. Greg Myers, "Discourse Studies of Scientific Popularization: Questioning the Boundaries," *Discourse Studies* 5, no. 2 (2003): 265–79; Massimiano Bucchi, *Science and Media: Alternative Routes in Scientific Communication* (London: Routledge, 1998); Sophie Moirand, "Communicative and Cognitive Dimensions of Discourse on Science in the French Mass Media," *Discourse Studies* 5, no. 2 (2003): 175–206.

24. Kohler, *Landscapes and Labscapes*, 7.

25. Robert E. Kohler, *Lords of the Flies: Drosophila Genetics and the Experimental Life* (Chicago: University of Chicago Press, 1994).

26. H.G. Wells, *Experiment in Autobiography: Discoveries and Conclusions of a Very Ordinary Brain* (Boston: Little, Brown, 1934/1984), 2–3.

27. Bruno Latour, *Science in Action*: *How to Follow Scientists and Engineers Through Society* (Cambridge: Harvard University Press, 1987), 33.

28. See Bruno Latour, *Science in Action*: *How to Follow Scientists and Engineers Through Society* (Cambridge: Harvard University Press, 1987), and *Pandora's Hope: Essays on the Reality of Science Studies* (Cambridge: Harvard University Press, 1999). In particular, see the first two chapters of *Science in Action*, "Literature" and "Laboratories," and the chapter "From Fabrication to Reality," in *Pandora's Hope.*

29. Lenoir, as a matter of fact, names Latour and Woolgar's *Laboratory Life* as a key example of this move.

30. Timothy Lenoir, "Inscription Practices and the Materialities of Communication," in *Inscribing Science: Scientific Texts and the Materiality of Communication*, ed. Timothy Lenoir (Stanford: Stanford University Press, 1998), 4.

31. Lenoir, "Inscription Practices," 4.

32. As Jameson explains, "Laws, labor, marriage, industrial and institutional organization, trade and exchange, even subjective raw materials such as characterological formations, habits of practice, talents, gender attitudes: all become, at one point or another in the story of utopias, grist for the Utopian mill and substances out of which the Utopian construction can be fashioned." Jameson, *Archaeologies of the Future,* 14.

33. Jameson, *Archaeologies of the Future*, xv.

BIBLIOGRAPHY

Aldiss, Brian. *Billion Year Spree: The True History of Science Fiction.* Garden City: Doubleday, 1973.

Butler, Marilyn. "*Frankenstein* and Radical Science." In *Frankenstein*, ed. J. Paul Hunter. London: Norton, 1996.

Davy, Sir Humphrey. *Elements of Chemical Philosophy.* Philadelphia: Bradford and Inskeep, 1812.

Forgan, Sophie, and Graeme Gooday. "Constructing South Kensington: The Buildings and Politics of T. H. Huxley's Working Environments." *The British Journal for the History of Science* 29, no. 4 (December 1996): 435–68. DOI: 10.1017/S0007087400034737.

Good, H.G. "On the Early History of Liebig's Laboratory." *Journal of Chemical Education* 13, no. 12 (December 1936): 557–62. DOI: 10.1021/ed013p55.

Hacking, Ian. "The Participant Irrealist at Large in the Laboratory." *The British Journal for the Philosophy of Science* 39, no. 3 (Sept. 1988): 277–94. DOI: 10.1093/bjps/39.3.277.

James, Frank. *The Development of the Laboratory: Essays on the Place of Experiment in Industrial Civilization.* London: Macmillan, 1989.

Jameson, Fredric. *Archaeologies of the Future: The Desire Called Utopia and Other Science Fictions.* London: Verso, 2005.

Knorr-Cetina, Karen. *Epistemic Cultures: How the Sciences Make Knowledge.* London: Harvard UP, 1999.

Kohler, Robert E. *Landscapes and Labscapes: Exploring the Lab-Field Border in Biology.* Chicago: University of Chicago Press, 2002.

———. *Lords of the Fly: Drosophila Genetics and the Experimental Life.* Chicago: University of Chicago Press, 1994.

Lefebvre, Henri. *The Production of Space.* Translated by Donald Nicholson-Smith. Cambridge: Blackwell, 1991.

Latour, Bruno. *Science in Action: How to Follow Scientists and Engineers Through Society.* Cambridge: Harvard University Press, 1987.

———. *Pandora's Hope: Essays on the Reality of Science Studies.* Cambridge: Harvard University Press, 1999.

Latour, Bruno, and Steve Woolgar. *Laboratory Life: The Construction of Scientific Facts.* Princeton: Princeton University Press, 1979.

Lenoir, Timothy. "Inscription Practices and the Materilaities of Communication." In *Inscribing Science: Scientific Texts and the Materiality of Communication*, edited by Timothy Lenoir, 1–19. Stanford: Stanford University Press, 1998.

Macherey, Pierre. *A Theory of Literary Production.* Translated by Geoffrey Wall. London: Routledge, 1978.

"Laboratory." *OED Online.* August 2018. Oxford University Press. http://www.oed.com.ezp2.lib.umn.edu/view/Entry/104723.

Prigogine, Ilya, and Isabelle Stengers. *Order Out of Chaos: Man's New Dialogue with Nature.* Toronto: Bantam, 1984.

Shapin, Steven. "The House of Experiment in Seventeenth-Century England." *Isis* 79, no. 3 (Sep., 1988): 373–404. DOI: 10.1086/354773.

Shelley, Mary. *Frankenstein.* Edited by J. Paul Hunter. New York: Norton, 1996.

Thomson, Sir William. "Scientific Laboratories." *Nature* 31 (1885): 409–13.

Welch, William. "The Evolution of Modern Scientific Laboratories." In Smithsonian Institution. Board of Regents., et al. *Annual Report of the Board of Regents of the Smithsonian Institution* 1895. Smithsonian Institution, 1846. https://library.si.edu/digital-library/book/annualreportofb1895smit, 495.

Wells, H. G. *Experiment in Autobiography: Discoveries and Conclusions of a Very Ordinary Brain.* 1934. Boston: Little, Brown, 1984.

Whitman, Frank. "The Beginnings of Laboratory Teaching in America." *Science* 8 (1898): 201–206.

Chapter Six

The Use of Forensic Techniques to Uncover Social Disorder in Caleb Carr's Alienist Novels

Kimberley H. Idol

In Caleb Carr's Alienist novels (*The Alienist*, 1994, and *The Angel of Darkness*, 1997), a team of criminalists living in New York City at the turn of the twentieth century utilizes current scientific and technological advances to hunt criminals. In the process they challenge existing ideas of cultural and social organization. New York City, already a powerful financial epicenter of the United States at this time, was experiencing a radical change in economic modes. A huge influx of immigration from Southern and Eastern Europe was altering the city's societal demographics. A massive rise in urbanism and an associated rise in the crime rate created a need for innovation in crime fighting techniques that, in turn, compelled law enforcement agencies to exploit technological advances in the forensic sciences.

In these novels forensic techniques are essential to the process of getting to the truth of the matter in terms of crime solving, catching the criminal, and in terms of assessing the nature of morality. They determine that the way to teach human beings how to fix what is wrong with society and help them solve more tangible short-term problems lies in the ability to trust the scientific method and to trust the objective investigative process. The protagonists in these novels were ruined people who have all found their way back to a productive place in society via the scientific method and who now completely trust that method and use it to solve the important riddles. All have suffered personal losses that temporarily turned them into drunks or criminals or caused psychological breaks. Carr is very careful to explain the techniques used by his investigators in layman's terms, and if he introduces more obscure terms, they and the history that leads to the development of their significance are fully explained. These novels lay the historical groundwork to works by authors such as Kathy Reich, Patricia Cornwell, and Beverly Connor because they trace the history of the investigative techniques and protocols on which more contemporary novels rely. Partially because of Carr's works, there is no longer a need to validate these procedures.

Carr reminds readers of his works that the introduction of scientific understanding into mainstream ideology was a rocky road. But because of the clear explanations of process, significance, and history, readers understand with ease how the science in these books works. Carr follows the path laid out in classics such as Mary Shelley's *Frankenstein* in that he examines the theme of the exploration of new science and belief in the power of science.

Carr's protagonists are forensic scientists, anthropologists, and police officers with groundbreaking investigative tools at their disposal. Dr. Laszlo Kreizler, the team's leader, is a post-Freudian psychologist (alienist) at a time when the science has achieved enough validation to be used to analyze and profile abnormal (criminal as well as insane) behavior. Dr. Kreizler's team also employs advances in the hard forensic sciences, novel and sophisticated, tested and untested methods of criminal apprehension: dissection, anthropometry or the Bertillon system (the use of meticulous physical measurements of body parts, especially the head and face, to produce a detailed description of a suspect and to determine whether suspects have been previously arrested), dactyloscopy (fingerprint identification), graphology (handwriting analysis), and ballistics, to name a few. These techniques are described in detail in terms of history, theoretical constructs, process, and levels of success achieved. The teammates scientifically test the merits of these techniques in the field. When the techniques fail or succeed, the team then assesses results, one example being the matter of anthropometry versus dactyloscopy.

Sara Howard, a police secretary, lists the countries in which anthropometry has been successfully used and the team reflects on its creator's credentials. Sergeant Marcus explains the technique's possible limitations, such as how difficult it is to get such exacting measurements as are required and notes that the technique can only work to locate individuals who already have records and that it might exclude suspects. When they assess dactyloscopy, also a controversial technique in this book's time period, Sara reveals her suspicions of a technique she feels has yet to be validated, while Marcus offers several examples of it being used successfully in other countries. The point of the debate is to reach a point when Kreizler and his team finally decide whether failure should kill further investigation into the use of new tactics or whether further testing is necessary to determine the value of these forensic techniques. Empiricism rules the day, although morality and suspicion also impact this team's ability to use novel modes of investigation.

Some of the team will encounter scientists who refuse to rely on dissection because cutting up a human corpse offends their moral sensibilities. But no matter how the arguments end, they are governed by the idea of rigorously testing and retesting procedures and ideas in order to determine validity. The conversation about fingerprinting and body measurements ends with an understanding that in order to maximize the possibilities of success for the whole team, the two techniques should be tested in the field and both kinds of data should be collected until one or the other proves its merit.[1]

A side effect of reliance on these scientific advances is an innovative interpretation of human nature and interpersonal relationships that suggests social systems themselves bear responsibility for creating the human monsters these detectives track. These investigations also result in a characterization of the criminal element as a natural expression of a whole system's dynamic nature, including its destructive tendencies. A central tension happens when the alienist's team posits these conclusions about interactive social systems that, in the opinion of New York civil authorities, threaten the status quo.

To provide more context, *The Alienist* is set after Theodore Roosevelt is installed as president of the NYPD Police Commission. Roosevelt's imperative is to professionalize and reform a historically corrupt organization that is primarily a partisan political task force by the time he takes control. He is experiencing pushback from powerful political and criminal interests, and because of this, he knows that his tenure will be limited. If he is to make any headway at all, he must proceed aggressively. His reliance on Dr. Kreizler and his colleagues furthers his goals, and indeed members are selected because they share Roosevelt's ideals and because they are outsiders to the system he means to reform.

Both of these stories are set in New York City in the years between 1896 and 1897. In *The Alienist*, Teddy Roosevelt tasks Dr. Kreizler's team (consisting of John Moore, a crime reporter; Sara Howard, a police secretary; Sergeants Marcus and Lucius Isaacson; and reformed criminals Steve Taggart and Cyrus Montrose) to conduct a surreptitious investigation of several murders that are being dismissed out of hand by the New York City police force. The murder victims are boy prostitutes, so their deaths barely merit police interest. Also, civic leaders express their belief that investigation of the crimes and the subsequent hunt for serial killer John Beecham could create the perception that there is a moral crisis in New York society and threaten the city's moral and economic status quo. These community leaders are particularly worried about what they call "immigrant uprising" fomented by "foolish notions" born in the ghettos of Europe—that is, socialism, liberalism, and the collective democratic impulse that is confronting the old European regimes in this period.

In Carr's second novel, *The Angel of Darkness*, team members of their own volition hunt Elisabeth (Libby) Hatch, a nurse who murders infants, and who has kidnapped Ana Linares, the fourteen-month-old offspring of a Spanish dignitary. Authorities are not involved because of the political ramifications of Ana's Spanish parentage during a time when the Spanish-American War is ramping up. Investigation of both these crimes brings the team into conflict with powerful public figures who share a specific vision of social order. Gangs who rule the area are also antagonistic to this group, although their leaders are more amenable to potential for social disorder because it offers potential political leverage. Specifically, J. P. Morgan, Archbishop Michael Corrigan, infamous Post Office censor Anthony Comstock, Episcopalian Bishop Henry Potter, ex–police chief Thomas Byrnes, Cornelius Vanderbilt II, Clarence Darrow, the Irish mob, and a street gang known as the Hudson Dusters antagonize Caleb Carr's heroes in both books.

This group of antagonists opposes Kreizler's scientific mode of investigation for a number of reasons. "We know of your investigation, and for a variety of reasons we want it stopped,"[2] says J. P. Morgan in the company of Comstock, two bishops, and Byrnes. Morgan explains that America and New York in particular are at a crossroads in which the dominant sources of income are shifting. To fuel private investment, this shift is serviced by the funneling of a huge influx of impoverished immigrants (cheap labor) into local industries whose owners want a docile workforce that accepts abysmal working and living conditions. In order to circumvent the inevitable ethnic conflicts of such a diverse working population, industrialists and their friends rely on propagation of values already familiar to lower-class workers, which includes the criminal class. Bishop Potter defines this ethical code as the "spiritual repose" that supports a "societal fabric" based on "the sanctity and integrity of the family, along with [acceptance of] each individual's responsibility before God and the law for his/her behaviour, [as] the twin pillars of our civilization."[3] The spiritual repose the bishop refers to means blind obedience to church and state. The societal fabric he refers to is the illusion of civility. Potter's concern is that if Kreizler and his team examine his value system closely, they will challenge the certainty of a family unit, for example, as an ultimate source of proper moral behavior. They might raise questions about the nobility of religious officials and their commitment to the community values that they want members of lower-class family units to support. The bishop is also worried about knowledge that challenges standard religious precepts because he envisions total social disarray as a result. In the police chief's mind the kind of scientific examination proposed by this team of scientists advances discomforting truths about criminal behavior.

As a student of William James (*The Principles of Psychology*, 1890)[4] and Franz Boas (*Race and Democratic Society*, 1945 [an anachronism]),[5] Dr. Kreizler asserts that current, presumably positive social constructs can naturally and powerfully encourage and/or subvert criminal behavior. He utilizes Boas's belief in empirical examination and cultural relativism to divine human behavior and James's idea that human nature is defined by a combination of instinct and experience. These ideas and Kreizler's confidence in psychological context support his belief that criminals are evidence of the general failure of society (and families in particular) to consistently provide morally uplifting environments. In doing so he challenges the established notion of responsibility as well as the bishop's emphasis on a very specific and established view of spiritual context for moral behavior. As a result of his work with the mentally disturbed, he also defines insanity in a disconcertingly narrow context, defining criminals, by and large, as reasonable and responsible members of society (in other appreciable aspects). "If the average person were to describe John Beecham in light of his murders, he'd say he were a social outcast, but nothing could be . . . more untrue. . . . He was its [society's] offspring, its sick conscience—a living reminder of all the hidden crimes we commit when we close ranks to live among each other."[6]

Dr. Kreizler is suggesting that John Beecham, the man murdering the boys, is not insane, but a reasonable result and reflection of the society that created him. He is also suggesting that insanity is a comforting solution too often applied to the problem of criminal behavior because it identifies miscreants as weird elements in a healthy social body that simply need to be excised. If mainstream society and its systems can be inherently corrupting influences, as Kreizler suggests, then criminals become reasonable results and logical extensions of bad relationships that are being touted as good ones by definition, and, therefore, the whole of society needs to redefine crime and the relationship between the criminal and his group of origin. "He [the serial killer] craved human society, craved the chance to show people what their 'society' had done to him. And the odd thing is, society craved him, too."[7] The criminal is a normal and necessary part of the system. He reveals the failures of the system to build healthy people and then bears total responsibility for the failure when the social body that intends to cleanse itself of its guilt condemns him. Without the criminal, society would be responsible for the boys' deaths and would need to evolve. The serial killer offers a scapegoating answer. His existence allows the status quo to continue unexamined and allows the pretense of stability to thrive.

The scientific mode of inquiry drives Dr. Kreizler's search for real answers, and Caleb Carr remains true to this theme throughout both stories. For Kreizler, there are reasonable means of defining criminality and determining levels of sanity, and he believes that rational investigation is the only way to prove his point.[8] Positing a distinction between immoral behavior and mental illness, Kreizler uses the term "explosive association"[9] and connects it to context. He suggests that insane individuals are those who cannot recognize or react to reality,[10] and sick but rational people are those who have been shaped by extreme environments and turned into savages, but who know that what they do is wrong. He then hypothesizes that if a criminal's behavior and mental state can be reasonably tracked as a cognitive result of a bad situation, then the offender's ability to rationalize the connections means that he or she is not pathologically insane.[11] Dr. Kreizler tests his theory of context at the Kreizler Institute for Children that rescues those in hopeless situations (like his driver Cyrus and the boy Stevie). The Institute provides research and carefully recorded results of the strength of his theories at work to law enforcement and to his colleagues.

The scientific method of investigation favored by Dr. Kreizler's team frightens their enemies. Even heads of law enforcement are deeply reluctant to engage in the battle: "There's no desire to investigate them [the mutilation and murders of transvestite boy prostitutes] in the department. Even if there were, none of our detectives is trained to make sense of such butchery,"[12] says Roosevelt. The insistence on examining crime scenes and collecting data offends the Victorian sensibilities of the police and of the political and religious authorities that encourage avoiding and eradicating evidence of ugliness in human nature rather than investigating it. Narrow minded and unskilled investigators in these books glance over a crime scene and judge the level of criminality by the victim's class and ethnicity; likewise, they experience a class and ethnic affinity where others like them could not possibly do wrong, and, if they do, then they are not bad people, but only somebody who has done a minimal bad deed. They believe that the real victims, the real sufferers, are always others like them because they can easily empathize with, if nothing else, their position in society. In contrast, Kreizler's team approaches a crime scene gingerly in order not to contaminate it. They objectively note, preserve, and categorize the types of evidence that will help them solve the crime. Objects are observed, recorded (photographically or in artist renderings). A slashed throat is examined, but not touched. The corpse's body temperature is taken to determine time of death, and all this data collection is done quickly and surreptitiously in order not to offend the police who'd rather clean the mess up.[13] Kreizler, certain that the scene has been violated by those who do not respect forensic science, writes a note to the police commissioner after leaving the scene:

ROOSEVELT: TERRIBLE ERRORS HAVE BEEN MADE . . . WE SHOULD BEGIN—THERE IS A TIMETABLE.[14]

When the police wipe away gross and offensive evidence that they should collect and examine at length in a laboratory setting, they feel justified. The forensic methods Kreizler and his team use are viewed with suspicion by the police force in part because the police in these novels judge crime philosophically. NYPD Sergeant Flynn links a dead boy's poverty to a madman's habits and solves the murder representatively. He rationalizes, "This piece of immigrant trash finally gets what's coming to it."[15] Prejudging motives and justifying violence according to class, race, and gender shuts down the inquisitive process. Once the boys are unworthy and destined for death, then the possibility of linked crimes becomes moot. In *The Alienist*, we see the following explanation (or rather justification) for a crime:

> ... it was no child, this one, not if childhood be judged by behavior ... "
> "'It'?" I said, wiping cold sweat from my forehead with the cuff of my coat. "Why do you call him 'it'?"
> Flynn's smile became a grin. "Sure, and what would you call it, Mr. Moore? It warn't no male, not to judge by its antics—but God didn't create it female, teither [*sic*]. They're all its to me, that breed."[16]

Here the sense is the child decided to become perverse. The fact that squalor, abuse, and abandonment common in the district were the source of the child's depraved existence and subsequent death does not compute for the policeman, although evidence suggests otherwise.

Once Libby Hatch is relegated to the category of caretaker who must, therefore, be ruled by a maternal instinct, then the facts of her homicidal actions no longer need to be charted. When the team starts to focus on Libby Hatch, Elizabeth Cady Stanton, without understanding all the facts, suggests that "no woman comes into this world with a desire to do anything but . . . create . . . and nurture . . . if that power is perverted, you may rest assured that a man is involved."[17] Stanton is suggesting environmental factors can limit women's growth, but not in ways that promote perversion. Like other characters in *The Angel of Death*, Stanton relies on sentiment to contradict the plausible theory that a mother who is also a nurse could be killing babies. For Stanton, if the facts argue another point, then they are wrong because the theory must stand. When Kreizler informs her that facts suggest that her version of femininity is invalid, she shuts him down.

Libby's crimes are not recognized as habitual acts, and James Beecham's crimes are considered to be one-offs because Libby's and James's groups of origin are not supposed to generate murderers, so society assumes that these criminals are incapable of killing for pleasure. In both cases, the families (and the larger social systems) that create these two serial killers seem normal, but in reality they are dysfunctional organizations.

In theory, according to the social leadership in these books, modern society is an institution in which decency is defended by a police force that fights crime and is defined by a Christian community that provides a moral center. But, once the scientific method is applied and these presumptions are tested, the results raise questions about these institutions because evidence is collected, collated, and analyzed according to strictly objective goals. The purpose of the investigation for these scientists is finding the truth rather than locating the pat answers that soothe worried minds.

The team uses a "reverse investigative procedure" to conduct its investigations. They develop a working hypothesis of the murderers' psychopathology, from physical evidence based on a premise of how normal human beings react to violence. "We start with the prominent features of the killings themselves, as well as the personality traits of the victims, and from those we determine what kind of a man might be at work."[18] This method inspires Detective Byrnes's deep fear, one shared by his fellows, that an "intellectual exercise" such as this would advance the dangerous idea that a solution is possible. He would prefer that the populace should only be advised that crime occurs when people break the law,[19] and, therefore, see it as a fact of life to be endured. If intellectual tools are available to all, then everyone (in theory) could solve this problem without a ruling class. The scientist's view is antithetical to Byrnes's standards and those of his ilk, many of whom are prominent socialite revolutionaries like Elizabeth Cady Stanton.

Dr. Kreizler's fundamental psychological pedagogy spells out a way to examine human relationships and human nature so that they are perfectly aligned with the investigative process of a team of individuals who believe wholeheartedly in using principles of the scientific method to hunt criminals. The Sergeants Marcus and Lucius Isaacson complement Kreizler's pedagogy with their use of novel forensic techniques of the day such as dissection, anthropometry, dactyloscopy, graphology, optography, and ballistics. By the early 1900s all of these techniques had achieved at least some scientific and social validation. And as critical as the disciplines themselves is the kind of discovery that their use promotes. These men are testing whether the new techniques work at all in a system governed by a strict peer review process. Testing ideas and criticizing the results in a group setting is a subversive protocol, so the two sergeants often work in private. Some of the techniques they use fail, but it is the impulse to test reality that marks this team as scientists of their day, not just their successes. Their failures are proof of the power of their methods since the policy of proving and disproving an idea is part of learning. Each of the procedures the sergeants use is viewed with suspicion in part because of a distrust of the outcomes, but also because of the social mores and superstitions their use flouts. This team is working on the edge of discovery.

In 1896 post-mortem examinations were controversial. Some believed that autopsies were sacrilegious. One of Libby Hatch's victims is not autopsied because his widow worries about harming her husband's soul. The lack of an ability to fully understand the breadth and depth of information available in autopsies and lack of training means that bad data is registered and valuable data is overlooked, which in turn renders the idea of an autopsy as less than a completely trustworthy scientific method, but that is the way of technological advances. Mistakes are made that result in devastating setbacks as each one compromises the team's credibility.

The Bertillon method has limits and results in misidentifications. Fingerprinting is a more reliable method of identification, but Kreizler's teammates do not know that yet. They use both methods as they build their data bank, which itself will be something to test. They know graphology might help them match authors to their texts, but they also try to divine personality traits from writing samples, which provides flawed results. They also use optography, the science of recovering the last image a dying man sees just before death. In all, sorting fact from superstition is also part of their job. They fail with the photographs, but succeed with ballistics. The photographs are often not sharp enough for their purposes and further, in terms of optographic use, the theory fails altogether. In terms of ballistics, Isaac and Marcus take the lead. They examine the gun in an attempt to disprove Libby Hatch's (Angel of Darkness) statement that an unknown villain shot her three children while they were seated in a carriage. The two officers determine possible trajectories by examining wounds and posit where victims were positioned. By examining the wounds in the children's bodies, they also determine that the bullets in Libby's gun caused the injuries. They then examine the lands and grooves in the gun barrel and match these patterns to those found on bullet fragments recovered from the scene. They also examine rust and powder buildup in the gun's chambers in order to determine how recently the gun was fired after its last cleaning. Libby's weapon is a six-shooter. Isaac and Marcus determine that it is missing three bullets. Two of the empty chambers are cleaner, they have less rust and powder deposits in them than does the third chamber, which is quite dirty, suggesting two bullets were fired at the same time, but not a third. Libby's fingerprints are found on the gun barrel, hammer, and trigger, but not on the chamber, so she could not have fired twice and reloaded. What the investigators finally ascertain using their examination procedures and some imaginative deduction is that one bullet passed through two bodies, proving Libby did murder her children with her gun.

When confronted with the question of who is committing murder, instead of guessing, the team builds an evidence base that generates a question-making process. By deconstructing crime scenes, personalities, and events and by staring closely at the perverse aspects of human society in order to track down their monsters, the investigators start to see how the monsters are the results of a society that makes them and actually needs them. Instead of aberrations in a system, Kreizler's team begins to see serial killers as manifestations of a deeply flawed set of social interactions that encourage monstrosity. They discover that these monsters are reflections of a society that lacks and needs critical examination.

Seen in this light, then, for example, the resistance to necropsy is representative of a desire to hide from the established and supported brutality that allows a system to exist in which children are abused and killed and then discarded on a regular basis. Once the young victims are dead, authorities, rather than seeing the corpses as evidence of how life on the streets of New York City is perverse, throw the bodies away. The children cannot be symptoms of slums ruled and funded by the Episcopalian Church, whose leaders wish the investigation to be stopped before it incurs civil unrest. When Cornelius Vanderbilt refuses to help Kreizler and hires Clarence Darrow to defend the baby killer, he plays his part in the process that protects and creates the killing creature Libby turns out to be. Vanderbilt's idea of family and his worldview is threatened if he accepts the fact that Libby is a dangerous predator, so he defends her to protect his idea of how the world works. Two men are direct victims of this dreaming state as a result. Libby slashes their throats and takes on the role of the mother figure of the Hudson Dusters, a gang of murderous children delivering a bizarre reflection of American family values truly at work in real time.

For many characters in *The Angel of Darkness*, Libby Hatch cannot be the inevitable product of a society and family setting in which killing babies is the resultant natural expression of the way women are harmed by unreasonable expectations. She must be a monster. Laziness is part of the reason mainstream investigators reject the scientific process as a means of inquiry, but their resistance is also the product of a concern that examination of the facts might reveal a shared responsibility originating in the normal dynamics of everyday violence and despair. "It creates certain difficulties, if we are forced to accept that our society can produce sane men who commit such acts."[20] It is easier to blame monsters rather than face the fact that "normal" human interactions are often destructive. Stories about dissolute dead boys being hunted by a bad man or about disappearing babies and a mother gone wrong are frightening and suggest that something is wrong at home. Turn a story about a headless body into one about a raving monster, and readers are entertained. Allow that the headless man was murdered by his wife and her lover and chopped up in order to facilitate disposal, then the story takes on a mundane taint that reveals more about marriages than monsters. Promote the marriage gone wrong story, then every marriage given the right circumstances has a dark potential, which contradicts the idea of a marriage as a relationship that always encourages decent and loving relationships.

When Kreizler's team checks for fingerprints on coat buttons to verify Libby's presence at a crime scene, one could say they are also localizing a problem. The process of Baby Ana's disappearance is aligned with a recordable series of human connections that provide evidence of human failure (not just perversion) that can and, therefore, should be carefully tracked. And the results of that hunt should be carefully recorded in order to see what is wrong with the world that left Ana, and the babies that died before her, exposed to the danger of a seemingly well-ordered and peacefully attuned society.

Ana's father beats her mother for suggesting that they call the police when their daughter is taken. When the baby is retrieved, politicians and policemen decide that it is safer for the mother and child to vanish rather than to be returned home to the husband (the Spanish dignitary), who wishes to retain the image of a family man and is unremorseful about his violence and callousness. Senor Linares's conclusion that it is better to let his baby die so that negotiations between the United States and Spain can proceed smoothly is considered wise rather than perverse according to the political powers that be. J.P. Morgan allows the team to proceed despite warnings from policemen and priests as long as his monetary concerns are not interfered with, but also as long as whatever information Kreizler uncovers does not teach society at large that the system its members are tied to is designed to make their lives darker.

> "Because it riles me." For the first time, Kelly's face went straight. "That's right, Doctor—it riles me. Those pigs back there get fed all that slop about society by the boys on Fifth Avenue just as soon as they're off the boat, and what do they do? They knock themselves out trying to eat every bit of it. It's a sucker bet, a crooked game, whatever you want to call it, and there's a part of me that wouldn't mind seeing it go the other way for a while."[21]

This Irish gangster says the murders are useful because they promote visible disarray and expose how New York society works below the surface. Kelly (a mobster) appreciates seeing the truth come to light because when it does, he is the man civil authorities rely on in order to make it seem as if order reigns. They will need the Irish gangster to use criminal means to make law and order look like it is working. It is important to note that the system is designed to keep a large body of the populace living in fear of crime, so it follows that criminals are vital components of a system of law and order.

Kreizler and his team suggest that an enlightened kind of power is available to the populace in terms of resolving crime; in so doing, they are also suggesting that perhaps the system they and their fellows are living in needs radical alteration. In essence, their use of technological advances espouses a general theory of problem solving. The system is broken, so it needs to be taken apart down to its most basic elements. These pieces need to be examined, reassembled, and evaluated in order to see how the pieces work as one and affirm how changes in general architecture alter system dynamics. Try again until you get it right—that's the message. An inherent sense of democracy is demonstrated in the process. Its users assume that all human beings can do this. They also presume that explanations are desired and necessary even if they seem dark.

Kreizler has a specific definition of pathological mental illness because, as he says, "a broad definition . . . might make society as a whole feel better but [does] nothing for mental science and only lessen[s] the chance that the truly mentally diseased [will] receive proper care and treatment."[22] In other words, a problem cannot be solved unless it is accurately defined. In an organic situation (such as one governed by social interactions) the ability to test and retest hypotheses until only the truth is left is essential to progress. This strategy makes Dr. Kreizler and his teammates more effective in terms of catching criminals than any other group in these books. Although the use of the scientific method is politically offensive in the eyes of legal and religious leadership, the scientific method in these stories demonstrates the inescapable accuracy by which this kind of inquiry can be used to assess real world situations. Use of it turns Kreizler's teammates into superheroes in terms of effectiveness in their world. They find the killers more quickly than anyone else, they predict their killers' actions, and they capture them while those who disdain their methods fail.

Solving social problems via scientific inquiry is a technique celebrated in both novels: each one focuses on investigating the damage done in the context of the supposed safety of a family structure. Family values are examined here: consistency, kindness, honesty, and social responsibility, to name a few. Beecham is abused by his mother as a child and later by a family outsider. Neither the family unit nor the society that considers the family unit one of the pillars of social decency saved him. Libby does not come from a violent family, but both her brother and her mother help hide her initial murder victims; she in turn mines the common notion of the fear of family traditions that is being examined. In another example, Beecham claims Sioux renegades murdered his parents. Hatch, in her turn, blames a black man for her children's deaths. When James Beecham and Libby Hatch use the mythology of an ethnic minority to avoid punishment, both rely on racism, another established pillar of American society, to support their actions. Their explanations are accepted because their answers don't upset the status quo despite letting serial killers run free among the children in these two cases.

Both of these stories conclude by leaving us with an understanding of New York society as a conglomeration of individuals who do not mix well with others and, as a result, force violent radical social interactions that drive change in order to relieve pressures built up behind a mountain of unworkable ideas regarding order and stability. Progress left uncontained can result in mutations (negative results) and forward movement (positive results). But when conservative forces inhibit natural growth, perversion is encouraged, and tracking its causes, by tracing backward from the hurricane to the butterfly, investigators reveal the breaks. These protagonists rely on forensic methods novel to their age, and in doing so they refute established understandings of human nature and urban order. They redefine the unraveling of New York's social systems as natural aspects that result in the creation of urban serial killers by employing faith in the scientific method and the forensic techniques novel to their age in their hunt for serial killers like Charles Beecham and Elisabeth Hatch.

NOTES

1. Caleb Carr, *The Alienist* (New York: Random House, 1994), 101–102.
2. Carr, *The Alienist*, 295.
3. Carr, *Alienist*, 297.
4. William James, *The Principles of Psychology: Volume One (Revised Edition)* (New York: Dover Publications, 2012), https://ebooks.adelaide.edu.au/j/james/william/principles/chapter4.html.
5. Franz Boas, *Race and Democratic Society* (New York: Biblo and Tannen (reprint), 1969.
6. Carr, *Alienist*, 481.
7. Ibid., 481.
8. Ibid., 28.
9. Ibid., 32.
10. Ibid., 85.
11. Ibid., 31.
12. Ibid., 19.
13. Ibid., 14–16.
14. Ibid., 16.
15. Ibid., 16.
16. Ibid., 15.
17. Caleb Carr, *The Angel of Darkness* (New York: Random House, 1996), 137.
18. Carr, *Alienist*, 301.
19. Ibid., 302.
20. Carr, *The Angel of Darkness*, 31.
21. Carr, *Alienist*, 276.
22. Ibid., 31.

BIBLIOGRAPHY

Boas, Franz. *Race and Democratic Society.* New York: Biblo and Tannen (reprint), 1969.
Boeing, Geoff. "Visual Analysis of Nonlinear Dynamical Systems: Chaos, Fractals, Self-Similarity and the Limits of Prediction." *Systems* 4, no. 4 (November 2016): https://doi.org/10.3390/systems4040037.
Carr, Caleb. *The Alienist.* New York: Random House, 1994.
———. *The Angel of Darkness.* New York: Random House, 1996.
———. "Myths and Criminal Masterminds." *New York Times*, July 25, 1997. https://www.nytimes.com/1997/07/25/opinion/myths-and-criminal-masterminds.html.
Csordas, Thomas J. "Morality as a Cultural System?" *Current Anthropology* 54, no. 5 (2013): 523–46.
Darrow, Clarence. "Why I Am an Agnostic: Including Expressions of Faith from a Protestant, a Catholic and a Jew." In *The Essential Words and Writings of Clarence Darrow.* New York Modern Library, 2007.
Freud, Sigmund. "Chapter 5." In *The Future of an Illusion.* London: Hogarth Press. (English translation), 1928. https://archive.org/stream/sigmund-freud-the-future-of-an-illusion/sigmund-freud-the-future-of-an-illusion_djvu.txt.
James, William. *The Principles of Psychology: Volume One (Revised Edition).* New York: Dover Publications, 2012. https://ebooks.adelaide.edu.au/j/james/william/principles/chapter4.html.

Lorenz, Edward N. "Deterministic Nonperiodic Flow." *Journal of the Atmospheric Sciences* 20
     (1963): 130–41.
———. "Can Chaos and Intransitivity Lead to Interannual Variability?" *Tellus* 42A (1990):
     378–89.
Serres, Michael. *The Natural Contract Studies in Literature and Science*. Translated by Eliza-
     beth MacArthur and William Paulson. Ann Arbor: University of Michigan Press, 1995.

Chapter Seven

Barbara Kingsolver's *Flight Behavior*

The Sciences in a Post-Fact World

Theda Wrede

Nature writer and environmental activist Terry Tempest Williams admonishes her readers—or, rather, "us," thereby including herself—to engage our imaginations to save species in peril and, as a result, save ourselves. The risk of passivity is too great, she implies: Where humans manipulate nature on a global scale, regardless of the costs to other species, loss becomes the only certainty. In *Flight Behavior*, Barbara Kingsolver outlines some environmental risks while focusing on the reasons many of us remain disengaged. First and foremost, she attributes the passive acceptance of environmental degradation to culture. In her 2012 interview with author Stephen L. Fisher, Kingsolver states that cultural differences fascinate her in the way they encourage a range of perspectives that occasionally clash quite forcefully: "People invest themselves differently in the same set of truths," she asserts, tracing the causes to "the dialectic between the truth we believe exists outside ourselves and the truth we invent for ourselves."[1] In the book, Kingsolver explores these contradictory truths as they are further shaped by class, gender, and race: When global climate change affects the habitual winter quarters of a large population of monarch butterflies in Mexico, forcing the insects to escape north to Appalachia, the local farming population interprets their arrival as a sign from heaven. The environmental and scientific communities disagree, however, suspecting the ominous environmental significance of such an event. Though this scenario recalls the age-old collision between science and religion, between empirical research and folksy superstition, Kingsolver shows that the playing field today has been transformed. In this world, scientists, treated as outsiders, must screen their activities to protect themselves from political spinning and misinformation, signs, both, of a shift in popular discourse from fact to "post-fact," from an authoritative, scientific truth to customized "truths" readily available from a smorgasbord of news, social media, and pseudo-news outlets. In exploring both, the possible causes and the implications of the current epistemological gap between media-generated opinion, propaganda, and their correlative, a growing popular skepticism of scientific truth, on the one hand, and, on the other, scientific reasoning, especially concerning the issue of global climate change, the novel is prescient of the social and political schisms that rupture contemporary America. Still, Kingsolver is not satisfied with portraying social conditions alone but, in writing the novel, takes action—and essentially calls her readers to action, too. Through the power of storytelling, *Flight Behavior* encourages readers' scientific understanding. In approaching the narrative as "laboratory literature" (lab lit for short), this chapter examines how the novel foregrounds the sciences—and science communication—in battling disinformation and political apathy, particularly with respect to the issue of global climate change, and proposes to overcome the uneasy dynamic between scientific knowledge and popular distrust of science. Where Kingsolver also offers a conceptual framework for the preservation of the land in the concinnity of scientific reasoning and ecofeminist values, I further take into account the ecofeminist values that may help defeat miscommunication, social division, and ideological disagreements while at the same time encouraging the protection of nature.

Given the role of climate change in *Flight Behavior*, much of the novel's criticism takes an ecocritical approach centered on the narrative's depictions of a changing climate and its effects on wildlife. Genre labels range from "climate fiction" (cli-fi for short) and "climate change novel" to "environmental apocalyptic." Frederick Buell places the novel within a tradition of narratives that portray a world dealing with environmental disaster—which includes Rachel Carson, Paul Ehrlich, and Donella Meadows—and suggests that, as an "environmental apocalyptic," it offers "prophetic revelation" to a chiefly unaware public.[2] In literature of this category, he explains, "environmental crisis has . . . moved from a passive constituent of the background to becoming a strange kind of entangling, nonhuman actor or active presence, one with which the characters engage, in a decidedly unequal *agon*."[3] Axel Goodbody and Sylvia Mayer, using the label "climate change fiction," focus on the characters' reactions to climate risk, revealing that risk awareness or, conversely, denial result largely from cultural and social contexts.[4] Stressing the political activism of Kingsolver's writing, Greg Garrard, in turn, argues the book as climate fiction contains qualities of both "conciliation" and "consilience," where the former registers Kingsolver's attempt to mediate between conflicting parties and ideologies vis-à-vis the evidence of climate change and the latter bridges disciplinary disagreement between science and the humanities and their interests, forms of knowledge, and belief systems.[5]

The author herself, however, prefers to call her work "realism" that is "based firmly in real science."[6] The narrative's emphasis on "realism" and "real science" as it pertains to strategies of successful science communication and environmental risk in the Anthropocene, is, effectively, the focus of the present chapter.[7]

In offering an absorbing story, the novelist makes the sciences—their methods and concerns—accessible to a non-expert audience and, true to her convictions, encourages environmental awareness. Indeed, this is not a new approach for Kingsolver. Several of her novels, often analyzed from an eco-feminist perspective, could be labeled "lab lit" where engaging storytelling serves to advocate scientific understanding and, important in Kingsolver, to promote environmental conservation: In her 1990 novel *Animal Dreams,* Codi Nolina discovers "poison ground" by microscopically testing the local water supply in the high school laboratory, which leads to an environmental movement that encompasses the entire community; in *Prodigal Summer* (2000), Deanna writes her college thesis on protecting coyotes and encourages predator protection in the wild. Indeed, the theme of our biological connection to others, including non-human others, runs through almost all of Kingsolver's work. Her most recent novel touches upon similar issues, though it is not as explicit in its environmentalist message: *Unsheltered* (2018) weaves contemporary social and environmental concerns together, comparing and contrasting them with those of the Gilded Age, and exploring the impacts of scientific findings in their respective eras. *Flight Behavior* offers no exception: The butterflies as indicators of environmental health suggest the manifold ways in which all aspects of nature are linked in a system. As a trained biologist, Kingsolver is at home with the scientific method, which she represents with detail, pitting science against the townsfolk's spiritual cravings and quest for absolution.[8]

SCIENCE COMMUNICATION AND ENVIRONMENTAL CRITICISM

The genre lab lit is increasingly garnering attention, even as some narratives captured under this umbrella are centuries old, such as Mary Shelly's *Frankenstein* (1818), which celebrated its bicentennial in 2018 and is the subject of Amanda Scott's chapter. (For the definition of lab lit and a general introduction to the genre, see the introduction.)

The sciences, however, often reject storytelling as a manner of communicating their findings—and the reasons are obvious: Science communication and narration diverge in their understanding of truth and how to arrive at truth. Where the sciences strive for objectivity in proving a hypothesis with facts and data, narratives are inherently subjective. These deviating approaches to truth, with one depending on deduction, the other on induction, are perceived by some as impediments to narrative science communication. Michael F. Dahlstrom explains:

> Because logical-scientific communication aims to provide general truths as an outcome, the legitimacy of its message is judged on the accuracy of its claims. In contrast, because narrative communication instead aims to provide a reasonable depiction of individual experiences, the legitimacy of its message is judged on the verisimilitude of its situations.[9]

Dahlstrom observes that the persuasiveness of narratives—through both pathos and ethos—makes counterarguments about their claims difficult. This actually renders them inappropriate for non-biased and objective science communication though communication experts and scientists today increasingly recognize their value in a world ever more dominated by social media platforms that compete for audiences. Narratives have key advantages compared to logical-scientific communication because of the ways audiences process information,[10] which, according to Dahlstrom, include the following factors: "motivation and interest, allocating cognitive resources, elaboration, and transfer into long-term memory."[11] Briefly, stories are an essential motivator in learning, drawing audiences in and engaging people's intellect, which, in turn, helps them comprehend and remember information. As the above quote suggests, scientific realism and verisimilitude—a life-like quality and implied possibility of being true—is the most crucial aspect in narrative science communication because it allows readers to assess the truthfulness of its messages. Research supports the growing acceptance of storytelling techniques in science communication, suggesting that professional science relies on narratives for communication among the members of the scientific community as well as with lay audiences.[12] Thus, narratives can serve the sciences.

Even though the acknowledgment of narrative science communication is fairly new, environmentalists and ecocritics have long openly employed storytelling to explore environmental issues, propose and defend earth-centered values, and encourage activism. If data as abstract information lacks significance for non-experts, stories give meaning, and using narrative in an environmentalist context is, therefore, neither new nor controversial. Ecocritic Scott Slovic and psychologist Paul Slovic write, "Stories have the power to help us understand large, complex problems—including environmental risks—that we cannot apprehend through quantitative information alone."[13] Because of the way in which human psychology operates, we are more attuned to emotional signals than to rational thought (particularly concerning risks and the awareness of risk), and stories, which evoke emotions and form images in our minds, help us process raw information and influence our decision making. Thus, though apparently paradoxical, "affect is a key ingredient of rational behavior," Slovic and Slovic contend.[14] Like Dahlstrom, Slovic and Slovic consequently urge "social and natural scientists, humanities scholars and artists" to come together to make tangible the environmental risks we face. [15] Similarly asking how we are to understand environmental problems and risks on a global scale if "nature" as an abstraction remains theoretical and remote in our everyday lives, Ursula Heise stresses the importance of specific narrative techniques:

> Literary and cultural scholars have produced a vast amount of research on the ways basic concepts such as nature, landscape, self and other, and the functioning of the human body in health and illness have been popularly envisioned by means of particular metaphors and stories in different cultures and at different historical moments. It stands to reason that such conceptualizations, which tend to be far more available to the general public than scientific information, play an important role in the selection and evaluation of risks. [16]

Imagery, in particular, helps reach audiences emotionally, aesthetically, and ethically by suggesting a concrete scenario and intimating, Heise writes, the "beauty and value of entire ecosystems such as tropical forests or oceans at risk."[17] In their cultural contexts, these images—especially "charismatic megafauna" like "panda bears, mountain gorillas, or whales"—have become emblematic of their rhetorical purpose while at the same time also expressive of the culture's narrative tradition.[18]

Ecofeminism also stresses the importance of narrative to promote an environmentalist ethics of care and mutual respect. Ecofeminism, a common critical approach to Kingsolver's oeuvre, has developed a substantial theoretical and literary body of work since the 1970s. Like its conceptual relative ecocriticism, ecofeminism is interdisciplinary, engaging the sciences and the humanities in a dialogue. Spearheaded by such theorists as Susan Griffin (*Women and Nature*, 1978), Mary Daly (*Gyn/Ecology*, 1978), and Carolyn Merchant (*The Death of Nature*, 1980), ecofeminism focuses, in broad strokes, on the parallels between the exploitation of the land and the oppression of women, based on historical and conceptual associations of women and the land. Like feminists, ecofeminists point to the hierarchical and dualistic paradigms of patriarchy which enable the subjugation of women and the land, often represented as female. Ecofeminists hold that western logocentrism serves patriarchal ideology and is at the root of conceptual binaries in the manner it disregards, even devalues, emotions, intuitions, and irrationality, which are traditionally associated with the feminine and nature. They further consider the factors of race, class, and ethnicity in the experience of oppression, which is essentially cumulative in its intersectionality, where forms of discrimination and oppression are mutually reinforced and shape an individual's experience.[19] Constructivist ecofeminists Karen Warren and Val

Plumwood offer alternative paradigms in ecofeminist narrative that values the feminine, emotions, nature, and all that patriarchy considers "Other." They encourage stories that appreciate subjective and emotional experiences and establish relationships between human and non-human others. They also promote an ethics of care and respect, mutuality, reciprocity, and love: Warren symbolizes this emotional relationship in a "loving perception" and a "loving eye"—"one that constantly 'must look and listen and check and question'"—to encourage a connection with nature.[20] Because these are human emotions, which both men and women can have, these experiences are not limited to women, though often thwarted in men by a culture that expects men to be detached and rational. Moreover, ecofeminist discourse seeks to empower those traditionally silent or silenced, not only the land but also those oppressed on grounds of gender, race, class, or ethnicity. Plumwood explains, "as ecofeminists we speak as those who are ourselves oppressed in a different area, as women, and we are able to transfer our understanding to the other's oppression."[21] Notably, it is important *how* stories are told. In "Climbing from Feminist Ethics to Ecofeminist Ethics," Warren tells about a rock-climbing experience that changed her attitude from conquest to respect and her relationship from disconnected to connected to the land. Thus, she argues, a key trait of ecofeminism is the ability to "conceiv[e] of oneself as fundamentally being in relationships with others, including the nonhuman natural world."[22] The ethical attitudes toward the other that result are those of caring. This attitudinal shift, strangely reminiscent of Aldo Leopold's famous crisis after the decisive moment of shooting a female wolf and seeing the "green fire" in her eyes die, grows out of a particular situation or experience (as portrayed in her above-mentioned account), Warren stipulates, rather than from imposition, as, say, by a moral principle.[23] Ecofeminist narrative therefore strives to articulate the individual experience, along with "a range of attitudes, values, beliefs, and behaviors" to validate what may otherwise "be overlooked or silenced by imposed ethical meaning and theory."[24] However, in expressing emotions and felt experiences, enacting a set of ethical values, building relationships, and contrasting perspectives in a "multiplicity of cross-cultural voices," ecofeminism clearly seems fundamentally at odds with the natural sciences and their imperative of objectivity, deductive reasoning, and emotional detachment.[25] Through narrative storytelling, Kingsolver's *Flight Behavior* makes concerns about global climate change real while bringing together scientific knowledge and ecofeminist ethics to promote scientific facts, on the one hand, and ecofeminist values, on the other.

A WORLD DIVIDED: LIFE IN RURAL APPALACHIA

Though the novel explores the causes of the uncustomary migration of a population of monarch butterflies from Mexico to the Tennessee Appalachian region and portrays in detail the work of the scientists who do the research, its focus is on a young mother who learns to embrace the sciences through her hands-on experiences in a field laboratory and thereby comes into her own. Dellarobia Turnbow grapples with such common issues as childrearing, homemaking, religion, and pleasing a husband in a loveless marriage. The tedium of this life turns out to be nearly unbearable, while the topic of science is far from her mind. Not only is she the book's protagonist, but she is also the narrative's perspective through the third-person limited point of view. In centering the novel on this fairly ordinary woman to whom readers can relate, Kingsolver eases her audience into the novel's larger concerns: the difficulty of the sciences in reaching a wider audience and the declining state of the environment.

The setting suggests the novel's dominant themes. In the opening pages, the author offers a glimpse of the isolation in which her heroine lives. If people are scarce, nature is abundant. Though her loneliness links Dellarobia, by default, to nature, it also symbolizes her oppression. Dellarobia's home somewhere on a country highway outside of town appears to be the last human outpost on the edge of the wilderness. Subject to nature's whims, human life here is engaged in a lasting battle with the elements. When the novel opens, the rain has been falling for months, ruining summer crops, "drowning" pastures, and forcing her to remain inside her house, which barely withstands the unusually wet climate.[26] However, it is not merely the ongoing rain but also the fertile vegetation that makes human life in this wilderness precarious: The surrounding mountains are covered in brambles and trees that quickly conceal any human trace.[27] True, Dellarobia's home offers a refuge from the elements and this unstoppable wilderness, but it also functions as her personal prison featuring only a limited, window-framed view. Similarly, the nearest township of Feathertown is a rural enclave whose remoteness in time and space is underscored by the small farms and clapboard houses scattered along the lone country road leading to a downtown with mostly unoccupied stores.[28] Cleary, the nearest commercial center, sporting modern shopping malls, chain restaurants, and even a college, is only fifteen miles away but figuratively decades ahead and clearly beyond the heroine's radar—or her ability to visit in her old and unreliable inherited station wagon.

Kingsolver magnifies the experience of personal entrapment through the various ways in which Dellarobia is oppressed. Her intersectionality—the multiple forms of oppression and exclusion—robs her of personal agency and is to blame for her limited worldview as well.[29] Her inadequate education, diminished finances, religion, and gender force her into a role she neither chose deliberately nor plays well: Only a decade ago, college-bound and dreaming of becoming an airline stewardess, Dellarobia had to give up her dream of freedom when she unintentionally became pregnant and married the man whose judgmental and narrow-minded family she must now endure.[30] The accidental quality of her life is underscored by her name: Intending to select a biblical name, her mother ironically chose "Dellarobia," which designates a type of natural-looking wreath with pine cones and acorns, thus foreseeing or possibly predestining her daughter's involuntary proximity to nature.[31] As the stay-at-home mother of a preschooler and a toddler, the twenty-eight-year-old is not only confined to the house (barring the occasional odd jobs on in her-laws' family farm) but also utterly dependent on her husband, whose income from gravel-truck driving is inconsistent, due to the incessant rain. But motherhood offers no solace; neither her family nor work on the small farm can provide Dellarobia the sense of purpose and connection that makes for a fulfilling life. On the contrary, Dellarobia feels "deep-mined" and "strip-mined" at once.[32] This metaphorical linking of motherhood and coalmining reinforces Dellarobia's oppression and foreshadows the novel's concerns with the exploitation of nature. At the same time, this imagery is suggestive of Dellarobia's alienation from nature. To the extent that the passage "correlate[s] maternal work and the protagonist's environmental estrangement," Heather Houser observes, "the novel reverses a powerful, pervasive trope that equates maternity with care for and closeness to the earth."[33] Whereas others in the community, held up by weekly church gatherings and sermons, appear to bear their burden stoically, Dellarobia is no saint, repeatedly succumbing to clandestine romantic distractions as a form of escape. Yet, religious tradition in the community approves of her choices: In realizing her traditional role as wife and mother, Dellarobia can at least live with the good conscience that she is fulfilling God's wish because marrying young "was the Lord's way for a girl with big dreams but no concrete plans, especially if a baby should be on the way"—even if it does not satisfy her personal needs or make her feel loved by her in-laws. Though clearly a representative of her community, Dellarobia also stands out from the other members: Physically marked by her flaming red hair, suggesting the trope of the witch or the wise woman in the woods, and exceptionally intelligent, she has potential to change and to resist the social expectations placed on her.[34]

Dellarobia is thus not a willingly acquiescent wife and daughter-in-law. Her frustrations with her limited opportunities affect her satisfaction with her husband, Cub, who, aware of his shortcomings, apologizes, "I'm sorry we're raising redneck children on a redneck paycheck."[35] Cub's lack of agency mirrors hers. Clearly, people do not choose their class or even community; still, his unquestioning acceptance of his station and the belief that "teams had been chosen" at birth aggravate Dellarobia.[36] While she is holding hopes for her son to attend college one day and hence emerge from his humble background, she also realizes that he, at age five, "was already behind."[37] At the same time, Dellarobia knows the importance of community by offering a sense of belonging and safety to the individual: "Humans are hardwired for social community," she muses.[38] Yet, if membership comes with certain privileges, it also makes demands, including for absolute loyalty to one's "clan."[39] Hinting at an insider-outsider dichotomy, she considers, "Reading the cues and staying inside the group, these are number-one survival skills in our species."[40] This insight, however, does not preclude Dellarobia from experiencing a sense of entrapment due to her class and gender.

Kingsolver focuses on a particular region and its culture and, in evoking stereotypes about Appalachia, reveals that the conceptual comingling of class identity, family ties, bloodlines, and region in America is ongoing. Surveying the history of class in America in *White Trash: The 400-Year Untold History of Class in America*, Nancy Isenberg suggests the symbolic significance of the American backcountry that is anchored in a heritage myth: "The backcountry of America never completely lost its regenerative associations. Appalachia remained in the minds of many a lost island containing a purer breed of Anglo-Saxon. Here, in this imaginary country of the past, is where the best of Jefferson's yeoman 'roots' could be traced."[41] While, according to Isenberg, this myth is adopted by both the middle and the working classes, albeit for different reasons, beliefs about class identity are further accentuated when ethnicity, lineage, and culture are intertwined with economic status. And this is where the Southern poor do not fare so well: "The language of class that America embraced played off English attitudes toward vagrancy, and marked a transatlantic fixation with animal husbandry, demography, and pedigree. The poor were not only described as waste, but as inferior animal stocks too."[42] In casting them as a distinct ethnicity or breed, the American dominant class at once ensured that class barriers remain firm and blamed the poor for their own poverty—poverty is thus not merely inherited but also a hereditary trait that ensures their victimhood. This rhetoric continues into the twenty-first century and is usually propagated by the media, which sees financial benefits in exploiting regional stereotypes: "the yuppies watched smart-mouthed comedians who mocked people living in double-wides who listened to country music," Dellarobia observes.[43] The consequences of accentuating the divisions between rural and urban populations, between the poor and the better-off in American society, are far-reaching: "With historically rooted impoverishment," Lloyd and Rapson write, "stereotypical images of the region 'constitute Appalachians as victims and obscure the possibilities for agency and empowerment.'"[44] Out of self-protection and in defense against the steady encroachment of the dominant culture, the economically strapped farmers of the novel hold on to their traditional set of values. And quite possibly, this clinging is typical of rural America in the late twentieth-century more generally, a sign of an effort to safeguard against the onslaught of twenty-first-century changes.

Not surprisingly, the local farmers despise outsiders, whether urban or foreign, and embrace the values of a pioneer past that have become symbolic of their distinct identity: hard work, religion, traditional gender roles, an overall antagonistic attitude toward nature, *and* a belief in the unutterable worth of country life. In Feathertown, the only thriving business is the Mountain Fellowship Church, and church attendance is one of the few manners of entertainment and a welcome diversion from the shearing, feeding, and inoculation of sheep; from the harvesting, cleaning, dying, and spinning of their wool; and from mending fences and other sorts of farm work. Indeed, church is the week's highlight. The Mountain Fellowship Church is quite an affair, bringing together the traditional and the modern and beckoning with promises not limited to personal salvation but encompassing the more mundane such as getting away from everyday chores, squalor, and drudgery: A "thriving little village" itself, the church taps into both spiritual and materialistic cravings with its clean appearance, modern conveniences, and up-to-date media. The in-house café presents a Starbuck's-like experience with its immaculate looks and appetizing fare: a space of comfort and escape from tedious household chores and children's messes. The large screens, reminiscent of those found in sports bars (which Feathertown lacks), add further value to this modern setting by offering the pastor's up-front personal touch. At the same time, the religious messages reassert traditional Christian values that penetrate all aspects of life, private and public alike, leaving little room for personal agency. [45]

A consequence of social circumstances and inherited values rooted in Christian beliefs, the townspeople's attitude toward nature is generally adversarial—a fact of which the church takes advantage—and exploitative, even if people occasionally embrace the wondrous. Thus, the financially strapped Turnbow family sells the trees growing on the mountain behind Dellarobia's house for lumber, regardless of the environmental impact clearcutting the mountain might have. This project, however, is suddenly halted because of the unexpected emergence of innumerable butterflies in the middle of the muddy and rainy winter. Though conflicting hypotheses exist, the idea that they represent a message from God prevails, not least because an explanation involving environmental issues would be difficult to maintain in this anti–climate change environment. Dellarobia, on her way to a romantic tryst, sees the butterflies first and thinks of Moses, assuming she is near a silent fire. [46] Biblical explanations then become jumbled with nebulous memories of scientific notions about the "new diseases" and "pests" that attack trees. [47] Neither explanation satisfies Dellarobia, who then considers that perhaps the occurrence carries spiritual significance meant only for her: "a vision of glory. . . . For her alone these orange boughs lifted."[48] The rest of the Turnbow family concludes more practically that the butterflies represent a supernatural attempt to prevent logging. They believe that the butterflies (which, they assume, would be "gumming up the [logging] equipment" or, worse, force the family to contend with "one of those government deals" that focus on endangered species) are symbols of a heavenly attempt to save the mountain.[49] Pastor Bobby Ogle, describing the event in church as a sign of "special grace," supports the miracle interpretation, which becomes the townsfolks' official explanation for the monarchs' existence on the mountain.[50]

As innocent as the religious interpretation appears, there is nothing guileless about the ways in which the media exploit the occurrence in their incessant quest for viewers. The first reporter, hailing from the nearby town of Cleary and working for a local newspaper, seems to be interested only in confirming regional stereotypes of Feathertown as full of "hicks."[51] She does not demonstrate an interest in the butterflies themselves and instead embraces the miracle angle, asking about Dellarobia, "who'd had a vision, who could see the future, who probably peed on dead flowers and made them bloom."[52] The tone of sarcasm suggests the respect such news-reporting should be accorded. Consistent with this approach is the reporter's press photograph portraying Dellarobia as "Our Lady of the Butterflies."[53] The miracle approach is later repeated by the News Nine TV reporter who is fascinated by the "phenomenon on your farm."[54] When Dellarobia, however, goes against the script and, at this later point in the narrative initiated into the scientific causes of such a migration, attempts to inform the public of the reasons for the butterflies' visit, this journalist spins the story out of context to suggest the young woman's suicidal intent providentially prevented by the butterflies. And although the channel provides interviews with other community members, all serve to affirm the view that Dellarobia had a vision, that she experienced a special blessing from God, while circumventing the real news concerning climate change. After all, sensationalist journalism attracts viewers—and climate change does not. Clearly, hampered by a dependence on viewers, the media can be counterproductive to science communication. Communication experts realize the tight interdependence between the mass media and their audiences, over whom they compete: Journalists must maintain a delicate balance between the "dual goals of reporting objective and accurate information," Dahlstrom explains, "[and] simultaneously remaining economically viable by earning and maintaining the fleeting attention of their audiences."[55] Besides audiences, the media depends on factors beyond the information to be distributed, including "upstream influences of organizational routines, external pressures, and internal goals of media industries [that] shape the messages and formats that eventually emerge for audience consumption."[56] As a result, Dahlstrom writes, "new stories are not preexisting units that journalists merely select for transmission, but rather, reality becomes news through a selective structuring that creates units that fit the organizational needs, such as timing of creation, ease of transmission, and audience expectations."[57] Because the mass media is the go-to place for information on science and related topics for most non-experts (and arguably, social media and a range of websites have today assumed this role), it has an enormous influence over popular ideas and beliefs about science-related topics. Thus, it can potentially benefit science education, but it can also have the adverse effect of reinforcing popular stereotypes and beliefs in a self-perpetuating and closed system so that new ideas and discoveries have difficulty penetrating. In addition, there is the issue of personal relevance: Generally, it is easier to believe a news story personifying events through a particular individual who invites sympathy and even identification than it is to trust abstract ideas about global climate change.[58] Or, as Garrard succinctly states, "It is not facts that people primarily believe . . . but other people."[59] In stressing the believable story of Dellarobia's psychic despair and neglecting the more terrifying news of environmental risk, the two news outlets featured in the novel not only shelter the population from an inconvenient truth but also boost existing prejudices against scientists.

Along with the media, the author identifies religious and educational politics as the culprits in the failure in communicating the magnitude of global climate change, especially to those who are most affected by it. In a 2012 interview Kingsolver observes, "The people who are already suffering the most from a drastically unpredictable, changing climate are conservative rural farmers, and these people are at this moment least equipped to understand climate change. I wanted to know how is this happening, why is this happening?"[60] The novel's farmers experience heavy losses from the rain: Because the summer's hay crop is rained out, and hay in the barns is starting to mold, they must buy expensive food from faraway states like Oklahoma. Even before the rain, the Turnbow family was heavily mortgaged and barely able to pay their bills, a situation that is only aggravated by the rain. Thus, the prospect of an income from logging offers, explicably, much hope.[61] Even as the mountain farmers in this impoverished region are disproportionately affected by climate distress and environmental despoliation, they doubt climate change, in spite of the fact that only fifteen years prior, it was a generally accepted scientific principle, Ovid Byron avers.[62] Kingsolver asks:

> How is it possible that many people can look at the same body of evidence—for example on climate change—and draw different conclusions? It's not about the evidence, it's about something else. That's the question this novel is pursuing; How do people decide what to believe when it comes to important matters? All of us like to believe we've made our minds up based on the sum of the evidence, but in fact we're mostly looking at the same evidence. So do we believe as we do because of fear of alternatives? Do we decide what to

believe by investing our trust in other people who make those decisions for us? What does this all mean, in a time when there are certain very large looming problems that have to be addressed, problems which some of us are simply deciding not to believe in?[63]

People's religious beliefs alone—which assign responsibility for climate change to God—are not exclusively to blame. The schools, too, are at fault because they utterly fail in science education.[64] Dellarobia recalls her science teacher's avoidance of his duties, playing basketball with the male students instead and occupying the girls with mindless study sheets. Perhaps the teacher's "hatred" of biology is an outgrowth of an increasingly common skepticism toward scientific facts, cause, also, of the current vehement denial of climate change.[65] In fact, as Lloyd and Rapson explain, teachers in Tennessee, though not encouraged to dodge the issue, are "legally bound to present climate change to students as controversial"—not as fact.[66] As a result, people are either confused or, as in Dellarobia's case, ignorant of the issue and their own implication in it. Denial of the problem is thus explicable. When given the option to "fight or flight," people will choose to "fly," Dellarobia observes.[67] Flight behavior, an allusion to the novel's title, is suggestive of cultural attitudes toward environmental disaster, particularly in an anti-intellectual environment that results from disempowerment and lacking privilege. Yet Kingsolver does not seek to take sides, asserting that she has "profound sympathy" for all her characters.[68] Rather, the author shows how cultural politics take advantage of people's fears and contribute to polarized views on the topic of climate change, which has hence transcended the sphere of science and entered political discourse, partisanship, and propaganda.[69]

Kingsolver's narrative defends the sciences against media bias through her heroine's direct encounter with scientific laboratory work. As the story progresses, Kingsolver increasingly juxtaposes both the media's self-serving spinning and the farmers' religious beliefs with scientific facts acquired through painstaking research, which in turn help explain the monarch butterflies' sojourn on the Turnbow mountain. Thus, eventually, science moves into the foreground—but not until readers have sufficiently developed an understanding of Dellarobia's situation. Then science comes as salvation, for Dellarobia at least. Along with a handful of students, Ovid Byron opens Dellarobia's horizons. Ovid's profession and degrees assure his expertise: He is an entomologist and ecologist as well as professor of biology at a university in New Mexico, and a government grant permits him to set up camp on the Turnbow property to conduct research. Kingsolver's descriptions of his research are precise, informed by her own science background: On the first day, the scientists count the butterflies on the ground by measuring equal squares. Later they count the butterflies on branches by shaking the insects onto tarps.[70] With mathematical precision and relying on specific formulas, they achieve a total count of butterflies per acre.[71] The measuring activities continue and include wingspans and "wet weights."[72] When they come upon a tagged butterfly, they trace its origin through a computer database.[73] Accurate measuring and exact data collection thus drive the scientists' efforts, who in turn rely on previous researchers' accuracy.[74] The scientists also have sophisticated and expensive gear: When setting up a lab in a sheep shed, they bring a Tissuemizer, freezer, Mettler balance, drying oven, and centrifuge to freeze and mix the butterflies and analyze their fat content; they also use a computer, GPS, calipers, scales, and other instruments required for their research.[75] As Dellarobia becomes involved in the activities, she is one of a growing number of participants that includes not only students but also volunteers from around the world whom Dr. Byron occupies in a citizen-science project. Initially relegated to keeping the sheep shed clean and organized, Dellarobia, who is now paid for her work, gradually advances to data recording in the lab and in the field, performing the same tasks as Dr. Byron's students: numbering aluminum pans, weighing the insects, and analyzing their fat content until eventually teaching others how to count inert butterflies on the ground.

Throughout the work, the professor himself, with his knowledge, skills, and discoveries, and most importantly passion for seeking truth, becomes the narrative's true hero. He recognizes the implications of his discoveries and explains important scientific processes. Thus, Ovid is enthusiastic when identifying the signs that a butterfly has mated, and he calls Dellarobia to witness tiny parasites on another butterfly, hypothesizing the link between the parasites and the monarchs' visit on the mountain[76]:

> Is the parasite sapping the monarch's strength and preventing a long migration? . . . We don't know. We are seeing a big increase in these parasite infestations. And we have recorded rising average temperatures throughout the range. Is the warmer climate giving the parasite an advantage? It's tempting to say this, but again, we don't know for sure. Not unless we can create experimental conditions that hold everything steady except for temperature. We cannot jump to conclusions. All we can do is measure and count. That is the task of science.[77]

Ovid reminds us that cause-and-effect and correlation are different, and scientific reasoning must make a clear distinction between the two.[78] The scientific method requires a set of hypotheses that are evaluated and tested—and the key is sticking to the facts, abiding by what is observable and measurable. Whereas religion depends on the strength of one's belief, the scientific method, Kingsolver demonstrates, places importance on precision, data-checking, and rigor.

Even as scientific arguments fall on deaf (or fearful) ears in places where climate change is a politically divisive issue and affected by, as much as it affects, subpar science education, media spinning, and the distrust in scientific endeavors, readers are encouraged to understand that the scenario Kingsolver depicts is possible, even likely. In an interview, the author asserted that the landslides in Mexico are real even as the butterflies as climate refugees in Appalachia are fiction.[79] In effect, the monarch colonies in Mexico that have been monitored since 1976 have decreased substantially over the past decade or so, due to environmental factors. Lincoln Brower, professor emeritus of zoology at the University of Florida and professor of biology at Sweet Briar College, discusses the complex migration pattern that takes three generations of butterflies from Mexico to Texas, the Great Salt Lake, New England, and Ontario until they finally return to their habitual roosting grounds in Mexico. Like his fictional counterpart, Dr. Brower arrives at his estimates of population losses not by guessing but by measuring. He explains the process as follows: "The way we measure the butterflies and the way we were able to get at the actual numbers, when you're looking at a colony, there are so many butterflies you can't possibly count them. But there was a storm in 2010, and the butterflies were dead on the ground up to three feet deep, and we were able to estimate that there are 50 million butterflies per hectare, which is about 20 million per acre." By no means do these numbers compare to the best year with "more than a billion butterflies overwintering in Mexico," however. Reasons for the decline are multifaceted, ranging from the destruction of milkweed, an essential nourishment for the butterflies, due to "herbicides and genetically engineered soybean and corn crops," Brower explains, to "habitat destruction on a grand scale" by increasing human encroachment.[80] The verisimilitude of Kingsolver's narrative, or "real-life likeness" and possibility of being true, adds to the novel's emotional and intellectual impact.

Thus, Kingsolver does not merely focus on the nitty-gritty details of scientific research but also considers the reasons for the unusual behavior of the butterflies as they point to global climate change: Readers learn that the butterflies visit Appalachia because rain, falling on clear-cut mountainsides, has created mudslides and affected habitat loss in their winter grounds in Mexico, decimating the butterfly population, even as their survival in Appalachia is jeopardized by cold temperatures and incessant rain.[81] If these conditions are signs of climate change, Kingsolver broaches a concern "among the most compelling issues now confronting science and society," Ann Hillier, Ryan Kelly, and Terrie Klinger observe.[82] As a scientist, Ovid does not doubt climate change because the facts are evident, and the process makes sense: "Think of condensation on a windshield," he explains to Dellarobia. "Multiply that times all the square meters above you, and it's a hell of a lot of water. It evaporates too quickly from the hot places, and floods the wet ones.

Every kind of weather is intensified by warming."[83] Even though this explanation sounds simple and plausible, it clearly requires an entire shift of mind for a whole population to accept the reality of climate change.

As Kingsolver tells the story of the butterflies and exposes the blurry thoughts and beliefs people have, marred, as they often are, by prejudices and fears, she also concedes that accepting a scientific worldview is not a simple task and has much to do with one's social and educational background. Again, the problem originates in cultural discrepancies, in a rigid division of "us" from "them."[84] Despite the professor's endeavors to initiate Dellarobia into the sciences, old assumptions and habits of thought, though usually embarrassing to her, frequently trump the new. Thus, Dellarobia continues to struggle with the idea that the butterflies have come, not as a sign of the "Lord mov[ing] in mysterious ways," or of beauty as a form of redemption, but because of climate distress.[85] But educational bridges are difficult to build when the privilege of the others is so obvious: Dr. Byron's cosmopolitan students have access to a range of experiences that are denied to Dellarobia and her children: airplane rides, international travel, and elite primary and secondary schools, just to mention a few.[86] Aside from these kinds of formal and informal education, the students' attire and gear, as well as their speech and attitude, distinguish them from the local population.[87] Meeting the offspring of the affluent middle class makes Dellarobia feel ashamed: "She felt herself looking at things through their eyes sometimes. . . . Their days here were like channel-surfing the Hillbilly Network."[88] Ever a keen observer of human nature, Kingsolver demonstrates that, rather than bridging the gap between the communities, an encounter of two social groups such as this highlights their differences, so that the epistemological gulf consequently widens: Because nobody wants to feel inferior, people in Feathertown resent the outsiders who come flocking to see the butterflies, who mock the townspeople for their distrust in science, and who even blame them for the environmental damages done. If the locals distrust the outsiders, then they also doubt their message.

Awareness of social disparity, contributing to an us-vs.-them thinking, is at the root of the problem of dissemination of scientific knowledge and may lead to the intentional misuse of facts and disinformation, on the one hand, and, on the other, a naive acceptance of false information. Still, as Kingsolver demonstrates, it is important to attempt to provide accurate scientific information to encourage understanding and, if needed, change. Yet, the real problem lies in technique: *how* to speak to a scientifically illiterate and science-wary population. The experts themselves, the scientists, are usually not trained to speak to general audiences, nor is this encouraged: "We are scientists," Ovid states. "Our job here is only to describe what exists."[89] He explains, "If we tangle too much in the public debate, our peers will criticize our language as imprecise, or too certain," which could imperil his reputation.[90] While Ovid is thus concerned, he is also the only person who could effectively get involved. Who has the authority to explain the problem and provide the scientific facts if not the scientist who is doing the research? When Ovid inadvertently, and rather reluctantly, gets drawn into the public debate after all, he must confront the very impediments to science communication. One of the greatest problems is the local news media, or more precisely, the conflict between the media's and the scientists' agendas. Right from the start, the interview with Tina Ultner held in Ovid Byron's lab suggests a clash of goals and the possibility for disinformation, which reinforces the professor's skepticism. Tina phrases her questions as if facts and data do not matter or, worse, do not exist: Stressing the beauty of the butterflies and insisting on the uncertainty that seemingly surrounds their migration, the reporter asks Ovid to explain, "in a nutshell," the reasons for their visit, thereby forestalling his attempt to give a clear scientific explanation while also denying him trustworthiness.[91] If all we have is uncertainty and doubt, all opinions are equal, yet none need facts to be sufficiently substantiated: Instead of a source of knowledge, the professor himself hence becomes a source of doubt.[92] As a result, Ovid's specific and evidence-based response to Tina's vague question about a possible "sign of some deeper problem with the ecology" falls on unresponsive ears.[93] While Tina thus goads him on throughout the interview, the professor becomes increasingly angered, though he knows full well to whom the reporter is ultimately responsible: "You are letting a public relations firm write your scripts for you," he accuses her, then adding, "You have no interest in real inquiry. You are doing a two-step with your sponsors."[94] Ovid points to the media's lack of responsibility when driven by concerns about the bottom line, rather than a desire to inform people, which is, of course, one of the reasons for the uncertainty that also surrounds the topic of global warming.[95] However, to survive in today's tough media market, the media must make certain concessions. Dahlstrom explains: "The concept of news values articulate[s] specific foci that have a better chance of attracting the attention of an audience. As such, news is packaged to match as many news values as possible, while downplaying or even ignoring other relevant aspects."[96] This creates an interdependence that is not only "delicate" but can also be noxious and self-reflexive. Tina's techniques of planting doubt where there should be none and of raising controversy over a scientifically proven issue contribute to more disinformation that makes her approach impenetrable to Ovid's science-informed measures and, instead, feeds into the echo-chamber of the mass media's self-repeating information cycle.

On the other hand, however, there are Ovid's professorial attitude, his professional jargon, and his apparent intellectual distance to the issue that actually hinder science communication. The sciences, and scientific discourse, have a long tradition of emotional detachment that has promoted scientific advances for the very fact that it leaves emotional considerations behind: "Terrible, beautiful, it's not our call," Ovid thus explains.[97] This emotional disconnect can easily be interpreted as a lack of feeling or empathy and worse, as arrogance toward those who feel passionately about the butterflies whether as signs of salvation or of doom. Combined with his use of scientific jargon, Ovid's professionalism can be perceived as an attempt to talk over the layperson's head, as speech meant only for the initiated few. Tina Ultner inadvertently frees him from these professional constraints, helping him express his feelings and use more accessible language so that his message becomes clearer to a non-expert audience. When Ovid, increasingly more frustrated, approaches Tina threateningly, "backing" her through the room, he precludes the interview from being aired on the TV channel.[98] But thanks to Dellarobia's friend Dovey, who witnesses and films the scene on her phone, then posts it on YouTube, the interview goes viral and makes Ovid instantly famous, affording him the kind of stardom that the climate science community, Kingsolver suggests, most likely will also recognize.[99] A quote by media expert Michael Dahlstrom can help elucidate the process that leads to this sudden popularity: "When the context moves from data collection to the communication of science to nonexpert audiences, stories, anecdotes, and narratives become not only more appropriate but potentially more important."[100] While the video thus "tells a story" of an upset and discouraged professor who passionately feels about the butterflies and the global disaster their visit portends, its success depends largely on the use of pathos to which humans are especially well attuned. But it also fulfills another requirement of storytelling: personification, essential in exploring abstract concepts because it invites the audience to "identify" and feel "empathy."[101] It is the professor with whom the audience is invited to identify and who, in the video, tells another story, using imagery, to relay the urgency of the situation: "We are at the top of Niagara Falls . . . in a canoe. . . . We got here by drifting. . . . We have arrived at the point of an audible roar. Does it strike you as a good time to debate the existence of the falls?"[102] Though Tina retorts flippantly, the analogy places in readers' minds an image that brings home the unsustainability of our current lifestyle. Ovid thus proves that even though there is nothing scientists can *do* to save the butterflies, *how* they tell the story of their plight makes a difference. Through pathos, storytelling, personification, and imagery, the video effectively communicates scientific facts: Even as the professor feels caught and duped, his passionate reaction helps convey his message better than any scientific lecture could have done in this age of social media, so that his yelling, aggression, personal attacks, and physical intimidations end up contributing to bringing his message across to a general audience.

Similar to the professor, Dellarobia tells the story of the butterflies' predicament convincingly because she understands *how* a story is told can matter more than *what* is told. In sharing, in her turn, her insights with a young audience of kindergarteners, she builds a relationship with the children through the use of pathos and ethos that makes them more receptive to the scientific facts. Compared to Ovid, Dellarobia has certain advantages: On the one hand, she knows and to some degree shares the community's cultural values and, on the other, as a mother, relates easily to the children. Not least, she is intimately connected to nature. Even though constructivist ecofeminists reject the view that women naturally have a closer bond with nature, the novel suggests that as a woman, wife, and mother Dellarobia has experiences that parallel the use and abuse of nature. These are not experiences conditioned by nature but by a culture that subjects women and nature alike to patriarchal oppression and capitalist exploitation.[103] They enable Dellarobia to experience empathy, rather than a desire to conquer and control, so that an emotional bond with nature can be formed. This bond is further galvanized by the intellectual discoveries this mother shares with her son: Dellarobia encourages Preston, her five-year-old, to discover nature in a common experience, figuratively bestowing her love for nature on him as a "present" by giving him "sight."[104] She also fosters his natural inquisitiveness by buying him a series of science books about animals, which they study together. Their shared curiosity spurs their increased attention to, caring for, and love of nature—ecofeminist attitudes necessary to develop a relationship based on mutual respect. As both mother and son learn about nature, Dellarobia realizes the importance of teaching children—the next generation—to value nature. Thus, she invites Preston's kindergarten class to the laboratory to learn about science. Kingsolver highlights the role of ecofeminist narration in a scene where Dellarobia tells the children a story about the insects. She does not spare them the more disturbing reality where logging, landslides, and pollution prevent the butterflies from returning to their customary habitat.[105] In teaching and narrating, Dellarobia acts as the sciences' and nature's "ambassador" who speaks a language that children can comprehend, thereby helping them relate to and care for the butterflies. Because for young children, the metaphorical walls often preventing adults from connecting with nature have not yet been built, there is hope that the younger generation will be more aware, less opportunistic, and more attuned to nature's needs. As Dellarobia learns to shed her own prejudices, she becomes instrumental in helping others envision an alternative: a rapprochement with nature. If there is no superhero to save the butterflies, at least there is someone to understand and narrate their plight.

Kingsolver's ecofeminist message is fully realized when her heroine saves a newborn lamb's life by merely following the instructions given in a science book.[106] This moment marks a newfound heroism, brought on by the confluence of knowledge, love, care, and sheer determination. Empowered by the experience, Dellarobia begins to envision a new beginning for herself, which entails the separation from her husband and the departure from her home and accustomed life in order to pursue a college degree and eventually seek out a professional career, possibly in veterinary medicine.[107] Goodbody explains this decision as "ecological enlightenment . . . mapped onto female emancipation."[108] At novel's end, readers are left with an image of Dellarobia witnessing her station wagon, the house, and even the fertile ground surrounding her being carried away by a flood of rainwater. The novel here comes full circle in its depiction of a watery mess caused by unexpected and erratic weather patterns that symptomize climate change. The flood's slow removal of human constructions that previously confined Dellarobia suggests the hubris inherent in a belief in the possibility of human domination of nature while acting also as a liberating force that washes away those things that constrict women in patriarchal society. Surprisingly, the flood also brings the barely surviving butterflies back to life: Having endured frost, ice, snow, and rain over the long winter months, they act "like a flood itself" and now soar freely in the sky.[109] In a final linking of Dellarobia (with her flaming red hair) to the surviving butterflies, the author suggests the vigor and the destruction lying at once in the elements of fire and flood: "the fire burst of wings reflected across the water, a merging of flame and flood. Above the lake of the world, flanked by white mountains, they flew out to a new earth."[110] This image suggests a cautious hope for the future: Both Dellarobia and the butterflies are survivors. Yet, as Garrard notes, this is not a "biblical redemption"; their survival in no way offers a guarantee that their lives will be easy from now on, and the notion of "a new earth" is left ambiguous.[111]

In *Flight Behavior*, Kingsolver renders scientific concerns through engaging storytelling, making a discipline that reputedly has difficulty reaching a broad audience relevant and palatable to lay readers. At the same time, she demonstrates how ecofeminist ethics—care, respect, and love for nature—can contribute to a more powerful science narrative. Indeed, pathos is effective, as Christopher Bergland confirms: "A growing body of research on the benefits of using narrative writing to create an emotional connection with empirical evidence" sheds light on the ways in which "feeling an emotional connection to science-based information can increase proactive behaviors."[112] Not only that, Kingsolver proposes that the geographic, social, racial, and gender divisions defining America in the twenty-first century can be dealt with through a shared quest for knowledge, where scientific insight helps the novel's heroine expand her intellectual horizons and change her entire worldview. She achieves this by experiencing science firsthand when working in Ovid Byron's laboratory. It is the daily routine of laboratory science that lets Dellarobia follow her dreams of a better future, enabling her to become an ambassador for both the environment and the sciences. Similarly, Kingsolver herself acts as a spokeswoman for nature and scientific reasoning, challenging her audience to reassess their values, to face the reality of climate change, and ultimately also to contribute to the protection of nature. As lab lit, then, *Flight Behavior* shows how the humanities can effectively collaborate with the sciences by making their concerns accessible and meaningful to non-expert readers.

NOTES

1. Stephen Fisher, "Community and Hope: A Conversation," *Iron Mountain Review* 28 (Spring 2012): 27.

2. Frederick Buell, "Global Warming as Literary Narrative," *Philological Quarterly* 93, no. 3 (Summer 2014): 262. *Academic Search Premier*, http://web.a.ebscohost.com.l ibproxy.dixie.edu.

3. Buell, "Global Warming as Literary Narrative," 265.

4. Sylvia, Mayer. "Explorations of the Controversially Real: Risk, the Climate Change Novel, and the Narrative of Anticipation," in *The Anticipation of Catastrophe: Environmental Risk in North American Literature and Culture,* ed. Sylvia Mayer and Alexa Weik von Mossner (Heidelberg: Universitätsverlag Winter, 2014), 39–58, and Axel Goodbody, "Risk, Denial and Narrative Form in Climate Change Fiction: Barbara Kingsolver's *Flight Behavior* and Ilija Trojanow's *Melting Ice,*" in *The Anticipation of Catastrophe: Environmental Risk in North American Literature and Culture,* ed. Sylvia Mayer and Alexa Weik von Mossner (Heidelberg: Universitätsverlag Winter, 2014), 39–58. In turn, Christopher Lloyd and Jessica Rapson consider the relationships between the local, global, and planetary environments and argue that they serve to enhance the novel's impact. The authors write, "Though rooted in a specific part of the rural South, Kingsolver's novel has an imaginative reach beyond its pages and locale. Its memory work, ever-moving whilst in place, speaks particularly to the era of the Anthropocene." See Christopher Lloyd and Jessica Rapson, "'Family Territory' to the 'Circumference of the Earth': Local and Planetary Memories of Climate Change in Barbara Kingsolver's *Flight Behaviour,*" *Textual Practice* 31, no. 5: 927, DOI: 10.1080//0950236X.2017.1323487.

5. Greg Garrard, "Conciliation and Consilience: Climate Change in Barbara Kingsolver's *Flight Behaviour,*" in *Handbook of Ecocriticism and Cultural Ecology,* ed. Hubert Zapf (Berlin: De Gruyter, 2016), 301, ProQuest Ebook Central. 31 Jan 2018.

6. Linda Wagner-Martin, *Barbara Kingsolver's World: Nature, Art, and the Twenty-First Century* (New York: Bloomsbury, 2014), 195. Nevertheless, if it is to be understood as realism, Linda Wagner-Martin faults the novel for its largely underdeveloped characters, especially Dellarobia who *"stops,* and so does her development," she writes (196): "Perhaps Kingsolver needed to say more herself about Dellarobia," she suggests, but she also understands that Kingsolver's primary concern lies elsewhere (194): "It may be said that in the twenty-first-century world, where all human concerns are likely to be global ones, this change, or shift, or reemphasis makes whatever Kingsolver attends to seem new, pertinent, and even prescient" (192). Thus, she suggests that *Flight Behavior* is evidence that Kingsolver has "relinquished the political realms of Patrice Lumumba and Leon Tolstoy [*sic*] [as in *The Poisonwood Bible* and *The Lacuna*] for the scientific worlds of biodiversity," even as she avoids categorizing the novel as climate fiction or otherwise (191).

7. "In 2000 in the IGBP *Global Change Newsletter*, Paul Crutzen and Eugene Stoermer suggested that in recognition of the enormous (and enormously negative) impact of humans on the planet, we needed a new term for the age in which we live, not the Holocene any longer but the Anthropocene" (Ace Pilkington, *Technologies of the Future: Opportunities and Perils* (Jefferson, NC: McFarland, forthcoming).

8. Barbara Kingsolver holds degrees in biology, which she obtained at DePauw University and at the University of Arizona. See "Barbara Kingsolver, the Authorized Site," Office of Barbara Kingsolver, accessed Jan. 30, 2018, www.kingsolver.com.

9. Michael F. Dahlstrom, "Using Narratives and Storytelling to Communicate Science with Nonexpert Audiences," *PNAS Proceedings of the National Academy of Sciences in the United States of America,* DOI 10.1073/pnas.1320645111. 15 Sept. 2014, accessed Jan 23 2018. The article does not contain page numbers.

10. María José Luzón, "Public Communication of Science in Blogs: Recontextualizing Scientific Discourse for a Diversified Audience," *Written Communication* 30, no. 4 (2013): 428–57, and Sophie Moirand, "Communicative and Cognitive Dimensions of Discourse on Science in the French Mass Media," *Discourse Studies* 5, no. 2 (2003): 175–206.

11. Dahlstrom, "Using Narratives and Storytelling to Communicate Science with Nonexpert Audiences."

12. G. Nigel Gilbert and Michael Mulkay, *Opening Pandora's Box: A Sociological Analysis of Scientists' Discourse* (Cambridge: Cambridge University Press, 2008); Rom Harré, "Some Narrative Conventions of Scientific Discourse," in *Narrative in Culture: The Uses of Storytelling in Sciences, Philosophy, and Literature,* ed. Christopher Nash (London: Routledge, 1994), 81–101; Greg Myers, *Writing Biology: Texts in the Social Construction of Scientific Knowledge* (Madison: The University of Wisconsin Press, 1990); Randy Olson, *Houston, We Have a Narrative: Why Science Needs Story* (Chicago: University of Chicago Press, 2015); Olga A. Pilkington, *Presented Discourse in Popular Science: Professional Voices in Books for Lay Audiences* (Leiden: Brill, 2018), 7, 9, 14–15, 159–74; Femke Reitsma, "Geoscience Explanations: Identifying What Is Needed for Generating Scientific Narratives from Data Models," *Environmental Modeling & Software* 25 (2010): 93–99.

13. Paul Slovic and Scott Slovic, "Numbers and Nerves: Toward an Affective Apprehension of Environmental Risk," in *The Feeling of Risk: New Perspectives on Risk Perception,* ed. Paul Slovic (New York: Routledge, 2010), 83.

14. Slovic and Slovic, "Numbers and Nerves: Toward an Affective Apprehension of Environmental Risk," 81.

15. Slovic and Slovic, "Numbers and Nerves: Toward an Affective Apprehension of Environmental Risk," 83.

16. Ursula Heise, *Sense of Place and Sense of Planet: The Environmental Imagination of the Global* (New York: Oxford University Press, 2008), 137.

17. Heise, *Sense of Place and Sense of Planet: The Environmental Imagination of the Global,* 137.

18. Heise, *Sense of Place and Sense of Planet: The Environmental Imagination of the Global,* 137–38. With a tradition going back to ancient Greece, the pastoral, for example, is particularly evocative and effectively used to contrast modern, urban, and blighted landscapes with the rural ideal: humans and nature living in harmony.

19. Intersectionality designates how racial and gender discrimination are cumulative. Kimberlé Crenshaw explains: "Black women are sometimes excluded from feminist theory and antiracist policy discourse because both are predicated on a discrete set of experiences that often does not accurately reflect the interaction of race and gender. These problems of exclusion cannot be solved simply by including Black women within an already established analytical structure. Because the intersectional experience is greater than the sum of racism and sexism, any analysis that does not take intersectionality into account cannot sufficiently address the particular manner in which Black women are subordinated." Kimberlé Crenshaw, "Demarginalizing the Intersection of Race and Sex: A Black Feminist Critique of Antidiscrimination Doctrine, Feminist Theory and Antiracist Politics," *University of Chicago Legal Forum* no. 1, article 8 (1989): 140, https://chicagounbound.uchicago.edu/uclf/vol1989/iss1/8.

20. Karen Warren, *Ecofeminist Philosophy: A Western Perspective on What It Is and Why It Matters* (Lanham: Rowman & Littlefield, 2000), 28.

21. Val Plumwood, "Androcentrism and Anthropocentrism: Parallels and Politics," in *Ecofeminism: Women, Culture, Nature,* ed. Karen Warren (Bloomington: Indiana University Press, 1997), 350.

22. Warren, *Ecofeminist Philosophy,* 103.

23. Often viewed as the turning point in Leopold's intellectual life, this moment marks a shift toward an environmental ethics that, growing over time, defines Leopold's legacy and is condensed in his "Land Ethic." Leopold describes the moment of shooting the wolf and seeing

it die in the chapter "Thinking Like a Mountain" of *A Sand County Almanac*, which also contains "The Land Ethic," today considered one of the most important writings in environmental ethics. Aldo Leopold, "Thinking Like a Mountain," *A Sand County Almanac* (New York: Ballantine Books, 1970), first edition 1949, 137–141.

24. Warren, *Ecofeminist Philosophy*, 104.

25. Warren, *Ecofeminist Philosophy*, 104.

26. Barbara Kingsolver, *Flight Behavior* (New York: Harper Perennial, 2012), 3.

27. Kingsolver, *Flight Behavior*, 3.

28. Kingsolver, *Flight Behavior*, 380.

29. Crenshaw stresses an initial focus on the mutually reinforcing intersections of gender and race, particularly for black women who were excluded from making compound claims in American antidiscrimination law, due to their dual oppression as women and people of color. Crenshaw suggests that approaches to intersectionality today vary across disciplines and may be even defined by individual scholars: She encourages readers to perceive intersectionality as "part and parcel" of "other like-minded approaches" and suggests that intersectionality "travels from its groundings in Black feminism to critical legal and race studies; to other disciplines and interdisciplines in the humanities, social sciences, and natural sciences . . . perhaps modifying how race, gender, and other social dynamics are conceptualized and intertwined or, alternatively, how the central subjects and social categories of intersectionality are identified" (792). The key feature of analysis should remain a focus on "sameness" and "difference" and "its relation to power" (795). Sumi Cho, Kimberlé Williams Crenshaw, and Leslie McCall, "Toward a Field of Intersectionality Studies: Theory, Applications, and Praxis," *Signs: Journal of Women in Culture and Society* 38, no. 4 (2013): 792–95.

30. Kingsolver, *Flight Behavior*, 305.

31. Kingsolver, *Flight Behavior*, 10.

32. Kingsolver, *Flight Behavior*, 26.

33. Heather Houser, "Knowledge Work and the Commons in Barbara Kingsolver's and Ann Pancake's Appalachia," *MFS Modern Fiction Studies* 63, no. 1 (Spring 2017): 102. DOI: 10.1353/mfs.2017.0006.

34. Kingsolver, *Flight Behavior*, 10.

35. Kingsolver, *Flight Behavior*, 161.

36. Kingsolver, *Flight Behavior*, 171.

37. Kingsolver, *Flight Behavior*, 172.

38. Kingsolver, *Flight Behavior*, 166.

39. Kingsolver, *Flight Behavior*, 166.

40. Kingsolver, *Flight Behavior*, 323.

41. Nancy Isenberg, *White Trash: The 400-Year Untold History of Class in America* (New York: Penguin Books, 2016), 270.

42. Isenberg, *White Trash*, xxviii.

43. Kingsolver, *Flight Behavior,* 166.

44. Lloyd and Rapson, "'Family Territory' to the 'Circumference of the Earth': Local and Planetary Memories of Climate Change in Barbara Kingsolver's *Flight Behaviour*," 915.

45. Kingsolver, *Flight Behavior*, 59.

46. Kingsolver, *Flight Behavior*, 14.

47. Kingsolver, *Flight Behavior*, 12.

48. Kingsolver, *Flight Behavior*, 15–16.

49. Kingsolver, *Flight Behavior*, 53.

50. Kingsolver, *Flight Behavior*, 72.

51. Kingsolver, *Flight Behavior*, 76.

52. Kingsolver, *Flight Behavior*, 76.

53. Kingsolver, *Flight Behavior*, 77.

54. Kingsolver, *Flight Behavior*, 200.

55. Dahlstrom, "Using Narratives and Storytelling to Communicate Science with Nonexpert Audiences."

56. Dahlstrom, "Using Narratives and Storytelling to Communicate Science with Nonexpert Audiences."

57. Dahlstrom, "Using Narratives and Storytelling to Communicate Science with Nonexpert Audiences."

58. Dahlstrom, "Using Narratives and Storytelling to Communicate Science with Nonexpert Audiences."

59. Garrard, "Conciliation and Consilience: Climate Change in Barbara Kingsolver's *Flight Behaviour*," 305.

60. Qtd. In Lloyd and Rapson, "'Family Territory' to the 'Circumference of the Earth': Local and Planetary Memories of Climate Change in Barbara Kingsolver's *Flight Behaviour*," 915.

61. Kingsolver, *Flight Behavior*, 332.

62. Kingsolver, *Flight Behavior*, 321.

63. Fisher, "Community and Hope: A Conversation," 30.

64. Kingsolver, *Flight Behavior*, 301.

65. Kingsolver, *Flight Behavior*, 222.

66. Lloyd and Rapson cite the Tennessee House Bill 368 (Senate Bill 893), which impedes accountable science instruction in Tennessee's public schools. Lloyd and Rapson, "'Family Territory' to the 'Circumference of the Earth': Local and Planetary Memories of Climate Change in Barbara Kingsolver's *Flight Behaviour*," 914.

67. Kingsolver, *Flight Behavior,* 231. Speaking about the psychology of risk, Axel Goodbody confirms this view: "Denial is a product of at least four different factors: it is a matter of the political and economic circumstances, a consequence of the world of lobby groups and the media, a product of social norms and a matter of individual psychology"—all of which are present in the novel (43). Drawing on Kari Norgaard's study on climate change in Norway and the United States, he specifies, "We block the topic from our minds in order to avoid feelings of fear, guilt and helplessness." Goodbody, "Risk, Denial and Narrative Form in Climate Change Fiction: Barbara Kingsolver's *Flight Behavior* and Ilija Trojanow's *Melting Ice*," 43.

68. Qtd. in Wagner-Martin, *Barbara Kingsolver's World: Nature, Art, and the Twenty-First Century*, 193–94.

69. Dahlstrom elucidates this relationship between climate science and political propaganda that is determined by fears of how the consequences may bear on us and how we humans are implicated in the process. He states, "Climate change provides an obvious context where conflicting narratives are present, including disjointed narratives of problem versus solution and polarizing partisan narratives that substitute for scientific understanding." Dahlstrom, "Using Narratives and Storytelling to Communicate Science with Nonexpert Audiences."

70. Kingsolver, *Flight Behavior*, 139, 142.

71. Kingsolver, *Flight Behavior*, 142.

72. Kingsolver, *Flight Behavior*, 149.

73. Kingsolver, *Flight Behavior*, 142–43.

74. Kingsolver, *Flight Behavior*, 144.

75. Kingsolver, *Flight Behavior*, 149, 217.

76. Kingsolver, *Flight Behavior,* 242–43.

77. Kingsolver, *Flight Behavior*, 244.

78. Kingsolver, *Flight Behavior*, 243.

79. Lloyd and Rapson, "'Family Territory' to the 'Circumference of the Earth': Local and Planetary Memories of Climate Change in Barbara Kingsolver's *Flight Behaviour*," 912.

80. Lincoln Brower, "Monitoring the Monarchs," *Science Friday*, NPR. 12 April 2013, www.npr.org/2013/04/12/17702957/monitoring-the-monarchs.

81. Kingsolver, *Flight Behavior*, 137–38.

82. Ann Hillier, Ryan P. Kelly, and Terrie Klinger, "Narrative Style Influence Citation Frequency in Climate Change Science," *PLoS One.* 15 Dec. 2016. DOI: 10.137/journal.pone.0167983.

83. Kingsolver, *Flight Behavior*, 280.

84. Kingsolver, *Flight Behavior*, 171.

85. Kingsolver, *Flight Behavior*, 148.

86. Kingsolver, *Flight Behavior*, 140.

87. Kingsolver, *Flight Behavior*, 323.

88. Kingsolver, *Flight Behavior*, 162.
89. Kingsolver, *Flight Behavior*, 148.
90. Kingsolver, *Flight Behavior*, 323–24.
91. Kingsolver, *Flight Behavior*, 364.
92. For more on the representations of scientists in the entertainment media, see Dahlstrom, "Using Narratives and Storytelling to Communicate Science with Nonexpert Audiences."
93. Kingsolver, *Flight Behavior*, 365.
94. Kingsolver, *Flight Behavior*, 368, 369.
95. Kingsolver, *Flight Behavior*, 368
96. Dahlstrom, "Using Narratives and Storytelling to Communicate Science with Nonexpert Audiences."
97. Kingsolver, *Flight Behavior*, 148.
98. Kingsolver, *Flight Behavior*, 368, 369.
99. Kingsolver, *Flight Behavior*, 393.
100. Dahlstrom, "Using Narratives and Storytelling to Communicate Science with Nonexpert Audiences."
101. Dahlstrom, "Using Narratives and Storytelling to Communicate Science with Nonexpert Audiences."
102. Kingsolver, *Flight Behavior*, 367.
103. For a discussion of this point, see Heather Houser, who indicates that motherhood and housework must be understood as a form of capitalist exploitation, not resistance to it, citing Marxist theorists Silvia Federici and Michael Hardt: "housework as the crucial factor in the definition of the exploitation of women in capitalism" because "capitalism requires unwaged reproductive labor in order to contain the cost of labor power." Qtd. in Houser, "Knowledge Work and the Commons in Barbara Kingsolver's and Ann Pancake's Appalachia," 105.
104. Kingsolver, *Flight Behavior*, 94.
105. Kingsolver, *Flight Behavior*, 355–56.
106. Kingsolver, *Flight Behavior*, 416.
107. Kingsolver, *Flight Behavior*, 419, 426.
108. Goodbody, "Risk, Denial and Narrative Form in Climate Change Fiction: Barbara Kingsolver's *Flight Behavior* and Ilija Trojanow's *Melting Ice*," 48.
109. Kingsolver, *Flight Behavior*, 433.
110. Kingsolver, *Flight Behavior*, 433.
111. Garrard, "Conciliation and Consilience: Climate Change in Barbara Kingsolver's *Flight Behaviour*," 310.
112. Christopher Bergland, "Storytelling Enhances the Influence of Science-Based Writing: Narrative Science Writing Engages Readers more than Expository Writing Styles," *Psychology Today*. Dec. 16, 2016, https://www.psychologytoday.com/blog/the-athletes-way/201612/storytelling-enhances-the-influence-science-based-writing.

BIBLIOGRAPHY

"Barbara Kingsolver: The Authorized Site." Office of Barbara Kingsolver. Accessed Jan. 30, 2018. www.kingsolver.com.

Bergland, Christopher. "Storytelling Enhances the Influence of Science-Based Writing: Narrative Science Writing Engages Readers more than Expository Writing Styles." *Psychology Today*. Dec. 16, 2016. https://www.psychologytoday.com/blog/the-athletes-way/201612/storytelling-enhances-the-influence-science-based-writing.

Brower, Lincoln. "Monitoring the Monarchs." *Science Friday*. NPR. April 12, 2013. www.npr.org/2013/04/12/17702957/monitoring-the-monarchs.

Buell, Frederick. "Global Warming as Literary Narrative." *Philological Quarterly* 93, no. 3 (Summer 2014): 261–94. Academic Search Premier. http://web.a.ebscohost.com.libproxy.dixie.edu/ehost/pdfviewer/pdfviewer?vid=4&sid=2975f49b-aaaa-4791-bb82-a004fefbb13a%40sessionmgr4010.

Cho, Sumi, Kimberlé Williams Crenshaw, and Leslie McCall. "Toward a Field of Intersection-ality Studies: Theory, Applications, and Praxis." *Signs: Journal of Women in Culture and Society* 38, no. 4 (2013): 785–810. DOI: 0097-9740/2013/3804-000.

Crenshaw, Kimberlé. "Demarginalizing the Intersection of Race and Sex: A Black Feminist Critique of Antidiscrimination Doctrine, Feminist Theory and Antiracist Politics." *University of Chicago Legal Forum*, no. 1, article 8 (1989): 139–67. https://chicagoun bound.uchicago.edu/uclf/vol1989/iss1/8.

Dahlstrom, Michael F. "Using Narratives and Storytelling to Communicate Science with Non-expert Audiences." *PNAS Proceedings of the National Academy of Sciences in the United States of America.* DOI 10.1073/pnas.1320645111. Sept. 15, 2014. www.pnas.org/content/111/supplement_4/13614.full . 23 Jan 2018.

Fisher, Stephen L. "Community and Hope: A Conversation." *Iron Mountain Review* 28 (Spring 2012): 26–32.

Garrard, Greg. "Conciliation and Consilience: Climate Change in Barbara Kingsolver's *Flight Behaviour.*" In *Handbook of Ecocriticism and Cultural Ecology*, edited by Hubert Zapf, 295–312. Berlin: De Gruyter, 2016. *ProQuest Ebook Central.* 31 Jan 2018.

Gilbert, G. Nigel, and Michael Mulkay. *Opening Pandora's Box: A Sociological Analysis of Scientists' Discourse.* Cambridge: Cambridge University Press, 2008.

Goodbody, Axel. "Risk, Denial and Narrative Form in Climate Change Fiction: Barbara King-solver's *Flight Behavior* and Ilija Trojanow's *Melting Ice.*" In *The Anticipation of Catas-trophe: Environmental Risk in North American Literature and Culture*, edited by Sylvia Mayer and Alexa Weik von Mossner, 39–58. Heidelberg: Universitaetsverlag Winter, 2014.

Harré, Rom. "Some Narrative Conventions of Scientific Discourse." In *Narrative in Culture: The Uses of Storytelling in Sciences, Philosophy, and Literature*, edited by Christopher Nash, 81–101. London: Routledge, 1994.

Heise, Ursula. *Sense of Place and Sense of Planet: The Environmental Imagination of the Global.* New York: Oxford UP, 2008.

Hillier, Ann, Ryan P. Kelly, and Terrie Klinger. "Narrative Style Influence Citation Frequency in Climate Change Science." *PLoS One.* 15 Dec. 2016. DOI: 10.137/journal.pone.0167983.

Houser, Heather. "Knowledge Work and the Commons in Barbara Kingsolver's and Ann Pancake's Appalachia. *MFS Modern Fiction Studies* 63, no. 1 (Spring 2017): 95–115. DOI: 10.1353/mfs.2017.0006.

Isenberg, Nancy. *White Trash: The 400-Year Untold History of Class in America.* New York: Penguin Books, 2016.

Kingsolver, Barbara. *Animal Dreams.* New York: HarperCollins, 1990.

———. *Prodigal Summer.* New York: Harper Perennial, 2000.

———. *Flight Behavior.* New York: Harper Perennial, 2012.

———. *Unsheltered.* New York: Harper Collins Publishers, 2018.

Lloyd, Christopher and Jessica Rapson. "'Family Territory' to the 'Circumference of the Earth': Local and Planetary Memories of Climate Change in Barbara Kingsolver's *Flight Behaviour.*" *Textual Practice* 31, no. 5: 911–31. DOI: 10.1080//0950236X.2017.1323487.

Leopold, Aldo. "Thinking Like a Mountain." *A Sand County Almanac.* New York: Ballantine Books, 1970.

Luzon, María José. "Public Communication of Science in Blogs: Recontextualizing Scientific Discourse for a Diversified Audience." *Written Communication* 30, no. 4 (2013): 428–57.

Mayer, Sylvia. "Explorations of the Controversially Real: Risk, the Climate Change Novel, and the Narrative of Anticipation." In *The Anticipation of Catastrophe: Environmental Risk in North American Literature and Culture*, edited by Sylvia Mayer and Alexa Weik von Mossner, 39–58. Heidelberg: Universitaetsverlag Winter, 2014.

Moirand, Sophie. "Communicative and Cognitive Dimensions of Discourse on Science in the French Mass Media." *Discourse Studies* 5, no. 2 (2003): 175–206.

Myers, Greg. *Writing Biology: Texts in the Social Construction of Scientific Knowledge.* Madi-son: The University of Wisconsin Press, 1990.

Olson, Randy. *Houston, We Have a Narrative: Why Science Needs Story.* Chicago: University of Chicago Press, 2015.

Pilkington, Ace G. *Technologies of the Future: Opportunities and Perils*. Jefferson, NC: McFarland, forthcoming.

Pilkington, Olga A. *Presented Discourse in Popular Science: Professional Voices in Books for Lay Audiences*. Leiden: Brill, 2018.

Plumwood, Val. "Androcentrism and Anthropocentrism: Parallels and Politics." In *Ecofeminism: Women, Culture, Nature,* edited by Karen Warren, 327–55. Bloomington: Indiana University Press, 1997.

Reitsma, Femke. "Geoscience Explanations: Identifying What Is Needed for Generating Scientific Narratives from Data Models." *Environmental Modeling & Software* 25 (2010): 93–99.

Slovic, Paul and Scott Slovic. "Numbers and Nerves: Toward an Affective Apprehension of Environmental Risk." In *The Feeling of Risk: New Perspectives on Risk Perception,* edited by Paul Slovic. Series: Earthscan Risk in Society. New York: Routledge, 2010.

Wagner-Martin, Linda. *Barbara Kingsolver's World: Nature, Art, and the Twenty-First Century*. New York: Bloomsbury 2014.

Warren, Karen. *Ecofeminist Philosophy: A Western Perspective on What It Is and Why It Matters*. Lanham: Rowman & Littlefield, 2000.

Williams, Terry Tempest. *Finding Beauty in a Broken World*. New York: Random House, 2008.

Chapter Eight

The Short Fiction of Andrea Barrett

Lab Lit as Sociology of Science

Stephanie Chidester

In her novels and short fiction, Andrea Barrett rarely places her characters in a laboratory setting, and her viewpoint characters are as likely to be surly teenagers or discontented housewives as they are to be formally trained scientists. Regardless, Barrett saturates her fiction with science, occasionally to excess. Kevin Baker observed in his review of *The Air We Breathe* that Barrett often "seems less interested in her story and characters than in her novel's metaphors and the science that generates them" and that she "feeds us historical and scientific information as strictly as her TB patients are made to eat regular meals."[1] Likewise, Thomas Mallon perceived "an artificiality" in the way Barrett interlaces science through her stories, as well as "a tendency to spell out connections the way one was taught to write 'Conclusion' before the last step of a lab report." However, Mallon goes on to acknowledge that "Barrett's scientific bent is sufficiently rare among fiction writers, and her concoctions so cunningly mixed, that dissatisfaction seems out of place."[2]

Barrett paints her fascination with science and natural history into each of the stories in her published collections *Ship Fever*, *Archangel*, and *Servants of the Map*. She explores the nature of scientific pursuit by populating her work with vibrant characters who are as captivated as she is by the natural world, and she examines human nature through the use of natural phenomena as metaphors for human experience. Although some of her characters perceive science as an elixir for enlightenment and social progress, and scientists as beings higher than the residue of humanity, Barrett takes a broader view. The historical figures and fictional characters she presents are innately flawed. They vary in competence, ethics, and intellect. Their vision is often blurred by ego, ambition, and bias. They blunder in their personal and professional lives, and they are frequently baffled by the vagaries of human nature.

The flaws Barrett depicts represent not only common aspects of human behavior but also specific social realities peculiar to the world of the laboratory. Such phenomena are the basis of a field of study called the sociology of science, which focuses on interactions among the individuals who conduct science. This field arguably originated with the writings of John Stuart Mill and currently includes the application of game theory to understand and improve interactions among members of research groups.[3] Barrett's works might be considered a fictional subgenre of the sociology of science. She uses narrative to reveal the human foibles, insecurities, and petty jealousy of individuals who aspire to an objective and rational approach to their world and their studies. Her narrative approach is consistent with what sociologists Gilbert and Mulkay call a "contingent repertoire"—an informal scientific discourse that is heavily dependent on "personal or social circumstances" and that portrays "scientists' actions . . . as the activities and judgements of specific individuals acting on the basis of their personal inclinations and particular social positions."[4] The personalities and sociality of those who conduct research are not easily discerned by lay persons, nor are these elements evident in traditional research publications. The genre of lab lit, on the other hand, and Barrett's writing especially, draws on this kind of personal experience because it allows for explorations of scientists not as a group, but as individuals.

SCIENTISTS AND THE NATURE OF SCIENTIFIC PURSUIT

Barrett's depiction of different types of scientific pursuit has a similar feel to her description in "The Island" of the life cycle of the *Aurelia* jellyfish. The professor expounds to his students that "each of the metamorphoses of the *Aurelia* . . . was once presumed to be a separate species. The hydroid phase was named *Scyphostoma*; the form with the buds stacked up was called *Strobila*. The first stage of the medusa . . . was called *Ephyra*. Only this stage you are seeing—the breeding adult—had the name *Aurelia*, although we now recognize all four as being forms of the same creature."[5] The scientists in Barrett's fiction undergo similar stages of development—the many permutations of avocational scientists in her fiction are analogous to the planulae, polyps, and strobilae, and the metamorphosis from amateur or student to formally trained scientist is analogous to the transformation of early ephyra to adult medusa.

Barrett's cast of characters includes not only formally trained, basic scientists, but also physicians and other applied scientists, self-taught naturalists, science enthusiasts, and others living on the fringes of the scientific community. In a few stories, historical scientists take center stage, as with Louis Agassiz in "The Island"[6] or Carl Linnaeus in "The English Pupil."[7] Fictional denizens of laboratories inhabit other stories, as with the geneticist Sam Cornelius[8] and the biochemist Rose Marburg.[9, 10] Constantine Boyd is a teenager who is passed between relatives in order to keep him safe from an abusive father, but who lands in Hammondsport, New York—a hub of applied science and innovation in the early development of aircraft.[11] Physicians and less formally trained healers are featured prominently in "Ship Fever"[12] and "The Cure."[13] Barrett explores the experiences and struggles of amateur or self-taught scientists in "Rare Bird,"[14] "Birds with No Feet,"[15] "Theories of Rain,"[16] and "Two Rivers."[17] Other stories feature lay persons as the principal characters. In "*Soroche*"[18] and "The Behavior of the Hawkweeds,"[19] for example, the viewpoint characters are housewives who are second-generation Americans of Eastern European descent, with blue-collar backgrounds and little opportunity for post-secondary education. Even these characters, however, are influenced by their experiences with or interest in natural phenomena and members of the scientific community.

The Life Cycle of the Scientist

Professional scientists appear in Barrett's fiction in many stages of training—as eager students and trainees, over-worked graduate and post-doctoral students, ambitious early- and mid-career researchers, and aging late-career scientists striving to remain relevant. As in the real-world culture of professional science, the progress of Barrett's characters through each phase of education and career is rarely smooth and uneventful, but rather entails significant conflict with mentors, colleagues, and students. Barrett illustrates the power differentials and struggles inherent in the strata of professional science through use of "conflict narratives," which include the phenomena of "disagreement . . . between a young and less experienced scientist and the more seasoned members of the scientific community."[20] Such narratives also involve "more experienced scientists" drawing upon their reputation and experience in order to "make assumptions and judgments, while . . . younger researchers do not have the luxury to make arguments based on intuition or personal beliefs."[21] Examples of these interpersonal dynamics between scientists are abundant in Barrett's fiction, perhaps most notably in "The Particles." Here, the reader follows not only the career of the narrator, Sam, but also those of his mentors and fellow students.

Barrett's presentation of three professional scientists who mentor students draws attention to the importance of social and managerial skills within the scientific community. Sam's first advisor, Axel, begins as an idealistic young scientist doing original work and relating easily to the students he mentors.[22] His style of mentorship is easy-going, and his relative inexperience as a

mentor is sometimes a detriment to his students. Sam, for instance, is sometimes allowed too much independence, as when he designs an experiment
independently and presents his preliminary findings during a summer research program, without seeking guidance from Axel beforehand. Axel re-
monstrates with Sam but encourages him to follow up on the research without evaluating the experimental design, which was flawed. The work is soon
discredited, and Sam's reputation is tarnished, in part due to Axel's inadequate oversight.[23] Axel is also depicted as somewhat impotent in his relationship to his colleagues. Although he describes himself as being "at the top of
the second tier" in his field, he lacks adequate influence to help Sam gain
entry to a reputable graduate program.[24] In late career, Axel has assumed a
subordinate role, following the most dominant of his former students rather
than continuing to lead: "Axel . . . increasingly relied on his connection to
Duncan . . . . Duncan and his colleagues shared fly strains with Axel's lab;
Axel and his students collaborated on papers with them, which helped them
all."[25]

Sam's subsequent advisor in graduate school has a more autocratic style:
Sam does not do any research that his advisor does not approve, nor does he
choose a thesis subject which he truly wanted to research; instead, he builds
upon his advisor's program of research.[26] In consequence, Sam feels stifled
and has less opportunity to develop the independence and other skills he will
need to transition to an early-career investigator. Sam's third mentor, Hermann Muller, provides a superior form of leadership and training. As an
undergraduate, Sam idolizes him, and as a graduate student, Sam opens up a
correspondence with Muller and receives helpful and objective feedback.[27]
Later, as a junior scientist working with Muller at an institute in Russia, Sam
recollects that "Muller proved to be an excellent guide. Not a teacher as Axel
had been; not really a friend . . . he was clearly Sam's superior, but he was
accessible and kind."[28]

Through her viewpoint character in "The Particles," Barrett also highlights the social and scientific perils encountered during early development
of science trainees and the early transition to early- and mid-career scientist.
Barrett presents Sam moving from his early years as a student when he is
viewed as a prodigy, through mid-career when he and his research are met
with hostility and skepticism. As the youngest member of Axel's research
group, Sam is eager to assist with real research but is instead assigned the
tasks no one else wants: washing laboratory glassware and preparing materials for more senior lab personnel.[29] In contrast, the graduate student Duncan
has the more glamourous work of breeding fruit flies and analyzing the
results of genetic experiments.[30] Sam advances to doing experimental work
after Duncan leaves the lab, but struggles for acceptance during his undergraduate and graduate education because of youthful blunders and underdeveloped social and political skills.[31] Whereas Duncan is politically adept

and seems to ascend effortlessly in his research career, Sam finds the world of research more difficult to navigate. He finds a modest faculty position after graduation and spends most of his spare time in his own laboratory, trying to build his program of research.[32] When he finds himself unemployed only three years after beginning his first job, he becomes increasingly disillusioned with the scientific community, which he bitterly describes as "little fiefdoms ruled by petty kings," where researchers are not "free to follow their best ideas."[33]

Sam adapts by seeking the more congenial social and scientific environment of Hermann Muller's research group in Russia. In this setting, Sam becomes more productive in his research, despite inhospitable living conditions and, later, endangerment by the overall sociopolitical climate present in Russia just prior to the Second World War.[34] In this episode, Barrett points out the impact on science of the social and political conditions present not just within the laboratory or university environment, but also in the macroenvironment of cities and nations.

Barrett further depicts Sam's mid-career experiences and his interactions between subordinates and colleagues in the international scientific community. Having returned to the United States, he becomes established in an academic research career; he enjoys mentoring students of his own, has a well-stocked laboratory, and feels a renewed enthusiasm and optimism about his work.[35] However, Sam's political and social ineptitude again earn him the disapprobation of his colleagues when he presents his controversial research and theories at the International Congress of Genetics. His peers react as if he has committed a heresy, and a colleague, instead of presenting his own research as scheduled, devotes that time to attacking Sam's work. Similar to the situation during his student years when he conducted and presented research without his mentor's oversight, Sam is again chastised by his former mentor Axel for not consulting with him beforehand.[36] Sam has failed to lay the political groundwork that might improve the likelihood of his research and theories gaining acceptance. Rather than collaborating with other influential scientists in his field, Sam prefers to work in the relative solitude of his own research group. In consequence, he finds little support when he presents his work to his international colleagues.

Barrett presents other mid- and late-career scientists in their sociopolitical milieux in "The Behavior of the Hawkweeds." The viewpoint character, Antonia, describes Gregor Mendel's endeavors to convince his contemporaries of the validity of his discoveries. She tells the story of how Mendel shared his work and theories with a more established and influential German scientist, Carl Nägeli.[37] Nägeli, however, dismissed the work because of contradictory evidence in hawkweeds, and then, after Mendel's death, published work that strongly resembled Mendel's without acknowledging his contribution.[38] After eight years of experimentation with peas, then presenting and publishing his findings, Mendel became discouraged when no one recognized the significance of his research. In the following years, according to Antonia's description, he abandoned his experiments and died unaware of how significant his work truly was.[39]

As counterpoint to Mendel and Nägeli, Antonia also recounts the waxing and waning of her husband's career in genetics. Like many young scientists, Richard starts out full of energy and enthusiasm. While in the Navy, he participates in research related to fungal species, tropical fungi, and afterward resumes his doctoral degree.[40] After graduation, he finds a faculty position, receives promotions, and works actively to produce and disseminate research. He is granted tenure and receives accolades for his work.[41] At this point, however, Antonia observes that he is driven more by ego than by love of science, and his relationships with his students have become dysfunctional: "I had seen him less than generous to younger scientists struggling to establish themselves. I had watched him pick, as each year's favored student, not the brightest or most original but the most agreeable and flattering."[42] The final section of the story shows the decline of Richard's career, when he is forced to retire and his work has been eclipsed by that of his most recent student: "The science of genetics is utterly changed and Richard has been forgotten by everyone."[43] Through such vignettes, Barrett illustrates how scientists' motives and worldviews may shift throughout their careers in consequence of their sociopolitical microenvironment. Motivation may shift from the desire to discover truth to the need to compete for eminence and funding. Dysfunctional interactions with colleagues may lead to discouragement and abandonment of promising lines of research.

In "The English Pupil," Barrett presents severely dysfunctional and harmful relationships between an established scientist and his protégés, and she provides another example of the role of ego in the world of science. Carl Linnaeus, suffering from physical and mental decline in advanced age, is the rambling narrator. He clings tenaciously to the remnants of his mind and memories, using deeply engrained habits of classification to recall people and places that try to slip beyond his reach. He experiences bursts of memory in which he recalls his work and the throngs of young scientists sent out in his service. He describes his relationship to his work and to his students in religious terms: "The world was an alphabet written in God's hand, which he . . . had been called to decipher. . . . The pupils he'd sent to all the corners of the world and called, half-jokingly, his apostles."[44] These young apostles, who martyr themselves to his cause, include Christopher Ternstrom, Fredrik Hasselquist, Pehr Forskal, Marten Kahler, and others whose names Linnaeus struggles to recall.[45] He reflects on the disparities in the human cost and the scientific gains: "The death of many whom I have induced to travel has turned my hair gray, and what have I gained? A few dried plants, accompanied by great anxiety, unrest, and care."[46] Here, the role of the established scientist is tantamount to that of a cult leader who has an almost sociopathic disregard for the well-being of his followers.

Barrett also portrays late-career scientists as more concerned with their personal legacy than with truth. They cling to their theories and perceive a need to defend their work against all challengers, without regard to emerging evidence. In short, they live in fear of what Thomas Henry Huxley called "the great tragedy of Science—the slaying of a beautiful hypothesis by an ugly fact."[47] This phenomenon is a motif in several of Barrett's stories. Her works feature younger scientists' attempt to knock senior colleagues—and their entrenched theories—from their pedestals, as well as senior scientists campaigning in defense of their work. Such is the case in both "The Ether of Space"[48] and "The Island." The former story begins with a description of Sir Oliver Lodge's reaction to evidence supporting Albert Einstein's theory of relativity. Disturbed by this evidence and the implications for his own theory of ether and the realm of spirits, Lodge flees the scientific meeting at which the evidence is presented. He is subsequently mocked by many of his junior colleagues as "the old man running from the new theory."[49] Lodge then embarks on a lecture tour, promoting his own philosophies and casting doubt on Einstein's emerging theory. Throughout his tour of the United States, a critic from the scientific community stalks him, loudly refuting his work and criticizing his attempt to integrate into his theories concepts that are not amenable to empirical proof.[50]

Lodge's experience is paralleled in many ways by those of Louis Agassiz in "The Island." Like Lodge, Agassiz reacts defensively to an emerging theory, in this case Darwin's theory of evolution and natural selection. Throughout the story, Barrett emphasizes his fame and renown by never referring to him by name; he is always "the famous professor" or simply "the professor."[51] Barrett also emphasizes Agassiz's age and declining cognitive capacity. Henrietta, for instance, reflects that, "in person, he looked older, and less robust, than the portraits in the newspapers"[52] and notes his difficulty in remembering names.[53] In the portions of the story told from Agassiz's perspective, the professor complains of worsening health, and feeling progressively more confused.[54] He is an effective and charismatic speaker, but often lectures on autopilot, which Agassiz acknowledges to himself: "He could do this in his sleep, and perhaps he was."[55] Like Lodge, Agassiz's late-career objective is to recruit new adherents, who will, he hopes, go forth and "spread his teachings."[56] Rather than searching out new evidence or continuing to test his own and others' theories, he has established a school of natural science on the island of Penikese in order to preach his own theories and to convince his students of the incorrectness of Darwin's.[57] As with Linnaeus, Agassiz sees himself as a prophet and his students as disciples, and perhaps this is unsurprising, since creationism is inherent in Agassiz's natural philosophy.[58] Some acolytes also hold him in such high esteem; in Henrietta's home, for instance, he is revered as a "household god," and "the attitudes passed to her by her mother and teachers [were] a kind of worship."[59]

Agassiz is harried throughout the story by students who continually challenge his stance in opposition to Darwin,[60] and the professor recalls a time when he was in their position, challenging old theories with new evidence: "Thirty years ago he'd taken the world by storm with his theory of glacial action; he had triumphed even over Mr. Darwin, convincing everyone that a sheet of ice had descended over Europe and North America, carving the landscape into its present forms."[61] The professor is acutely aware of the relative positions he and his students occupy in the life cycle of the scientist and suspects that many of his students secretly agreed with Darwin, but "None of them knew, as he did, how the theories seized on with such enthusiasm by one generation might be discarded scornfully by the next."[62] He suspects that even his outwardly loyal former students are torn between loyalty to him and their personal inclination to follow the evidence supporting newer theories.[63]

Depictions of conflict among scientists in Barrett's fiction call attention to phenomena integral to the sociology of science, in particular the "immense impact of human interactions on the process and outcome of a scientific project."[64] Through these interactions, Barrett underscores the essential role in science of the undervalued skill sets of social and emotional intelligence, as well as leadership and management abilities. As Cohen and Cohen point out, the increased focus on the sociology of science during recent decades has brought to light the importance of expanding scientific training to include not only the philosophy and methodology of a specific research discipline, but also interpersonal and managerial skills crucial to the effectiveness of scientific endeavors.[65]

Ability and Credibility

Barrett examines issues of ability and credibility through her depictions of further conflicts between professional scientists and science enthusiasts with a wide range of backgrounds and training. These issues are increasingly relevant today with the promotion of citizen science and maker culture, particularly in the fields of natural science, computing, and technology.[66,67,68] Ready access to 3-D printers, fab labs, and programming resources have opened the door to DIY innovations in science and technology.[69,70] Citizen scientists also contribute significantly to data acquisition in the natural sciences through online platforms such as iNaturalist, which enables participants to upload images and observations about numerous plant and animal species.[71] These online platforms enable collaboration between professional and amateur scientists, as with a recent publication by Drury et al., in which formally trained scientists collaborated with thousands of amateur naturalists to study the wing phenotypes of damselflies.[72]

As she explores these issues, Barrett asks what it means to be a scientist, and who qualifies for that title. In her stories with a contemporary setting, the answers seem rather clear-cut and entail university education and training under the mentorship of a senior scientist. Even then, however, the boundaries occasionally shift with changes in scientific trends. Rose Marburg, for example, doesn't consider the descriptive research of earlier decades—such as Peter Kotov's work in entomology—to be real science.[73] In Barrett's stories with settings and characters from earlier generations, the lines between science as vocation and avocation are blurred, and the reader must weigh the relative merits of extensive informal training and formal academic credentials. Historically, a university education has not always been requisite for membership in the scientific community. Prior to and during the early years of the Industrial Revolution, it was more the rule than the exception for scientists to establish themselves through "self-education and private experiment."[74,75] Antonie van Leeuwenhoek, Michael Faraday, Benjamin Franklin and Thomas Edison, for instance, had little or no formal training,[76,77,78] and the nineteenth century is littered with American and British naturalists who were largely self-taught.[79,80] Nevertheless, many such autodidacts struggled to gain recognition and respect as scientists, and Barrett depicts this struggle in her fiction.

When Alec Carriere, the protagonist of "Birds with No Feet," embarks on his quest to become a natural scientist, he points to the precedent of autodidacts in his chosen discipline.[81] Barrett introduces the historical naturalist Alfred Russel Wallace into the story in order to illustrate differences in their motivations and their capacity for theoretical thinking. A review of Wallace's background reveals a history not dissimilar to the fictional Alec's.[82] The two arise from similarly disadvantaged backgrounds, and both seize opportunities to improve themselves through personal study and informal tutelage of experts from within the scientific community. Both begin their journeys more as collectors than scientists. However, whereas Wallace begins with an interest in ideas of speciation, Alec is focused on adventures to be found in "wild places" and naturalism as a pathway to wealth, prestige, and personal freedom. He hopes to earn enough money from his collecting expeditions that he will have opportunities to do independent work of his own,[83] but he never devotes much time to systematically recording and analyzing his observations. Barrett is not subtle in many of her comparisons. Like Wallace, Alec loses the specimens he collected in his first journey when the ship on which he sails catches fire. Also like Wallace, Alec is struck down by a malaria-like illness during a subsequent expedition. After the first catastrophe, Alec's primary concern is the financial loss and disruption to his plans. Wallace, on the other hand, grieves the loss in a deeper way: "each specimen lost represents a double death. Our hunting always had a point; each bird we shot and butterfly we netted was in the service of science. But burnt, they now serve no one."[84] Whereas Alec marvels over the variety of his beetle collection, Wallace looks at the same collection and stuns Alec with a commentary on this evidence of speciation.[85] Alec recovers from an episode of fever to find that not only has Wallace suffered likewise, he has at the same time had an epiphany regarding speciation and drafted a paper in which he proposes the mechanism of natural selection independently of Darwin's coinciding work.[86] Alec, in contrast, has not even begun to develop this sort of theoretical thinking. Instead of learning and speculating about his discoveries, "his journals had deteriorated into little more than a tally of species, interspersed with fumbling descriptions of places and people."[87] It is possible, of course, that this young man might develop a scientific mindset given the opportunity for sufficient study, experience, and mentorship. However, he is discouraged and dismayed by constant self-comparison to the brilliant Wallace and abandons his dream entirely after encountering further adversity at home.[88]

In "Servants of the Map,"[89] Barrett again takes up this theme with her character Max Vigne, a surveyor with the British Trigonometrical Survey of India. In England, Max was an amateur botanist, and he sees the survey expedition as an opportunity to gain experience as a naturalist.[90] He does not possess the brilliance of a Wallace or a Darwin, but he is intelligent, devotes a great deal of time to study, and eventually progresses beyond the amateur mindset of a collector.[91] Of necessity, since he hasn't the resources to preserve and ship specimens home to England, his recorded observations are elaborate and include detailed drawings and descriptions of plant species and their ecological niche.[92] Max also benefits from the long-distance mentorship and encouragement of an established naturalist, Joseph Hooker.[93] Despite this encouragement, he wrestles with doubt about his aptitude for science. To his wife he writes: "Have I any scientific talent at all? Dr. Hooker says I do, he has been most encouraging. If he is right, then my separation from you means something, and the isolation . . . and the long hours of extra work. But if I have no real gift . . . then I am wasting everything."[94]

Initially, Max shows little interest in the theory or philosophy of the discipline. He attempts to read Darwin's *Origin of Species* during the early days of the expedition, but the book proves too challenging for him and he gives it up in favor of more foundational works by Hooker and Asa Gray.[95] Eventually, however, he returns to Darwin, better prepared by his studies and observations to understand the theory.[96] With this new perspective, he gains a deeper understanding of the context of Hooker's *Journals*, and begins to grasp what it means to be a scientist, as evidenced by his questions about ecology and adaptation: "How do the species that have arisen here differ from those in other places? How do they make a life for themselves, in such difficult circumstances?"[97] Throughout the story, however, it is clear that Max is motivated by more than just a passion for natural science. He explains to Clara that a significant part of his attraction toward this work and the scientists who have paved the way previously is "the way they defend each other so vigorously and are so firmly bound."[98] Tied up in his determination to pursue a career in botany is the hope that it will bring him the acceptance and close, meaningful relationships he craves. The lifestyle that accompanies the work is also part of the appeal; he is compelled equally by the experiences and trajectories of Dr. Hooker, the shady but adventurous Dr. Chouteau, and even the man whose remains Max found during the survey and whose last words he absorbed.[99] Ultimately, Max is driven as much by his quest for freedom and self-discovery as he is by scientific curiosity.

In other stories, Barrett highlights situations in which informal training and extensive experience are not adequate for inclusion in the scientific community. Antonia in "The Behavior of the Hawkweeds" relates the experience of her grandfather, who learned horticulture and heredity as a young boy from Gregor Mendel in the monastery gardens at Brno.[100] Mendel, impressed with the boy, ensured he had opportunities for basic education.[101] Antonia recalls that as an émigré in America who spoke little English, her Tati first worked at a menial job making buttons in an immigrant community, but he was eventually able to secure a job at a nursery, a position he enjoyed but which was likely beneath his true ability.[102] When the nursery underwent a change in management, the new supervisor "lost no time telling Tati that he had a master's degree from a university out west, and it was clear from his white lab coat and the books in his office that he thought of himself as a scholar. . . . he treated Tati like a common laborer."[103]

"Inconvenient Women"

In her treatment of informal training and lack of acceptance in the world of science, Barrett gives considerable attention to the experiences of women whose scientific ambitions are impeded by gender bias, poverty, and inadequate access to higher education. In bringing these conditions to light, Barrett is in line with the views of modern feminists such as Karen Warren, Val Plumwood, and Donna Haraway, who advocate for an inclusive approach to science that grants greater access to women and minorities.[104,105,106]

In "Ship Fever" and "The Cure," the character Nora Kynd pursues healing through the only means open to her. Despite lacking basic education, she learned herbal remedies and principles of quarantine and infection control from her grandmother in Ireland.[107] During the typhus epidemic on Grosse Isle in 1847, Dr. Grant perceives her as dedicated and useful but without formal training,[108] and his fellow physicians would prefer that she not assist with the epidemic, even though they are completely overwhelmed and nurses are in short supply.[109] While Nora is certainly illiterate, she is by no means untrained, which Dr. Grant acknowledges privately in his journal: Nora's grandmother "seems to have practiced something very close to the quarantine procedures we've tried and failed to employ here."[110] Later, she is mentored by the traditional healer Fannie McCloud, serving immigrants who do not have other access to medical care. Fannie also teaches her to read and write, opening the door to further study through reading.[111] Subsequently, Nora moves to the Adirondacks to reunite with her younger brother, and she finds purpose in working with the tuberculosis patients who flock there seeking the fresh cold air they hoped would aid their recovery.[112] Her skill continues to go unrecognized by physicians such as Dr. Fuller, who sneers at her: "What do you know about phthisis? It takes a good solid classical education and medical school and some years in a hospital after that before you can even think of understanding this disease." Then, ironically, he goes on to claim that the disease is not contagious but is a heritable disorder.[113]

This motif recurs in "Rare Bird," which is set in the mid-eighteenth century. Sarah Anne is a highly intelligent, unmarried woman whose father tutored her in natural history and who continues her studies through extensive reading.[114] Barrett describes Sarah Anne as the true successor to her father's intellectual pursuits, albeit without the financial means or social advantages to further them. Not only does Christopher, her less gifted brother, inherit their father's entire estate, but he is also granted the advantage of a Cambridge education as well as the friendship and respect of his late father's naturalist friends.[115] Sarah Anne yearns for opportunities to discuss and investigate questions about the natural world but is hampered by her brother's oppressive treatment and his insistence that she confine herself to a conventional female role in his household. The naturalists who gather in her home for dinner and conversation no longer contribute to her informal education, but rather dismiss or humor her when she interjects an opinion.[116] Sarah Anne finds an outlet for her scientific curiosity only after a chance introduction to another woman who shares her passion for natural history and scientific inquiry.

The story "Two Rivers" includes an amateur paleontologist, Grace, who collects fossils in the Dakota Badlands during the 1850s, with the support of her older sister Miriam.[117] Grace was educated in an academy for the deaf which emphasized the study of natural science, but she had no opportunity for university education.[118] Although Grace and Miriam have the freedom and financial resources to pursue their interest in fossils, they still struggle for recognition and encounter resistance from male colleagues and associates. All the fruits of their labors are sent to a formally trained paleontologist for analysis, who hoards the credit, acknowledging their contribution to his published findings only in a condescending footnote.[119] Miriam describes the attitudes of the soldiers and scientists with whom they work in the Badlands as "all of them . . . wishing the inconvenient women would leave."[120]

Another example of the barriers faced by women in science is the character Phoebe Wells Cornelius in "The Ether of Space." Although Phoebe earned a degree in astronomy at Cornell in the early 1900s, she is denied employment commensurate with her credentials. She is first underemployed as a "computer"[121] and is later able to participate in the sort of research for which she was trained only through her marriage to a fellow astronomer.[122] With the death of her husband, she loses access to such opportunities and is unable to secure employment in astronomy or even computing. She eventually establishes herself as a writer of popular science articles and books, but her meager earnings are inadequate to support herself and her son without help from her parents.[123] She tries to maintain a collegial relationship with her husband's former student Owen, whom she considers a peer in their discipline rather than a superior.[124] This assumption proves unfounded when she receives a letter from him containing feedback she perceives as impertinent and even disrespectful.[125]

Phoebe's situation is echoed in "The Island," where the professor's wife is an author in her own right and an active participant in field work with her spouse.[126] However, her independent ambitions, if any, are subsumed into her famous husband's interests. The professor considers her as a sort of votary in his service and is disappointed in the changes in their relationship that accompany her increased competence and confidence. Part of the appeal he sees in his teaching on Penikese is the prospect of students—particularly female students such as Henrietta—who treat him with the adulation he received from his wife earlier in their marriage.[127] Far from being a mere adjunct to the professor, she has contributed significantly to his success through more than her participation in his research endeavors. Henrietta marvels that the professor persuaded someone to donate an island to him in addition to the yacht and many other resources needed for the summer school,[128] but Barrett reveals later that this is largely due to the social and political aptitude of his wife.[129]

In "The Behavior of the Hawkweeds," Antonia also sees marriage as a means of gaining access to the world of genetics, at least tangentially. While young, she learned horticulture from her grandfather, who, in turn, was tutored in his boyhood by Gregor Mendel. Her hopes for college education were aborted when her father's death necessitated her return to work.[130] Just as she lost her mentor with the death of her grandfather, she loses the opportunity to pursue her interest in genetics further with the death of her father. She energetically courts Richard, a budding geneticist. In an effort to increase her appeal in his eyes, Antonia plies him with her cooking and emphasizes their shared interest in genetics, though she downplays her experience, saying only that she learned the basics of horticulture from her grandfather. [131] In order to increase her appeal, she offers Richard a sort of scientific dowry in the form of the family connection with Mendel and the historical documents her grandfather left behind. [132] Through her marriage Antonia gains a garden in which to work and opportunities to interact with Richard's colleagues during dinner parties and other social events. [133] Not surprisingly, Antonia does not find this fulfilling. Her successes in overseeing the household and acting as hostess she describes indifferently; as her husband ascends in his career and becomes increasingly pompous, Antonia experiences a corresponding diminution in her own satisfaction with life. [134]

Marriage is presented as a barrier to pursuing scholarly interests in several of Barrett's stories. Clara Vigne, the wife of Max in "Servants of the Map" and "The Cure," is also a botany enthusiast. In fact, Max's courtship of Clara was shaped by field outings in which they studied native plant species. [135] Max's unilateral decision to perpetuate his solo adventures and study of natural history precluded any opportunities Clara might have had to pursue her own interest, since she was left behind to manage their household and young family on her own. Clara's feelings about this situation are hinted at in "The Cure," after Ned tells her of a friend who was very thankful for his sister, who had assumed all the responsibilities of his household, leaving the friend free to explore the world *ad lib.* Clara's bitter response to this is: "Who *wouldn't* be grateful?" [136] Max's fulfillment comes at the expense of hers, a truth that he acknowledges obliquely in his egotistical assertion that "This is his story, his life unfolding. The women will tell the tale of these months another way." [137] While Max may romanticize himself a "servant of the map" or of science, the true servants of these endeavors are his wife and daughters, who support him in the background.

In "Theories of Rain," set in 1810, Lavinia's adoptive aunts view marriage as akin to slavery and anathema to scholarly endeavors. They intend, Lavinia reports, to "preserve me as they've preserved themselves. Not the children born every year, half or more of them to die; not the daily bowing down, the loss of my own thoughts and my independence; not the loss of my mind . . ." [138] In "The Island," set in 1873, students Henrietta and Daphne perceive similar hazards. Henrietta believes that marriage is incompatible with her ambition to pursue a career in natural history and education, and she considers her mother—another natural history enthusiast—as a case in point: "her mother, with all the miscarriages and stillbirths she'd suffered . . . had taught her more than she'd meant." [139] Daphne, similarly, declares her intent to remain single and explains that she is working to rid herself of an unwelcome suitor, after which she means to author a text on insects. [140] Interestingly, Barrett also creates a male character—Stuart in "Two Rivers"—whose marriage and family responsibilities prevent him from engaging in his scientific avocation. [141]

Barrett includes few examples of women who soar to lofty heights in the world of science, but there is at least one who fully realizes her ambitions. Rose Marburg is a rising star in her discipline; in "The Mysteries of Ubiquitin," at the age of thirty, she had "grants, . . . an embarrassingly large research budget, . . . was the youngest Senior Fellow at the Institute," and was on the verge of winning a prestigious award for her program of research.[142] But even Rose stays single for most of her career: "She didn't socialize with [her colleagues]. She was single, she lived by herself. . . . She had no friends, no pets, at the moment no lover. The lab was . . . the only place in the world where she felt at home."[143] She embarks on a long-term relationship only after retiring early from her research career and taking up teaching in her hometown of Hammondsport.[144] Her loneliness dispelled, Rose finds acceptance in the community where she grew up and companionship with Harry and the dog that used to be her father's.[145]

The Myth of Objectivity

Henrietta Atkins in "The Island" recounts her early instruction in science regarding the importance of objectivity in scientific inquiry: *"The 'I,' . . . has no place in scientific study."*[146] Barrett illustrates the difficulty of achieving this ideal in practice, since every person observes the world from a unique, human perspective. In their search for truth and reality, Barrett's characters are hampered by implicit bias, emotions, and unfounded assumptions. This is most apparent when her characters are reacting to paradigm shifts or controversial new theories, as with Sir Oliver Lodge reacting to the theory of relativity or Louis Agassiz to the theory of evolution by natural selection.

In "The Ether of Space," the premature death of Lodge's son has reinforced his need to embrace a philosophy that allows for an unseen world inhabited by spirits of the dead. Not content with expressing faith or belief in this unseen world and in the possibility of communication with the dead, Lodge attempts to put it forward as science despite a lack of empirical proof.[147] Other scientists in this story approach their discipline with various admixtures of emotion, faith, and empiricism. In a meeting where evidence is presented in support of Einstein's theories, the scientists in attendance initially respond to this evidence not with reasoned discussion but with emotion: "Half of us sighed as the other half gasped, some thrilled and some appalled and some split between the two; the older members were really upset. I could feel . . . something that shook me."[148] Characters speak of believing in theories rather than accepting them based on incontrovertible evidence. The press responds to Einstein's work with biased remarks disparaging not the theory but the German nationality of the scientist who formed it.[149]

During Lodge's lecture tour, his ideas evoke similar responses from his audiences. This tour occurs in the aftermath of the First World War, with its devastating casualties, and Lodge's message—asserting the existence of ether that is inhabited by spirits of the dead who seek to communicate with the living—holds tremendous appeal for the masses of people who have lost loved ones to the war.[150] The protagonist of the story, Phoebe, has experienced the loss of her husband, Michael, from an illness, but Lodge's theory repels rather than attracts her, once she learns more about his ideas of communication with the dead.[151] Phoebe struggles to reconcile Lodge's belief in the supernatural with his prior exemplary work in physics, and she finds herself blocked in her attempts to add a chapter on Lodge to the popular science book she is authoring. However, Phoebe herself is impeded by emotion and bias. She recognizes that her reaction to Lodge's lecture was on par with Lodge's reaction to evidence supporting the theory of relativity.[152] A sense of loyalty to her husband's memory prevents her from reading and evaluating Lodge's *The Ether of Space* for herself, even though she acknowledges her obligation as a scientist to investigate and examine evidence carefully. Michael had emphatically rejected Lodge's ventures into the realm of metaphysics, and Phoebe refuses to open the book even while she attempts to write about Lodge's theories.[153] Ultimately, her teenage son, Sam, succeeds where she has failed. Phoebe later learns that Sam has found Lodge's tome in the library, read it, and come to an understanding not only of his own struggle with his father's death, but of Lodge's persistent belief in the metaphysical. Sam perceives it as a showcase for the impact of emotion on science[154] and arrives at the conclusion that all scientific endeavors, from initial curiosity to hypothesis testing and theory formation, are rooted in human experience and emotion.[155]

Similarly, the worldview and theories of Agassiz in "The Island" are rooted in his theology.[156] He cites divine authority[157] and quotes his own work as though it is scripture in its own right.[158] Henrietta observes this mingling of religion with scientific study and feels that it is not in harmony with an empirical approach.[159] Elsewhere, characters treat science as a sort of religion itself, applying religious concepts and jargon to the methods, theories, and community of science. In "The Particles," Sam notes that some ideas and theories are considered "heresy" in the scientific community, evoking visceral reactions.[160] He also refers to "beliefs that were quickly becoming conventions" in the discipline of genetics and mistakenly assumes that the admonition "to question everything" allows for questioning and testing those beliefs.[161]

This motif of bias and emotion influencing scientists and their work appears frequently in "The Particles," where scientists' reactions are often governed by petty jealousy and unconscious motivations. Sam asserts that he is motivated only by a drive to uncover the realities of genetic inheritance,[162] but the questions he asks and the choices he makes are influenced by a deep-seated desire for approval and connection.[163] His theories about developmental timing in genetics are heavily informed by his need to understand the impact of his father's death during his boyhood and his early mistakes related to the premature dissemination of research findings.[164]

Other examples of mixed motives in this story include scientists' intense focus on advancing their reputations and prestige, even when that conflicts with the goal of uncovering truth and advancing science in their discipline. Duncan is perhaps the most unprincipled of the lot. After Sam presents controversial experimental findings as a student during a summer research program, Duncan is moved at least partially by jealousy to halt his own research and conduct other experiments in an effort to disprove Sam's work and then discredit him in print.[165] Duncan's reaction is far beyond what was merited by the circumstances, and he effectively destroys Sam's reputation and opportunities for placement in a reputable graduate program.[166]

The actions of Duncan and other colleagues resemble primate or pack behavior rather than the higher capacities of modern humans. Duncan, who sees himself as an alpha male, is driven to beat down all challengers and is more interested in maintaining his position than in fairly evaluating evidence.[167] The characters' mating behavior is also suggestive of pack dynamics. Ellen initially pursues Sam because of phenotypic traits that suggest he is a superior mate, including his intelligence and early successes as well as his stature and temperament.[168] After Duncan first sabotages Sam's work and reputation, Ellen abandons Sam to seek out more successful and fertile scientists.[169] Duncan then asserts his dominance over Sam in his personal life by marrying and successfully reproducing with Sam's former lover.[170] On the rescue ship, Duncan monopolizes the attention of the female students on board, and interrupts whenever he notices Sam interacting with women.[171] Duncan also demands the allegiance of Axel, the former leader, and does everything he can to prevent Sam from strengthening his relationship with Axel.[172] Furthermore, although Duncan was not a victim of the ship that was torpedoed, he nevertheless appoints himself as spokesman for the survivors, collating their stories and retelling them with his own biased spin when members of the press are clamoring for firsthand accounts of the tragedy.[173]

Barrett also presents political ideologies and agendas as barriers to objectivity and freedom in scientific inquiry. In "The Behavior of the Hawkweeds," a cohort of students in the 1970s protests the uses to which science is put in contemporary American society: "Science confined to the hands of the technocracy produces nothing but destruction."[174] In "The Particles," Sam notes that due to the political climate after World War I, "no one wanted to hear that inheritance wasn't everything, or that race and class characteristics passed on through generations might be altered."[175] Sam also describes the intrusion of political ideologies into a scientific meeting in Russia. His mentor speaks in refutation of unsubstantiated opinion that was presented as scientific fact, and "some in the audience actually hissed, and . . . after

Lysenko responded by dismissing all of formal genetics, those same people stood and cheered."[176] Similarly, after Andreas Kammerer falsifies evidence in support of Lamarckian inheritance, Russian propagandists seize on the story and spin conspiracy theories that Kammerer's research was faultless and that he fell victim to "a sinister German who tampered with his specimens" to discredit his work.[177] The situation worsens to the point that the lives and careers of the scientists at the institute are endangered when public sentiment turns against them: "Geneticists had failed, Sam read in the papers, to serve the state by providing the collectives with new crops and livestock that could thrive in difficult climates and relieve the food shortages."[178]

Likewise in "Servants of the Map," Max Vigne is dismayed when he realizes that the ultimate purpose of his surveying work is not geographic discovery or advancements in natural science. Instead, the maps generated "would be printed, distributed to governments, passed on to armies and merchants and travelers. Someone, someday, would study them as they planned an invasion, or planned to stop one."[179] In "Archangel," decisions related to medical treatment for combat injuries are dictated by military regulations and political necessity. Psychological trauma is considered cowardice. Soldiers who claim injury without obvious physical trauma—as with Havlicek's spinal injury and Constantine's embedded shrapnel—are stigmatized as malingerers and subject to punishment.[180] Military discipline occasionally takes the form of court-martials, but it also occurs in subtler ways, as when officials deny medical treatment to a group of soldiers suspected but not convicted of mutiny.[181]

Something similar happens in "Ship Fever," where Barrett's focus is the politics of immigration and public health. The health crisis originates in Ireland, during a blight which destroys the potato crops.[182] The British government distributes "unground Indian corn" that only sickens those who consume it, but they do little else to intervene, leaving the poor to die of starvation; meanwhile, "ships . . . sail daily for England with Ireland's produce, which might have been used to feed the starving."[183] In Canada, ports of entry are flooded with Irish immigrants fleeing famine and a typhus epidemic in their homeland. However, they carry the disease with them, and typhus spreads rampantly among the passengers, who are crammed into steerage decks and cargo holds in the most unsanitary of conditions, with little to eat and no clean water.[184] Efforts to control the epidemic on Grosse Isle are hindered by the political climate, which is rife with anti-immigrant sentiment, and by the military command of the quarantine station. Dr. Lauchlin Grant quickly learns after arriving at the station that questions are not welcomed and that those in command prioritize "discipline, the chain of command, [and] the appearance of priority" over the welfare of the immigrants or reforms that might improve quarantine procedures.[185] He later comes to the conclusion that "what's going on here has nothing to do with science and everything to do with politics."[186] When a friend criticizes the management of the quarantine, Lauchlin retorts bitterly that neither the government nor charitable organizations have cooperated to provide them with the basic supplies, personnel, and facilities needed to operate the station.[187]

MEANING AND IDENTITY

Central to the themes in Barrett's short fiction are questions of identity. The essential questions that drive her characters include who they are and who they are becoming, what it means to be human, and how they can construct meaning from their lives. Max Vigne might be speaking for Barrett's entire cast of characters when he asks, "Who am I? Who am I meant to be?"[188] These questions not only influence the science conducted by the characters, but the characters' understanding of science also informs their search for identity and self-understanding.

"Servants of the Map" is in large measure about Max Vigne's quest for self-discovery. In the beginning, the persona he presents to Clara and others is that of a morally upright husband and father making sacrifices to provide for his family.[189] Max shares his thoughts and history more freely with the reader than he does in his letters to family, and he reveals a more complex character than the image he tries to project. He reflects that he has never felt like he truly belonged anywhere after the death of his mother,[190] and because he chooses to leave Clara and his daughters, the reader may assume he doesn't even feel he belongs in his own home. Indeed, as the story progresses, it's clear he has concealed part of his motive for going in the first place, perhaps from himself as well as from Clara. Despite the sprinkling of gallant sentiments in his letters to Clara, what he fears most are the demands and responsibilities of domestic life.[191] Max wants to fit in, to find acceptance from his fellow surveyors. However, for as long as he clings to the morally upright persona, he meets with rejection.[192] Whereas Max was initially appalled by the promiscuity of his companions in their casual gratification of sexual urges,[193] he feels increasingly tempted to engage in such behavior himself,[194] and eventually he seeks comfort in a mistress.[195] This is what ultimately earns him the respect of his fellow surveyors, and "it is this knowledge that breaks the last piece of his heart."[196]

Other aspects of Max's identity are based on his nationality and his philosophical worldview, which includes assumptions of the fixed nature of species. His pride as a citizen of the great British empire and his membership in the Trigonometrical Survey of India suffer after hearing in detail about atrocities committed during the Indian Rebellion of 1857.[197] His vision of the world and of nature are transformed through his study of *The Origin of*

Species.[198] During his experiences far from home, Max undergoes a sort of metamorphosis. He seems to feel he is evolving into someone else entirely, adapting to the extremes in his physical and psychosocial environment, and he drops hints of these changes in his missives to Clara.[199] He becomes increasingly self-absorbed and sees his personal transformation as justification for his neglect of Clara and abandonment of his mistress.[200] Finally, he suggests to Clara that they "start over . . . someplace new. Somewhere I can be my new self, live my new life, in your company."[201]

At the beginning of "Ship Fever," Dr. Lauchlin Grant is experiencing a crisis in his career and identity. He is perpetually discontented with his life—longing for Susannah (now married to his friend Arthur Adam) and bemoaning his stalled research program and non-existent medical practice.[202] He feels keenly his lack of success in Quebec and craves respect and acknowledgment for his professional accomplishments.[203] His self-esteem at a low ebb, he wonders if he might find new purpose in a career in public health.[204] However, this change in course fails to bring either professional recognition or personal fulfillment; he instead finds himself entrenched in a stifling hierarchy with little tolerance for independent thought.[205] Just before his death, Lauchlin fears that his entire existence—from his childhood experiences to his professional training and subsequent endeavors—has been devoid of meaning, and he wonders if he might have found meaning by taking opportunities to appreciate "the beauty of daily life," in the way he did as a child when his mother was still alive.[206] He then experiences an epiphany about the interconnectedness of the human family and the meaning to be found in his apparently futile efforts on Grosse Isle: "these people he'd been caring for were, if not exactly him, extensions of him, and he was an extension of them. It was life, simply life that they had in common, and if he could have had his life back he could be happy with anything."[207]

In *Soroche*, the viewpoint character's sense of identity and the choices she makes are heavily influenced by what she learns about natural history and by her experience with altitude sickness, which becomes a metaphor for experiences in her marriage. Zaga, the working-class granddaughter of Lithuanian immigrants,[208] is lifted to dizzying social heights through marriage to a much older, wealthy man.[209] Barrett tells the story as a series of reflections and memories after Zaga is widowed and while she is attempting to sort out who she is and what she values, separate from her husband, Joel. During their marriage, Zaga was treated as an accoutrement to Joel's life, not as an equal or partner with goals and dreams of her own. This is typified by their delayed honeymoon at an Andean ski resort, which Joel selfishly plans to suit his own interests and abilities, ignoring the mismatch with Zaga's.[210] Whereas her husband prioritizes his wealthy lifestyle, including his art collection, expensive home, vacations, and social life,[211] Zaga prefers the quiet intimacies of everyday life and desires acceptance, love, and children of her own.[212]

During the delayed honeymoon in the Andes, Zaga is made miserable not only by the presence of his two teenaged children, who resent her,[213] but also by a combination of morning sickness and *soroche*, or altitude sickness.[214] The doctor who treats her for these maladies keeps her company while her husband and stepchildren are enjoying themselves on the ski slopes,[215] and during the course of their conversations, Zaga learns more about physical and social altitude sickness. The doctor describes the social equivalent of *soroche* when he recounts an episode from Darwin's scientific expedition on the *Beagle*.[216] The story he tells revolves around four people—two men and two children—snatched by the crew from Tierra del Fuego. In what may have been an ill-conceived social experiment, the Fuegians were pampered and acculturated to British life, then years later returned to their homeland along with various gifts and implements of European civilization.[217] The doctor tells how Darwin returned during a later voyage, to find that the child they had named Jemmy Button, now an adult, had rejected the gifts and European lifestyle and had completely reintegrated himself into Fuegian society.[218]

While Zaga's interactions with the doctor are brief in the timeline of the story, the impact reverberates for years to come. Zaga begins to see herself and her background as incompatible with her husband's sphere. She is physically unable to tolerate the altitudes of the Andean ski resort, while her husband and stepchildren are unphased by the heights.[219] She miscarries the baby conceived with her wealthy, sophisticated husband.[220] She never truly acclimates to her elevated social station and never gains acceptance from her husband's children or peers.[221] When she is widowed, she is bereft of social support and ill-equipped to manage the wealth she has inherited; her own relatives provide no comfort, but instead offer criticism and ask for handouts.[222]

Zaga proceeds to follow the pattern set by Jemmy Button; she is swindled out of part of her inheritance and compulsively gives away most of the remainder. She describes feeling "a fever that came over her . . . a burning in her fingertips, which could only be relieved by writing checks" and afterward "the antic joy of flinging her old life to the winds."[223] She perceives the wealth she inherited as lifeless and meaningless and her house and possessions as reminders of loss, unhappiness, and the person Joel wanted her to be.[224] Having cast off every trace of Joel's transformative influence, she returns to her less exalted social sphere; what she might have found meaningful in her marriage had already been taken from her—the child she miscarried and the children she would never have because her husband refused to try again thereafter. In her old neighborhood, she reclaims her identity and finds acceptance and contentment with her family.[225]

In the "The Littoral Zone," the two principal characters struggle to understand themselves and the impulses that dissolved their marriages and disrupted their children's lives. The phenomenon referenced by the story's title becomes a metaphor for the characters' experiences and behavior after two scientists—Ruby and Jonathan—act on a mutual attraction. Barrett defines the littoral zone as "that space between high and low watermarks where organisms struggled to adapt to the daily rhythm of immersion and exposure."[226] Ruby and Jonathan feel no attraction to each other initially, although they have a shared interest in marine biology.[227] They are brought together, however, by shared hardship; their littoral zone initially consists of primitive living conditions on an island marine station with ample poison ivy and no running water.[228] Their first real conversation takes place only after nearly two weeks filled with hard work, sunburn, students, insects, sleep deprivation, and social isolation.[229] Barrett suggests that their sudden attraction seems partly attributable to their shared suffering and their efforts to adapt to these extreme conditions: "Neither likes to think about how much of the thrill of their early days together came from the obstacles they had to overcome."[230]

Emotionally, they do not escape the littoral zone when they leave the island. The challenging ecology they face afterward consists of "mortgages, bills," guilt, and families in turmoil.[231] Once Ruby and Jonathan marry and their lives settle into a routine, the attraction wears thin, but they maintain the pretense because otherwise their mutual sacrifices would be devoid of meaning.[232] This may be considered yet another type of littoral zone, in which pretense is an adaptive mechanism the two employ constantly in order to survive in the no-man's land where they find themselves.

Family relationships are another important factor in identity, a point brought home by the interrelatedness of Barrett's characters and stories. Eudora MacEuchern in "Archangel" is the granddaughter of Nora Kynd ("Ship Fever" and "The Cure") as well as Max and Clara Vigne ("Servants of the Map" and "The Cure"). Phoebe Wells and her son Sam Cornelius ("The Ether of Space" and "The Particles") are descendants of Lavinia and Frank Wells ("Theories of Rain"). Not only are Rose and Bianca Marburg ("The Marburg Sisters," "The Forest," and "The Mysteries of Ubiquitin") related to the Vignes, Kynds, and MacEucherns through their father, but they are also related to Caleb and Miriam Bernhard ("Two Rivers") through their mother's line.[233] More obscurely, they are connected to members of the Wells family, particularly Erasmus, Cornelius, and their mother Lavinia ("The Cure" and "Theories of Rain"); among the family heirlooms that Rose's mother had saved were "one ancient, tiny lady's boot, black and moldy"[234] and missing a button[235]—the boot Lavinia wore during her visit with William Bartram in "Theories of Rain."[236]

Just as the reader may identify the characters in terms of their relationships to others, the characters likewise try to understand who they are in the context of their family origins and professional relationships. Many of Barrett's characters have been impacted by the loss of a parent early in life, and that impact may manifest in a variety of ways. That loss may spark questions about heredity and environment, or it may influence decisions about careers and lifestyles. Loss sometimes drives the survivors to try to regain that lost connection in any way they can, and it often impairs the survivors' ability to connect to others in meaningful ways.

When Lauchlin Grant's mother died during a cholera epidemic, he also effectively lost his father, who became withdrawn and angry.[237] Lauchlin's childhood friend Susannah lost both parents in the same epidemic, and this shared suffering increases his attachment to her, despite the separation that occurs when both children are sent away to live with other relatives.[238] Lauchlin's relationship with his father, on the other hand, is further weakened not only by the separation but also by his perception that he shares no common interests with his father; he declines to join his father's lumber business and instead seeks out connections to his mother.[239] His mother's death inspires him to become a physician and to research treatments for infectious diseases: "A substance as useful as atropine or quinine might reveal itself to him, if he were diligent."[240] When he returns to Quebec, Lauchlin gravitates toward Susannah, who represents another tie to the time before the deaths of her parents and his mother, and the two share an uneasy friendship.[241] Susannah's work is also motivated by her early losses; although she lacks formal training in medicine or nursing, she feels compelled to assist in caring for victims of the latest epidemic.[242] Eventually, she convinces Lauchlin to apply his training to more than research, and his work at the quarantine station brings him face to face with memories of his mother's death.[243]

Sam Cornelius, whose father died after contracting measles, initially clung more tightly to his mother, who would tell him stories about his father and the scientific work of his ancestor Copernicus Wells.[244] However, when his mother withdraws into her work, Sam eventually withdraws from her in turn.[245] As a teenager, Sam yearns for his father, and later he wonders about similarities between himself and his father. He puzzles over how different his mother is from his grandparents. In his reflection, he sees features that he attributes to his father and mother but also some that make him wonder about unknown relatives—especially those related to his late father.[246] These questions and observations evolve into scientific curiosity about genetics and inheritance. When he learns that he is probably infertile, this also affects his vision of himself, and he is disturbed by the idea that when he dies, "everything that had led to his father and mother and converged in him would be extinguished."[247]

In the absence of strong bonds with his biological family, Sam seeks out substitutes, and he thinks he has found that in Axel's research group. This sense of family increases when Axel teaches him about his "scientific pedigree," tracing a line beginning with Charlie Spacek and Axel himself and continuing through Thomas Morgan, William Brooks, and Louis Agassiz.[248] In some ways, Sam identifies more with his scientific family than with his biological family, and he is aware of an intense longing for his mentor's approval.[249] He sees Axel less as a professional mentor than a father; he is disappointed when Axel marries and starts his own family and when Axel treats him only as a former student or friend.[250]

Max Vigne finds meaning in his "tangential" relationship to the explorer Gregory Vigne, whom he tries to emulate,[251] and his memories of his late mother are fundamental to his identity. Max recalls her sharing with him her love of nature and telling him "there is something special in you. . . . In the way you see."[252] As he pursues his avocation of botany, he remembers more about his mother and believes increasingly that the essence of his identity had its roots in those early interactions with his mother; he perceives that being forced prematurely into adult responsibilities diverted him from his intended life course, and that his current exploration and studies have restored him to his true identity and purpose in life.[253]

Lavinia in "Theories of Rain" and Caleb in "Two Rivers" are siblings who are separated after their parents die. Lavinia clings tenaciously to the memory of her brother and the family who perished from yellow fever, and she resents the adoptive aunts who took her and "stripped" away her true identity.[254] For Lavinia, every thought and written word is a means of reaching out to her brother across time and space. She addresses him, asking, "Wherever you are, do you too look at the world and ask question after question?"[255] Though she cannot see him, she senses his presence "not as a human voice but as a pulsing hum, lower in pitch than the tree frogs' note, higher than the cicadas; pure intonation, no information."[256] Because it was raining when she watched her brother disappear, she associates rain and the phases of water with life transitions and with possibilities for change.[257] She's charmed by the less rational theories of rain that spark the imagination, including the one in which physical objects form from lapidary juice.[258] If this is possible, then why not imagine that her brother could rematerialize in the rain? She is also fascinated with the concept of attraction, and she makes comparisons with meteorological phenomena such as electricity, lightning, and the attraction between water molecules in her endeavors to understand the physical and intellectual attraction she feels for James and Frank, respectively, the long-distance familial attraction she feels for her brother, and the repulsion she feels for her adoptive aunts and their utilitarian worldview.[259]

Caleb, on the other hand, is more accepting of his adoptive family, though his thoughts never stray far from the parents and sister he lost. He is attached to his adoptive parents, but occasionally feels an impulse to deny the relationships and reclaim the parents who died.[260] He occasionally notices a personal trait that could not have been acquired from Samuel, and he asks, "Where had this come from?"[261] His first days with his adoptive father he describes as a sort of brainwashing, in which Samuel keeps him awake late into the night with lessons that mix natural history and theology, though Caleb is "swooning with lack of sleep."[262] Intrigued by Samuel's topics, Caleb nevertheless "[wonders] if he might not vanish himself, his former ways and habits buried beneath the flow of Samuel's ideas."[263] Samuel later confesses his intent to remake Caleb "in [his] own image."[264] Caleb's expedition to search for fossils in Kentucky's Big Bone Lick occurs after his wife's death and after a summer filled with dreams in which she appeared "holding his sister Lavinia."[265] The trip is almost a compulsion, driven by those dreams and his need to "make sense of his history with Samuel."[266] His journey leads him to Miriam and Grace, through whom he feels an almost tangible connection with Lavinia. They both resemble his lost sister physically, with their pale hair, and Grace in particular shares his affinity for finding fossils, just as his own child might.[267] Caleb compares his growing attachment to Grace to his feelings of falling in love with paleontology, then with Miriam, and before them both, with Lavinia.[268] Poignantly, after he says farewell to Miriam and Grace, he recalls that "Lavinia, who'd been folded into a stranger's arms when he last saw her . . . had twisted her head as the wagon began to roll and gazed directly at him," and at that moment, Grace echoes that memory, turning to watch him fade into the distance.[269]

THE SOCIOLOGY OF SCIENCE

On the surface, Barrett's stories are vehicles for sharing her fascination with natural phenomena and events in science history. Barrett acknowledges this fascination and that she gets her inspiration from "old books, old bones, fossils, feathers, paintings, photographs, museums of every kind and size, microscopes and telescopes, plants and birds."[270] Her *Ship Fever* collection was the product of "intense research into the history of natural science and medicine."[271] However, as many critics have noted, Barrett's primary concern in her short fiction is the social context in which science takes place and the role of human nature in the generation of knowledge.[272] Laura Van den Berg, for instance, observes that "the stories confront the knotty relationship between humans and the natural world and, in turn, the complexities of the characters' relationships with each other."[273] Similarly, Charles May concludes that her stories are ultimately about "the vulnerable human element behind the scientific impulse."[274]

Lab lit has great potential for exploring the many tribes of science and issues of concern to sociologists of science. Barrett takes full advantage of the potential offered by this genre. Regardless of the scientific content or historical context of her short fiction, her characters are always seeking to understand themselves and to construct meaning from their relationships, their experiences, and their world. Science is often the lens they use to sharpen their perspectives, but their human nature can distort and blur their view through that lens. They are both hampered and driven by basic impulses such as jealousy, competition and fear. Barrett may fill her fiction to the brim with elaborate details of natural science and science history, but in each work, she ultimately focuses the reader's attention on the human being within the scientist and the network of personalities within the world of scientific inquiry.

NOTES

1. Kevin Baker, "Waiting to Exhale," *New York Times,* Sept. 30, 2007.

2. Thomas Mallon, "Under the Microscope," *New York Times*, Jan. 28, 1996.

3. Helen Longino, "The Social Dimensions of Scientific Knowledge," in *The Stanford Encyclopedia of Philosophy*, ed. Edward N. Zalta. https://plato.stanford.edu/entries/scientific-knowledge-social/.

4. Nigel G. Gilbert and Michael Mulkay, *Opening Pandora's Box: A Sociological Analysis of Scientists' Discourse* (Cambridge: Cambridge University Press, 1984), 57.

5. Andrea Barrett, "The Island," in *Archangel* (New York: W. W. Norton & Company, 2013), 113.

6. Barrett, "The Island," in *Archangel,* 73–127.

7. Andrea Barrett, "The English Pupil," in *Ship Fever* (New York: W. W. Norton & Company, 1996), 34–46.

8. Andrea Barrett, "The Particles," in *Archangel* (New York: W. W. Norton & Company, 2013), 129–86.

9. Andrea Barrett, "The Mysteries of Ubiquitin," in *Servants of the Map* (New York: W. W. Norton & Company, 2002), 171–94.

10. Andrea Barrett, "The Marburg Sisters," in *Ship Fever* (New York: W. W. Norton & Company, 1996), 123–58.

11. Andrea Barrett, "The Investigators," in *Archangel* (New York: W. W. Norton & Company, 2013), 1–32.

12. Andrea Barrett, "Ship Fever," in *Ship Fever* (New York: W. W. Norton & Company, 1996), 159–253.

13. Andrea Barrett, "The Cure," in *Servants of the Map* (New York: W. W. Norton & Company, 2002), 195–272.

14. Andrea Barrett, "Rare Bird," in *Ship Fever* (New York: W. W. Norton & Company, 1996), 59–79.

15. Andrea Barrett, "Birds with No Feet," in *Ship Fever* (New York: W. W. Norton & Company, 1996), 103–22.

16. Andrea Barrett, "Theories of Rain," in *Servants of the Map* (New York: W. W. Norton & Company, 2002), 99–120.

17. Andrea Barrett, "Two Rivers," in *Servants of the Map* (New York: W. W. Norton & Company, 2002), 121–70.

18. Andrea Barrett, "*Soroche*," in *Ship Fever* (New York: W. W. Norton & Company, 1996), 80–102.

19. Andrea Barrett, "The Behavior of the Hawkweeds," in *Ship Fever* (New York: W. W. Norton & Company, 1996), 11–33.

20. Olga A. Pilkington, *The Language of Popular Science: Analyzing the Communication of Advanced Ideas to Lay Readers* (Jefferson, NC: McFarland, 2019), 85.

21. Pilkington, *The Language of Popular Science: Analyzing the Communication of Advanced Ideas to Lay Readers*, 85.

22. Barrett, "The Particles," in *Archangel*, 144.

23. Barrett, "The Particles," in *Archangel*, 158–64.
24. Barrett, "The Particles," in *Archangel*, 164.
25. Barrett, "The Particles," in *Archangel*, 169.
26. Barrett, "The Particles," in *Archangel*, 169.
27. Barrett, "The Particles," in *Archangel*, 149.
28. Barrett, "The Particles," in *Archangel*, 171.
29. Barrett, "The Particles," in *Archangel*, 147.
30. Barrett, "The Particles," in *Archangel*, 148–49.
31. Barrett, "The Particles," in *Archangel*, 158–64.
32. Barrett, "The Particles," in *Archangel*, 169.
33. Barrett, "The Particles," in *Archangel*, 170–71.
34. Barrett, "The Particles," in *Archangel*, 171–75.
35. Barrett, "The Particles," in *Archangel*, 176–77.
36. Barrett, "The Particles," in *Archangel*, 152.
37. Andrea Barrett, "The Behavior of the Hawkweeds," in *Ship Fever* (New York: W. W. Norton & Company, 1996), 21.
38. Barrett, "The Behavior of the Hawkweeds," in *Ship Fever*, 22–23.
39. Barrett, "The Behavior of the Hawkweeds," in *Ship Fever*, 22.
40. Barrett, "The Behavior of the Hawkweeds," in *Ship Fever*, 17.
41. Barrett, "The Behavior of the Hawkweeds," in *Ship Fever*, 25.
42. Barrett, "The Behavior of the Hawkweeds," in *Ship Fever*, 27.
43. Barrett, "The Behavior of the Hawkweeds," in *Ship Fever*, 32.
44. Barrett, "The English Pupil," in *Ship Fever*, 39.
45. Barrett, "The English Pupil," in *Ship Fever*, 40–43.
46. Barrett, "The English Pupil," in *Ship Fever*, 46.
47. Thomas Henry Huxley, *Address to the British Association for the Advancement of Science* (London: Taylor and Francis, 1870), 11.
48. Andrea Barrett, "The Ether of Space," in *Archangel* (New York: W. W. Norton & Company, 2013), 33–72.
49. Barrett, "The Ether of Space," in *Archangel*, 35.
50. Barrett, "The Ether of Space," in *Archangel*, 64.
51. Barrett, "The Island," in *Archangel*, 74.
52. Barrett, "The Island," in *Archangel*, 74.
53. Barrett, "The Island," in *Archangel*, 86.
54. Barrett, "The Island," in *Archangel*, 81, 83, 86, 107.
55. Barrett, "The Island," in *Archangel*, 82, 119.
56. Barrett, "The Island," in *Archangel*, 118.
57. Barrett, "The Island," in *Archangel*, 78–79, 82–84, 97–98, 100, 102, 108–09.
58. Barrett, "The Island," in *Archangel*, 81.
59. Barrett, "The Island," in *Archangel*, 85, 106.
60. Barrett, "The Island," in *Archangel*, 97, 109, 114–15, 118, 120.
61. Barrett, "The Island," in *Archangel*, 121.
62. Barrett, "The Island," in *Archangel*, 109.
63. Barrett, "The Island," in *Archangel*, 94.
64. Carl M. Cohen and Suzanne L. Cohen, *Lab Dynamics: Management and Leadership Skills for Scientists*, 3rd ed. (New York: Cold Spring Harbor, 2018), xv.
65. Cohen and Cohen, *Lab Dynamics: Management and Leadership Skills for Scientists*, ix, xv–xvi.
66. Sean F. Johnston, "Vaunting the Independent Amateur: *Scientific American* and the Representation of Lay Scientists," *Annals of Science*, 75, no. 2 (2018): 97–119, doi:10.1080/00033790.2018.1460691.
67. Liz Dowthwaite and James Sprinks, "Citizen Science and the Professional-Amateur Divide: Lessons from Differing Online Practices," *Journal of Science Communication* 18, no. 1 (2019): doi:10.22323/2.18010206.

68. Susana Nascimento and Alexandre Pólvora, "Maker Cultures and the Prospects for Technological Action," *Science and Engineering Ethics* 24, no. 3 (2018): 927, doi:10.1007/s11948-016-9796-8.

69. Susana Nascimento and Alexandre Pólvora, "Maker Cultures and the Prospects for Technological Action," 934–36.

70. John Tierney, "The Dilemmas of Maker Culture," *The Atlantic,* April 20, 2015, https://www.theatlantic.com/technology/archive/2015/04/the-dilemmas-of-maker-culture/390891/.

71. Jonathan P. Drury and colleagues, "Continent-Scale Phenotype Mapping Using Citizen Scientists' Photographs," *Ecography* 42 (2019): 1–2, doi:10.1111/ecog.04469.

72. Drury et al., "Continent-Scale Phenotype Mapping Using Citizen Scientists' Photographs," 2–5.

73. Andrea Barrett, "The Island," in *Archangel*, 187.

74. Michael D. Stephens, "The Role of the Amateur in Nineteenth Century American and English Scientific Education," *The Vocational Aspect of Education* 34, no. 87 (1982): 1, doi:10.1080/10408347308001591.

75. Olga A. Pilkington, *Presented Discourse in Popular Science: Professional Voices in Books for Lay Audiences* (Leiden: Brill, 2018), 4–12.

76. Brian J. Ford, "The van Leeuwenhoek Specimens," *Notes and Records of the Royal Society of London* 36, no. 1 (Aug. 1981): 38.

77. John Meurig Thomas, "Faraday and Franklin," *Proceedings of the American Philosophical Society* 150, no. 4 (Dec. 2006): 523–24.

78. Randall E. Stross, *The Wizard of Menlo Park: How Thomas Alva Edison Invented the Modern World* (New York: Three Rivers Press, 2007), 4.

79. Elizabeth Keeney, *The Botanizers: Amateur Scientists in Nineteenth-Century America* (Chapel Hill: University of North Carolina Press, 1992), 5–13.

80. Stephens, "The Role of the Amateur in Nineteenth Century American and English Scientific Education," 2.

81. Barrett, "Birds with No Feet," in *Ship Fever*, 104.

82. Andrew Berry, "Alfred Russel Wallace—Natural Selection, Socialism, and Spiritualism," *Current Biology* 23, no. 24 (2013): R1066-R1069, doi:10.1016/j.cub.2013.10.042.

83. Barrett, "Birds with No Feet," in *Ship Fever*, 103.

84. Barrett, "Birds with No Feet," in *Ship Fever*, 110.

85. Barrett, "Birds with No Feet," in *Ship Fever*, 113.

86. Barrett, "Birds with No Feet," in *Ship Fever*, 114–17.

87. Barrett, "Birds with No Feet," in *Ship Fever*, 117.

88. Barrett, "Birds with No Feet," in *Ship Fever*, 120–22.

89. Andrea Barrett, "Servants of the Map," in *Servants of the Map* (New York: W. W. Norton & Company, 2002), 17–69.

90. Barrett, "Servants of the Map," in *Servants of the Map*, 25, 34.

91. Barrett, "Servants of the Map," in *Servants of the Map*, 24–26, 61–62.

92. Barrett, "Servants of the Map," in *Servants of the Map*, 45, 49.

93. Barrett, "Servants of the Map," in *Servants of the Map*, 34, 42–43, 49, 58.

94. Barrett, "Servants of the Map," in *Servants of the Map*, 55.

95. Barrett, "Servants of the Map," in *Servants of the Map*, 24.

96. Barrett, "Servants of the Map," in *Servants of the Map*, 62.

97. Barrett, "Servants of the Map," in *Servants of the Map*, 68.

98. Barrett, "Servants of the Map," in *Servants of the Map*, 43.

99. Barrett, "Servants of the Map," in *Servants of the Map*, 57.

100. Barrett, "The Behavior of the Hawkweeds," in *Ship Fever*, 21.

101. Barrett, "The Behavior of the Hawkweeds," in *Ship Fever*, 21

102. Barrett, "The Behavior of the Hawkweeds," in *Ship Fever*, 13–14.

103. Barrett, "The Behavior of the Hawkweeds," in *Ship Fever*, 14–15.

104. Karen Warren, *Ecofeminist Philosophy: A Western Perspective on What It Is and Why It Matters* (Lanham, MD: Rowman & Littlefield, 2000).

105. Val Plumwood, "Androcentrism and Anthropocentrism: Parallels and Politics," *Ecofeminism: Women, Culture, Nature,* ed. Karen Warren (Bloomington: Indiana University Press, 1997).

106. Donna Haraway, *A Cyborg Manifesto: Science, Technology, and Socialist-Feminism in the Late Twentieth Century* (Minneapolis: University of Minnesota Press, 2016).

107. Barrett, "Ship Fever," in *Ship Fever*, 194–96.

108. Barrett, "Ship Fever," in *Ship Fever*, 229.

109. Barrett, "Ship Fever," in *Ship Fever*, 200.

110. Barrett, "Ship Fever," in *Ship Fever*, 194.

111. Barrett, "The Cure," in *Servants of the Map*, 106–07.

112. Barrett, "The Cure," in *Servants of the Map*, 214–15, 220–22, 231–32.

113. Barrett, "The Cure," in *Servants of the Map*, 254.

114. Barrett, "Rare Bird," in *Ship Fever*, 60–61.

115. Barrett, "Rare Bird," in *Ship Fever*, 60.

116. Barrett, "Rare Bird," in *Ship Fever*, 61.

117. Barrett, "Two Rivers," in *Servants of the Map*, 123–24.

118. Barrett, "Two Rivers," in *Servants of the Map*, 125, 169.

119. Barrett, "Two Rivers," in *Servants of the Map*, 124.

120. Barrett, "Two Rivers," in *Servants of the Map*, 170.

121. Barrett, "The Ether of Space," in *Archangel*, 39.

122. Barrett, "The Ether of Space," in *Archangel*, 39–40.

123. Barrett, "The Ether of Space," in *Archangel*, 45, 47.

124. Barrett, "The Ether of Space," in *Archangel*, 46.

125. Barrett, "The Ether of Space," in *Archangel*, 65.

126. Barrett, "The Island," in *Archangel*, 75.

127. Barrett, "The Island," in *Archangel*, 81.

128. Barrett, "The Island," in *Archangel*, 78.

129. Barrett, "The Island," in *Archangel*, 97.

130. Barrett, "The Behavior of the Hawkweeds," in *Ship Fever*, 17.

131. Barrett, "The Behavior of the Hawkweeds," in *Ship Fever*, 17.

132. Barrett, "The Behavior of the Hawkweeds," in *Ship Fever*, 23.

133. Barrett, "The Behavior of the Hawkweeds," in *Ship Fever*, 25.

134. Barrett, "The Behavior of the Hawkweeds," in *Ship Fever*, 25.

135. Barrett, "Servants of the Map," in *Servants of the Map*, 25.

136. Barrett, "The Cure," in *Servants of the Map*, 246.

137. Barrett, "Servants of the Map," in *Servants of the Map*, 67.

138. Barrett, "Theories of Rain," in *Servants of the Map*, 114.

139. Barrett, "The Island," in *Archangel*, 100.

140. Barrett, "The Island," in *Archangel*, 99.

141. Barrett, "Two Rivers," in *Servants of the Map*, 140–41.

142. Barrett, "The Mysteries of Ubiquitin," in *Servants of the Map*, 185.

143. Barrett, "The Marburg Sisters," in *Ship Fever*, 130.

144. Barrett, "The Marburg Sisters," in *Ship Fever*, 149.

145. Barrett, "The Marburg Sisters," in *Ship Fever*, 157.

146. Barrett, "The Island," in *Archangel*, 98.

147. Barrett, "The Ether of Space," in *Archangel*, 43.

148. Barrett, "The Ether of Space," in *Archangel*, 34.

149. Barrett, "The Ether of Space," in *Archangel*, 35.

150. Barrett, "The Ether of Space," in *Archangel*, 42–43, 54–55.

151. Barrett, "The Ether of Space," in *Archangel*, 43–45.

152. Barrett, "The Ether of Space," in *Archangel*, 48.

153. Barrett, "The Ether of Space," in *Archangel*, 50, 52.

154. Barrett, "The Ether of Space," in *Archangel*, 70.

155. Barrett, "The Ether of Space," in *Archangel*, 71.

156. Barrett, "The Island," in *Archangel*, 84, 90, 95.

157. Barrett, "The Island," in *Archangel*, 82, 91, 107.

158. Barrett, "The Island," in *Archangel*, 82, 121.
159. Barrett, "The Island," in *Archangel*, 102, 111
160. Barrett, "The Particles," in *Archangel*, 156.
161. Barrett, "The Particles," in *Archangel*, 157.
162. Barrett, "The Particles," in *Archangel*, 157, 163.
163. Barrett, "The Particles," in *Archangel*, 156, 182.
164. Barrett, "The Particles," in *Archangel*, 177–78, 183.
165. Barrett, "The Particles," in *Archangel*, 162.
166. Barrett, "The Particles," in *Archangel*, 163–64.
167. Barrett, "The Particles," in *Archangel*, 152, 162, 182.
168. Barrett, "The Particles," in *Archangel*, 161–62.
169. Barrett, "The Particles," in *Archangel*, 164–65.
170. Barrett, "The Particles," in *Archangel*, 165.
171. Barrett, "The Particles," in *Archangel*, 138–39, 167–68, 179–81.
172. Barrett, "The Particles," in *Archangel*, 149, 152, 154–55, 180.
173. Barrett, "The Particles," in *Archangel*, 185–86.
174. Barrett, "The Behavior of the Hawkweeds," in *Ship Fever*, 26.
175. Barrett, "The Particles," in *Archangel*, 157.
176. Barrett, "The Particles," in *Archangel*, 174–75.
177. Barrett, "The Particles," in *Archangel*, 173.
178. Barrett, "The Particles," in *Archangel*, 174.
179. Barrett, "Servants of the Map," in *Servants of the Map*, 57.
180. Barrett, "Archangel," in *Archangel*, 196.
181. Barrett, "Archangel," in *Archangel*, 215–17.
182. Barrett, "Ship Fever," in *Ship Fever*, 160.
183. Barrett, "Ship Fever," in *Ship Fever*, 160.
184. Barrett, "Ship Fever," in *Ship Fever*, 177–78, 183.
185. Barrett, "Ship Fever," in *Ship Fever*, 199.
186. Barrett, "Ship Fever," in *Ship Fever*, 229.
187. Barrett, "Ship Fever," in *Ship Fever*, 217.
188. Barrett, "Servants of the Map," in *Servants of the Map*, 55.
189. Barrett, "Servants of the Map," in *Servants of the Map*, 27, 32–33, 43, 49.
190. Barrett, "Servants of the Map," in *Servants of the Map*, 26, 49, 50, 60.
191. Barrett, "Servants of the Map," in *Servants of the Map*, 65.
192. Barrett, "Servants of the Map," in *Servants of the Map*, 23–24, 32.
193. Barrett, "Servants of the Map," in *Servants of the Map*, 32–33.
194. Barrett, "Servants of the Map," in *Servants of the Map*, 33–34.
195. Barrett, "Servants of the Map," in *Servants of the Map*, 63–65.
196. Barrett, "Servants of the Map," in *Servants of the Map*, 66.
197. Barrett, "Servants of the Map," in *Servants of the Map*, 48–49.
198. Barrett, "Servants of the Map," in *Servants of the Map*, 62.
199. Barrett, "Servants of the Map," in *Servants of the Map*, 31, 54.
200. Barrett, "Servants of the Map," in *Servants of the Map*, 67.
201. Barrett, "Servants of the Map," in *Servants of the Map*, 69.
202. Barrett, "Ship Fever," in *Ship Fever*, 167–68, 171.
203. Barrett, "Ship Fever," in *Ship Fever*, 173, 175.
204. Barrett, "Ship Fever," in *Ship Fever*, 171–73.
205. Barrett, "Ship Fever," in *Ship Fever*, 186.
206. Barrett, "Ship Fever," in *Ship Fever*, 238–39.
207. Barrett, "Ship Fever," in *Ship Fever*, 239.
208. Barrett, "*Soroche*," in *Ship Fever*, 85, 88.
209. Barrett, "*Soroche*," in *Ship Fever*, 85.
210. Barrett, "*Soroche*," in *Ship Fever*, 81.
211. Barrett, "*Soroche*," in *Ship Fever*, 80, 84, 86, 90.
212. Barrett, "*Soroche*," in *Ship Fever*, 85, 99–100, 101–02.
213. Barrett, "*Soroche*," in *Ship Fever*, 81–82, 86.

214. Barrett, "*Soroche*," in *Ship Fever*, 81–83.
215. Barrett, "*Soroche*," in *Ship Fever*, 82–83, 87–89, 91–92, 100–01.
216. Barrett, "*Soroche*," in *Ship Fever*, 89, 92–94, 99–100.
217. Barrett, "*Soroche*," in *Ship Fever*, 93–93.
218. Barrett, "*Soroche*," in *Ship Fever*, 92–94, 100.
219. Barrett, "*Soroche*," in *Ship Fever*, 94, 100.
220. Barrett, "*Soroche*," in *Ship Fever*, 101.
221. Barrett, "*Soroche*," in *Ship Fever*, 80, 81, 84, 86, 87, 95, 100–02.
222. Barrett, "*Soroche*," in *Ship Fever*, 90–91, 97–98.
223. Barrett, "*Soroche*," in *Ship Fever*, 95, 98.
224. Barrett, "*Soroche*," in *Ship Fever*, 80, 84, 93, 96, 97, 99–100, 101–02.
225. Barrett, "*Soroche*," in *Ship Fever*, 98–100.
226. Andrea Barrett, "The Littoral Zone," in *Ship Fever* (New York: W. W. Norton & Company, 1996), 51.
227. Barrett, "The Littoral Zone," in *Ship Fever*, 48, 50–51.
228. Barrett, "The Littoral Zone," in *Ship Fever*, 48.
229. Barrett, "The Littoral Zone," in *Ship Fever*, 48–50.
230. Barrett, "The Littoral Zone," in *Ship Fever*, 55.
231. Barrett, "The Littoral Zone," in *Ship Fever*, 47, 48, 53.
232. Barrett, "The Littoral Zone," in *Ship Fever*, 51, 53–58.
233. Elizabeth Gaffney, "Andrea Barrett: The Art of Fiction CLXXX," *The Paris Review* 168 (Winter 2003): 84–85.
234. Barrett, "The Mysteries of Ubiquitin," in *Servants of the Map*, 182.
235. Barrett, "The Cure," in *Servants of the Map*, 232
236. Barrett, "Theories of Rain," in *Servants of the Map*, 117.
237. Barrett, "Ship Fever," in *Ship Fever*, 203.
238. Barrett, "Ship Fever," in *Ship Fever*, 164.
239. Barrett, "Ship Fever," in *Ship Fever*, 203.
240. Barrett, "Ship Fever," in *Ship Fever*, 166.
241. Barrett, "Ship Fever," in *Ship Fever*, 162–63, 166.
242. Barrett, "Ship Fever," in *Ship Fever*, 166, 207, 218
243. Barrett, "Ship Fever," in *Ship Fever*, 166–68, 182, 236, 238.
244. Barrett, "The Ether of Space," in *Archangel*, 38–39.
245. Barrett, "The Ether of Space," in *Archangel*, 47, 48.
246. Barrett, "The Particles," in *Archangel*, 142.
247. Barrett, "The Particles," in *Archangel*, 168.
248. Barrett, "The Particles," in *Archangel*, 145–46.
249. Barrett, "The Particles," in *Archangel*, 156.
250. Barrett, "The Particles," in *Archangel*, 164, 168, 169, 182.
251. Barrett, "Servants of the Map," in *Servants of the Map*, 22, 57.
252. Barrett, "Servants of the Map," in *Servants of the Map*, 26, 49.
253. Barrett, "Servants of the Map," in *Servants of the Map*, 55–56.
254. Barrett, "Theories of Rain," in *Servants of the Map*, 102, 106, 109.
255. Barrett, "Theories of Rain," in *Servants of the Map*, 118.
256. Barrett, "Theories of Rain," in *Servants of the Map*, 119.
257. Barrett, "Theories of Rain," in *Servants of the Map*, 109, 111, 113, 119–20.
258. Barrett, "Theories of Rain," in *Servants of the Map*, 110.
259. Barrett, "Theories of Rain," in *Servants of the Map*, 107, 111, 116.
260. Barrett, "Two Rivers," in *Servants of the Map*, 131, 133.
261. Barrett, "Two Rivers," in *Servants of the Map*, 131, 132.
262. Barrett, "Two Rivers," in *Servants of the Map*, 127–29.
263. Barrett, "Two Rivers," in *Servants of the Map*, 130.
264. Barrett, "Two Rivers," in *Servants of the Map*, 158.
265. Barrett, "Two Rivers," in *Servants of the Map*, 141.
266. Barrett, "Two Rivers," in *Servants of the Map*, 142.
267. Barrett, "Two Rivers," in *Servants of the Map*, 165.

268. Barrett, "Two Rivers," in *Servants of the Map*, 168.
269. Barrett, "Two Rivers," in *Servants of the Map*, 168–69.
270. Andrea Barrett, "The Sea of Information," *The Kenyon Review* 26, no. 3 (Summer 2004): 8.
271. Samuel Baker, "PW Interview: Andrea Barrett: Images of Science Past," *Publishers Weekly*, Aug. 10, 1988: 364.
272. Robert K. Merton, *The Sociology of Science: Theoretical and Empirical Investigations*, ed. Norman W. Storer (Chicago: University of Chicago Press, 1973).
273. Laura Van den Berg, "About Andrea Barrett," *Ploughshares* 33 (Fall 2007): 210.
274. Charles E. May, "Andrea Barrett," in *Critical Survey of Short Fiction, Vol. 1*, ed. Charles E. May (Ipswich, MA: Salem Press, 2012), 107.

BIBLIOGRAPHY

Baker, Kevin. "Waiting to Exhale." *New York Times*. Sept. 30, 2007. https://www.nytimes.com/2007/09/30/books/review/baker.html.

Baker, Samuel. "PW Interview: Andrea Barrett: Images of Science Past." *Publishers Weekly*, Aug. 10, 1988: 363–64.

Barrett, Andrea. *Archangel*. New York: W. W. Norton & Company, 2013.

——. *Servants of the Map*. New York: W. W. Norton & Company, 2002.

——. *Ship Fever*. New York: W. W. Norton & Company, 1996.

——. "The Sea of Information." *The Kenyon Review* 26, no. 3 (Summer 2004): 8–19. http://www.jstor.org/stable/4338598.

Berry, Andrew. "Alfred Russel Wallace—Natural Selection, Socialism, and Spiritualism." *Current Biology* 23, no. 24 (2013): R1066-R1069. doi:10.1016/j.cub.2013.10.042.

Cohen, Carl M. and Suzanne L. Cohen. *Lab Dynamics: Management and Leadership Skills for Scientists*. 3rd ed. New York: Cold Spring Harbor, 2018.

Dowthwaite, Liz, and James Sprinks. "Citizen Science and the Professional-Amateur Divide: Lessons From Differing Online Practices." *Journal of Science Communication* 18, no. 01 (2019). doi:10.22323/2.18010206.

Drury, Jonathan P., Morgan Barnes, Ann E. Finneran, Maddie Harris, and Gregory F. Grether. "Continent Scale Phenotype Mapping Using Citizen Scientists' Photographs." *Ecography* 42 (2019): 1–10, doi:10.1111/ecog.04469.

Ford, Brian J. "The van Leeuwenhoek Specimens." *Notes and Records of the Royal Society of London* 36, no. 1 (Aug. 1981): 37–59. https://www.jstor.org/stable/531656.

Gaffney, Elizabeth. "Andrea Barrett: The Art of Fiction CLXXX." *The Paris Review* 168 (Winter 2003): 57–99.

Gilbert, Nigel G., and Michael Mulkay. *Opening Pandora's Box: A Sociological Analysis of Scientists' Discourse*. Cambridge: Cambridge University Press, 1984.

Haraway, Donna. *A Cyborg Manifesto: Science, Technology, and Socialist-Feminism in the Late Twentieth Century*. Minneapolis: University of Minnesota Press, 2016.

Huxley, Thomas Henry. *Address to the British Association for the Advancement of Science*. (London: Taylor and Francis, 1870). https://babel.hathitrust.org/cgi/pt?id=chi.18287997;view=1up;seq=5.

Johnston, Sean F. "Vaunting the Independent Amateur: *Scientific American* and the Representation of Lay Scientists." *Annals of Science* 75, no. 2 (2018): 97–119, doi:10.1080/00033790.2018.1460691.

Keeney, Elizabeth. *The Botanizers: Amateur Scientists in Nineteenth-Century America*. Chapel Hill: University of North Carolina Press, 1992.

Longino, Helen. "The Social Dimensions of Scientific Knowledge." In *The Stanford Encyclopedia of Philosophy*. Summer 2019 ed., edited by Edward N. Zalta. https://plato.stanford.edu/entries/scientific-knowledge-social/.

Mallon, Thomas. "Under the Microscope." *New York Times*, Jan. 28, 1996. https://www.nytimes.com/1996/01/28/books/under-the-microscope.html.

May, Charles E. "Andrea Barrett." In *Critical Survey of Short Fiction, Vol. 1*, edited by Charles E. May, 106–10. Ipswich, MA: Salem Press, 2012.

Merton, Robert K. *The Sociology of Science: Theoretical and Empirical Investigations*, edited by Norman W. Storer. Chicago: University of Chicago Press, 1973.

Nascimento, Susana, and Alexandre Pólvora. "Maker Cultures and the Prospects for Technological Action." *Science and Engineering Ethics* 24, no. 3 (2018): 927–946, doi:10.1007/s11948-016-9796-8.

Pilkington, Olga A. *The Language of Popular Science: Analyzing the Communication of Advanced Ideas to Lay Readers*. Jefferson, NC: McFarland, 2019.

Pilkington, Olga A. *Presented Discourse in Popular Science: Professional Voices in Books for Lay Audiences*. Leiden: Brill, 2018.

Plumwood, Val. "Androcentrism and Anthropocentrism: Parallels and Politics." *Ecofeminism: Women, Culture, Nature*, edited by Karen Warren, 327–55. Bloomington: Indiana University Press, 1997.

Stephens, Michael D. "The Role of the Amateur in Nineteenth Century American and English Scientific Education." *The Vocational Aspect of Education* 34, no. 87 (1982): 1–5. doi:10.1080/10408347308001591.

Stross, Randall E. *The Wizard of Menlo Park: How Thomas Alva Edison Invented the Modern World*. New York: Three Rivers Press, 2007.

Thomas, John Meurig. "Faraday and Franklin." *Proceedings of the American Philosophical Society* 150, no. 4 (Dec. 2006): 523–41. https://www.jstor.org/stable/4599022.

Tierney, John. "The Dilemmas of Maker Culture." *The Atlantic*, April 20, 2015, https://www.theatlantic.com/technology/archive/2015/04/the-dilemmas-of-maker-culture/390891/.

Van den Berg, Laura. "About Andrea Barrett." *Ploughshares* 33 (Fall 2007): 207–12. https://www.jstor.org/stable/40354154.

Warren, Karen. *Ecofeminist Philosophy: A Western Perspective on What It Is and Why It Matters*. Lanham, MD: Rowman & Littlefield, 2000.

Chapter Nine

The Honest Look at
Science and Poetry

Elaine Pearce

Sometimes we think of scientists as super-human beings, people who are almost god-like in their ability to be the gatekeepers of detailed and specific knowledge. They are the seekers of truth, the discovery makers and the innovators, our best hope for a better future. In short, they are not like us. They work in specialized settings, in university research facilities or corporate laboratories, studying, observing, moving systematically from Point A to Point B. To the general public, it may seem that scientists inhabit a serene world of intellectual endeavor, closeted away in sterile, state-of-the-art laboratories, separated from everyday burdens. Some view scientists as an additionally rarefied species of academic, insulated by laboratories and technical vocabularies, focused on experiments and equipment, removed from campus politics and power struggles. Scientists are certainly not immune to the challenges imposed upon other academics. "Aspiring scientists are encouraged to attend conferences; get doctorates and post-doc's from, and become professors at, prestigious universities; bring in research support; get published; get tenure; get more funding; get appointed to boards; get noticed; and get prizes."[1] The corporate world of research science is equally demanding.

Jennifer L. Rohn's *The Honest Look* corrects common misconceptions about science and scientists held by many people outside the scientific community. "It provides an authentic peek into the backgrounds, histories and motivations of those who work in corporate science."[2] Her scientists live and work in the real world, a world that includes personal and professional conflicts, budget restrictions, and time restraints. They experience pressures that may interfere with practicing pure scientific research and create moral and ethical dilemmas. Reality is far different from idealized notions of science

175

and scientists. Concentrating on scientific activities in a realistic manner, the novel strives to illuminate the obscure world of science and teach its fundamentals by examining the intricacies of scientific work. It also deals with "the creative tension between thinking and feeling in everything from . . . [the sciences] to art to ourselves."[3]

Almost all of the major characters in the novel are scientists who work at NeuroSys, a British-owned biotech company located in a small village in the Netherlands a quick train ride away from Amsterdam. NeuroSys is a state-of-the-art facility funded by a multi-millionaire seeking a cure for Alzheimer's to avenge his wife's death from the disease. It is here that the reader discovers the complex process of scientific research. Claire Cyrus, the latest addition to NeuroSys, quickly finds out that corporate research science, while not necessarily of "the every-man-for-himself mentality of the university," is far from the community of "white-coated scientists" who labor in earnest "toward a common goal, suffused in a glow of camaraderie"[4] that she had envisioned. Like most of the other members of the company, Claire is a cell biologist, but she is different from the others in that she is one of only three people in the world who can operate the company's newly acquired Interactrex 3000, a room-size machine created to peer inside living cells, extract microscopic proteins from them, and analyze those proteins. Claire and the machine she has nicknamed *"Raison D'être"* or "the Raisin"[5] can "watch proteins interact in real time."[6]

Rohn describes this complicated process and cell proteins in a way that is easy to understand and imagine. It seems almost like a video game with Claire stalking a cell, using a joystick to guide a needle to zap the cell and suck up an infinitesimal amount of the fluid inside. A "droplet, a billionth of the size of one raindrop but packed . . . with hundreds of proteins, invisible Legos which, in intricate, infinite combinations, [could] construct absolutely anything: a claw, a hair . . . a leaf, an ear of corn, a blue whale."[7] In a split second the Interactrex can sort proteins for identification.

Claire and the Interactrex are not immediately accepted by the rest of the researchers. The Interactrex is an expensive machine whose acquisition negated purchases for other departments. Another reality of scientific research. It is costly. Most scientific research cannot be performed adequately without money, lots of it. There are facilities to be built, equipment and supplies to be purchased, support personnel to be hired, salaries to be paid. Corporate scientists are expected to turn a profit sooner or later. The Interactrex might well be resented, even seen as a "big, money-sucking black hole."[8] In the minds of most of the company, it has yet to prove itself. Similarly, Claire in her first post-doc job must also prove herself. Her natural reticence, her workaholic hours, and her professional and personal insecurities make her seem antisocial or disdainful of others.

It is tempting to say that in the course of the novel Claire, the central character of *The Honest Look*, experiences a transformation and shifts from being a scientists to becoming poet. However, it is not a transformation that a reader encounters but another side of the heroine, a facet of her being that was always there but was suppressed. At the end of the novel, Claire is a renewed and a complete self; her equilibrium is restored, but this happens only after she realizes how truly intertwined and similar art and science are.

In order for the reader to better understand Claire, Jennifer Rohn flashes back to her formative years, emphasizing the importance of her father and his influence on her life. Instead of reading children's books to her, Claire's father read aloud whatever he was reading—fiction, non-fiction, drama, and, most importantly, poetry; much as Atticus Finch in *To Kill a Mockingbird* would read the nightly paper as his daughter, Scout, followed along. Like Scout, Claire learned to read at an early age. Eventually, her love of all things written focused on poetry, and reading and writing it became her first great love. Honing her skill with language, Claire began her observations of the world as a child. Walking with her poet father, she learned to watch closely in order to play well the game that was their private domain. "Tell me the colour of the parked car we just passed,"[9] and Claire would search her mind for the object, remember its details, select and discard possibilities, as she endeavored to describe it from a different angle, a view that avoided the commonplace and captured the richness of its essence. Claire's father did not praise all of her efforts, as parents are inclined to do with young children. More often, he challenged her to see the world with fresh eyes, to reject the easy, the obvious, the cliché. The more they played the game, the more she became her own critic, developing her own internal voice of challenge, creating original ideas and thus earning a deserved praise rather than a hollow one.

Her first separation from that life, a separation from parents, comes when she leaves for university, a common occurrence for young people on their journey of self-discovery. It is more than a physical separation for Claire. Her father always hoped that she would choose "a profession" using "the art of words."[10] Claire believed the study, teaching, and writing of poetry would be her professional niche. She surprises herself and her father by pursuing a different course of study. Instead of a career in literature, she opted for the sciences, ultimately obtaining her doctorate in cell biology. This choice separated her from the self of her childhood and initiated the suppression of her artistic side.

The decisions that Claire makes in this uncharted territory of science lead her to loneliness and isolation. She leaves the university in England to work for a research company in the Netherlands, a country in which she knows no one. She is further isolated because she does not know the language, is tolerated as a foreigner but not welcomed, and is viewed with a certain amount of distrust by her new colleagues. In this liminal world, she forges a new identity. Initially, her only friend is the Interactrex 3000. The Raisin is beautiful, sleek and trim, one-fifth the size of the first Interactrex prototype whose enhanced collection program Claire developed. It is Claire's ally and companion.

Rohn gives the Raisin human characteristics. It sighs, moans, and confirms. It is jealous and unrepentant. It chirps reprovingly and winks out messages. Claire talks to it, feeds it, and touches it with affection. She is less upset by the negative reception that she receives from the other scientists at NeuroSys than she is by their resentment of the Raisin, feeling it necessary to defend the Raisin's honor and abilities. Her desire to come up with a brilliant idea for Alzheimer's research is, in part, to showcase the Raisin's talents and vindicate it. Even when she seemingly concedes that the creature is a machine, she reveres it as a fine instrument. Just before using it to perform an important procedure, she prepares "like a concert pianist."[11] This kind of relationship between a researcher and his or her apparatus is common in lab lit, where an "apparatus . . . is not just a well-described background to the narrative action. It serves as a way of characterization and, at times, appears as a character itself. There is also a pronounced trend to present the affectionate relationships between researchers and their equipment."[12]

Claire's other companions are poetry and science, her first and second love. Poetry commutes to work with her in the form of some well-worn book or another. Lines from famous poets fill her mind, order her experiences, express her thoughts in better words than she can herself. Its familiarity supports her like a lifelong friend. Yet, she is now at outsider to this comfortable world. As a practitioner of science, Claire fills her days and directs her work by its laws. Science is a neat, orderly profession. Results can be replicated. Hypotheses proven or disproved. "Truth and precision created by an imprecise human mind."[13]

Gradually, Claire acquires additional companions. Most are scientists. One is not. It is not surprising that Rachel May—a graphic designer, female friend, confidant, and admirer—can see Claire far more objectively than she can see herself. (We are all our own harshest critics.) Rachel and Claire are similar. They are both attractive, intelligent, and observant. Even in the simplest setting, coffee with a friend, Rachel's senses seem to be on high alert, touching, feeling, eyeing, critiquing. She "filtered the world through crafted objects just as Claire" used to use words to do so.[14] But Rachel also has traits Claire does not possess, traits she admires. Rachel is well known among the British ex-pats of Amsterdam and seems universally popular, appealing to people from all walks of life, "united only by the arbitrariness of language."[15] Rachel is at ease with herself and her environment and in control. Claire's friendship with Rachel allows her a space in which to relax, not subject to the scrutiny and criticism of NeuroSys. Their conversations also give us insight into "the nuances of Claire's research as she explains them to" Rachel.[16]

Interactions with the others, male scientists, ultimately help Claire to clarify and solidify her values. Dr. Ramon Ortega is the comfort mentor, kind, gentle, serving her the special Spanish coffee of her childhood. A founding partner of the company, he is a dedicated family man with a consistent work schedule that takes him home at the end of each day to his wife's excellent cooking. Dr. Joshua Pelinore, very tall and very pale, has been schooled by his observations of animals and human beings and can calm horses, hysterical undergraduate interns, and Claire's first-day panic attack. Dr. Alan Fallengale seduces Claire with his physical beauty, his brilliance, and his coldness. With his upper-class accent, Alan, another founding partner, is charming when he chooses to be, caustic when he chooses not to be charming, and mercurial. He has expensive tastes and desires the finest wines, furniture, and art. It is also rumored that he is a womanizer.

The way these men perform science does much to reveal their characters. Joshua started out as an experimental biologist but was "drawn . . . into the world of bioinformatics. Only other computer folk could understand the innovative way Joshua blended instincts with hard mathematics to infer biology from DNA code."[17] Ramon, pulled into an administrative role, would send the scientists in his lab home at the same hour each day to allow himself a private hour of solitary research, to "putter around in the laboratory . . . working . . . with his hands instead of his head. He did small experiments, he did them lovingly and painstakingly, and he did them one at a time. . . . 'It's not so much about generating data. . . . It's more about keeping my hand in, keeping my instincts sharp. Trying out new techniques. . . . It gives me fresh ideas; it keeps me young—and flexible.'"[18] Alan, an excellent scientist, is "'as sharp as a [*sic*] eagle. . . . He's clever enough to both have a preconceived idea and not miss the warning signs when he's wrong.'"[19]

How will Claire fit in? She has come to believe that there are "different sorts of scientists, from visionary Darwins (like Alan and Ramon) to people like [herself], all the way down to" the lab technicians "and every shade in between. In the scientific community, everyone had their value."[20] For Claire, being a true scientist means more than performing someone else's experiments, testing someone else's hypotheses. Claire's greatest challenge and her greatest uncertainty is ideas, specifically the talent of generating new ideas. Even though she was hired primarily to operate the Interactrex 3000, her job description requires she "possess the creativity to realize a self-conceived programme of basic research."[21] An extremely competent scientist who can systematically and logically execute the processes necessary to further ideas, Claire questions her own scientific creativity, feeling that she is not capable of originating the ideas for a successful line of scientific inquiry.

Despite many efforts to come up with a brilliant idea, she repeatedly draws a blank.

Her meticulous work refining the ideas of other researchers makes her a valuable asset to the scientific community, but it does not sufficiently satisfy her intellectual hunger, a hunger that comes from a bright, inquisitive mind rather than ego. Scientific research, like art, differs from other occupations and activities that are purposeful but not creative. Purposeful activity is "activity engaged in and consciously controlled so as to produce a desired result. . . . The agent envisages the result he desires to produce and has it consciously in view, and he believes that if he acts in certain ways the result desired will be produced."[22] The act of testing a hypothesis may resemble purposeful activity, but the steps necessary to generate that hypothesis depend on scientific inspiration, idea, and research. For Claire, any professional pressure to produce new ideas is secondary to her own desires to experience that creative pleasure, to justify to herself her love of science and her career choice. Reviewing the research on the Universal Aggregation Principle, the basis for NeuroSys's soon-to-be tested drug, Claire marvels, "Such a simple idea . . . a beautiful idea . . . an idea . . . that might end up curing Alzheimer's. What must it feel like to be the originator of such a powerful discovery?"[23]

Ultimately, she finds out what it feels like to be the originator of a powerful idea. Coming out of nowhere while she was doing routine tasks, "the idea was born. . . . And not just a filling-in-the-gaps idea, but a trail-blazing idea. An idea that, if true, would kick off an entirely new avenue of research." The idea was beautiful in its simplicity and perfectly suited to the Raisin's capabilities. She was surprised that she hadn't thought of it earlier.[24] Interestingly enough, Claire conceives this scientific idea only after her poetic voice reawakens. For six years she had silenced that voice and the voice of her father echoing in her head. She channeled her time, talents, and energy into the practical realities of studying science, completing undergraduate and graduate school, researching, investigating, helping Maxwell, her PhD supervisor, perfect the Interactrex 3000. It had been an either-or proposition, and she had made an active choice. Instead of choosing her passion for her profession, she had chosen science for its predictability, relegating poetry to the sidelines. Now both her poetic voice and her father's are alive again.

After her inner poet is reawakened, her outer scientist is ignited. "Claire was now completely captivated by her research." Never before had she experienced "the crushing momentum familiar to a certain class of scientist who, once they sense the nearness of truth, cannot rest until it is captured."[25] This drive is completely overwhelming and compelling. Everything else—even eating and sleeping are subjugated to it. This is like Claire's need to write poetry. Having neglected poetry for so long, she is not sure that she can still do it, yet when she starts writing again, she is completely absorbed in the poem for hours at a time, her whole body focused on the art of writing, forgetting to eat, allowing no interruptions.

"Do Art and Science live in very different domains, or are they the same domain but seen through different filters? . . . What can happen when . . . relationships between art and science . . . grow and new kinds of thinking . . . emerge from a blend of two cognitive realms?"[26] Claire Cyrus clearly demonstrates that science and art are not in opposition. "Poets and scientists both seek to observe, explain, and understand the world around them."[27] The skills that make a poet are equally beneficial for a scientist to possess. Claire's early training with her father, the game they played on their walks together, taught her more than a mental agility with language. It "released in her some ability to see the truth about objects or people that no one else seemed to notice."[28] The ability to observe is a defining skill for a scientist. "I'm a scientist—I observe," declares Claire.[29] Because they are human, scientists are not infallible. They must guard against personal bias. They must observe critically and carefully the results their experiments produce. "Preconceived notions can blind the eye to things that don't quite fit, to signals that are trying to tell you you're on the wrong track."[30] A poet must have the same clarity of vision. Claire could just as easily have said, "I'm a poet—I observe." To be valid, a poet's images must ring true. They must chime with the reality readers know to be true.

Poets and scientists need to be creative, to generate new ideas. Both the creative artist and the scientist originate "something the like of which did not exist before. . . . In the creative process, two moments may be distinguished, the moment of inspiration, when the new suggestion appears in consciousness, and the moment of development or elaboration. The 'moment' of development may last a long time, of course, even years."[31] For Claire, the development of the idea is the same whether she is writing poetry or performing research. She is completely focused on the task at hand in an almost trance-like state. When she writes poetry, she spills word after word onto the page, possibilities to be sorted, analyzed, selected, or discarded. When she performs scientific research, she must figure out how to structure experiments properly, analyze data and interpret it. In both instances she employs divergent thinking that culminates in convergent thinking as results are narrowed and refined, choices made, answers found.

Alan Fallengale prides himself on being a gifted scientist. He enjoys and values the creativity of science, but he does not value Claire's poetic creativity, seeing it as a dalliance, a distraction from her focus on science that is preventing her from becoming a brilliant scientist. His scientific ideas are sparked by examining and contemplating the ideas of other scientists. Claire's ideas come from her own observations and seem to spring unbidden from her mind, pushing to get out. They are more like a "spontaneous overflow . . . recollected in tranquility."[32] Regardless of what generates their respective ideas, both are equally viable. Alan does not realize that writing poetry is actually healthy for Claire, keeping the pathways of thought open and recharging her creativity. "Poetry . . . involves a high level of abstraction in language and ideas, and it requires specific critical thinking skills and deeper comprehension."[33] Abstraction of ideas and critical thinking skills are necessary components of scientific research. Scientific knowledge and completed poems do not magically appear fully formed. The creative process is vital in each. Is creativity in science essentially different from creativity in the arts? *The Honest Look* suggests that it is more similar than different.

The greatest similarity between science and poetry is purpose. Both disciplines have the same end, the discovery of truth. Science is a means of discovering truths in the natural world that are verifiable through duplicated experimentation. It is a logical, systematic progression from step A to step B to Step C. "How can a *scientist* lie about the truth? Otherwise what is the point of doing science."[34] Discovering one scientific truth "leads to more questions and further truths demanding to be revealed in turn."[35] Truth is the raison d'être of science. Poetry is the same. It too is the search for truth. Poetry is about discovering and presenting universal truths about the human condition. It may be more of a subjective truth, but it is a truth all the same. If science is organized knowledge, it is equally possible to see poetry as organized understanding. "The head and the heart are not just compatible but codependent . . . even the most rational approach to the pursuit of truth inevitably requires the capacity for self-reflection and all of the poetry that comes with it."[36]

In *The Honest Look* truth and beauty are linked. "'Beauty is truth, truth beauty,'—that is all / Ye know on earth, and all ye need to know."[37] When she sees living cells for the first time, Claire falls in love "with the vast and unknowable beauty of life" to be found in and through science, and marvels "how this strange carpet of luminous bubble-wrap [could] equate to the smooth surface of someone's skin, or the curve of a heart or the cornea of an eye."[38] Being susceptible to the charms of beauty is an occupational hazard for poets, and even though beauty and the appreciation of beauty are thought to be more in the realm of poetry, Claire, with a poet's eye, can also see the beauty of the natural world, the beauty of logic, and the beauty of discovery.

The quest for truth and beauty has led Claire through the world of corporate scientific research and back to poetry. The world of science has tested her resilience, challenged her psyche, and ultimately made her realize the value and power of poetry. It is only by accepting both her scientific and artistic side that Claire restores her equilibrium. Kat Arney correctly notes that *The Honest Look* is about interaction,[39] but it is also about integration or reintegration at least for Claire as she sorts out her values, her talents, and ultimately her identity. Reading *The Honest Look*, "we gain an appreciation for the dedication it takes to be a scientist: frustrating dead-ends alternating with marathon work sessions stretching late into the night for weeks on end, the complex collaborations with brilliant and ambitious . . . people."[40] Jennifer Rohn "shows us that science, far from being the soulless recording of facts, can be fascinating, unpredictable and powerful."[41] We also discover that "we will do better science and understand ourselves better, morally and otherwise, if we adopt a holistic perspective and not a reductive one."[42] *The Honest Look* is the quintessential lab lit novel.

NOTES

1. David S. Caudill, "Expertise, Lab Lit, and the Fantasy of Science Free from Economics," *Cardozo Law Review* 33, no. 6 (August 2012): 2475–476.

2. GrrlScientist, "The Honest Look [book review]," *The Guardian*, February 7, 2011, www.theguardian.com/science/punctuated-equilibrium/2011/feb/07/5.

3. Stephen Abbott, "Why I Love Tom Stoppard," *Middlebury Magazine* (Spring 2017): 28.

4. Jennifer L. Rohn, *The Honest Look* (Cold Springs Harbor, NY: Cold Springs Harbor Laboratory Press, 2010), 9.

5. Rohn, *The Honest Look*, 2.

6. Lynne Herndon, "Science, Meet Poetry," *Cell* 143, no. 7 (December 23, 2010): 1039.

7. Rohn, *The Honest Look*, 36.

8. Rohn, *The Honest Look*, 39.

9. Rohn, *The Honest Look*, 27, 29.

10. Rohn, *The Honest Look*, 28.

11. Rohn, *The Honest Look*, 93.

12. Olga A. Pilkington, "Popular Science versus Lab Lit: Differently Depicting Scientific Apparatus," *Science as Culture* 26, no. 3 (2017): 229–300.

13. Rohn, *The Honest Look*, 16.

14. Rohn, *The Honest Look*, 49.

15. Rohn, *The Honest Look*, 48.

16. GrrlScientist, "The Honest Look [book review]."

17. Rohn, *The Honest Look*, 20.

18. Rohn, *The Honest Look*, 84.

19. Rohn, *The Honest Look*, 85.

20. Rohn, *The Honest Look*, 46–47.

21. Rohn, *The Honest Look*, 4.

22. Vincent Thomas, "Creativity in Art," in *Creativity in the Arts*, ed. Vincent Thomas (Englewood Cliffs, NJ: Prentice-Hall, 1964), 98–99.

23. Rohn, *The Honest Look*, 38.

24. Rohn, *The Honest Look*, 59.

25. Rohn, *The Honest Look*, 83.

26. Jack Ox and Richard Lowenberg, "What Is the Challenge of Art/Science Today and How Do We Address It?" *Leonardo* 46, no. 1 (2013): 2.

27. Sylvia M. Vardell, "Connecting Science and Poetry," *Book Links* (November 2013): 16.

28. Rohn, *The Honest Look*, 31.

29. Rohn, *The Honest Look*, 89.

30. Rohn, *The Honest Look*, 85.

31. Thomas, "Creativity in Art," 98, 104.

32. William Wordsworth, "Preface to the *Lyrical Ballads*," in *English Romantic Poetry and Prose*, ed. Russell Noyes (New York: Oxford University Press, 1956), 365.

33. Vardell, "Connecting Science and Poetry," 16.

34. Rohn, *The Honest Look*, 124.

35. Rohn, *The Honest Look*, 83.

36. Abbott, "Why I Love Tom Stoppard," 28.

37. John Keats, "Ode on a Grecian Urn," in *English Romantic Poetry and Prose,* ed. Russell Noyes (New York: Oxford University Press, 1956), 1193–194.

38. Rohn, *The Honest Look*, 35.

39. Kat Arney, "Book Review: The Honest Look by Jennifer L. Rohn," 2 Nov. 2010, https://katarney.com/2010/11/02/book-review-the-honest-look-by-jennifer-l-rohn/ accessed 4 July 2018.

40. GrrlScientist, "The Honest Look [book review]."

41. Daisy Brickhill, "Science and Sensibility," *Au Science Magazine* 3 (March 2012): 26.

42. Hans Oberdiek, "Midgley, Mary. *Science and Poetry*," *Ethics* (October 2003): 189.

BIBLIOGRAPHY

Abbott, Stephen. "Why I Love Tom Stoppard." *Middlebury Magazine* (Spring 2017): 28.

Arney, Kat. "Book Review: The Honest Look by Jennifer L. Rohn." November 2, 2010. Accessed 4 July 2018. https://katarney.com/2010/11/02/book-review-the-honest-look-by-jenni
fer-l-rohn/.

Brickhill, Daisy. "Science and Sensibility." *Au Science Magazine* 3 (March 2012): 26.

Campbell, Joseph. *The Hero with a Thousand Faces.* Novato, CA: New World Library, 2008.

Caudill, David S. "Expertise, Lab Lit, and the Fantasy of Science Free from Economics." *Cardozo Law Review* 33, no. 6 (August 2012): 2471–497.

GrrlScientist, "The Honest Look [book review]." Feb 7, 2011, *The Guardian*, www.theguardian.com/science/punctuated-equilibrium/2011/feb/07/5.

Herndon, Lynne. "Science, Meet Poetry." *Cell* 143, no. 7 (December 23, 2010): 1039. DOI 10.1016/j.cell2010.12.006.

Keats, John. "Ode on a Grecian Urn." In *English Romantic Poetry and Prose*, edited by Russell Noyes, 1193–94. New York: Oxford University Press, 1956.

Oberdiek, Hans. "Midgley, Mary. *Science and Poetry*." *Ethics* (October 2003): 187–89.

Ox, Jack, and Richard Lowenberg. "What Is the Challenge of Art/Science today and How Do We Address It?" *Leonardo* 46, no. 1 (2013): 2

Pilkington, Olga A. "Popular Science versus Lab Lit: Differently Depicting Scientific Apparatus." *Science as Culture* 26, no. 3 (2017): 285–306 http://doi.org/10.1080/09505431.2016.1255722.

Rohn, Jennifer L. *The Honest Look.* Cold Springs Harbor, NY: Cold Springs Harbor Laboratory Press, 2010.

Thomas, Vincent. "Creativity in Art." In *Creativity in the Arts*, edited by Vincent Thomas, 97–109. Englewood Cliffs, NJ: Prentice-Hall, 1964.

Turner, Victor. *The Ritual Process: Structure and Anti-Structure.* New York: Routledge, 1969.

Van Gennep, Arnold. *The Rites of Passage.* Chicago: University of Chicago Press, 1960.

Vardell, Sylvia M. "Connecting Science and Poetry." *Book Links* (November 2013): 16–18.

Wordsworth, William. "Preface to the *Lyrical Ballads*." In *English Romantic Poetry and Prose*, edited by Russell Noyes, 365. New York: Oxford University Press, 1956.

Chapter Ten

Addressing the Gender Gap in STEM through Theater

Eileen Trauth and Suzanne Trauth

STORYTELLING FOR SOCIAL CHANGE

This chapter tells the story about a collaboration between a scientist and a playwright to use literary fiction as a way to create awareness, stimulate attitude change, and inspire action about who can become a scientist. The purpose of this collaborative effort is to use theater to give voice to the subtle, emotional, and often subconscious forces that act upon young women, and that help to explain the underrepresentation of women in STEM: science, technology, engineering, and mathematics[1] The rationale for pursuing this departure from scientific writing is the belief that an artistic rendering of this topic through lab lit is an effective way to create awareness about the biases that exist in society and that are transmitted through cultural norms and values. These biases, in turn, influence gender roles and become the barriers that are both imposed upon and internalized by young women. Hence, a medium of creative artistic expression, such as theater, is particularly suited to representation of the subtle and emotional dimensions of these barriers because it enables one to "show it, don't say it." The major outcome of this collaboration is the play *iDream*[2] that tells a story about experiencing, internalizing, and overcoming barriers to inclusion.[3] It has been performed in multiple venues since 2012. An extension of the playwriting project is the more recent collaborative development of short scripts intended for audience interaction via live theater or digital media. The ultimate objective of all these theatrical products is to stimulate conversation about one's hopes and dreams, and how they can be achieved—or contravened.

This essay traces, from earliest insights to the present, a project to characterize the world of information science and technology, the people who work in this field and what they do in their everyday lives, and to highlight some of the reasons for the underrepresentation of women and other marginalized groups in this STEM field. While lab lit often employs the novel as its literary genre, this essay demonstrates how theater is a valid literary genre for lab lit as well. It begins by tracing the process of developing and performing *iDream*. This is followed by a discussion of the ways in which *iDream* attains the goals of lab lit. The essay concludes by looking forward to follow-on dramatic works that extend our corpus of lab lit.

THE *IDREAM* PROJECT

The scientific research that inspired the play project came from a qualitative field study of 123 women working in the contemporary information science and technology (IT) profession in the USA.[4] These women were asked to tell their life stories about preparing for, entering, and working in this scientific field. During open-ended interviews that ranged from one to three hours in duration, the women discussed their life stories and the individual journeys that led each of them to their current positions in the IT field. They discussed their demographics, the type of work they did, personal characteristics, significant others in their lives, and influences from the larger society regarding gender roles and working in a technical field. At the outset of each interview Eileen explained her interest in understanding the various ways in which women were exposed to, experienced, and responded to gender barriers throughout their careers.[5]

This research was guided by a gender theory that she developed: The Individual Differences Theory of Gender and IT. According to this theory the gender imbalance in the IT field can be explained by the interaction of three sets of factors (theoretical constructs). The first is the variability of individual identity: demographic characteristics (such as age, ethnicity, sexual orientation, socio-economic class),[6] and type of IT work (such as computer hardware development, software design, or IT user support). The second factor is varied individual influences: personal characteristics (such as personality traits, abilities, and self-esteem) and personal influences (such as role models and mentors). The third factor is variety of environmental influences (such as differing cultural norms about gender roles).[7]

During the interviews the women talked about the IT field as a man's world, pressures on women in the IT field, and how these pressures affect their professional development and working lives. They also talked about the relationship between working in the IT profession and a woman's gender self-image. Finally, they talked about the variety of ways in which women in the IT profession cope with the challenges presented to them.

While this research was being conducted, Eileen Trauth did not expect her results to have a direct impact on those who were experiencing the biases and barriers, nor on those who could change this situation. She had not envisioned developing a play script as a way to enact change regarding gender barriers. However, Eileen had been thinking about the use of literary genres to spark interest in scientific careers (and barriers to entering them) since the early 1990s when she witnessed the influence of the hit television series *LA Law* on increased law school enrollments.

As her research progressed, the evocative and emotionally compelling nature of the women's stories became ever more apparent to her. Meanwhile, Suzanne Trauth has written plays which incorporate scientific themes about the environment (*Katrina: The K Word*) and nuclear energy (*La Fonda*) and has employed field interviews to inform her playwriting (*Katrina: The K Word*). As sisters, Eileen and Suzanne often talked about their respective projects and began to consider the possibility of writing a play (Suzanne's domain) based upon Eileen's scientific research.

With a grant from the National Science Foundation (NSF) they embarked upon a project to write and perform an original play—*iDream*—that translated Eileen's research findings into theater. The goal was to disseminate Eileen Trauth's research findings to a wider audience in order to have an impact on those who were experiencing biases and barriers, and those who could do something about it. Thus, the play would create awareness, stimulate attitude change, and inspire action about the IT profession and who can participate in it.[8] Creating awareness means that the audience would believe what is presented in the play about biases and barriers affecting women in IT. But these research results would be *shown* to the audience through dramatic portrayal rather than being *told* to them through some scientific publication. Stimulating attitude change means that the audience would care about this topic of gender biases and barriers in scientific careers. Inspiring action means that the audience would be motivated to do something to address these biases and barriers. For young people, it would mean resisting the biases that would hold them back. For adults (parents, teachers, counselors) it would mean doing their part to remove these barriers. The NSF funding supported development of a play script and the production of a series of staged readings in order to obtain developmental audience feedback that would inform subsequent revisions of the script. That project is completed, and the play script is currently available at the *iDream* website for those interested in reading or producing the play.

The characters, plot, and dialogue of the play come from Eileen Trauth's research[9] on the gender imbalance in the IT field.[10] The characters in the play embody the struggles of those who are marginalized in the IT field by virtue of gender in combination with ethnicity and socio-economic status, but who seek inclusion and equality in the information society.[11] This dramatic presentation of the universal themes of experiencing and overcoming barriers to inclusion is intended to have universal appeal beyond the context of this project (i.e., gender barriers in STEM).

In the play, three young women are high school students confronting an uncertain future: whether or not to go to college, what they might study, and how to make that happen. Khadi, who is African American, becomes interested in computer engineering and robotics, but she lacks sufficient mentoring because her father is deployed in the military overseas, and her mother works two jobs. She also has responsibility for taking care of her younger brother while her mother is at work. Theresa, who is Latina and interested in gaming and computer science, is caught in a dilemma. On the one hand, there is her family's expectation that she will earn money immediately after graduation to help support her family. On the other hand, there is her desire to attend college and delay earning money. Amanda, who is white, becomes interested in cybersecurity, but she lives with her single mother who didn't graduate high school and has low expectations for her daughter. The three young women are encouraged in their efforts by Ms. Donahue (Ms. D), the dynamic teacher of their Digital Design course who recently left industry to become a high school computer science teacher. Supporting members of the cast introduce the biases and barriers that might hold Khadi, Theresa, and Amanda back from achieving their respective dreams. As *iDream* unfolds, we see them begin to discover their places in the world even as they struggle with personal, societal, family, and academic obstacles that threaten to prevent them from following their dreams.

There are two intended audiences for the play. Teenagers constitute the primary intended audience—those who might be experiencing and internalizing barriers to participation in the IT field. The secondary intended audience consists of significant adults in teenagers' lives: parents, teachers, coaches, guidance counselors, and others who are in a position to influence them. Hence, while performances of this play are intended for younger audiences, in order to make the play appealing to adults as well, some themes that were intended primarily for this secondary audience were also embedded in the play script. An example is an adult's effort to hold a young person back from pursuing a dream out of a desire to protect her from the same trauma she experienced.

To date there have been ten staged reading performances of *iDream*. The play premiered in Washington, DC in June 2012 with professional (i.e., Equity) actors. It was the keynote event for a conference of several hundred scientists sponsored by the National Science Foundation. The attendees were all engaged in NSF-funded STEM research. This performance was followed by five staged readings of the play in October 2012, again with professional actors. Three were in New Jersey and two were in Pennsylvania. Each of these initial performances was followed by audience talkback sessions held immediately afterward. Following each event, the script was revised. The final version of the play was completed in 2013 and, under the terms of the grant, was made available to the public.[12] Subsequent performances have been at universities in Nebraska, Utah, and Ohio. A full production is currently under development in Australia.

THEATER AS LAB LIT

iDream adds to a body of theatrical works that speak to STEM topics. As mentioned above, Suzanne Trauth's play *Katrina: The K Word*[13] engages with elements in the natural environment, and her play *La Fonda*[14] is about nuclear science. Another play on a similar topic is Herb Du Val's *Einstein at Cutchogue*.[15] Additionally, Vince LiCata wrote the play *DNA Story*[16] to teach non-scientists about DNA structure and X-ray crystallography.[17] Playwright Lauren Gunderson has written two plays about women scientists. *Silent Sky*,[18] based on real characters, tells the story of women astronomers who have been often overlooked in the history of this scientific area. And her play *Ada & the Engine*[19] is about Ada Lovelace (daughter of Lord Byron)—who lived from 1815 to 1852 and is considered to be the world's first computer programmer—and Charles Babbage, who developed the analytical engine, a prototype of the modern computer.

iDream enacts the goals of lab lit by using the creative and expressive genre of theater to depict the culture of science and those who work in it. The play, through characters, plot, and dialogue, teaches science fundamentals, illuminates the world of science, and shows characters as (current and would-be) scientists. Further, the play's storyline and characters also show the connections between the scientific field of information science and technology, on the one hand, and art and music, on the other.[20]

One of the main characters, Ms. D, has just left her job working for an IT company to become a high school teacher. Several scenes take place in her course, Digital Design. In some scenes she is explaining the field to her students. She makes connections between information technology and artistic endeavors such as visual art and music by showing how IT skills can be combined with these interests. She takes the students on a field trip where they learn about the field of robotics. She also assigns a project to identify and interview computer and information scientists to learn about what these people do in their everyday work. In another scene the students are studying for a test in which they reveal what they are learning about the IT field.

THERESA: Come on. We've got to get serious. We have a test Monday.
KHADI: Everyday use of IT?

AMANDA: Tweeting and texting.
KHADI: Robots cleaning up the BP oil spill.
THERESA: Computer games like Bubble Shooter that you can play on an iPhone or more complex games like Starcraft II that took about 10 years to create.
AMANDA: Using intelligence information to like find out where terrorists are hiding. Or developing software to protect yourself from identity theft.
THERESA: Business use?
AMANDA: Robots in factories.[21]

A major objective of the play was to open up the world of IT professionals and enable the audience to see possible IT careers. *iDream* depicts the world of information science and technology to a lay audience through the devices of classroom scenes described above and through the story arc about the evolving interest in an IT career by three young women in the course: Khadi, Theresa, and Amanda.

All of the main characters in *iDream* are scientists or would-be scientists. Ms. D, the teacher, is a computer scientist who recently left her work in the information technology industry after twenty years to teach high school computer science. Over the course of the play, the three girls, who are high school students in Ms. D's class, learn about the work of computer science and engineering. This occurs, in part, from a school assignment. They are told to find a computer professional working in an area that interests them and to interview the person in order to learn about her or his work.

MS. D: Here is your "careers in IT assignment." Take notes. I want you to go on the Internet and find someone who has a career that looks interesting to you. For example, Khadi could look into robotics and Titus could look into digital media.
AMANDA: Like how do we do that?
MS. D: Google a company or a university and find someone to interview. Email or Skype them. Find out what the person does and what kind of education he or she has.
TITUS: Then what do we do?
MS. D: Ask if they like what they do and why or why not. You might even score a summer internship.[22]

The assignment is a device to introduce the actual scientific work of computer professionals. Through this school assignment Khadi, Theresa, and Amanda become interested in their respective future scientific careers: robotics, computer gaming, and cybersecurity. But even as they are becoming exposed to the world of information technology careers, they are experiencing barriers to pursuing them.

THERESA: Papi tells me to get my nose out of the books and learn to do something practical so I can earn money for the family.

KHADI: Dad would say "yeah" but Mom is worried about money. I would need a scholarship or something.
AMANDA (mimics her mother): Mom says, "I'm not wasting good money on college when I'm not sure you'll even graduate high school." [23]

As Ms. D introduces the world of computing, she also shows the way in which scientists can engage in artistic practice as well. The course in which the students first learn about careers in this scientific field is not called "computer science" but rather "digital design," thereby invoking art. This was a conscious decision on the part of Ms. D in order to connect the IT field to a variety of artistic endeavors.

DARRYL: Yo, Ms. D, what's my field of interest?
MS. D: You could look into music technology. [24]

Over the course of the play, we learn that Darryl could connect computer science to music, Titus could express his artistic talents through digital media, and Theresa could learn how to design computer games by studying computer science in college.

Evidence of the success of the play in achieving its goal of portraying the culture of this scientific community came from audience responses during post-performance talkback sessions. Members of the audience believed that *iDream* "spoke" to them. [25] A mother commented that she didn't realize how broad the IT field was. Other audience members indicated that seeing the play changed their perceptions about who can pursue IT careers; they became more aware that the IT field is available to women and other underrepresented groups. One audience member commented on the accessibility of the presentation of IT careers in the play. One student liked the presentation of careers, saying that young people play video games, but they don't usually think about how they're made. A woman in the audience commented that after experiencing the play, she now knows that information professionals do more than just develop software. A young woman who was part of an inner-city teenage audience related the character of Theresa in the play to her brother, who has an interest in gaming and graphic design. She intends to tell her brother he could make a career out of developing video games. A high school teacher said she appreciated that the play portrays the struggles of students at home and the different cultures represented; it better prepared her to understand and help get students to graduate. Several audience members recommended that all high school students see the play. A college professor recommended that all first-year college students see the play in order to help clear up the confusion about STEM. A student in the audience asked that the script be made available to schools so that *they* could perform it. As a result of seeing the play, a mother asked about courses for her daughter to take that would help her to address gender bias in the IT community.

The interconnection of scientific and artistic practice permeates the entire project—a scientist (Eileen Trauth) works with a playwright (Suzanne Trauth) to tell a story about scientific findings through the medium of theater. As argued above, artistic practice—in the form of theater—can be employed to stimulate awareness, understanding, and activism about barriers to women in technological fields. Sociological knowledge about structural barriers to social inclusion reported in scholarly publications is generally inaccessible to the lay person. The scientific model of research dissemination leaves little room for the expression of subtlety, nuance, emotion, and holistic representation. However, theater employs dramatic ways of communicating research findings about the barriers imposed and internalized by women who aspire to technological careers. It offers a creative, dramatic outlet to give voice to the powerful emotions expressed by women about gender barriers in the IT field that would be silenced in conventional scientific journals. [26]

CONCLUSION

Theater provides ways of knowing about the world of science that go beyond cognition to empathy, contextual understanding, and the interconnectedness with culture and the environment. [27] As such, the intent of writing and performing *iDream* was twofold. One was to depict the world of information science and technology and those who work in it. Through the classroom scenes' assignments and story arc the audience is able to peer inside this scientific world to see the scientific work that is performed and the scientists who do it. The other intent was to employ a creative and expressive genre to portray the subtle experience of barriers to participation in this scientific field and the subconscious internalization of them. During the talkback sessions, audience members who had experienced being devalued as persons or as women of color were emotional in their responses; they related the characters to their own lives. Some female audience members related the play to their own experiences of gender stereotyping and being dissuaded from IT careers, or not being given the same opportunities as their male counterparts. One woman audience member said she could very much identify with Theresa because it brought back to her memories of her responsibility as the oldest child in her family. She was expected to help the family rather than undertake a career. But the play also depicts how these barriers can be recognized and overcome. As *iDream* progresses the audience witnesses the influence of supportive others on Khadi, Theresa, and Amanda—girlfriends, boyfriends, parents, teachers, and scientists themselves—and the blossoming of personal agency as a result.

The choice of theater to create awareness, stimulate attitude change, and inspire action about the IT profession and who can participate in it comes from theatre's superior ability to dramatize the ways in which young women are experiencing, internalizing, and overcoming barriers to inclusion. Using the literary genre of theater, in contrast to scientific publication, to communicate the results of research about the field of information science and technology, and barriers to entering it, expands reach beyond a scientific community to a lay audience. The project is a way of translating to a public audience what has been learned from research about barriers to the recruitment and retention of women information technologists.[28]

An additional goal in writing this play was to extend awareness and understanding beyond the experience of the play through post-performance discussions and workshops.[29] Such an outreach program involving *iDream* performances and post-performance IT career workshops was enacted in 2017 by the Hope Road Organization in Dayton, Ohio.[30] Young actors from Hope Road Organization, the community group, presented a staged reading of the play, thereby facilitating awareness about the issues. Following the performance was a panel discussion that focused on some of the issues that were raised in the play. Then, in the lobby outside the theater, local universities had set up information tables so that audience members leaving the theater could learn more about information technology careers and ways to prepare for them. This form of IT career outreach was a concrete example of the way in which the play can facilitate action inspired by watching a performance.

Performances of *iDream* with follow-on career workshops is but one way in which Eileen and Suzanne Trauth are using theater as lab lit to address the gender imbalance in science, technology, engineering, and mathematics. They have recently embarked upon another, related, theatrical lab lit project that broadens access to the story begun in *iDream*. This is being achieved by writing short scripts that build upon and extend the characters and storyline of the play. These scripts are also incorporating interactive features to enhance audience engagement with the subject matter. These short scripts are intended to be performed as interactive video storytelling or by students, themselves, as live theater.

NOTES

1. Eileen Trauth, "*iDream*: Addressing the Gender Imbalance in STEM through Theatre," Webinar Presentation to Society for Information Management STEM Outreach, September 26, 2016; Eileen Trauth, "*iDream*: Addressing Gender Barriers in STEM through Theatre," Presentation to Course: Transdisciplinary Creativity: Eco-social Justice Art, The Pennsylvania State University, University Park, PA, October 25, 2017; Trauth et al., "Using Theatre for Social Transformation," Presentation at 7th Conference of the European Research Network, Sociology of the Arts, Vienna, Austria, September, 2012.

2. More information about this play can be found at http://iDreamThePlay.com.

3. Eileen Trauth and Suzanne Trauth, *iDream* (New York: Writers Guild of America East, 2017), http://iDreamThePlay.com.

4. "A Field Study of Individual Differences in the Social Shaping of Gender and IT," National Science Foundation, #0204246.

5. For further explanation see: Eileen Trauth, "Odd Girl Out: An Individual Differences Perspective on Women in the IT Profession," *Information Technology & People, Special Issue on Gender and Information Systems* 15, no. 2 (2002): 98–118; Eileen Trauth and Jeria Quesenberry, "Are Women an Underserved Community in the Information Technology Profession?" Proceedings of the International Conference on Information Systems. Milwaukee, WI, December 2006.

6. For examples see: Lynette Kvasny, Eileen M. Trauth, and Allison Morgan, "Power Relations in IT Education and Work: The Intersectionality of Gender, Race and Class." *Journal of Information, Communication and Ethics in Society Special Issue on ICTs and Social Inclusion* 7, no. 2/3 (2009): 96–118.

7. Eileen Trauth, Jeria Quesenberry, and Haiyan Huang, "Retaining Women in the U.S. IT Workforce: Theorizing the Influence of Organizational Factors," *European Journal of Information Systems* 18(2009): 476–97.

8. "Addressing Gender Barriers in STEM through Theatre of Social Engagement," National Science Foundation, #1039546.

9. Eileen Trauth, "Odd Girl Out"; Eileen Trauth, "Are There Enough Seats for Women at the IT Table?" *ACM Inroads* 3, no. 4 (2012): 49–54; Eileen Trauth, "The Role of Theory in Gender and Information Systems Research," *Information & Organization* 23, no. 4 (2013): 277–93; Trauth, "iDream: Addressing Gender Barriers in STEM through Theatre."

10. For more information about this research see http://eileentrauth.com.

11. For more information see: Eileen Trauth, "A Research Agenda for Social Inclusion in Information Systems," *The Data Base for Advances in Information Systems* 48, no. 2 (2017): 9–20.

12. The play script and reading/performance licenses can be downloaded at http://iDreamThePlay.com.

13. Lisa S. Brenner and Suzanne M. Trauth, *Katrina: The K Word.* In *Katrina on Stage: Five Plays,* edited by Lisa S. Brenner and Suzanne M. Trauth (Chicago, IL: Northwestern University Press, 2011), 203–47.

14. Suzanne Trauth, *La Fonda* (National New Play Exchange, 2017), https://newplayexchange.org.

15. Herb Du Val, *Einstein at Cutchogue.* Personal copy from author.

16. Vince LiCata, *DNA Story.* Personal copy from author.

17. Trauth and LiCata, "Communicating STEM through Theatre," Presentation at Alliance for the Arts in Research Universities, Ames, IA, November, 2014.

18. Lauren Gunderson, *Silent Sky* (Dramatists Play Service, Inc., 2015), http://www.dramatists.com.

19. Lauren Gunderson, *Ada & the Engine* (National New Play Exchange, 2015), https://newplayexchange.org.

20. Jennifer Rohn, "What Is Lab Lit (the genre)?" *Lablit.com.* 2005 http://www.lablit.com/article/3.

21. Eileen Trauth and Suzanne Trauth, *iDream* (New York: Writers Guild of America East, 2017), http://iDreamThePlay.com.

22. Ibid.

23. Ibid.

24. Ibid.

25. Eileen Trauth et al., "*iDream*: Addressing the Gender Imbalance."

26. Eileen Trauth, "Cultivating Creative Information Practice: The Yin and Yang of the Research Process," Panel at iConference 2012, Toronto, CA, February, 2012.

27. Karen Keifer-Boyd et al., "STEAM Curricula: Adding Art to STEM," Presentation at Teaching Creativity in Higher Education: Current Trends and Critical Encounters, Wake Forest University, Wake Forest, NC, March, 2011.

28. Conrad Shayo et al., "Alternative Ways of Connecting IT Researchers with Target Public Audiences," Proceedings of the ACM SIGMIS Computers and People Research Conference, Milwaukee, WI, May–June, 2012.

29. Trauth, Eileen. "*iDream*: Addressing the Gender Imbalance in STEM through Theatre." Webinar Presentation to Society for Information Management STEM Outreach, September 26, 2016.

30. See: http://www.hoperoad.org.

BIBLIOGRAPHY

Brenner, Lisa S., and Suzanne M. Trauth. *Katrina: The K Word.* In *Katrina on Stage: Five Plays,* edited by Lisa S. Brenner and Suzanne M. Trauth, 203–47. Chicago, IL: Northwestern University Press, 2011.

Du Val, Herb. *Einstein at Cutchogue.* Personal copy from author. 2015.

Gunderson, Lauren. *Ada & the Engine.* National New Play Exchange, 2015. https://newplayexchange.org.

———. *Silent Sky.* Dramatists Play Service, Inc., 2015 http://www.dramatists.com.

Keifer-Boyd, Karen, Eileen M. Trauth, and Jennifer Wagner-Lawlor. "STEAM Curricula: Adding Art to STEM." Presentation at Teaching Creativity in Higher Education: Current Trends and Critical Encounters, Wake Forest University, Wake Forest, NC, March, 2011.

———. "STEAM Embodied Curricula: Creativity through Translate-ability, Sense-ability, Response-ability." In *Connecting Creativity Research and Practice in Art Education: Foundations, Pedagogies, and Contemporary Issues,* edited by Flávia Bastos and Enid Zimmerman, 88–94. Reston, VA: The National Art Education Association, 2015.

Kvasny, Lynette, Eileen M. Trauth, and Allison Morgan. "Power Relations in IT Education and Work: The Intersectionality of Gender, Race and Class." *Journal of Information, Communication and Ethics in Society Special Issue on ICTs and Social Inclusion* 7, no. 2/3 (2009): 96–118.

LiCata, Vince. *DNA Story.* Personal copy from author. 2009.

Rohn, Jennifer. "What Is Lab Lit (the genre)?" *Lablit.com.* 2005. http://www.lablit.com/article/3.

Shayo, Conrad, Kate Kaiser, Eileen Trauth, and Frank Lin. 2012. "Alternative Ways of Connecting IT Researchers with Target Public Audiences." Proceedings of the ACM SIGMIS Computers and People Research Conference, Milwaukee, WI, May–June, 2012.

Trauth, Eileen M. "Are There Enough Seats for Women at the IT Table?" *ACM Inroads* 3, no. 4 (2012): 49–54.

———. "Cultivating Creative Information Practice: The Yin and Yang of the Research Process." Panel at iConference 2012, Toronto, CA, February, 2012.

———. "*iDream*: Addressing Gender Barriers in STEM through Theatre." Presentation to Course: Transdisciplinary Creativity: Eco-social Justice Art, The Pennsylvania State University, University Park, PA, October 25, 2017.

———. "*iDream:* Addressing the Gender Imbalance in STEM through Theatre." Webinar Presentation to Society for Information Management STEM Outreach, September 26, 2016.

———. "Odd Girl Out: An Individual Differences Perspective on Women in the IT Profession." *Information Technology & People, Special Issue on Gender and Information Systems* 15, no. 2 (2002): 98–118.

———. "Plan, Play, Pressure, Pause: Engaging Creative Information Practices." Panel at iConference 2013, Ft. Worth, TX, February, 2013.

———. "A Research Agenda for Social Inclusion in Information Systems." *The Data Base for Advances in Information Systems* 48, no. 2 (2017): 9–20.

———. "The Role of Theory in Gender and Information Systems Research." *Information & Organization* 23, no. 4 (2013): 277–93.

Trauth, Eileen M., Michel Avital, Julie Kendall, Ken Kendall, and Richard Boland. "Out of the Box and onto the Stage: Enacting Information Systems Research through Theatre." Proceedings of the Thirty-Third International Conference on Information Systems, Orlando, FL, December, 2012.

Trauth, Eileen M., Curtis Cain, K.D. Joshi, Lynette Kvasny, and Kayla Booth. "The Influence of Gender-Ethnic Intersectionality on Gender Stereotypes about IT Skills and Knowledge." *The Data Base for Advances in Information Systems* 47, no. 3 (2016): 9–39.

Trauth, Eileen, Karen Keifer-Boyd, and Suzanne Trauth. "*iDream*: Addressing the Gender Imbalance in STEM through Research-Informed Theatre for Social Change." *Journal of American Drama and Theatre, Special issue, Alt Inq: Scientific Research and Inquiry in American Theatre* 28, no. 2 (2016): http://jadtjournal.org/category/vol-28-no-2.

Trauth, Eileen, and Vince LiCata. "Communicating STEM through Theatre." Presentation at Alliance for the Arts in Research Universities. Ames, IA, November, 2014.

Trauth, Eileen, and Jeria Quesenberry. "Are Women an Underserved Community in the Information Technology Profession?" Proceedings of the International Conference on Information Systems. Milwaukee, WI, December, 2006.

Trauth, Eileen M., Jeria L. Quesenberry, and Haiyan Huang. "Retaining Women in the U.S. IT Workforce: Theorizing the Influence of Organizational Factors." *European Journal of Information Systems* 18 (2009): 476–97.

Trauth, Eileen, and Suzanne Trauth. *iDream*. Writers Guild of America East, 2017 (WGAe # 1237535). https://iDreamThePlay.com.

Trauth, Eileen M., Suzanne Trauth, Karen Keifer-Boyd, and Jennifer Wagner-Lawlor. "Using Theatre for Social Transformation." Presentation at 7th Conference of the European Research Network, Sociology of the Arts, Vienna, Austria, September, 2012.

Trauth, Suzanne. *La Fonda*. National New Play Exchange, 2018. https://newplayexchange.org.

Chapter Eleven

Using Science in Writing Mystery Novels

Beverly Connor

Lab lit encompasses all genres of novel writing from mainstream to mysteries. It isn't science fiction, though a science fiction novel could come under the lab lit umbrella. The important factor is the integration and realistic portrayal of science and scientists in the story. The plot, setting, and characters have to be immersed in and influenced by the world of science. And the science cannot be made up. Just as researchers cannot falsify lab data in their research, lab lit writers cannot make up scientific facts and procedures for their fiction. The challenges and solutions of how to incorporate science into a novel are the focus of this essay.

All characters that inhabit the world of a novel must have credibility. This is certainly true of a character who is a scientist. An author cannot slap a scientist sticker on the forehead of a character and not have him or her behave like a scientist. A person who works in the sciences as a professional has years of education in the understanding of the scientific method and deep knowledge of her particular discipline. Scientists think in terms of their subjects. They have special languages that define and describe their subjects. All disciplines have their own terminology.

A fundamental rule in fiction writing is: character drives plot[1] A character who is not credible as a scientist cannot power a plot that has science as a major component. Often in the lab lit genre, major plot points[2] involve science. One can say that, like characters, science also drives the plot. Correspondingly, the setting has to reflect the particular scientific interest in the novel. So what the writer focuses on is (1) character: the scientist; (2) dialogue: the scientist's special terminology and syntax; (3) plot: driven by the scientist and science; (4) setting: infused with science; and (5) activity: scientists actually doing science. Weave all these elements together seamlessly, and the writer creates a satisfying lab lit read.

Amid all these factors the author must follow the rules of novel writing. A good novel pulls readers into its world and does not voluntarily let them leave. This is where the challenge of putting science into a novel begins. Every scientific discipline's knowledge builds upon itself. One has to know the basics in order to understand the advanced elements. If a reader thinks an author made up some bit of science, the author did not adequately give the reader the basics. After all, science can seem like magic if one doesn't know how she got here from over there.

I write two mystery series, both with protagonists who are scientists. One is an archaeologist and a physical anthropologist, the other is a forensic anthropologist and director of a museum. Science is integral to both series. Both characters are experts in their fields. It isn't enough that my archaeologist, Lindsay Chamberlain, knows that a specific Native American archaeological site had five structures, the occupants stored their pots on shelves, and which deer remains were hunted in the summer and which in the winter. Readers must understand how she knows what she knows. I have to figure out clever ways to keep readers up to speed without bringing them out of the story, without them feeling like the narrator is just giving exposition. A novel can't feel like a textbook, nor can it feel like the old grade B science fiction horror movies where the scientist explains correctly with hardly any data what is going on. I don't want my novel to look like a new car that has been totaled and put back together using different colors of doors and bumpers. No author can have readers stop reading and say, "She's just telling me how this works." How-this-works must be a seamless part of the world of the novel.

In the following scene from the novel *The Boric Acid Murder: A Gloria Lamerino Mystery (The Periodic Table Series Book 5)*, chapter 2, by Camille Minichino, meting out information is handled by conversation between Gloria Lamerino, the main character, who is a scientist, and Berger, who is a detective and a minor character. The information is important because it could contain a clue and a possible plot point. Matt, another main character, is not a scientist but a detective like Berger. Matt serves here as a naive character who knows very little science but needs to understand this particular bit of information, requiring that the science be simplified and clarified for his—and the reader's—benefit. The book is written in first person. The segment is narrated by Gloria Lamerino:

> "Am I the only guy here who doesn't know what boron is?" Matt asked after Berger and I spent a few minutes discussing how a work-related controversy could have led to Yolanda's murder.
> Matt and I both knew Berger would appreciate an opportunity to use his one year of college chemistry.[3]

Berger is a minor character in this novel and in this scene it is his job to provide the reader with basic knowledge that is reasonable for him to know—he has had college chemistry. For example, Berger knows basic facts about boron: it "is the fifth element in the periodic table. . . . And the most common boric acid is H_3BO_3: 'Boron was discovered by Humphry Davy in 1808. . . . The main use of boron compounds is as a bleaching agent in detergents.'"[4]

Several things happened in this passage. Detective Berger supplied basic information on boron. The reader now knows what it is. Matt further reinforces that by mentioning a common product that is familiar to everyone—20 Mule Team Borax. Matt is learning and the reader is learning. The passage is interspersed with comments, thoughts, and feelings so the reader does not get a constant narrative on boron. The interruptions—along the lines of "Most scientists I'd worked with would never pass a test on historical trivia. It was the present that mattered"[5]—along with the dialogue also provide opportunities to familiarize the reader with the personalities of the characters and show character development as time goes on in the story. At the end of the passage, when it is crucial to know how boron can be used in nuclear reactors, Berger passes the knowledge baton to Gloria, the actual scientist. The next passage shows how the scientist has deeper knowledge and understanding of the subject. The author gets to the real point of how boron is important and how it may be a clue to the murder that took place a short time before. At this point, Gloria explains:

> Boron is what we call a neutron poison. . . . It absorbs neutrons. That means it doesn't allow them to interact with each other, or with whatever other nuclei are in the way. . . . We need to be able to control the reactions of the neutrons. Putting a neutron absorber like boron into the system does that for us. Usually components will be made of boron, and a solution of boric acid will be used in cooling and waste systems.[6]

Again the passage is interrupted with interjections from the other two characters so the information is broken up and readers feel they are witnessing a conversation among three of the characters and not listening to a lecture. Having detective Berger give the basic information, and Matt adding the comment about 20 Mule Team Borax, readers feel a familiarity with boron when Dr. Lamerino explains its use in a nuclear facility.

Analogies are another way of helping readers understand scientific information. Comparing the science with something readers are familiar with is a fast way to bring them information about a bit of science that might otherwise be difficult.

The Oak Ridge National Laboratory (ORNL) adjoining my hometown of Oak Ridge, Tennessee, is home to Summit, the world's fastest supercomputer. Summit can make 200 quadrillion calculations per second—a number that few people can wrap their brains around. Steve Lohr, a *New York Times* reporter, won a Pulitzer Prize for explaining things well—Explanatory Reporting—taking difficult subjects and clarifying them. He wrote about Summit and described that huge number this way: "A person doing one calculation a second would have to live for more than 6.3 billion years to match what the machine can do in a second."[7]

Still a mind-boggling number, yet one that illuminates clearly what Summit can do, and it leaves the reader impressed with the machine's capabilities.

In *Dead Hunt: A Diane Fallon Forensic Investigation*, part of the plot hinges on epigenetics,[8] a wonderfully fascinating DNA topic that is not well known. A quantity of blood is discovered in Diane Fallon's apartment, a quantity too large to suggest anything but the death of the person who lost the blood. The main character, Diane Fallon, a forensic anthropologist and museum director, is in trouble at this point. Jin, Diane's employee and the head of the DNA lab, calls a meeting of the principals involved in the hunt for Clymene, an escaped murderer, the person whose blood is all over Diane's apartment floor. Jin is about to explain the concept of epigenetics—which will turn the plot around and lead it in a different direction.

> "Any idea what this is about?" Garnet gestured to the Christmas trees and the lined-up chairs.
> "Not a clue," said Diane. "Jin," she said. "What's this about?"
> "All in good time," he said, grinning.
> He was so hyperactive the marshals might think he had been drinking too much caffeine, but Jin was always like this. Whatever he was up to, he had told neither Neva nor David. This would be interesting.
> "I'm sure you all are wondering why I called this meeting," said Jin. "We're going to have a short workshop on genetics."
> "What?" said Deputy Marshal Dylan Drew. "You called us here for a workshop?"
> "Now, please bear with me, because the payoff is great," said Jin. "There's been some interesting progress made in the world of genetics lately. What I want to talk to you about is epigenetics. Epigenetics studies the changes in gene expression that don't require changes in the base sequence of the DNA itself."[9]

Already Jin the DNA expert has started out his talk with a statement that other scientists in the area, but no one else, can understand. But the reader suspects that since he has brought charts and tabletop Christmas trees with him, the information will become clear. The secondary characters, in essence, let the reader know that it is all right not to understand at this point. The interchange also highlights the personalities of the characters.

"Okay, son," said Deputy Marshal Chad Merrick, "you've lost me already. What the hell are you talking about and how does it affect me and my partner here? And can you please stop pacing and moving around?"

"He can't," said David.

Neva shook her head. "Nope, he really can't."

Jin ignored his coworkers. "I'm talking about making changes in the way genes . . ." He seemed to be searching his brain for a word. "The things that make genes function differently when the basic DNA is still the same."

"Not helping," said Merrick.

"That's why I got the Christmas trees," said Jin.

"I've been sitting here worrying about that," said Drew. [10]

After the playful interchange, we begin getting to the analogy and how it will help explain epigenetics.

"Say you have a gene for lung cancer but it is turned off, not doing anything. But because of your environment, say one full of secondhand smoke, a certain chemical group hooks onto your chromosome . . . like the decorations hooked onto a Christmas tree . . . and turns the gene on and you get cancer.

"Let's say these two identical Christmas trees were bought at the same place but taken to two different homes where they were decorated differently. The trees look different to us because of what's hanging on them, but underneath they are just alike. That's like two people with the same DNA who have lived in different environments."

Jin held a red tree ornament in one hand and a blue ornament in the other. "For two DNA sample profiles that look just alike on the base indicators, you can do an epigenetic profile, which means taking a little wider focus on the DNA structure, and see these differences," he said, indicating the different colored ornaments. [11]

Now, like the characters in the story, the reader is understanding the concept of epigenetics. Diane, who understands epigenetics, now sees what it means for her predicament.

The hairs on the back of Diane's neck stood up. She glanced over at Kingsley, who looked wide-eyed. Chad Merrick straightened up in his chair. "This has to do with Clymene or we wouldn't be here. Are you saying Clymene is a twin?"

"No, not a twin," said Jin, grinning.

Now Diane was confused. That is exactly what she thought he was saying. So did Kingsley and the others.

David looked at her as if to say, *I can't do anything with him.*

The marshals frowned at Jin. [12]

The explanation of the science is frequently interrupted by other elements in the story so that the narrative doesn't get too tedious and bring the reader out of the story. Here it is Jin's personality and the way he likes his information to unfold that interrupts.

"Let me tell you what got me to thinking about this," he said.

"If it clears things up, go to it, son," said Merrick. [13]

The science of DNA is not the only science being explained in this scene. The science of crime scene analysis [14] and how the characters who work to solve puzzles come to know what they know is also a part of the scene.

"Too many things didn't add up. For one thing, why didn't anybody in Dr. Fallon's apartment building hear anything? Were they all drugged? Let me tell you, if the odd couple across the hall heard a life-and-death struggle going on, they would have been over there, and so would the people from downstairs. And why was Dr. Fallon drugged to make her sleep through the whole thing? You have to ask yourself that."

Jin paused and looked out at his audience who were giving him their attention in hopes it would be made clear why they were sitting there listening to him.

"We study blood patterns in this unit," continued Jin. "If you have enough blood, it can tell you all kinds of things, from the shape of the drops to the pattern on the walls. And Lord knows there was a lot of blood. One thing I noticed was the cast-off blood pattern indicated a beating, not a stabbing, but what we found was a cleaned-up knife.

"And what about all that blood? We found no arterial spray, no spurting. Not too unusual. People can just lie there and bleed out after an attack, but what did the perp do while that was happening? Sit in Dr. Fallon's living room and wait? Then finally, at four pints of blood on the floor, got tired of waiting and dragged the body out? Why didn't we find more blood on the way to Dr. Fallon's car? Even if Clymene's heart had stopped, she would still have been leaking blood from her wounds. We only had a smear."

They all leaned forward, attentive now. Diane wasn't sure where he was going, but his analysis of the crime scene was interesting.

"But what really got me to thinking was, why clean the knife with kerosene . . . which is better than bleach, by the way, for getting rid of blood. Why clean the knife and then leave it in the trunk to be found alongside the blood? That made no sense. Then it hit me. They weren't trying to hide what was on the knife, but what *wasn't* on the knife." Jin paused for dramatic effect.

"Skin cells," Jin said. "It was a serrated knife. There should have been a lot of skin cells if it was the murder weapon. We found no skin cells."

"I take your point," said Garnett, "but what does this mean?"

"I'm getting to that," said Jin. "All of these questions led me to go back and resample the blood and do an epigenetic profile. And lo and behold . . ."

Jin flipped over a page on the chart, showing a drawing that looked to Diane to be an outline of the blood pattern on her living room floor. But Jin had drawn another pattern inside the outline.

"The blood on Dr. Fallon's floor came from two contributors with the same DNA. The blood was poured out of two containers that left overlapping patterns something like this." He traced the patterns on the chart with his finger.

"But the real kicker . . . Are you ready for this? I told you it would be great . . . Both blood sources matched Clymene's DNA . . . but neither matched her epigenetic profile. It wasn't her."

All eight of them sat staring at Jin as he lifted the piece of white fabric, revealing a third Christmas tree. This one was decorated with candy canes. There was silence for several moments. Finally Kingsley spoke up after looking open-mouthed at the three trees.

"Are you saying she is a triplet?" Kingsley said.

Jin's grin broadened. "She could be one of a set of quintuplets as far as we know. I just have three contributors."

"More important, are you saying she's alive?" said Merrick.

He and Drew exchanged glances and leaned forward as if somewhere in the three trees they might catch a glimpse of her.

"She could have gotten hit by a truck this morning and be dead, but she didn't die in Dr. Fallon's apartment," said Jin. "No one did, as far as the evidence shows. But two very anemic people left there."[15]

Scientists tend not to go beyond their data. It becomes a personality characteristic for some of them. In writing about characters who are scientists, having them act and think like scientists even in informal situations strengthens their credibility with the reader.

Then, at the end of the scene, Jin gives the reader a last bit of information about epigenetic profiles that further adds an important clue:

The two marshals did not look happy. "Can you tell us anything that will help us find her?" said Merrick.

"Nothing definite," said Jin. "But I can tell you something interesting." He brought the third tree around and set it beside the other two. "This is Clymene," he said of the tree with the candy canes. "The other two, the one with the red ornaments and the one with the blue ornaments, are her two sisters. There's been a lot of twin studies in epigenetic research. Twin babies have, as you would expect, very similar epigenetic profiles. The older they get, the more different experiences they have, the more divergent their profiles become. That's especially true in twins that have been separated at birth or at some other point in their lives. Clymene's two sisters have similar profiles to each other. Clymene's is very different."

"Clymene was separated from her two sisters at some point," said Kingsley. He was literally on the edge of his seat. "Is that what you are saying?"

"Yes," said Jin. "I don't know if that will help catch her, but I think it is interesting."[16]

Jennifer L. Rohn's novel, *The Honest Look,* takes a different slant on the description of science. Her main character, Claire Cyrus, a scientist, has the soul of a poet. Her descriptions of equipment, cells, her thought processes are described not in crisp descriptions, but softer images, like a Monet painting, and the reader can see it, see what she sees. The whole book is poetic prose that shows the reader a different way to look at science. One sees how Arts and Sciences came to reside in the same college at universities.

Here the analogy of spaces in the wall and cells flow like lines of poetry culminating in an idea of a medical breakthrough.

> She had part of her attention on a line of poetry she was worrying in her head, and part of an ear on the crickets, whose song this morning sounded a bit different, a bit muffled, a bit shifted towards the right of the room. She was wondering if the group—herd? swarm? school?—was in the wall itself, and if so, whether that space had different layers or compartments, spaces within spaces within spaces, cul de sacs formed by insulation or ductwork, each with its own unique acoustics. And then something about this possibility reminded her of the complicated three-dimensional set-up of spaces and tubes within cells, with their wonderfully old-fashioned yet evocative names: the endoplasmic reticulum; the Golgi Apparatus; the mitochondrial christae. Not full of migrating crickets, but of proteins, shuttling in and out of the vast microscopic motorway system, slip roads and roundabouts and tunnels and bridges, keeping everything running smoothly. And there, just then: the idea was born. Not about stroke, but about Alzheimer's disease. And not just a filling-in-the-gaps idea, but a trail-blazing idea. An idea that, if true, would kick off an entirely new avenue of research. And it was so simple, and so suited to the Raison's[17] strengths, that she was surprised she—or Alan or Ramon—had not thought of it before.[18]

The first example, from *The Boric Acid Murder*, illustrates the use of three characters, one of whom is the scientist, to illuminate a topic. The second example, from *Dead Hunt*, uses analogy to do the same thing—clarify science. There are other ways. The writer can simply have the scientist explain a concept, simplifying it, and still break up the scientific narrative so the passages don't seem like exposition.

Rohn in *The Honest Look* uses analogy in a different way. The analogy and the science become a dreamy thought process of the main character, yet still paint a clear and compelling picture for the reader.

Knowledge is one of the traits of a believable scientist character. When Gloria Lamerino from *The Boric Acid Murder* said she was "a little rusty" yet came through with a description of what boron does in connection with nuclear power plants, it was clear that "a little rusty" means something different to an expert than to a novice. In *Dead Hunt*, the DNA expert Jin's difficulty beginning his lecture with a simple explanation of epigenetics and his unwillingness to go beyond his data in fact showed his expertise to the reader. Simple descriptions and dialogue can reveal a character's facility with his or her knowledge and, woven throughout the novel, give the character growing believability as a scientist.

The characters' scientific knowledge and their facility with it, intertwined with revelations through narration and dialogue, contribute to the creation of a seamless, science-oriented novel. Having the scientific information actually furthering the plot creates a story where the science does not sound like it is from a textbook or tacked on as an afterthought. Jin moved the plot forward with every revelation of the DNA found in the blood samples from his boss's apartment and sent the plot in a different direction from where it began.

Setting is another element a novel needs to create a real world inside the story. Without a clear description of setting, readers have no bearings on where they are. For lab lit, adding the trappings of science—the laboratory, the equipment, the things that all scientists need to do their work—completes the scientific universe created between the covers of the book.

One compelling method of showing a setting is by listing things. Lists are a wonderful way of allowing the reader to stand in a room and look around at all the incredible things residing there. In *The Name of the Rose* by Umberto Eco, William of Baskerville is a nascent scientist in the year 1327. He values logic and loves the empiricism of Roger Bacon. He uses his unique perspective and skills to solve a murder at an abbey. In this passage he is visiting an infirmary—quite like a laboratory—with his ward, Benedictine novice Adso of Melk. Adso is the narrator.

> We had reached the infirmary. Venantius's body, washed in the balneary, had been brought there and was lying on the great table in Severinus's laboratory; alembics and other instruments of glass and earthenware made me think of an alchemist's shop (though I knew of such things only by indirect accounts). On some long shelves against the wall by the door was arrayed a vast series of cruets, ampoules, jugs, pots, filled with substances of different colors. "A fine collection of simples," William said. "All products of your garden?" "No," Severinus said, "many substances, rare, or impossible to grow in this climate, have been brought to me over the years by monks arriving from every part of the world. I have many precious things that cannot be found readily, along with substances easily obtained from the local flora. You see . . . aghalingho pesto comes from Cathay: I received it from a learned Arab. Indian aloe, excellent cicatrizant. Live arient revives the dead, or, rather, wakes those who have lost their senses. Arsenacho: very dangerous, a mortal poison for anyone who swallows it. Borage, a plant good for ailing lungs. Betony, excellent for fractures of the head. Mastic: calms pulmonary fluxions and troublesome catarrhs. Myrrh . . ."[19]

The reader sees Severinus's laboratory clearly. The equipment, the herbs come into focus simply because Severinus lists their presence. Adso's awe at these things brings wonder to the scene as does William's critical and suspicious eye.

In *Dead Secret*, I describe Diane Fallon's crime lab by using a long list with the intent of creating that same exciting sense of wonder at the shiny setting of the laboratory.

> The room was a warren of glassed-in workspaces outfitted with all the modern forensic equipment for various kinds of microscopic analysis, gas chromatog-

raphy, spectral analysis, electrostatic detection and computer analysis. The computers held national and international databases for fingerprint and DNA identification, as well as databases for fibers, shoe prints, bullet casings, tire treads, paint, hair, cigarette butts and several others that David had added. In addition, the computers had software that matched, categorized, imaged, mapped and correlated all manner of data. [20]

The magic of a crime lab is not simply in the wizardry of the characters' ability to draw critical information from scant, often skewed data, but in the machines they use, the databases that many readers didn't even know existed. It is a peek into a fascinating world of specialized methods, technology, and vast storehouses of accessible data relating to crimes and crime solving.

Setting interacts with characters and can be almost a character in itself. In *Skeleton Crew: A Lindsay Chamberlain Novel*, the setting dramatically impacts the plot as much as character. Lindsay and her forensics crew are excavating a Spanish galleon off the coast of Georgia in a cofferdam—a donut-shaped structure built in the ocean enclosing the ship that allows the archaeologists to work in the dry. [21] In this novel, the site, the cofferdam, the barrier islands, the ocean are the setting, and each place is like an organism with its own behavior patterns. This excerpt introduces the cofferdam and the site with its wonders and dangers.

The sun was just high enough that it made a diffuse golden avenue across the glittering blue-green ocean as the boat Lindsay rode in approached the cofferdam. The oval dam five miles out in the Atlantic Ocean off the coast of one of Georgia's barrier islands was a structural marvel that held back the ocean and allowed archaeologists to work on the ocean floor as if it were dry land.

The boat docked outside the dam where a young Native American held out his hand and helped her onto the dock. Luke Youngdeer, his name tag read.

"Dr. Chamberlain, welcome aboard." He grinned at her with even, white perfect teeth and nodded toward the pilot of the boat. "He'll take your luggage to the barge."

Lindsay looked up at the metal outside wall of the dam extending some nine feet above the waterline. "Wow, this is big!"

"Wait until you get inside," Luke said.

Lindsay climbed a metal staircase to the top of the dam and stood on the wide ring of sand shaped like an oval racetrack that filled the space between the two steel bulkheads of the cofferdam. The structure reminded her of the walls of a castle, protecting the keep within from the rising surge of water without. She looked down into the dry center of the dam at a large pump that, like the fifth Chinese brother who could hold the ocean in his mouth, had sucked out the water and revealed the ocean bottom and its wondrous treasures.

The Spanish galleon *Estrella de España*, once 123 feet from stem to stern, lay on her side, buried in the ocean bottom. When they had first uncovered her, she could have been a giant creature that had been laid to rest in a flexed position with the frames as ribs and the keel as a backbone. Now, with layers of silt and sand and her hull removed, she looked like any other archaeological excavation, with grid squares and walkways. But it was not hard for Lindsay to visualize the ship upright and new, in full sail gliding across the water.

The remains of the ship and its cargo were crisscrossed with scaffolding that kept the weight of the crew and equipment off the fragile wreck as it was being excavated. Several crew members were already stretched out on the planks, working under the tall roof shading the site. [22]

Lindsay Chamberlain is an archaeologist and in each novel works at a different site. Here she is involved in underwater archaeology as well as working inside the cofferdam. It is a wondrous setting, but the crew are working inside an anxiety-producing structure. The cofferdam has continuously running pumps to pump the water out because, as well built as it is, water seeps in and waves crash over the walls. And although it is big, it becomes claustrophobic after a while. In this place, they are doing their science. Excavating is not simply digging up ancient remains, but doing so in a careful and structured way so that each item is documented and very little data is lost. It is an outdoor laboratory. The archaeologists take various samples to look for pollen, bacteria, plant remains, protein antigens, and anything else that might be recoverable. They are doing this in a place that by its nature produces anxiety. Creating such a setting and having scientists do their work there is effective in the framework of a novel. It also makes the work of science as integral to the story as any other element of a novel.

We have discussed ways to provide scientific information without bringing the reader out of the story, ways to show that the scientist has credentials, how being a scientist can affect dialogue, how science can affect plot and scientific setting. These things all make the story a credible read. There is another thing that the writer must do in a lab lit novel: have the scientists do work—actual scientific work—and it must be work that pushes the plot along. In the Lindsay Chamberlain novel *Airtight Case* all of these elements are woven tightly together—and that is the goal: a tight fit.

The setting is a dig site, in particular, the excavation of a lead coffin in a trash pit. [23] The scientist in the scene is a minor character but plays an important part. She does the work and explains it. The scene becomes a plot point.

Juliana Skyler, expert in nondestructive evaluation, sat cross-legged in the pit with the coffin. "What we are going to do here," she told the archaeology crew with elaborate gestures, "is to see if the coffin is in good enough condition to be lifted out of the ground."

"If it isn't?" asked Drew.

"We'll have to open and analyze it here. Simply put, what we're going to do now is send different kinds of energy through the coffin. If the coffin is in absolutely perfect condition, whether it's heat, or sound, or electromagnetic currents being introduced, they will go through relatively undistorted." She moved her hands smoothly along the top of the coffin. "However, if there are flaws or weaknesses, the various currents and eddies will be distorted." She moved her hands across again, occasionally wiggling her fingers. "The degree or pattern of distortion tells us how serious the weakness is." Skyler spoke as if she had explained it a hundred times.[24]

Skyler does her work and the test shows that they can move the coffin. It is at this time that Skyler makes a discovery.

> They slowly moved it across to the waiting trolley. It was like watching the tiny Sojourner Rover inch along on Mars. Lindsay let out a breath when it was finally settled securely on its transport.
>
> "Well, who is that?" asked Juliana Skyler, standing on the edge of the pit, looking in. "The grave digger?"
>
> Lindsay threaded her way through the onlookers to the edge of the pit and followed Skyler's gaze. There in the bottom, crushed, displaced, and the color of the surrounding brownish red dirt, looking like a macabre bas-relief Picasso, were the remains of a skeleton. Were it not for the curve of a rib and the relative length of the femur, it would have been hard to tell they were the bones of a human, having been flattened for two centuries by the heavy weight of the coffin. Lindsay squatted for a closer view.
>
> "Is it human?" asked one of the men who had just hoisted the coffin onto the trolley.
>
> "Yes, it's human," answered Lindsay.
>
> Lewis had come up and squatted beside her. "Who is it?" he asked.
>
> Lindsay turned her attention to him for several seconds, a smile playing around her lips. "I don't know."
>
> "Could it have fallen out the bottom of the coffin?" asked Kelsey.
>
> "I think I would have detected that kind of breach in integrity," commented Juliana Skyler.
>
> The inescapable truth was that the coffin had been put in place on top of other remains.
>
> "Is it contemporaneous with the coffin?" asked Lewis.
>
> "Lewis. I'm squatting here looking at the bones for the first time, just like you are. How am I supposed to know?"
>
> Lindsay stood and dusted her hands. She glanced at the pit wall and the black charcoal layer only partially uncovered.
>
> "Probably is contemporaneous," she said. "We're still in the trash pit."[25]

It is the intricate weaving of the novel elements and the science that makes a lab lit novel work. Readers who choose the lab lit genre of novel want the science; they want to learn new and cutting-edge things. They also want to be absorbed in a good read. They want to be trapped by the spell of the book. Writers who have science in their books have to satisfy all these needs for the book to work. That is the challenge.

NOTES

1. Anne Lamott, *Bird by Bird: Some Instructions on Writing and Life* (New York: Anchor Books, 1995), 54; Sol Stein, *Stein on Writing*, (New York: St. Martin's Press), 49; Sol Stein, *How to Grow a Novel: The Most Common Mistakes Writers Make and How to Overcome Them*, 127.
2. A plot point is an event in a novel that takes the plot in a different direction.
3. Camille Minichino, *The Boric Acid Murder*, chapter 2.
4. Ibid.
5. Ibid.
6. Ibid.
7. Carmine Gallo, "How Expert Explainers Put A Mind-Boggling Supercomputer Into Human Terms."
8. Beverly Connor, *Dead Hunt*, chapter 32.
9. Ibid.
10. Ibid.
11. Ibid.
12. Ibid.
13. Beverly Connor, *Dead Hunt*, chapter 33.
14. Henry Lee et al., *Crime Scene Handbook* (New York: Academic Press), 2001.
15. Beverly Connor, *Dead Hunt*, chapter 33.
16. Ibid.
17. Claire's equipment that she named *Raison D'être*
18. Jennifer L. Rohn, *The Honest Look,* chapter 9.
19. Umberto Eco, *The Name of the Rose,* 107–08.
20. Beverly Connor, *Dead Secret*, 197–98.
21. "Discovery and Investigations: The Recovery of La Belle," *Texas Beyond History*; https://texasbeyondhistory.net/belle/excavations.html.
22. Beverly Connor, *Skeleton Crew*, 3–5.
23. R.C. Robbins et al. "Analysis of Ancient Atmospheres," *Journal of Geophysical Research* 78 (24), 1973: 5341–344; "Project Lead Coffins: The Search for Maryland's Founders. An Interdisciplinary Inquiry," Historic St. Mary's City https://www.hsmcdigshistory.org/pdf/Project-Lead-Coffins.pdf.
24. Beverly Connor, *Airtight Case*, 330–331.
25. Ibid., 343–45.

BIBLIOGRAPHY

Connor, Beverly. *Airtight Case: A Lindsay Chamberlain Novel.* Nashville: Cumberland House, 2000. Reprint, Oak Ridge, TN: Quick Brown Fox, 2013.
Connor, Beverly. *Dead Hunt: A Diane Fallon Forensic Investigation.* New York: Penguin, 2008. Reprint, Oak Ridge, TN: Quick Brown Fox, 2013.
Connor, Beverly. *Dead Secret: A Diane Fallon Forensic Investigation.* New York: Penguin, 2005. Kindle edition.
Connor, Beverly. *Skeleton Crew: A Lindsay Chamberlain Novel.* Nashville: Cumberland House, 1999. Reprint, Oak Ridge, TN: Quick Brown Fox, 2014.
"Discovery and Investigations: The Recovery of La Belle." *Texas Beyond History*; https://texasbeyondhistory.net/belle/excavations.html.
Eco, Umberto. *The Name of the Rose.* New York: Harcourt Brace Jovanovich, 1983.
Gallo, Carmine. "How Expert Explainers Put a Mind-Boggling Supercomputer Into Human Terms." *Forbes*, June 11, 2018, https://www.forbes.com/sites/carminegallo/2018/06/11/how-expert-explainers-put-a-mind-boggling-supercomputer-into-human-terms/.
Lamott, Anne. *Bird by Bird: Some Instructions on Writing and Life.* New York: Anchor Books, 1995.

Lee, Henry, Timothy Palmbach, and Marilyn T. Miller. *Crime Scene Handbook*. New York: Academic Press, 2001.

Minichino, Camille. *The Boric Acid Murder: A Gloria Lamerino Mystery. (The Periodic Table Series Book 5)*. New York: St. Martin's Press, 2002. Kindle edition.

Nessa, Carey. *The Epigenetics Revolution: How Modern Biology Is Rewriting Our Understanding of Genetics, Disease, and Inheritance*. New York: Columbia University Press, 2012. Kindle edition.

Project Lead Coffins: The Search for Maryland's Founders, An Interdisciplinary Inquiry, Historic St. Mary's City. https://www.hsmcdigshistory.org/pdf/Project-Lead-Coffins.pdf.

Rohn, Jennifer L. *The Honest Look*. Cold Spring, NY: Cold Spring Harbor Laboratory Press, 2011. Kindle edition.

Robbins, R.C., L.A. Cavanagh, L.J. Salas, Elmer Robinson. "Analysis of Ancient Atmospheres." *Journal of Geophysical Research* 78 (24), 1973: 5341–344.

Stein, Sol. *How to Grow a Novel: The Most Common Mistakes Writers Make and How to Overcome Them*. New York: St. Martin's Press, 2014.

Stein, Sol. *Stein on Writing*. New York: St. Martin's Press, 2014.

Chapter Twelve

Lab Lit

Illuminating a Hidden World through the Medium of Fiction

Jennifer L. Rohn

GENESIS AND INCUBATION

Fiction brings hidden worlds to life. Growing up as an avid reader of a wide array of novels, from mysteries, adventure stories, and romances to science fiction and classic works of literature, I took delight in immersing myself in the extreme diversity of past, present, and future worlds on offer. I also wrote from a young age, keeping a daily diary and creating literary worlds of my own.

In parallel, I grew to love the sciences, and studied hard throughout school and university to become a research scientist. My chosen specialty was biology, and while I'd been fascinated by visible nature as a child—insects, plants, stars, rocks—I soon homed in on the microscopic. Viruses and bacteria teem in their trillions under the surface of our everyday lives, and I wanted to understand how they worked, and to join the ranks of those laboring to find cures.

Despite my chosen research vocation, I still continued to use the written word as an outlet for my imagination, and to make sense of my life in a scribbled account confessed to an invisible audience.

I began a PhD at the Department of Microbiology at the University of Washington in Seattle in 1990, researching the fluid and mutable genetics of a common cat virus capable of inflicting tumors. Although the course of study was intense, time-consuming, and intellectually overpowering, the storyteller in me was frequently distracted by the surrounding laboratory culture. When I put on my white coat and slipped into the brightly lit world of shining glassware, stringent chemicals, and stainless-steel machines humming with a life of their own, I felt immediately at home.

My lab mates became a surrogate family, and my department, a small village where everyone knew everyone else's business. There, myths, superstitions, gossip, romance, petty feuds, and lore proliferated like bacterial cultures in a petri dish. I don't think I ever laughed as often or as hard as during those graduate school years, or shed so many tears—of frustration, heartache, anxiety, youthful uncertainty. Everything was heightened in that pressure-cooker of an environment.

It was—is—a world like no other, and scientists are the larger-than-life characters who populate this narrative. Simultaneously singular, and completely ordinary, scientists are driven and passionate, curious and smart, ambitious and competitive, critical and zany, earnest philosophers and practical jokers. Despite our focus in the lab world, we are passionate about other things too—literature, the arts, indie films, politics, fashion, gardening, music. The choice of music in the lab is, in fact, a fiercely fought battle. Both scientists and non-scientists, we move in and out of the lab world seamlessly, shedding our white coats and slipping into the real world at the end of a long day, anonymous "normal people" whom no one could pick out of a lineup; we become lovers and friends, parents and children, scout leaders and soccer coaches, neighbors and citizens.

As I am a chronic chronicler, forgive me for now telling a pivotal true tale that I have related in various outlets at various times. A few years into my PhD research, a colleague passed me a battered paperback novel doing the rounds in the labs. Dog-eared and margin-scribbled, with some passages highlighted in lurid yellow, it was a novel called *Cantor's Dilemma* by the late Carl Djerassi.

I was struck almost speechless by what I found within—not because the writing was particularly earth-shattering, but because it was a novel *about my world*. A novel about science. A *normal* novel, not science fiction with spacecraft, three-headed aliens or a near-future dystopia. Just a tale about a jobbing scientist, working in an actual, present-day lab. A professional going about his business, facing plot complications that can only happen in labs but which are entirely familiar if you are of that world, in a way that would also resonate with the uninitiated.

Based on the annotations within, and the enthusiasm with which the book was being shared, I wasn't the only trainee scientist excited by the unusual content. (The highlighted passages weren't racy sex scenes but instances of explicit biochemistry. One marginalia even enthused, *I did this exact experiment last week!*) I immediately went to the nearest bookshop to find more examples like it—and drew a blank. A genre without a name is not categorized in a helpful section; any examples could be dispersed absolutely anywhere. More research was clearly required to locate these needles in an immense literary haystack.

Thus began my quest, over the next decade or so, to seek out and read novels about scientists. In searching online and skulking in secondhand bookshops and libraries, I came up with about eighty examples during that period. There had to be more, surely: science is a global profession employing millions, and its outputs underpin all of the technology that fuels our modern lives—transport, infrastructure, medicine, food production, commerce. It's been estimated that 130 million books have been written to date.[1] There are many thousands of novels about detectives, doctors, artists, lawyers, people who work in offices or coffee shops or in retail—and, of course, about writers themselves. But where were all the scientist protagonists in everyday stories about modern life? Why were these characters invisible—except occasionally on the big screen, when they were often stereotyped beyond recognition?

Names are powerful, so namelessness is a weakness. In 2005, I decided to name the nameless genre and promote it in the hopes of attracting writers to this fertile and colorful world ripe for fictionalization. In some ways this was more of a rebranding exercise: Djerassi had used the term "science-in-fiction" to describe his work.[2] But I found the label too easily confused with science fiction, an allied but distinct genre that, in being so popular, did not need any cheerleading. (Indeed, science fiction can be off-putting to some readers, so—with apologies to science fiction authors everywhere, including some I consider my own heroes—it wasn't necessarily helpful to conflate the two.)

LAB LIT—AND LABLIT.COM—IS BORN

Back in 2005, I chose the term "lab lit"[3] to name the nameless genre because of its playful parallels with the then-trending, catchy term "chick lit." I also appreciated the word play of the double meaning of *lit*, as my mission was to illuminate the hidden world of laboratory life and introduce this culture to outsiders through the lens of fiction. In the same year, I founded a website, LabLit.com, to curate the main list of novels and to enfold it within an inspirational online magazine dedicated to scientific culture.[4] As its logo, I chose a slightly open door spilling out light into the darkness. This symbol was inspired by how evocative scientific institutions look at night when viewed from the street below—all those mysterious lit-up windows seem like portholes to a mysterious world, both enticing and impossibly strange from the outside.

What is lab lit, then, and what is it not? Here is the consensus definition currently on *Wikipedia*:[5]

> Lab lit (also "lablit") is a loosely defined genre of fiction, distinct from science fiction, that centers on realist portrayals of scientists and on science as a profession. . . . Unlike science fiction, lab lit is generally set in some semblance of the real world, rather than a speculative or future one, and it deals with established scientific knowledge or plausible hypotheses. In other words, lab lit novels are mainstream or literary stories about the practice of science as a profession. They may or may not center exclusively on the science or the workplaces of scientists, but all tend to feature scientists as central characters.[6]

The LabLit.com article introducing the list of books further explains:

> The action does not have to take place in a laboratory per se, just anywhere where scientists are doing what they do, such as a field station. Although some science fiction does indeed have elements of "lab lit," and the boundaries can be fuzzy, this list is meant to feature real scientists in the real world.[7]

The naming of lab lit started a small but growing movement dedicated to easing more science and scientists into mainstream fiction. The genre, and website, have been mentioned in the *New York Times*,[8] the *Boston Globe*,[9] and on US National Public Radio[10] to name a few media outlets. The name is now used generally, not just by me; released into the wild, it has thrived. Gratifyingly, new lab lit novels seem to be on the rise,[11] including those penned by famous authors; Barbara Kingsolver, Ian McEwan, Allegra Goodman, Tracy Chevalier, Elizabeth Gilbert, Joyce Carol Oates, and others have all published works featuring scientists as central characters, some historical and some wholly imagined.

The best outcome of the website's founding has been the nominations that have poured into my editorial inbox from all over the world, alerting me to books that I have missed in my years of research, including those in foreign languages. Thirteen years on from the founding of LabLit.com, the list now includes nearly three-hundred examples.[12] This is still an astonishingly small number, so a lot of work remains to be done. But my personal journey has come a long way from *Cantor's Dilemma*.

THE POWER OF SCIENCE NARRATIVES

The rarity of lab lit is also its advantage: authors can cover original ground not revisited thousands if not millions of times before throughout the centuries. The scientific profession offers a colorful setting: science takes place not just in labs, but in field stations, in outer space, in the seas and deserts and jungles, and within giant telescopes on remote mountainsides. It is complicated by competitive, all-too-human practitioners, often embraces deep ideas, is rich in opportunities for metaphor, and is punctuated by ethical landmines. The interface between science and society is often fraught, as the implications of research ripple far beyond the research team which produces the findings. Finally, science narratives can dispel the harmful illusion that science is "black and white" and progresses solely in a linear fashion, as opposed to the messy, argumentative way that it actually unfolds, at the whim of fashion and funding, and rife with accidental serendipity, blind alleys, and abandoned theories.

So what is lab lit fiction good for?

First and foremost, although some literary writers look down on this concept, I believe that the main role of fiction is to entertain. I see little point in the sort of novel that is conceived of as "serious" or "experimental art" but which no one really enjoys reading—but that's a personal view.

If we take as a baseline assumption that novels are meant to entertain and inspire, I am not therefore a big fan of the use of lab lit fiction as a pedagogical tool to "teach" people about scientific facts. However, a good lab lit story will manage to slip in facts or ideas that a reader might not have known—but this is not unique to a science novel; it's almost de rigueur for good fiction generally.

Nor do I think that lab lit should be used as propaganda—to "preach," for example, about how we should allow unfettered research or always support what scientists do, or as a recruitment tool to entice the next generation into the profession. I have encountered scientists who feel uncomfortable when scientist characters in novels are portrayed doing something morally wrong, or when a lab lit novel highlights the many unpleasant and sometimes outright unaspirational aspects of an academic career in science. While fiction's role is to entertain, it does not follow that it must make people feel comfortable; again, one hallmark of good fiction is probably shaking people out of their comfort zones.

What lab lit fiction *can* do is to portray scientists as human beings, with all of their good points and foibles fully on display: the good, the bad, and the ugly. This, I believe, is one of the most powerful beneficial side effects of a good lab lit novel.

CENTURIES-OLD STEREOTYPES

Why is showing scientists as human beings a good idea—or to rephrase the question, why should we care if scientists are portrayed inaccurately, or not portrayed at all?

It all comes down to the problematic stereotype of scientists. In 1957, the anthropologist Margaret Mead published a study of 35,000 North American high school students who were simply asked: "When I think of a scientist, I think of . . ."[13] The answers variously described a middle-aged or elderly man in a white coat wearing glasses, who was unkempt, often with a beard.

He was said to be surrounded by bubbling test tubes, and to be boring, working all the time, and neglecting his family. Women did not feature in the answers.

Although the stereotype has improved somewhat in recent years, a quick Google image search of "scientist" will still throw up a large number of mad or evil-looking male scientists with messy hair, spectacles, and a beard, familiar to anyone who's been exposed to films or comics over the past century.

Some traces of the scientist stereotype are ancient and probably originated in ancient Greece. For example, the playwright Aristophanes lampooned Socrates, his contemporary, in *The Clouds*. Socrates and his crowd were portrayed as intellectuals who were meddling in the sphere of the gods, and the play has been said to reflect "humankind's ambivalence toward knowledge and the limits we feel that we must set in our pursuit of it."[14]

Similarly, the myth of Daedalus casts an unflattering light on the Cretan inventor; he tests feather and wax wings on his son Icarus, who, in turn, inevitably flies too close to the sun and plummets to his death.[15] This myth highlights the Greek concept of "hubris": if you stray into the territory of the gods, you will get burned. It also nicely encapsulates the sense, still very much with us today and rehashed ad nauseam in science fiction B-movies, that scientists, even well-meaning ones, are toying with potentially dangerous knowledge that "man was not meant to know," and are at risk of losing control of their own experiments. Much later, the behavior (and physical appearance) of the alchemists probably did much to fuel the stereotype of strange, meddling, and dangerous men of science.[16] And of course, the Manhattan Project, culminating in the destruction of Hiroshima and Nagasaki, would not have done much to dispel this impression.

Anyone who has been to the cinema in the past three decades will have noticed a renaissance in Hollywood scientists, who are now diverse in gender and race, and impossibly young and beautiful—many with designer spectacles. As a plus, thanks to the growing trend for science consultants, they and their science are also more realistic.[17] But the underlying sense of hubris and losing control of experiments still plays out in many films about scientists. A good example of this is the 2007 film *I Am Legend*.[18] The premise is that a highly effective and feted gene therapy for cancer based on the measles virus suddenly mutates and spreads, transforming all who contact it into monsters. Although the scientist in question—played by Emma Thompson—is worlds away from the physical stereotype of a B-movie scientist, the underlying message is that she has lost control of her experiment and (almost) destroyed the world. Her smug hubris and arrogance is almost palpable in Thompson's brief cameo appearance.

Movies are just a bit of fun. Again, why should scientists care what people think of them? The answer is that science promises solutions for many of society's most urgent problems, and scientists have many important messages to share with the public. For example, childhood vaccines are safe and effective, but people are turning away from them in droves, trusting fear-mongering conspiracy theorists more than trained experts. As a result, out-breaks of potentially deadly diseases are killing children in isolated pockets of the world. Similarly, the bulk of scientists believe that climate change is caused by human activity and that not reversing its effects will have serious ecological consequences, but this message is not heeded by a large number of people, including some in positions of authority with the power to regulate in favor of mitigating global warming.

People don't trust the message if they don't trust the messenger. So a pervasive view that scientists cannot be trusted with their own experiments, and that they are meddling with dangerous things in hidden, inscrutable labs, will not make them reassuring emissaries for evidence-based information crucial for saving lives and improving conditions on this planet. People fear what they don't understand, and if they don't understand what drives scien-tists and the fact that they are human, they won't be as likely to heed. On the other hand, scientists merely showering people with facts and figures, under-lining their academic credentials, and expecting people to listen because "we know best" is a recipe for disaster in the current era of "fake news" and rampant distrust of experts. Instead, as unpalatable and unscientific as it might seem, scientists might have to take a leaf out of the charismatic snake-oil peddler's book and work on their image.[19]

So what is the best way to shatter the stereotypes that hold scientists back from getting their important messages across? It is clearly important for scientists to engage with the public, getting out of their labs and presenting their work in an arena where the dialogue can be two-way. Science commu-nication is big business now, and most researchers are aware of their obliga-tions in this sphere. Even the bodies that dispense research grants are now expecting their fundees to make an effort.

I would argue, however, that these traditional efforts are not enough. And here is where the lab lit project comes into its own. Fiction is an excellent stealth medium for imparting the idea of the human face behind science. A museum exhibition about science, or a non-fiction popular science book, might attract thousands of people, but it's likely that this audience is already primed to be sympathetic to the topic. Not only, then, are they preaching to the converted, but such efforts will inevitably, with some exceptions, center on the knowledge, not the people who have gathered it. In contrast, one Hollywood blockbuster featuring a well-drawn scientist could attract mil-lions, including a large proportion who are indifferent, or even antagonistic, to the idea of scientists and science. Packaged into an entertaining story, scientist protagonists can be seen as humans—flawed, well meaning, con-flicted—and their motivations can be laid bare.

Scientists, with a very few well-known exceptions, are largely invisible in public life. By infiltrating popular culture—even in fictional form—their increasing familiarity may well go a long way toward changing the image of the profession. In doing so, it may be possible to counter the growing tide of internet-based charlatans whose seductive, non-scientific, and sometimes actively harmful messages are currently swamping out the politely academic arguments that society needs to hear.

INTRODUCING THE CASE STUDY

I don't want to spoil the lab lit story that follows by dissecting it too much in advance. This work is inspired by a real-life controversy, now largely laid to rest, about a virus called XMRV, which I describe in the afterword. Suffice it to say that I have always been interested in the non-scientific impulses that motivate scientists and those who support science. It is probably safe to assume that "knowledge for knowledge's sake" is not the primary driver for most researchers. I am also interested in the common phenomenon of hypothesis bias, which happens when people want so badly to believe in their own theories that they ignore evidence to the contrary and carry on trying to "prove they are right" long after they should have gracefully surrendered. No one should be surprised by either concept, given that scientists are human beings, but the myth of stoic, almost robotic objectivity remains strong, and it is one of the main barriers holding scientists back from being effective messengers.

LATENT

A Short Story by Jennifer L. Rohn

I searched for the paper every morning, scouring the online journals and abstract listings. I knew it would come out eventually.

And then, one day, there it was, in a journal whose name was so prestigious that merely appearing within its pages could jump-start an entire scientific career. Although I had been expecting it, the absence of my name from the author list was a kick in the stomach.

Scrolling down with beating heart, I took it all in: my idea, my methods, many of my data figures . . . and my painful, inexorable conclusions, all beautifully framed and embedded in the most compelling of narratives. Not exactly fiction, but nevertheless as idealized as a Photoshopped selfie.

At the very end, under the heading of acknowledgments, my name was finally mentioned. Thanks were owed, apparently, for my "helpful advice and discussion."

And that is how the discovery would always be remembered—the triumph of someone else only peripherally involved. It happens all the time: science swallows up individuals and spits out mythology. Truth is forged by the telling. The facts may be pure, but the history of their generation is a white lie.

And surprisingly, it works—it always has. It sends men to the moon, detects bosons, cures cancer.

But it's best to look the other way when there's collateral damage.

The world is full of questions. And I'm not talking the sort whose answers appear upside-down in small print at the bottom of next week's crossword puzzle. I'm talking about questions whose answers are so tenuous that you're not even sure the initial question was valid. I'm talking about questions that throw back a hundred possible answers, or a thousand, except that there's no way to tell which of them are correct. Oh, they're all answers all right, but they probably aren't answers to the question you thought you were asking in the first place.

Looking right, then left, then right—then a quick left again—I cross the road. The street is empty, but though I've lived in this country for nearly twelve years, I still have no visceral certainty in the flow of its traffic.

It's one of those tricky late-autumn London afternoons: four o'clock but already full dark, the body clock swindled into premature hunger and the urge to head underground for the journey homeward. And the emptiness is a trick, too: a few seconds later the road refills with cabs, sliding around the corner I've just crossed, bumper to bumper like ebony beads on a string. Ahead, I dodge a sudden surge of pedestrians in the city's winter uniform of drab black. My right hand holds closed the collar of my own similarly colored V-necked overcoat, tailored more for feminine style than protection as rain-flecked air funnels down the university thoroughfare.

Some answers, I think, are like chestnuts. I remember the first time William took me nut hunting up in Yorkshire. In the country where I grew up, we had plenty of horse-chestnut trees, but true chestnuts had long since been wiped from the map by fungal blight. William's northern woods had been silent, long lazy hills of sparse growth, a thin, flame-colored canopy allowing dusty streaks of sunlight. The chestnut trees were disproportionately large for such a flimsy forest: golden bark crisscrossed with undulating lines; vast yellowing leaves, the pointed ovals drooping from branches and forming a thick layer underfoot.

William taught me how to push a stick through the rich leaf mold under the trees, turning over soil shot through with moss, bark, and sinister pale toadstools until the gleaming nuts, burnished like alien artifacts, were released, along with the ancient smell of the leaf litter, damp and brown and redolent of fairy tales about children losing their way, of changelings and enchantments and merry men. He told me not to bother with the nuts still in their fearsome green cases, but using two sticks I soon devised a way to impale their soft, prickled innards until the shining objects would slither out, imagining as I did a long chain of women stretching back to Paleolithic times working out that same technique as their William counterparts focused on the easier prizes, or forewent unglamorous gathering altogether in favor of bludgeoning unsuspecting mammals in the next grove.

I pass one of the many private gardens that dot this city, a fenced rectangle of deep unpopulated green. I can smell hardcore autumn seeping through the pointed iron bars, and then a whiff of floral scent, something pink-blushed ivory and delicate. In this mild climate, things can bloom all year long, evidence of spring hopelessly mixed up with winter in a way that just feels wrong to me—in a way that contaminates an otherwise solid body of evidence.

I'm on my way to an informal job interview, but I don't feel even the slightest twinge of nervousness. Not anymore. I've been at this game for so long that I know exactly what I am: a highly skilled gun-for-hire. I won't even consider working for someone who doesn't instantly recognize my worth. If the fit isn't right, I'll find something else. William would be relieved—but then again, maybe he wouldn't. Maybe I'll actually manage to convince him that my ass-backward plan is sound.

I may not be nervous, but I do feel the usual quick-step of curiosity. Curiosity, my stock in trade. My modus operandi. The place will look like every other laboratory I've worked, and my possible future colleagues much like those of the past. Interchangeable, William always says whenever he sets foot into whatever domain I'm currently perched. But the questions will be different, and the vast array of answers, and the stratagems they will employ to throw me off the scent. And because of the unconventional scheme that I have cooked up on William's behalf, everything will be entirely one-eightied: my desires, my expectations, my approach. The textbooks say there's only one method, but the textbooks are crap. Trust me: the only thing scientific about the scientific method is that it's done by scientists. The rest is desire, intuition, narrative-tweaking, and retrospective rationalization.

I negotiate a zebra-crossing, locking the grudging cab driver in eye-contact, signaling mutually assured destruction. The lemon globes flash on their grayscale barber poles, light fuzzy-focused in the drizzle.

Sometimes we carry the answer inside us, with no idea that it's lodged there all along, a quiet secret that might never be discovered if no one thinks to ask the right question.

****

He makes me wait fifteen minutes on the leather sofa on the first landing, a red two-seater creased by the ghosts of a thousand PhD wannabes and bored biotech sales reps. At least it's the man himself who finally arrives, not a harried post-doc pressed into service to make him look important. As he sticks out his hand and murmurs apologies, I take in the sharp jacket and designer spectacles: cut glass and jade-colored struts disappearing into a well-clipped haircut. Unusually, he doesn't look older than his university webpage would have us believe.

"You look younger than I thought you would," he says—a mind-reader? Did I want to work for a mind-reader?

The handshake is firm, not too long, not too short.

"I moisturize," I say.

He smiles, beckoning me down the corridor. In my peripheral vision, the labs are bright outposts on my left and right, their yellow fluorescence bleeding into the darkened tunnel we navigate. I see young people in standard tableau: crouching over apparatus, pipetting into patient rows of tubes, surfing the internet.

"I didn't mean to be rude," he says. "It's just your CV—it's . . . "

"Epic?"

"Something like that." The smile grows twitchy in profile—a man laughing at himself. Very English. "You've got more papers than I do, you know."

"I know. They're just nowhere near as exciting. Also, I'm older."

"You didn't have to tell me that—HR regulations and all that."

"I'm sure any idiot could subtract the year I got my PhD and work it out."

He shrugs. "True—it's all bollocks anyway. Here we are."

The office is tiny, scarcely room for the second chair. But he has a shockingly expensive looking computer screen and, out of the Art Deco windows, a strategic view of the Quad. Undergraduates swarm the pavement, heads down in the rain—a mix of hair, hats, umbrellas, headscarfs, and the odd hijab from this angle. Before I turn back to my quarry, I catch sight of a spiral of leaves meandering through empty air into darkness. A warm breathiness in one corner: an overworked inkjet printer on standby.

His chair creaks as he leans back—the aforementioned epic CV suddenly in his hand.

"It's all very impressive," he says. "But what's the real story? Why aren't you a lab head by now?"

I wonder if this man might be too sharp for his intended role in my plan. "Nothing sinister," I say. "I just have no interest in becoming a pencil-pusher."

"Touché. Although I do still dabble with the occasional experiment, you know."

"I don't want to 'dabble,'" I say. "I'm an excellent scientist. When I do something in the lab, it works. If you put me in an office and ask me to write grants, sit on committees, and lecture students, it would be a waste of my talents."

He studies me. But everything I've said so far is true, so my expression is above reproach.

"Are you sure this isn't just post-hoc rationalization? You couldn't cut it in academia, so you've reinvented yourself as the person who never wanted it in the first place."

If he weren't so astute, I'd almost label him a jerk. "I had an offer from Imperial College once," I say. "I turned it down."

"Why did you apply, then?"

"I didn't," I say. "They wanted to create a position for me."

He asks for the details, and I give him the name of the department head without qualm. This, too, is the truth—though I have no doubt he'll follow up the reference. This man, I sense, is not one simply to leave bluffs uncalled.

****

William never lets me get away with things either. When he first brought up the topic that ultimately led to my idea and the job interview, a few weeks earlier, we were jammed into a corner down at a pub near Paddington, close to where my previous lab lurked in all its soot-stained Victorian glory. I thought I'd tell him it was all bullshit and that would be that. After all, I was the scientist with all the qualifications, which no amount of search-engine savvy could replace.

Where was Carina that evening? Dubai? Riyadh? Abu Dhabi? Someplace hot and sandy at any rate, with alien skyscrapers and artificial islands, indoor ski resorts and discreet speakeasies, wearing a culturally sensitive headscarf and stilettos. Carina was often out of the country, chasing a dwindling seam of black ooze while her company scrambled to come up with some green alternative. Her affliction was incubating but had yet to really slow her down. William continued to beg her to start cutting back on the stressful foreign trips, lest it exacerbate her illness; I prayed that she'd keep on telling him to fuck off—for all sorts of reasons.

She must have been away, or William wouldn't have been allowed to come out.

William set two pints down between us and, without preamble, asked what I planned to do in my next stint.

When I shrugged, he added, "It's about time to look, isn't it?"

"No rush," I said. "I'll probably start scanning ads in a few weeks."

William has this earnest look that kills me. The unexpected thing is that I can even fall for it anymore. To be sure, earnestness was a much-prized quality in my youth, when I was a tentative undergraduate pining after self-important boys with long hair and political ideals, who professed to care deeply about ethical issues unfolding in countries I might struggle to pinpoint on a map. Lean, scraggly boys whose ribs and elbows pressed into me as I jostled for position in various dorm room beds.

When I first met William, I noticed the eyes first: citrine-brown, almost glowing with idealistic warmth. Unlike the scraggly boys, this seemed to be genuine: if he said he thought that Uganda needed more wells, he wouldn't talk about it; he'd be on the next plane out with a shovel.

"You've obviously got something on your mind," I said.

"Do you ever . . . " He rubbed stubble—wheat, ginger, and gray—with an absent thumb. "Do you ever think about working on something for a reason? In the lab, I mean?"

"I always work on things for a reason. AIDS, influenza, cervical cancer. Textbook good causes." I swallowed a surge of irritation along with the lager. Irritation, my inevitable response to undue earnestness these days. "Saving the world, you might even call it."

"But that's not really why you do it," he said. "You do it because you like the challenge of a new problem. You don't actually care about the patients, do you? Or at least, that's not your primary driver."

"So? Does that disqualify me from being a bona fide do-gooder?" I whizzed a beer mat at him. *Snick*—he caught it midair, slapped it down onto the table.

"Temper, temper."

"Cut me some slack," I said. "I'm a poorly remunerated scientist, not an evil hedge-fund manager."

"Willful misinterpretation," he said, with his referee-flashing-the-red-card look.

"So what *do* you mean?"

"I'm not disputing that your research leads to good things and ultimately helps people," he said. "You know I'm not. But I'm simply wondering if you might one day like to get a bit more . . . personal."

I still wasn't with him, though I was definitely developing the impression that I wouldn't like wherever it was when I finally caught up.

"You've got this amazing talent," he continued. "But you could be more . . . targeted."

"Targeted," I said. And then, "Oh no. No, you don't. No way."

"Why not?" Those amber eyes, wide and—damn him—earnest.

"But you know I don't know anything about multiple sclerosis."

His turn to shrug, now. "It's just a new puzzle, a new challenge. It's a disease like cervical cancer, with molecular circuitry gone awry. Why couldn't you contribute?"

"It may have escaped your notice that I'm a *virologist*, Will."

"Exactly," he said. "Which is why it's such a great idea."

This was when he rummaged in his canvas courier bag and extracted a copy of the *Lancet* article.

And thereby forged my first acquaintance with Professor Graham Bryck.

The concept of William briefing me on an item of science, no matter how new and obscure, made me feel uncomfortable. It's not that he's not an intelligent man—far from it. Before assuming the presidency of Defeat Multiple Sclerosis, he'd earned his living as an up-and-coming human rights barrister. But one thing you could never accuse William of was being untargeted, impersonal; Carina's diagnosis was all the incentive he'd needed to infiltrate DMS's rather unprofessional London headquarters in his limited spare time and work his way up through the ranks, making himself so indispensable that the trustees were ultimately happy to throw money at him to keep his talents in-house full-time. What charity wouldn't relish someone as charismatic and *earnest* as William at its fore? Besides, in the disease charity world, having a partner with the affliction wasn't seen as a conflict of interest; it was almost de rigueur.

What made me uncomfortable was that my superior knowledge of science was the sole axis of power that I still held over him. In every other way that counted, he had me on my knees. Even that largely irrelevant superiority gave me some semblance of holding my own hand on the rudder—take that away and I was lost at sea. And now here I was in the pub, about to be caught off-guard.

"When you helped me read up on MS," William said, "there wasn't a lot of consensus about what causes it."

This was an understatement. I recalled that session at my computer, about a year previously. William had long since familiarized himself with popular accounts of the disease, but soon after we met, he asked me to take a look at the latest published scientific literature and give my expert opinion of where things stood in the field. The overwhelming memory I retained from that session wasn't one of curiosity, but guilt. Guilt at the sudden, uncharitable surge of hope when he first stammered the news to me, when I thought that Carina might be close to death. And guilt, equally refined, at my disappointment when further knowledge disabused me of that little fantasy.

"DMS is open-minded," William continued. "We don't give research grants disproportionately to one camp over any of the others."

"You must really be spreading yourselves thin." I remembered how many diverse but poorly substantiated theories had been summarized in those review articles we'd pored over: vitamin D deficiency, stress, diet, hormones, infections, vaccinations; a handful of mutations on chromosome six; all, some, or none of the above.

"This is one of the things I'd like to change," he said. "If we could only back a winner, we'd get there so much faster."

Get there. As if a cure for MS were just a sleepy hamlet at the end of a long day's drive on the M1. As if it wouldn't take twenty years to sort out the biology, and another twenty to design and test a drug that might actually work. As if a hundred other diseases, far more straightforward, weren't still languishing in want of a therapeutic agent despite decades of research and billions of pounds of grant money. As if—respectable endowment portfolio and celebrity endorsements notwithstanding—DMS's annual research budget wasn't a tiny fraction of the spending power it might take to make this possible.

As if any of his efforts could ever help Carina in her lifetime.

"Let me guess," I said. "You've stumbled onto a new horse."

He nodded, finally surrendering the printout to me. The look on his face pained me: excitement mingled with irrepressible hope. I bowed my head over the article's abstract, struggling to skim it in the face of my own mixed emotions. He knew I hated to be disturbed while reading, but couldn't stop his commentary from spilling over as I attempted to screen out his voice and the noisy pub babble behind it.

"It's a new agent," he said. "They're calling it HMSV—that's short for Human Multiple Sclerosis Virus."

"Rather optimistic of them, isn't it?"

He ignored my sarcasm. "They found it in 72 percent of patients with MS, compared with 5 percent of healthy controls."

"That seems way too high," I muttered, flipping a few pages to the relevant section. Eager to get the upper hand once again, to restore my rightful place in the balance of things. How had they determined infection? Ah— standard PCR, no bells or whistles. They'd been looking for a particular herpes virus, and this new bug had popped up instead. The article was a short communication designed to get groundbreaking news out as quickly as possible, so it wasn't possible to work out from the sparse description of their experiments exactly what anti-contamination measures they'd taken. "And, God—only eighteen patients? How did this paper ever get into the *Lancet* in the first place?"

"It's statistically significant," he said, pointing at the error bars on the graph.

I had no doubt they'd found a statistics test that claimed it was, but I didn't want to piss William off. I'd prefer escorting him back from this cruel detour as gently and painlessly as possible.

"I know it's early days," he said, "but Graham says they've now tested a larger group, nearly a hundred, and the correlation is bearing up. He says there's another lab in Norway that's seen the same thing."

"*Graham*?" I took a look at the last name in the author list, the one with all the footnotes and fancy acronyms after it. "You're on a first-name basis with this guy?"

Professor Graham Bryck, head of a department in a prominent medical school in New York. I'd never heard of him, but that didn't mean much. We virologists were tribal, keeping to our own particular microorganism, getting quietly drunk at the gala dinners of our own bespoke conferences. Of course we all shared the same virology journals, but we seldom bothered reading up on anything but the most closely related viruses in other fields. The variety out there was staggering.

"I spoke to him on the phone earlier," he said. "He was very forthcoming. In fact, he's promised to fly over and address the board in a few weeks' time, combine it with another trip to London he's been planning."

"Smells cash, does he?"

"Very possibly. Isn't that what you scientists do: smell cash and follow it?"

"I suppose." I got to the end of the piece, looked up. "In my opinion, I think it's just too preliminary to place your bets on, Will. Looks like they've got a lot less than some of the more speculative theories out there."

"But it's the first fresh lead in years."

"Fresh doesn't mean reliable, you know."

"I know. But hell—it's something, and it would be stupid for us to just ignore it."

I studied him, trying to work out why he was swallowing this paper so credulously. William was still, at heart, a lawyer: skeptical beyond all reason, and wanting his life served up in evidence-based portions, all things neatly substantiated and defensible.

"There's still something you're not telling me, isn't there?" I said.

After a pause, he nodded. He'd taken the printout back and was clutching it like a talisman, while the rest of him bristled with the untold, almost to the point of explosion. "On the phone—Bryck mentioned that they've managed to culture HMSV in the lab."

I make a noncommittal noise. If true, though, it was a pretty big achievement. Herpes viruses can be very fussy in that department, and they couldn't have had more than a few months to play with it to judge by the hasty feel to the *Lancet* article.

"He says it's susceptible to anti-herpes drugs currently on the market for other herpes," he went on. "In the petri dish, at least. Which means . . . "

At that point all of William's hopes and credulity unfolded like a map before me on top of the weathered pub table: all his secret wishes—his one biggest wish—laid bare. The cure for Carina might already exist; it might be a quick clinical trial away, not the uncertain end of a generational slog.

"*If* HMSV actually is the causative agent," I warned him. "*If* the damage it causes is reversible once you cure the virus. *If*—"

"Yes, yes, yes." An edge to his voice, now. "I know all that. But if Bryck can muster enough support, he should be able to get permission to conduct a trial with one of the approved drugs for herpes simplex—acyclovir, say. DMS can help lobby the appropriate bodies on whichever side of the Pond works best. And with my influence, I can probably get Carina enrolled in it." He lowers his voice. "Bryck thinks he might even be able to ensure she's in the experimental group, not the control—though of course you couldn't breathe a word of that to her or anyone else."

He desperately wanted my approval, for me to share in his happiness. He wanted my blessing. Instead, I had to cover up the fact that I was simmering like a petulant child, one step away from kicking over his precarious Lego construction out of sheer spite.

****

"Yours is a pretty risky career strategy, though," my prospective future employer says at the interview. "How can you be so sure you'll keep getting those short-term appointments? The older you get, the fewer fellowships you're eligible for."

"There's always money for great post-docs like me. I never have a problem."

"Hmm." His gaze drops back to the stapled sheaf of paper, my entire adulthood summarized into a neat series of accomplishments. "You've got lots of experience, which could probably be applied to any project, but your main thrust is virology. As you know, that's not what we do in my lab."

Here's my opening, and I don't hesitate: "And that's precisely the key weakness in your scientific approach."

He blinks, pauses. "I don't know what you mean."

"It's the elephant in the lab. As long as you ignore it, it undermines your reputation."

Awareness, now: "You're talking about HMSV."

I nod.

He struggles to keep a neutral expression, but meanwhile, his forefinger assaults the chair arm in a brisk staccato. A man like him, I speculate, does not like loose ends. A man like him doesn't want to step through a fractured plank in his scientific empire, sending splinters of wood flying. In the year since the first report, there has been a steady trickle of support for the renegade new view beneath the more dominant naysayers. As long as the medical journals continue to publish speculative pieces about the virus, and small case studies supporting it, his own theories will be ever so slightly destabilized. Never mind that the majority view followed his perspective. Scientific opinion is not a democracy; you can't establish truth with a simple majority, *all in favor?* No, you only need one maverick with gravitas to set the entire edifice toppling. And gravitas is one quality that Graham Bryck, chief witness for the underdog prosecution, is not lacking.

Plus, Bryck adores chatting to journalists. And as for the journalists, there is nothing they adore more than a health conspiracy theory.

"Let me get this straight," he finally says. "You honestly think you can debunk HMSV once and for all?"

"Not HMSV itself," I say. "There's no reason to think the virus itself doesn't exist in the human population at a low level. In fact, it's probably rather common, given how much of it Bryck keeps finding in patients."

He makes a face, and I continue: "If it's endemic, it's always going to mess up standard tests if contamination isn't properly controlled. But I'm quite sure I can detect it using techniques far more accurate and sensitive than what Bryck's been using—and detect it *properly*, with no background contamination. You see that stint I did at Porton Down?" I lean forward, point out the relevant publication in my CV. "I came up with that method: it's virtually foolproof. I could detect the equivalent of one virus particle floating around in the English Channel of closely related variants."

He considers. "If it's such a great method, why aren't Bryck and his disciples using it?"

I want to say that there's no need for Bryck to change his methodology if it's giving him the answer he wants. Instead: "It's a pretty minor journal and a completely different virus—easy to miss if you're not very diligent on your reading. But what Bryck is really lacking is a proper group of patients—a massive and diverse group like yours. You could have the best detection system in the world, but if you don't have enough relevant patient material to do it justice, your statistics are always going to be crap."

"Hmm." He's staring off into the middle distance—nodding ever so slightly. "So using your technique, and my samples, you reckon we can blast Bryck's theory out of the water once and for all?"

"Provided you're right, of course."

He thinks I'm joking. "Naturally I'm assuming you don't actually believe Bryck's theory."

I laugh: "Certainly not."

Here, I've allowed myself the first lie of the interview. Actually, it's not strictly a lie: the truth is that I don't believe HMSV causes multiple sclerosis, and—despite the flimsiness of the evidence to date—I don't believe it doesn't. I don't *believe* anything, period. My mind is completely open about this issue. I want to come at this using the scientific method as it was meant to be used: I want to know the truth, not confirm something that I already believe, or be disappointed when my hunch is proved wrong. All very quaint, I know, and not particularly like me. But I have so much vested interest in the outcome that it's the only way I can devise to help out my friend without going a little bit insane with all the second-guessing.

But no point in giving my stance away. This man doesn't want a devil's advocate in his crew: he wants a convert.

"Okay, here's the deal," he says at last. "I'm intrigued, there's no denying it. The idea of bringing Bryck down has undeniable appeal, and anything that can consolidate the field and limit the number of theories will only help consolidate the grant money too."

He means there will be more in the pot for his chromosome six theory, of course. And who can blame him?

"But?" I hazard.

"*But* . . . the fellowship I've advertised is attached to a grant specifically geared toward looking at the genetics. While I'm not always a slave to the black-and-white details of what research goes on in my lab . . ."

"You really do need someone to work on the genetics," I finish, to his apologetic nod.

"And you don't have the experience I need for that approach—especially the animal work. I'm sure you could learn, but the contract is only two years, so I want someone quick off the mark."

The idea of failure had not even occurred to me, although somewhere behind the sting, I can sense the sweet relief of being off the hook. It had all been an incredibly stupid plan, after all.

And then, he throws a curve ball:

"I do happen to have a bit of extra space," he says. "Half a bench free and no one on the horizon after we fill the genetics post. If you were somehow able to secure your own funding, you'd be very welcome to come here and do your worst. I know money is tight, though: have you seen any suitable fellowships going?"

I manage to suppress the smile. "Actually, now that you mention it, I think I might have a bit of an idea."

****

The steamed-up door with its cheerful tinkle gives way to the pandemonium of Dante's Inferno inside. I raise a hand to Dante himself, who is up to his elbows tossing pesto-drenched pasta in a tub behind the glassed-in refrigerated counter, and he shrugs and wiggles his Einstein eyebrows in return. The chatter of students is a collective roar, pans clatter in the unseen kitchen, and the baby-blue espresso machine hisses like a steampunk apparition. It's a shock to see Carina sitting next to William in our usual corner booth. She's frowning at the menu and hasn't seen me yet, but William makes eye contact straightaway, his posture struggling to convey some sort of apology, some sort of "it wasn't my idea" disclaimer.

It's funny, actually, but it's only at this moment I realize that William and I have an unspoken pact to keep Carina well clear of me—of us. After all, why should her presence need apologies, under normal circumstances? When did our frequent, affectionate threesome—drinks, coffee, films, dinner at mine or theirs—gradually dissolve into avoidance? Of course William and I know roughly when, and exactly why—but for the first time I wonder what explanation Carina has been given for our effective estrangement. Her traveling schedule has grown increasingly busy, so maybe she hasn't even noticed. Maybe it's just something that, for her, seems a natural progression.

As I weave through a crowd of undergraduates queuing at the counter, Carina spots me and her face glows with pleasure. My answering smile comes as a thoughtless reflex and before I know what's happening, I'm at the booth and she's up, grasping my shoulders and planting an almost-kiss on either side of my face, that whispery maneuver that only Europeans can pull off without looking self-conscious. Her aura is redolent of delicate floral scent, and wisps of silvery black hair escape from the shiny mass coiled on top of her head. She is also unseasonably tanned, her healthy olive skin masking the secret within. As always, even though we are exactly the same age, I feel scruffy and childish in comparison, like she's the grown-up and I'm just some perpetual post-grad.

"My dear, it has been too long." She studies me with those calm almond-shaped eyes as I sit, then appeals to her husband: "How long, William?"

Dante's wife Adriana appears to take our coffee orders, disrupting the need to incriminate ourselves. At least eighteen months, easily: not so straightforward to explain when you look at it head-on. As Carina and Adriana babble in Italian, I wriggle out of my coat and avoid William's eye. My boot clunks against something under the table: a carry-on wheelie suitcase. That, combined with Carina's tailored but rumpled suit, tells me she must have decided on a spontaneous meet-up with William on her way home from the airport.

Adriana takes Will's order for a Peroni and mine for a double espresso and melts away. Carina regroups and opens her mouth to tackle my inexplicable absence, but William rallies and gets in first:

"So what's the big surprise?"

"Surprise?" Carina looks from him to me.

"She asked me to meet her here because she had some news," William explained.

"And I am crashing the gate," she says, putting lacquered fingertips to her lips. "I did not realize . . . I mean, if it's personal . . ."

There is a gleam in her eye that suggests she thinks I'm about to confess to a lab-rat lover, at long last—that there is hope for me yet.

"It's just about science," I tell her. "And it's perfect that you're here, because it's partly about you."

William, who's been scrunched in the corner, sits up straighter.

"You've spoken to Lafayette," he breathes. "You're going to Dundee!"

"Lafayette?" Carina says. "Who's he?"

"*Charlotte* Lafayette," William says. "A newish group leader at Dundee, lately from UCLA. She studies herpes simplex viruses, but has just collaborated with the Norwegian group on HMSV—nice short communication in the *BMJ*, out next month. She's hiring. She's—"

"That's not it," I say. Dundee? For Christ's sake, that's out in the middle of fucking nowhere, so far up on the map in Scotland that it might as well be in the Arctic Circle.

"Oh." William pauses, and then his eyes widen. "Don't tell me . . . but Joanne, that's amazing!"

"What is?" Carina demands, as confused as I am.

He turns to his wife, takes her hand in his. The diamond glints in its chunky barricade of white-gold rings—I'm not even in the room.

"Joanne's going to New York," William says, as if I'm some holy pilgrim. "She's managed to finagle a job with Graham Bryck himself."

"Will—"

"She'll be our agent on the inside!" he says. "I never dreamt this would be possible, but now that it's happened, I see it's the ideal scenario."

As they both turn to me expectantly, I find that I'm having trouble breathing.

"It's not with Bryck," I finally manage to get out. "I've found something appropriate here in London."

"But there's no one working on HMSV in London," he says, frowning. "Lafayette is the only one in the UK, and of course Bryck himself—well, I hadn't considered this, but it's perfect. I'm sure it's not too late to arrange something."

The fact that he could consider a three-thousand-mile distance from him "perfect" is not something that I'm doing a good job processing.

"I'm not going to Dundee, and I'm certainly not going to New York!"

"But, Joanne, it's—"

"William, for shame!" Carina's tone surprises me, and the violence with which she frees her hand from his grip. "Listen to yourself! You can't just expect Joanne to move to another country for the sake of one of your crazy schemes."

"Scientists move around," he said defensively. "It's part of the profession. She's done stints all over the world."

"But this is her home, now." Behind her anger, I hear exasperation—and a sympathy for me that makes me feel like dirt.

"It's not as if she has real ties, though . . . a family . . . " He dwindles off into an awkward pause. At that moment, I think I hate him.

Carina gives him a brief but pointed piece of her mind, something in Italian, and he sits back like he's been slapped in the face. In the resulting silence, she flashes me a look—*these stupid men, eh?*—and says, more gently, "Tell us what you've come up with, Joanne. I'm sure it's wonderful."

It's all ruined, now: ruined by William's sulking and Carina's unexpected alliance. But I open my mouth and the story comes out: dull, matter-of-fact. Scientific. Hearing the words now, and knowing what William really wants, I can't recapture the same sense of purpose. The whole plan just sounds like evasion and wishful thinking, its backwardness not clever but just misguided.

When I mention my prospective future employer's name, William pounds a fist on the table.

"Keiron *Kelvin?* But he's the enemy!"

"Enemy?" Carina says. "I didn't know it was a war."

I smile, despite myself. "You'd be surprised."

She smiles, too. "Perhaps your science business is more interesting than I'd been led to believe. Tell me about this Kelvin—I've heard the name but I can't remember which one he is." Unlike her husband, Carina prefers to remain ignorant of the science behind her condition. She has great respect for the medical profession and is happy to be steered by the Harley Street neurologist who looks after her—except when he urges her to cut back on her travel, that is.

"Kelvin is a bloody-minded fool on a wild goose chase," William mutters.

"Kelvin," I say, "is a highly respected professor who doesn't believe the theory that MS is caused by a virus—a dissenting view which he has no qualms about emphasizing in public."

William glares at me.

"He has also been amassing many years' worth of evidence that the disease is genetic, caused by the patients' own immune systems," I go on. "It's solid work, published in good journals."

"So you don't think the virus causes MS either?" she asks.

"I don't know one way or the other," I say, not looking at William. "Nobody does."

"But you think the immune system theory holds more promise?"

"No, not that either," I say. "The point about the Kelvin lab is that they have an amazing group of patients, from a number of countries around the world—thousands of patients. And they've been tracking them for more than ten years, taking bloods at regular intervals. If I worked in his lab, I could have access to these patients too—this is something that Lafayette and Bryck, and even the Norwegian group, can't touch."

"But you'd be working on his genetic angle, right, so it wouldn't help address the virus theory," William says.

"Wrong," I say. "This is what I've been trying to tell you. I've sold him on the idea that he needs me to rule out this pesky virus angle once and for all. All I need is some funding, and I'm in."

"Rule out . . ." William pauses, then slowly meets my eye. "Or in."

"Exactly," I say. "We let the science decide, one way or the other. If you and Bryck are right, it shouldn't take me very long at all to find that out. And if you're wrong . . . "

"Then DMS can focus their efforts on something more promising," William says, but I can tell he thinks this contra view is just a formality. "I'll see what I can do."

"Where are you going?" Carina says as I shoulder myself into my coat. "What about your coffee?"

I throw a five pound note on the table. "I've just remembered something I've forgotten to do in the lab." I need to escape—from Carina's kindness, from William's callous betrayal. "Another time soon, okay?"

In the days of the scrawny boys, I would have been trapped, transfixed in misery and unable to leave the table until the entire thing had played out. I might even have perversely relished that misery. Now, at least I have the grace and wisdom to know how to leave when I want to.

And to not look back.

****

As a child, I brimmed with the urge to discover. It is difficult now to recapture this feeling, the sensation of mysteries hidden everywhere: in the black stamens buried deep within a tulip; in the way globules of dew rolled in perfect spheres when I tilted the leaf of a nasturtium; the hole through which a straggling file of ants would vanish. Together with my friend Antonia, we'd track up the small creek that ran through the pine forest of our adjacent back yards—in a land of big skies, four seasons, no terraced rows, and few fences. Each expedition felt like the first time, as if we hadn't prowled every square inch a hundred times already. We'd walk through the ancient hemlock grove, the needles brushing cool against our faces, then skirt the plowed fields further back, willing the overturned earth to reveal the pink knapped flints of arrowheads.

My mother, too, was complicit. She'd get Dad to drill holes in jam jar lids so that I could capture fireflies in the long grasses and crowd them all together, giving off their acrid scent. She'd put droplets of pond water under her old brass microscope and I'd stare until the tiny creatures would fry from the heat of the lamp, leaving me with a tinge of nausea as they suffered—but not enough nausea to prevent me from doing it all over again. She pointed her telescope at the moons of Jupiter as they wavered in the oculars like pennies at the bottom of a fast-running rill.

Back then, these natural mysteries were freely interspersed with the paranormal in a way I was not yet sophisticated enough to differentiate. I frightened myself reading tales about planes lost in the Bermuda Triangle. I suspected that fairies might make their home in Dad's prized patch of lily-of-the-valley. Even into my teens, I was still a little bit afraid of the sprawling basement with its dark corners, and the ghosts of previous residents that might lurk there.

In the face of all these unknowns, I thought that the scientific method was nothing more than extra-keen observation. I thought that if I collected enough moths and beetles in my nets, or rocks and shells in a shoe box, that some great wisdom would just settle onto me, that I could call myself a scientist. I had no way of knowing that all knowledge was based on previous knowledge, a previous knowledge that would have to be learned, understood, dissected, memorized. I had no way of knowing about hypotheses, or about the mind-numbing drudgery of testing them over and over. I had no way of knowing that what was important was not the superficial appearance of things, but of what went on underneath.

"But you haven't lost that thrill of discovery completely, have you?" he asked me. "Underneath the mind-numbing drudgery, I mean."

I can still see the intent way he was looking at me: a microscopist who'd found his dream specimen.

"Because," he added, "you don't look like the sort of person who would just go through the motions."

"With respect, how could you possibly know what sort of person I look like, after five minutes of small-talk?" I was flattered, but didn't want him to know.

He tapped a finger to his temple. "I have my ways."

I wouldn't normally be that interested in prolonging any interaction with a lawyer, but I was a little drunk, and he was so sexy I decided to waive my moral objections. We'd struck up that first conversation while trying to get a broken cork out of a bottle of cheap vin de pays in the kitchen of a flat in Kensal Rise, where a rather decent party was just starting to thin out.

"You must know a more scientific way to go about this," he said as I tried to push the fragment through with a bread knife. "Something involving nano-technology, or robots."

"Unfortunately, I left my nano-robotic cork extraction apparatus back in the lab."

"So what do you do all day—meddle with things man wasn't meant to know?"

"Only when I'm not working on my clone army. A-ha!" The cork shot through the bottleneck, along with a hundred corky fragments.

"Don't worry," he said. "They'll float, and we can skim them out of our glasses with a spoon."

"Elementary, my dear . . . what did you say your name was again?"

"I didn't," he said. "But it's William."

****

I retreat along the dark sidewalk, using my purposeful movement to shed memories. Memories of my first meeting with William, of the painful scene in Dante's just a moment ago. Of all the scenes of secret pleasure and pain in the two years between.

My gaze sweeps automatically along the concrete pavement, scouring its pixels for interesting patterns. It's a habit I picked up years ago. I was often alienated at school—the occupational hazard of a smart-ass who didn't like to pretend she wasn't smart—so I would pass the interminable hours of outdoor recess prowling the perimeter fence, looking for treasure along the concrete edge of the playground. Amid the crabweed, bottle caps, twist-ties, candy wrappers, and other detritus, I was convinced there would be something worth finding: coins, at the very least, or even something as momentous as a lost diamond ring. I can't remember a single face of a single teacher from the seven years I attended elementary school, but I can still see the ground around that fence in vivid detail, its weeds poking through the wire rhomboids of the fencing: asters, dandelions, yarrow, chicory.

The funny thing is, I can't remember now if I actually ever found anything, even so much as a dull silver quarter. Instead, my lack of success only made me look harder. I realize for the first time that this tenacity is exactly the same impetus that I've relied on for the past two decades in my career as a scientist.

I laugh to myself—at myself—and pull my scarf more snugly around my throat. The cold has deepened, and the London night smells of snow.

****

It all transpires as I predicted: DMS is happy to fund my fellowship in the Kelvin lab once William gives it his backing, and in less than a week I'm starting in my new laboratory, preparing to find out once and for all whether Graham Bryck's pet virus causes multiple sclerosis.

I just want to get on with it. Instead, I know from many years' experience what awaits me: the tedious machinations of the university flexing its bureaucracy to the fullest. Health and safety inductions; tours of the building and all of its fire escapes; interminable form-filling; passport and visa checks; allergy tests; the assignment of a file drawer, a locker, a desk, a workbench, and, if I'm lucky, some grudging space in a lab freezer and fridge. There will probably be a coffee or lunch with the rest of Kelvin's team. Depending on the mix of dominant personalities, this will be either awkward or enjoyable.

I'm easy, either way. I've worked in labs with people hardly on speaking terms, and labs full of camaraderie where late experiments would morph naturally into nights out on the town. One of my talents is the ability to blend in and adapt to whatever psychosocial vibe happens to be on the ascendant. But the most important thing right now is to get the bullshit out of the way so that I can regain my usual autonomy. I loathe this feeling of being dependent on others, of drifting helplessly in an unfamiliar space.

In just a few days, I'm all systems go, queen of my domain—I have remade my scientific home at yet another new bench. The lab is rich and well-appointed, the blood bank is beautifully organized, and the company is surprisingly decent: geneticists, it turns out, are far less morose than virologists. Most importantly, Kelvin is not a micromanager, and I'm left alone to just get on with it.

The fellowship is for a year, but in the end it only takes me two months of preparation and pilot tests to get to the point when I am ready to perform the pivotal experiments.

There is a particular feeling I get just before an experiment. It doesn't matter if it's a trivial one, designed to fill in the picture of something I think I already know, or a major fact-finding expedition, as it is now, embarking into new territory. Somehow, an entire world waits for me on the other side. It's almost like the Bermuda Triangle—you lose yourself in the question, and it's all a bit mysterious and scary, and if you're very lucky it won't be like most of your other doomed journeys and you'll actually come out the other side with a small piece of understanding.

It's just after lunch when the answer finally comes. The lab is full to capacity: music blares, students laugh and banter, world-weary post-docs block it all out with headphones. Three poorly balanced centrifuges are howling in the corner; the fume cupboard alarm is going off because it's been on the blink for weeks and no one can be bothered to put in a request for repair.

I call up the realtime PCR results on the screen, and everything else vanishes in a bubble of expectation. Seeing the pattern instantly in the swoop of colored lines, I force myself to breathe deeply and maintain skepticism. I pull up a spreadsheet and crunch the numbers: the pattern holds true. All the controls have worked, the stats are sparkling clean, the deviations negligible. It's the kind of textbook graph that you almost never obtain in real life. Filtered through the blind eyes of a machine, untainted by human interpretation, it is the closest to Truth with a capital T that you are ever likely to get in your lifetime.

Truth is, of course, beautiful.

It also hurts.

"This can't be right," William says, transfixed by the printout I've given him. His knuckles are white.

"It's right," I say, gently. "The stats are rock solid. I've repeated it five times. There are more than six-hundred patient samples."

"No." For the first time, I hear the anger over the pub's white noise. "You can't publish this. You must have made a mistake."

"I haven't. And it's important that everyone knows as soon as possible that HMSV doesn't cause MS. Particularly the patients."

He doesn't appear to be listening. "Have you showed anyone this? Does Kelvin know?"

"No," I say, so confused that I almost stammer, "I've kept it under wraps like we agreed. But surely now—"

He slams the papers down on the café table between us, so loudly that a few other customers look round.

"You won't tell anyone about this, Jo, do you understand?" His voice is dangerously quiet now. "Bryck has just got the clinical trial approved. He starts recruiting patients in April."

"But—"

He considers me, eyes fiery. And then, they widen. "I should have realized that you have a conflict of interest. I should *never* have let you—"

"*What?*"

"It's all clear now," he spits out. "You don't want the virus theory to be true because you don't want Carina to be cured! You fabricated the data to try to shut down Bryck."

His words ring out and seem to echo against the inside of my skull.

"This is ludicrous, Will." I am angry now, as well, so angry that I'm close to tears.

"It's over, Jo," he says. "Destroy the data as soon as possible. Destroy it, or I swear to you . . . you'll be sorry."

I want to laugh at his melodrama, but he swipes his coat up and pushes through the crowd.

Inside me, there are no answers, only a numb sense of finality.

The next morning when I arrive at the lab, Kelvin is waiting for me. He calls me into his office.

A few minutes later, I'm back outside in the quad, completely adrift and clutching the cardboard box containing my few personal effects. My face burns in the frigid air. DMS has terminated my fellowship, and Kelvin— apologetic and embarrassed—tells me I can no longer be in his lab.

I somehow know that he knows I'm not the sort to go to HR with a complaint; science closes ranks on misfits and whistleblowers with ruthless efficiency. Gallantly, he's offered to write me a reference, but I demur: I have been with him so short a time that I don't even need to mention it on my CV. The entire episode will be swallowed up as if it had never occurred, ironed smoothly out of the narrative of my life as surely as my affair with William.

Except: I have deliberately left the data on the computer attached to the PCR machine. My notebook, rich with meticulous detail, is resting there enticingly alongside.

Kelvin thinks I've only set the stage, but if he's as curious as I suspect him to be, then treasure awaits.

****

The cab drops me off at a modern brick building on the edge of a campus in the far north of England.

I straighten my interview suit, slam the taxi door, and stride purposefully toward the entrance.

AFTERWORD

There are a host of human diseases whose cause remains obscure despite decades of research. As understanding the underlying molecular mechanism for a disorder is the key to a cure, any breakthroughs are usually widely reported and followed with keen interest by patients and their advocates. Discovery that a pathogen, such as a virus or bacteria, is responsible for a disease of unknown etiology is often the best possible news: while indwelling genetic disorders can remain elusive to treatment, we already know how to cure many pathogens, as well as how to prevent them with vaccination.

In 2006, a virus called XMRV was found to be strongly associated with the incidence of Chronic Fatigue Syndrome (CFS), a baffling and debilitating disorder. The media went into overdrive, hopes were raised, and other laboratories scurried to replicate the results. To make a long story short, the connection between the virus and CFS proved to be the result of a contamination derived from laboratory mice, brought about by the generous tendency of laboratories to share useful materials and, in doing so, disseminating any underlying latent biological entities worldwide.[20]

My then-publisher, John Inglis of Cold Spring Harbor Laboratory Press, suggested that this sort of scenario was ripe for a fictional take. There are, of course, other prominent examples of the public's hopes being raised by scientific claims, such as autism being caused by the MMR triple vaccine. Tales such as these highlight how science is not just confined to the laboratory: aided by the media, the government, and public pressure, the messages soon escape and are used (or abused) by society. To maintain some control of how these messages are framed, scientists have to fight their corner and work on their image, credibility, and (eminently non-scientific) powers of persuasion in an increasingly noisy and contentious space.

NOTES

1. Ben Parr, "Google: There Are 129,864,880 Books in the Entire World," *Mashable*, August 6, 2010. www.mashable.com/2010/08/05/number-of-books-in-the-world/?europe=true#YIDlvSA7GmqL.

2. Nicholas Wroe, "Master of Reinvention," *The Guardian*, August 26, 2000. www.theguardian.com/books/2000/aug/26/4.

3. Jennifer Rohn, "Experimental fiction," *Nature* 439 (January 2006): 269.

4. Jennifer Rohn, "Welcome to LabLit.com: Our Lights Are Now On," *Lablit.com*, March 7, 2005. http://www.lablit.com/article/1.

5. Wikipedia is used as an example of consensus definition since until the present volume there were no systematic scholarly explorations of the genre. Neither the *Oxford English Dictionary* nor *Webster's Dictionary* supply a definition.

6. "LabLit: Wikipedia," *Wikipedia*. Accessed July 25, 2018. www.en.wikipedia.org/wiki/Lab_lit.

7. "The Lab Lit List," *Lablit.com*. Accessed July 25, 2018. http://www.lablit.com/the_list.

8. Katherine Bouton, "In Lab Lit, Fiction Meets Science of the Real World," *New York Times*, Dec. 3, 2012. www.nytimes.com/2012/12/04/science/in-lab-lit-fiction-meets-science-of-the-real-world.html?_r=0.

9. Delia Cabe, "Dissecting Science Scandals & Lab Culture," *Boston.com*, August 17, 2010. www.boston.com/community/blogs/creative_type/2010/08/the_plot_usually_goes_like.html.

10. Heather Goldstone, "10 LabLit Picks You Won't Want to Miss," *WCAI Living Lab Radio*. April 30, 2014. www.capeandislands.org/post/10-lablit-picks-you-wont-want-miss#stream/0.

11. Jennifer Rohn, "More Lab in the Library," *Nature* 465 (June 2010): 552.

12. "The Lab Lit List," Lablit.com. Accessed July 25, 2018.

13. Margaret Mead and Rhoda Métraux, "Image of the Scientist among High-School Students: A Pilot Study," *Science* 126 (August 1957): 384.

14. Dene Grigar, "Transgressing the Limits," *The Scientist* (August 3, 2006). https://www.the-scientist.com/daily-news/transgressing-the-limits-47314.

15. Ovid, "Metamorphoses," in *Metamorphoses (Oxford World's Classics) Paperback*, Reissue edition, ed. E. J. Kenney, trans. A. D. Melville (Oxford: Oxford University Press, 2008), 177–78.

16. Roslynn Haynes, "From Alchemy to Artificial Intelligence: Stereotypes of the Scientist in Western Literature," *Public Understanding of Science* 12, no. 3 (July 1, 2003): 243–53.

17. Declan Fahy, "Hollywood's Newest Hero Stereotype: The Scientist," *Washington Post*, November 13, 2014. www.washingtonpost.com/posteverything/wp/2014/11/13/hollywoods-newest-hero-stereotype-the-scientist/?noredirect=on&utm_term=.65aefd054fea.

18. Jennifer Rohn, "Unexpected Side-Effects," *LabLit.com*, January 6, 2008. www.lablit.com/article/338.

19. Jennifer Rohn, "Scientists Can't Fight 'Alternative Facts' Alone," *The Guardian*, January 25, 2017. www.theguardian.com/science/occams-corner/2017/jan/25/alternative-facts-experts-scientists-fight-alone-humanities.

20. Robin A. Weiss, "A Cautionary Tale of Virus and Disease," *BMC Biology* (27 September 2010) 20108:124, www.doi.org/10.1186/1741-7007-8-124.

BIBLIOGRAPHY

Bouton, Katherine. "In Lab Lit, Fiction Meets Science of the Real World." *New York Times*. Dec. 3, 2012. Accessed Jun. 5, 2017 http://www.nytimes.com/2012/12/04/science/in-lab-lit-fiction-meets-science-of-the-real-world.html?_r=0.

Cabe, Delia. "Dissecting Science Scandals & Lab Culture." *Boston.com*. Aug. 17, 2010. Accessed Oct. 7, 2018. www.boston.com/community/blogs/creative_type/2010/08/the_plot_usually_goes_like.html.

Fahy, Declan. "Hollywood's Newest Hero Stereotype: The Scientist." *Washington Post*. Nov. 13, 2014. Accessed Jun. 10, 2017. www.washingtonpost.com/posteverything/wp/2014/11/13/hollywoods-newest-hero-stereotype-the-scientist/?noredirect=on&utm_term=.65aefd054fea.

Goldstone, Heather. "10 LabLit Picks You Won't Want to Miss." *WCAI Living Lab Radio*. Apr. 30, 2014. Accessed Apr. 5, 2018.www.capeandislands.org/post/10-lablit-picks-you-wont-want-miss#stream/0.

Grigar, Dene. "Transgressing the Limits." *The Scientist*. Aug. 3, 2006. Accessed Sep. 17, 2018. https://www.the-scientist.com/daily-news/transgressing-the-limits-47314.

Haynes, Roslynn. "From Alchemy to Artificial Intelligence: Stereotypes of the Scientist in Western Literature." *Public Understanding of Science* 12, no. 3 (Jul. 1, 2003): 243–53.

"LabLit: Wikipedia." *Wikipedia*. Accessed Jul. 25, 2018. www.en.wikipedia.org/wiki/Lab_lit.

"The Lab Lit List." *Lablit.com*. Accessed Jul. 25, 2018. http://www.lablit.com/the_list.

Mead, Margaret, and Rhoda Métraux. "Image of the Scientist among High-School Students: A Pilot Study." *Science* 126, no. 3270 (Aug. 30, 1957): 384–90.

Ovid. "Metamorphoses." In *Metamorphoses (Oxford World's Classics) Paperback*, Reissue edition, edited by E. J. Kenney, translated by A. D. Melville. Oxford: Oxford University Press, 2008.

Parr, Ben. "Google: There Are 129,864,880 Books in the Entire World." *Mashable*. Aug. 6 2010. Accessed Jan. 6, 2018. www.mashable.com/2010/08/05/number-of-books-in-the-world/?europe=true#YIDlvSA7GmqL.

Rohn, Jennifer. "Experimental Fiction." *Nature 439* (January 2006): 269.

———. "More Lab in the Library." *Nature* 465 (Jun. 3, 2010): 552.

———. "Scientists Can't Fight 'Alternative Facts' Alone." *The Guardian*. Jan. 25, 2017. Accessed Sep. 20, 2018. www.theguardian.com/science/occams-corner/2017/jan/25/alternative-facts-experts-scientists-fight-alone-humanities.

———. "Unexpected Side-Effects." *LabLit.com*. Jan. 6, 2008. Accessed Sep. 9, 2018. www.lablit.com/article/338.

———. "Welcome to LabLit.com: Our Lights Are Now On." *Lablit.com*. March 2005. http://www.lablit.com/article/1.

Weiss, Robin A. "A Cautionary Tale of Virus and Disease." *BMC Biology* (Sep. 2010): 124. www.bmcbiol.biomedcentral.com/articles/10.1186/1741-7007-8-124.

Wroe, Nicholas. "Master of Reinvention." *The Guardian*. Aug. 26, 2000. Accessed Jun. 5, 2018. www.theguardian.com/books/2000/aug/26/4.

Conclusion

Lab Lit

Teaching Accessible Science

Olga A. Pilkington

Fiction influences fact when it comes to practicing science. Numerous sociological explorations of laboratory life, culture, and publication practices reveal that science and literature share affection for narrative.[1] Scientists use fictional models and engage in imaginary scenarios (thought experiments) probably just as often as novelists, poets, and playwrights.[2] The public, too, it appears, prefers to look at science through the lens of fiction.

As Peter Weingart and Petra Pansegrau observe, "It is evident that only very few actual scientists are well known among the broader public (exceptions include Albert Einstein and, more recently, Stephen Hawking). Fictional 'scientists,' by contrast, such as Dr. Faust, [Dr.] Frankenstein, Dr. Seltsam and Dr. Caligari, are very well known."[3] In fact, as Amanda Scott points out in her essay on *Frankenstein*, the power of fiction is such that it creates perceptions and interpretations of science that may not always be realistic but yet last for centuries. "Popular images of science and scientists are influenced far more by fictitious characters than by real people"—this is the assumption Weingart and Pansegrau introduce to their readers after surveying conference papers "concerning the meaning of literature and film for the public perception of science and scientists, their effect on the formation of popular images of science."[4] This is also a point many of the essays in this book illustrate. It appears that the public is, in fact, curious about science, yet it does not always have reliable guides to help it traverse the world of science.

When college students not majoring in science are asked what science means to them, most respond with images that recall grade school chemistry experiments and have very little to do with modern scientific activities.[5] This is a clear indication that non-professionals associate science with the laboratory. However, as Matt Hadley shows, the notion of the laboratory in our culture extends well beyond the scientific lab. The kind of laboratory a modern scientist may occupy still remains a mysterious space, and popularizations of science do little to explain actual research procedures.[6]

It is also easy to blame Hollywood[7] and bad science teachers for the public's confusion when it comes to understanding what scientists really do. A more realistic answer, on the other hand, has to do with the accessibility of science. By accessibility I mean learning about science and understanding science in such a way that is meaningful to individuals of various walks of life. To a person interested in geology or biochemistry, the accessibility of science may manifest as a well-stocked lab; to an English or a sociology major, the accessibility of science may mean being able to dissect the motives of individual researchers—a very different kind of equipment is required for this task, the kind a science lab does not supply.

With the current emphasis on STEM (Science, Technology, Engineering, Math), the accessibility of science in many modern educational institutions is increasingly being defined in narrow ways—as an accessibility of laboratory resources and funding. This leaves those not choosing a professional scientific career without a path to meaningful interactions with science. And in a rapidly advancing technological society this is a major disadvantage if not an outright danger. Theda Wrede's chapter addresses the consequences of an intellectually and technologically fractured society. Writing about Barbara Kingsolver's novel *Flight Behavior*, Wrede explains, "In centering the novel on . . . [a] fairly ordinary woman to whom readers can relate, Kingsolver eases her audience into the novel's larger concerns: the difficulty of reaching a wider audience with science and the declining state of the environment." Later in her essay, Wrede discusses Kingsolver's presentation of people deprived of scientific knowledge: "Kingsolver increasingly juxtaposes both the media's self-serving spinning and the farmers' religious beliefs with scientific facts acquired through painstaking research, which then help explain the monarch butterflies' sojourn on the Turnbow mountain. Thus eventually, science moves into the foreground." However, before the message that it brings can be heeded, people need to find personal points of access to science. Introducing science through hands-on experience, as happens in *Flight Behavior*, is an effective way. At the same time, in addition to STEM programs, offering explorations of scientific facts and issues through humanities might appeal to students who do not considers themselves "scientifically minded" or who have had prior negative experiences with science classes.

Another possible problem with a STEM-exclusive approach to science is the exclusion of certain groups from STEM education programs. Eileen Trauth and Suzanne Trauth suggest addressing the gender gap in STEM through theater. They demonstrate that "an artistic rendering of this . . .

[issue] is an effective way to create awareness about the biases that exist in society and that are transmitted through cultural norms and values." The Trauths argue that a dramatic rendering of scientific issues "teaches science fundamentals, illuminates the world of science, and shows characters as (current and would-be) scientists. Further . . . storyline and characters also show the connections between . . . [a] scientific field . . . on the one hand, and art and music, on the other."

Attention to the humanities is equally important as a solid basis for science and technology. Today, the laments for the death of the humanities have given way to cautions that technology and science may become meaningless and even dangerous when people who engage in these fields do not consider the social contexts in which their advancements will inevitably function. Mark Zuckerberg, with his lack of formal education, especially in the humanities, has become the go-to example of a brilliant technological mind that could be even more successful had he been able to contemplate human relationships and interconnections on a deeper level. Evan Osnos, after interviewing Zuckerberg about a number of current social issues, found him "straining, not always coherently, to grasp problems for which he was plainly unprepared. . . . These are not technical puzzles to be cracked in the middle of the night but some of the subtlest aspects of human affairs, including the meaning of truth, the limits of free speech, and the origins of violence."[8]

Gianpiero Petriglieri, writing for the *Harvard Business Review* website, calls Zuckerberg and those like him "unprepared overachievers." The unpreparedness, he argues, stems from the lack of education in one particular field—the humanities. "Many a tech titan . . . would have been helped by an extra humanities class . . . or social science course: those staples of liberal arts education meant to prepare future leaders to wrestle with the dilemmas and complexities of human lives and societies. It is impossible to attend a management or technology conference these days without hearing some version of that call for more humanism in tech."[9]

Lab lit is an excellent bridge between the humanities and the sciences, and some colleges and universities already use the genre to foster interdisciplinary connections for their students. It is, very likely, not surprising to anyone that MIT would recognize the importance of such interactions. They have been supporting a successful creative writing program for years. MIT's writing programs (undergraduate and postgraduate) focus on science writing (fiction and non-fiction), among other things, and the faculty include a healthy mix of writers, social scientists, and computer scientists, as well as professors with training in physics.[10] Another example is Brown University's Science and Technology Studies program, which functions under the direction of John Richards, a professor of history.[11] The University of Pennsylvania and the University of Note Dame offer science and literature courses,[12] as do the University of North Carolina at Chapel Hill,[13] the University of Nevada, Las Vegas,[14] and the University of Michigan's Lyman Briggs College.[15] Undergraduates at New York University can take a course titled "Lab Lit."[16] Dixie State University in St. George, Utah, is designing a Medical Humanities program.[17] For many of these schools, classes on literature and science are parts of a requirement for a degree that incorporates the sciences and the humanities.

The need for meaningful science becomes more apparent as we come up against the consequences of a society that advances technologically at a magnificent speed. It is just as crucial for a scientist to understand the ethical, cultural, and social consequences of research as it is for a non-professional to comprehend the basic scientific principles behind the latest discoveries and cures. All of us, no matter our interests or professions, are responsible for the world that we are creating. This world depends on science. Thus, we all should have some kind of access and means for meaningful interactions with the subject.

Human beings tend to create social power structures with restricted access. Science has started out as one such power structure.[18] However, the modern public rightfully demands its share and tries to insert itself into the production of science. Those outside scientific institutions and laboratories can no longer afford to remain passive consumers. Lab lit is one way in which the public can engage with science on a meaningful level, and a college classroom is a perfect environment to foster it.

An interdisciplinary program in science and literature, like the ones mentioned above, might not be feasible for many institutions of higher education; however, any literature class can incorporate a lab lit text. As the range of essays in this volume demonstrates, lab lit can fit within explorations of nineteenth-, twentieth-, and twenty-first-century literatures. It can become part of a drama, sociology, history, or humanities class. As a tool for communication of science and science accessibility, lab lit is invaluable because this literature offers a variety of characters through whom different people can relate to science in their own unique ways. In addition to introducing and explaining science, these texts discuss universal issues of power and mortality, love and gender, responsibility to self and to society, and the list goes on. Lab lit looks at various issues through a unique lens of science and in the process personalizes science, makes it meaningful, and, therefore, accessible to people who may never have had a chance or a desire to enter a laboratory.

The essays in this book offer a number of possible access points to science. Psychology or criminal justice students might be drawn to Kimberley Idol's examination of Caleb Carr's novels, in which "forensic techniques are essential to . . . crime solving, catching the criminal and in terms of assessing the nature of morality. They determine that the way to teach human beings how to fix what is wrong with society and help them solve more tangible short-term problems lies in the ability to trust the scientific method and to trust the objective investigative process."

Drama and creative writing classes would find ways to connect with scientific issues using Eileen Trauth and Suzanne Trauth's essay or Beverly Connor's and Jennifer Rohn's insights on writing lab lit. For example, Connor shares her knowledge of characters, setting, and plot devices specific to lab lit. She writes, "Having the scientific information actually furthering the plot creates a story where the science does not sound like it is from a textbook or tacked on as an afterthought." Jennifer Rohn notes that "a good lab lit story will manage to slip in facts or ideas that a reader might not have known—but this is not unique to a science novel; it's almost de rigueur for good fiction generally."

Dean Conrad and Lynne Magowan's look at *The Andromeda Strain* as well as Ace Pilkington's chapter with its discussion of *Jurassic Park* might be gateways to science for students of film. Before offering a detailed analysis of the movie, Conrad and Magowan caution that "lab lit is tricky territory for those filmmakers attempting faithfully to bring its literature to the screen."

Elaine Pearce's analysis of *The Honest Look* is likely to appeal to English majors as it draws explicit connection to literature. Those looking for literature-inspired explorations of science will find interesting Amanda's Scott's approach to Mary Shelley's *Frankenstein*. Scott offers her readers, among other things, a look at *Frankenstein* in terms of "'Romantic Science,' namely scientific inquiry informed by Romantic ideals." Ace Pilkington's chapter tackles, perhaps, the biggest question about lab lit—how is it different from science fiction? And while the introduction provides a cursory answer, his chapter goes in depth, explicating not only lab lit and science fiction in terms of genre criticism but also taking a look at other related generic fictions such as techno-thrillers.

This collection is intended as an introduction into lab lit. It is not a survey of the most recent titles; rather, it offers a look at what has been happening within this genre for a number of years. Some of the essays address works already familiar to most students, while others draw attention to lesser known titles.

That is not to say that the latest developments in lab lit are of no consequence. In fact, lab lit is gaining popularity, and writers choose the genre to launch their careers: Andrea Rothman's successful debut with *The DNA of You and Me* (2019) is an excellent example. Lab lit is also becoming mainstream, and in addition to its authors winning prestigious literary prizes, the genre sells! For example, an Amazon best book of April 2018 was *The Overstory*, an eco-epic by Richard Powers. The same book was also Amazon's top twenty pick for the year 2018 in Literature and Fiction. Lab lit is also branching out into poetry (e.g., *Laboratorio: Poems from the Mullard*

Space Science Laboratory, edited by Simon Barraclough, 2015) and graphic novels (e.g., Jim Ottaviani and Leland Myrick's 2013 bestseller *Feynman* is followed by *Hawking* in 2019).

No matter the form a lab lit work takes, for students, exposure to the genre can often trigger new thought patterns and help make connections among various scientific disciplines and the humanities. In fact, interdisciplinary research designs are gaining popularity. For example, Benjamin Winterhalter, writing for *The Atlantic*, highlights a doctoral student from Berkeley, who "was studying modernist literature (e.g., James Joyce, Virginia Woolf, Ezra Pound) by studying neuroscience." Winterhalter explains the research project this way, "In essence, . . . literary modernism's insights about the relationship between abstract thoughts and tangible objects are now being understood by neurological research." Here is the elaboration from Matt Langione, the doctoral candidate: "This thesis of Ezra Pound's that poetry should yoke ideas to particular objects—so that the thing and the thought are brought together in a single manifold . . . actually anticipates a very recent neuroscientific insight, which is that, in certain aesthetic states, processing and perception happen in the same cortical centers of the brain."[19]

The idea of examining science in an interdisciplinary context is not without precedent. Before lab lit ever became a noticeable genre of literature, there was the literature and law movement. As David S. Caudill notes, quoting Gavin Little's *Literature and Legal History*, "Literature may not only accurately elucidate the atmosphere of a period, but shape 'the development of the popular imagination of law, and that of lawyers themselves.'"[20] However, Caudill continues to observe that in the law and literature movement, the role of verisimilitude is not prominent, "thus, the utility of the law and literature movement, and the value of the insights offered by paying attention to literature about law and lawyers, is rarely a function of how realistically or accurately the legal system (and its processes and actions) are represented."[21]

According to Caudill, lab lit parallels the law and literature movement not only in its interdisciplinary approach but also in its relationship with truth. That is, some lab lit representations of science are accurate while some are stereotypical and uninformed. He writes, "The broader notion of using literature to 'illuminate' science is rarely based on the scientific accuracy of literary narratives." The examples to support this statement that Caudill offers are taken from the film industry of the 1940s.[22] Lab lit of the present, on the other hand, and according to Caudill himself, is a much more realistic genre.[23] As Jennifer Rohn notes in the reflective component of her case study, sometimes "scientist characters in novels are portrayed doing something morally wrong, or a lab lit novel . . . [may highlight] the many unpleasant and sometimes outright unaspirational aspects of an academic career in science."

As a genre in the spectrum of science writing (see my essay in this collection),[24] lab lit helps bring to light some features of scientific reality that other scientific texts do not necessary dwell on—the role of laboratory animals, for instance. Eva Hayward argues, in her article for *Cultural Anthropology*, that such interactions are not one-way, with the human scientists impacting the non-human test subjects. She argues that interactions with laboratory animals go deeper and impact human researchers beyond the obvious retrieval of test results. Examining a marine biology lab, she notes that, at first glance, "the power of who observes and who is observed is tentacled through machines and expertise at ever-changing scales and grains of resolution." However, the domineering power of humans is illusory. She continues her observations: "But all these forces are quite literally impressed on organisms such that bodies (human, animal, machine) carry the markings, the fleshly and instrumental inscriptions, of the other. I am reminded of *Sensory Exotica* by Howard C. Hughes (1999). Working through the biomechanics of animal senses, Hughes maintains that technologies such as sonar and electroreception bespeak a human envy of nonhuman sensoria."[25]

Lab lit covers the relationships between human scientists and their research subjects and laboratory apparatus in minute detail, creating the illusion not only of the physical manipulation of various machines or instruments or animals but also of the emotions and thoughts that such interactions promote (see, for example, Susan Gaines's *Carbon Dreams*, Allegra Goodman's *Intuition*, or Jennifer Rohn's *The Honest Look*). In these instances, lab lit shows what the mutual impressions that Hayward talks about look like, feel like, and how they impact both the observer and the observed.

For example, when Allegra Goodman describes her characters handling laboratory mice, she uses fairly simple, action-filled sentences that create a solemn atmosphere and indicate the high level of focus on the part of the scientists:

> These animals were already quite sick. Tumors bulged grotesquely, as if the mice had swallowed marbles. . . . As Feng examined the mice in one cage, Marion studied those in another. In silence, Feng and Marion held each mouse gently, with gloved thumb and forefinger grasping the fold of skin behind the neck. . . . The mice in two groups with the virus had already died, and those in the third group were close to death as well. Marion could not help [staring] for a moment at the waste. She wasn't proud of sacrificing living creatures for the idle repetition of failed experiments.[26]

It is obvious that Marion and Feng are affected by their interactions with the animals. They try to be respectful and careful. Goodman makes sure that her readers understand that "Marion was an attentive and compassionate investigator, almost fond of her small charges, proud and careful of them—not as if they had rights or souls, but as a craftsman might treat precious tools."[27]

It is easy to assume that the interactions between laboratory animals and scientists leave physical marks on the animals only; after all, it is the animals who are injected with viruses, probed, and finally autopsied. At the same time, as Hayward points out, the interactions quite often affect both the subject and the researcher physically. She calls this affect "an impression." She explains, "Impression registers the reciprocal nature of being touched in the act of touching, as well as the double meaning—as in 'having an impression of' or 'making an impression on me'—of knowing and being."[28] Goodman does not implicitly describe an act of mutual physical impressions between the scientists and their mice, but she does allude to a very likely possibility: "Positioned on their backs, the mice flailed their legs helplessly and could not turn or bite while Marion and Feng measured their tumors with tiny calipers."[29] As it is in this example, mutual impressions are not always desirable for the researchers; this does not, however, negate their existence and consequences.

Apart from laboratory animals and apparatus, non-scientists also make significant contributions to research and discoveries. Jennifer Rohn's *The Honest Look* gives a clear example of one type of such contributions— human organs donated for research. At one of the key points in the novel, the scientists learn that they will soon have fresh human brain cells available to them to test their Alzheimer's drug.

The interpretation of this news by the characters in the novel might seem heartless and cruel at first glance to a reader not familiar with the world of laboratory drug trials: "'And there's another piece of news, which Alan asked me to pass on, since he's tied up in a meeting. . . . There's been a death at the hospice,' he said simply, 'There'll be a slight delay—I understand they're waiting for the daughter to fly up from Pretoria before they switch off life support.' . . . 'Expect the samples on Thursday.'"[30] The tone and syntactic simplicity of this announcement is similar to Goodman's handling of the researcher-to-mice interactions. Matter-of-factness and lack of emotion punctuate both. Both the mice and the human are precious tools. In fact, at one point, one of the scientists gets impatient waiting for the brain to arrive at the laboratory and expresses his frustration in a way that the others condemn: "'This waiting around doesn't help matters. But the patient's daughter's instructions were very clear.' He made a face. 'It shouldn't matter—her mother is dead whether she's on the machine or not.'"[31]

The reaction to death and its physical and emotional impressions may seem unfamiliar to some lab lit readers. However, such reactions are realistic. Examining and discussing them is one way to access the world of science. The very differences between the characters' and the readers' reactions and understandings create points of accessibility, making science meaningful to people who do not practice it. In this regard, the realism of lab lit may push some of the readers away from the characters, but it will also pull them closer to science by engaging them emotionally. Emotional connection to science for non-specialists, research suggests,[32] is a possible point of meaningful access. For example, Marco Caracciolo suggests upon examining Ian McEwan's novel *Saturday* that "the sense of experiencing a storyworld through the consciousness of a character [means] developing a feeling of 'closeness' to that character." This kind of closeness can, in turn, lead to empathy, and the readers who started out resentful toward researchers' attitudes to organ donors may develop a sense of empathy. In Caracciolo's words, "Empathy, as a form of perspective-taking, can be identified as the psychological mechanism behind" the closeness to fictional characters. [33]

Another example of lab lit's realism is the economics of science. It is the aspect of lab lit that Caudill discusses in detail as a realistic and crucial part of the scientific world. Looking at the economics side of science allows for social and ethical debates, which many lab lit works present and encourage. The presence of the financial side of conducting research in lab lit adds another layer of verisimilitude to the genre. These works attempt to show not only realistic scientists and scientific processes but also to bring to light the social realities of being a scientist.

Thus lab lit is interdisciplinary not only because it is a genre that juxtaposes fiction and reality but because it reveals the interconnectedness of the human quest for knowledge. Because of this, it offers a number of access points to science and not all of them straight through the laboratory. In other words, scientific discourse can take many shapes. Current research in the area of communicating science to the public shows that "there is a diffuse border between different discourses of science." [34] Usually this means that popular science and professional science are not as far apart as we may think. On the other hand, statements like these also mean that literature has a place in disseminating science, that knowledge about the world is not confined to a handful of narrowly specialized disciplines but accessible through a variety of avenues. Lab lit offers possible ways into science.

While we would like to see this volume in the classroom in addition to a scholar's library, it is not intended as a teacher's guide in the sense that it does not include possible discussion topics or writing prompts. Rather, in putting these essays together, our goal was to introduce lab lit as a genre and show a range of its possibilities. Yet, we believe that the selection of texts and the issues they cover (both scientific and social) would make this book compatible with a variety of subjects and pedagogical approaches.

For literature instructors, teaching lab lit does not have to differ from teaching any other kind of genre text. Instructors of hard sciences will find that the very subject matter of these texts offers them an advantage and a way into the world of literature. Just as a bridge can be crossed in either direction, lab lit works as an introduction to literature for scientists equally well.

The structure of this book, if used in a classroom, affords flexibility. Any of the chapters and the lab lit texts behind them can lead to a meaningful and accessible encounter with science and literature. However, for students not inclined to read longer texts, Jennifer Rohn's short story (part of the case study) might be a more manageable first step. Stephanie Chidester's essay and the collection of Andrea Barrett's short fiction that it focuses on could also be excellent starting points.

In the end, this book offers two kinds of introductions—on the one hand, it may be used to welcome science and its issues into a literature or a humanities classroom; on the other hand, the scholarly investigations of lab lit texts offered in this collection show that lab lit is a fully developed literary genre with a variety of forms, practitioners, and audiences. It is our hope that these essays will encourage not only debates about science and its place in society but also become starting points for further scholarly examinations of lab lit.

NOTES

1. See Rom Harré, "Some Narrative Conventions of Scientific Discourse," in *Narrative in Culture: The Uses of Storytelling in Sciences, Philosophy, and Literature*, ed. Christopher Nash (London: Routledge, 1994), 81–101; Olga A. Pilkington, *Presented Discourse in Popular Science: Professional Voices in Books for Lay Audiences* (Leiden: Brill, 2018); Femke Reitsma, "Geoscience Explanations: Identifying What Is Needed for Generating Scientific Narratives from Data Models," *Environmental Modeling & Software* 25 (2010): 93–99.

2. Anouk Barberousse and Pascal Ludwig, "Models as Fictions," in *Fictions in Science: Philosophical Essays on Modeling and Idealization*, ed. Mauricio Suárez (London: Routledge, 2009), 56–73; Ann-Sophie Barwich, "Science and Fiction: Analysing the Concept in Science and Its Limits," *Journal for General Philosophy of Science* 44 (2013): 357–73. DOI 10.1007/s10838-013-9228-2; Joseph Rouse, "Laboratory Fictions," in *Fictions in Science: Philosophical Essays on Modeling and Idealization*, ed. Mauricio Suárez (London: Routledge, 2009), 37–55; Mauricio Suárez, "Fictions in Scientific Practice" *Fictions in Science: Philosophical Essays on Modeling and Idealization*, ed. Mauricio Suárez (London: Routledge, 2009), 3–15; Adam Toon, *Models as Make-Believe: Imagination, Fiction and Scientific Representation* (New York: Palgrave Macmillan, 2012).

3. Peter Weingart and Petra Pansegrau, "Introduction: Perception and Representation of Science in Literature and Fiction Film," *Public Understanding of Science* 12 (2003): 227–28.

4. Ibid., 227.

5. Dorothy Rosenthal, "Images of Scientists: A Comparison of Biology and Liberal Studies Majors," *School Science and Mathematics* (Apr. 1993): 212–16.

6. Olga Pilkington, "Popular Science versus Lab Lit: Differently Depicting Scientific Apparatus." *Science as Culture* 26, no. 3 (2017): 285–306.

7. See, for example, David A. Kirby's *Lab Coats in Hollywood: Science, Scientists, and Cinema*. He writes, "Cinematic inaccuracies impact public perceptions of science. Cinematic science *can* play a crucial role in influencing public discourse about science" (112).

8. Cited in Gianpiero Petriglieri, "Business Does Not Need the Humanities—But Humans Do," *Harvard Business Review*, Nov. 2, 2018. Accessed Nov.8, 2018. https://hbr.org/2018/11/business-does-not-need-the-humanities-but-humans-do

9. Gianpiero Petriglieri, "Business Does Not Need the Humanities—But Humans Do."

10. "Comparative Media Studies/Writing," Massachusetts Institute of Technology, 2018. Accessed Nov. 2, 2018. https://cmsw.mit.edu/education/writing/.

11. "Science and Technology Studies Faculty," Brown University, 2018. Accessed Nov. 1, 2018. https://www.brown.edu/academics/science-and-technology-studies/faculty.

12. "Department of English," University of Notre Dame, 2018. Accessed Nov. 3, 2018. https://english.nd.edu/people/faculty/literature-and-science/; "Lance Wahlert/Department of English," Penn Arts & Sciences, 2018. Accessed Nov. 1, 2018. https://www.english.upenn.edu/

people/lance-wahlert; "Bethany Wiggin/Department of English." Penn Arts & Sciences, 2018. Accessed Nov. 1, 2018. https://www.english.upenn.edu/people/bethany-wiggin.

13. "Interdisciplinary Minor in Medicine, Literature, and Culture," Honors Carolina, The University of North Carolina at Chapel Hill, 2018. Accessed Nov. 4, 2018. http://honorscaroli na.unc.edu/academics/interdisciplinary-minor-in-medicine-literature-and-culture/.

14. "Felicia Florine Campbell," University of Nevada, Las Vegas, 2018. Accessed Nov. 2, 2018. https://www.unlv.edu/people/felicia-florine-campbell.

15. "Courses." Lyman Briggs College. Michigan State University. Accessed Nov. 3, 2018. https://www.lymanbriggs.msu.edu/current_students/courses.cfm.

16. "Lab Lit: Fact, Fiction, and the Narratives of Science," The Gallatin School of Individu-alized Study, New York University. Accessed Nov. 3, 2018. http://gallatin.nyu.edu/academics/courses/2016/SP/IDSEM-UG1769_001.html.

17. AmiJo Comeford, e-mail message to author. Nov. 6, 2018.

18. Pilkington, *Presented Discourse in Popular Science*, 4–11.

19. Benjamin Winterhalter, "The Morbid Fascination with the Death of the Humanities," *The Atlantic*, June 6, 2014, https://www.theatlantic.com/education/archive/2014/06/the-mor bid-fascination-with-the-death-of-the-humanities/372216/.

20. David S. Caudill, "Expertise, Lab Lit, and the Fantasy of Science Free from Econom-ics," *Cardozo Law Review* 33, no. 6 (2012), 2484–485.

21. Ibid., 2485.

22. Ibid., 2487.

23. Ibid., 2487–491.

24. See also Pilkington, *Presented Discourse in Popular Science*.

25. Eva Hayward, "Fingeryeyes: Impressions of Cup Corals," *Cultural Anthropology* 25, no. 4 (2010): 580.

26. Allegra Goodman, *Intuition* (New York: The Dial Press, 2006), 26.

27. Ibid., 23.

28. Hayward, "Fingeryeyes: Impressions of Cup Corals," 581.

29. Goodman, *Intuition*, 26.

30. Jennifer Rohn, *The Honest Look* (Cold Spring Harbor, NY: Cold Spring Harbor Labora-tory Press, 2010), 257–58.

31. Ibid., 271.

32. Olga Pilkington, "Popular Science as a Means of Emotional Engagement with the Scien-tific Community," *International Journal of Science Culture and Sport* 4, no. 1 (2016): 118–25 http://dx.doi.org/10.14486/IntJSCS466; Marco Caracciolo, "Phenomenological Metaphors in Readers' Engagement with Characters: The Case of Ian McEwan's *Saturday*," *Language and Literature* 22, no. 1 (2013): 60–76; Esther Laslo, Ayelet Baram-Tsabari, and Bruce V. Lewen-stein, "A Growth Medium for the Message: Online Science Journalism Affordances for Explor-ing Public Discourse of Science and Ethics," *Journalism* 12, no. 7 (2011): 847–70; María José Luzón, "Public Communication of Science in Blogs: Recontextualizing Scientific Discourse for a Diversified Audience," *Written Communication* 30, no. 4 (2013): 428–57; Sophie Moi-rand, "Communicative and Cognitive Dimensions of Discourse on Science in the French Mass Media," *Discourse Studies* 5, no. 2 (2003): 175–06; Alexandra Supper, "Sublime Frequencies: The Construction of Sublime Listening Experiences in the Sonification of Scientific Data," *Social Studies of Science* 44, no. 1 (2014): 34–58; Jon Turney, "The Abstract Sublime: Life as Information Waiting to Be Rewritten," *Science as Culture* 13, no. 1 (2004): 89–103.

33. Caracciolo, "Phenomenological Metaphors in Readers' Engagement with Characters: The Case of Ian McEwan's *Saturday*," 61.

34. Luzón, "Public Communication of Science in Blogs: Recontextualizing Scientific Dis-course for a Diversified Audience," 429.

BIBLIOGRAPHY

Barberousse, Anouk, and Pascal Ludwig. "Models as Fictions." In *Fictions in Science: Philosophical Essays on Modeling and Idealization*, edited by Mauricio Suárez. London: Routledge, 2009.

Barwich, Ann-Sophie. "Science and Fiction: Analysing the Concept in Science and Its Limits." *Journal for General Philosophy of Science* 44 (2013): 357–73.

"Bethany Wiggin/Department of English." Penn Arts & Sciences, 2018. Accessed Nov. 1, 2018. https://www.english.upenn.edu/people/bethany-wiggin.

Caracciolo, Marco. "Phenomenological Metaphors in Readers' Engagement with Characters: The Case of Ian McEwan's *Saturday*." *Language and Literature* 22, no.1 (2013): 60–76.

Caudill, David S. "Expertise, Lab Lit, and the Fantasy of Science Free from Economics." *Cardozo Law Review* 33, no. 6 (2012): 2471–497.

"Comparative Media Studies/Writing." Massachusetts Institute of Technology, 2018. Accessed Nov. 2, 2018. https://cmsw.mit.edu/education/writing/.

"Courses." Lyman Briggs College. Michigan State University. Accessed Nov. 3, 2018. https://www.lymanbriggs.msu.edu/current_students/courses.cfm.

"Department of English." University of Notre Dame, 2018. Accessed Nov. 3, 2018. https://english.nd.edu/people/faculty/literature-and-science/.

"Felicia Florine Campbell." University of Nevada, Las Vegas, 2018. Accessed Nov. 2, 2018. https://www.unlv.edu/people/felicia-florine-campbell.

Goodman, Allegra. *Intuition*. New York: The Dial Press, 2006.

Harré, Rom. "Some Narrative Conventions of Scientific Discourse." In *Narrative in Culture: The Uses of Storytelling in Sciences, Philosophy, and Literature*, edited by Christopher Nash. London: Routledge, 1994.

Hayward, Eva. "Fingeryeyes: Impressions of Cup Corals." *Cultural Anthropology* 25, no. 4 (2010): 577–99.

"Interdisciplinary Minor in Medicine, Literature, and Culture." Honors Carolina. The University of North Carolina at Chapel Hill, 2018. Accessed Nov. 4, 2018. http://honorscarolina.unc.edu/academics/interdisciplinary-minor-in-medicine-literature-and-culture/.

"Lab Lit: Fact, Fiction, and the Narratives of Science." The Gallatin School of Individualized Study. New York University. Accessed Nov. 3, 2018. http://gallatin.nyu.edu/academics/courses/2016/SP/IDSEM-UG1769_001.html.

"Lance Wahlert/Department of English." Penn Arts & Sciences, 2018. Accessed Nov. 1, 2018. https://www.english.upenn.edu/people/lance-wahlert.

Laslo, Esther, Ayelet Baram-Tsabari, and Bruce V. Lewenstein. "A Growth Medium for the Message: Online Science Journalism Affordances for Exploring Public Discourse of Science and Ethics." *Journalism* 12, no. 7 (2011): 847–70.

Luzón, María José. "Public Communication of Science in Blogs: Recontextualizing Scientific Discourse for a Diversified Audience." *Written Communication* 30, no. 4 (2013): 428–57.

Moirand, Sophie. "Communicative and Cognitive Dimensions of Discourse on Science in the French Mass Media." *Discourse Studies* 5, no. 2 (2003): 175–206.

Petriglieri, Gianpiero. "Business Does Not Need the Humanities—But Humans Do." *Harvard Business Review*, Nov. 2, 2018. Accessed Nov. 8, 2018. https://hbr.org/2018/11/business-does-not-need-the-humanities-but-humans-do.

Pilkington, Olga A. "Popular Science as a Means of Emotional Engagement with the Scientific Community." *International Journal of Science Culture and Sport* 4, no. 1 (2016): 118–25.

———. "Popular Science versus Lab Lit: Differently Depicting Scientific Apparatus." *Science as Culture* 26, no. 3 (2017): 285–306.

———. *Presented Discourse in Popular Science: Professional Voices in Books for Lay Audiences*. Leiden: Brill, 2018.

Reitsma, Femke. "Geoscience Explanations: Identifying What Is Needed for Generating Scientific Narratives from Data Models." *Environmental Modeling & Software* 25 (2010): 93–99.

Rohn, Jennifer. *The Honest Look*. Cold Spring Harbor, NY: Cold Spring Harbor Laboratory Press, 2010.

Rosenthal, Dorothy. "Images of Scientists: A Comparison of Biology and Liberal Studies Majors." *School Science and Mathematics* 93, no. 4 (Apr. 1993): 212–16.

Rouse, Joseph. "Laboratory Fictions." In *Fictions in Science*, edited by Mauricio Suárez. New York: Routledge, 2009.

"Science and Technology Studies Faculty." Brown University, 2018. Accessed Nov. 1, 2018. https://www.brown.edu/academics/science-and-technology-studies/faculty.

Suárez, Mauricio. "Fictions in Scientific Practice." In *Fictions in Science: Philosophical Essays on Modeling and Idealization*, edited by Mauricio Suárez. London: Routledge, 2009.

Supper, Alexandra. "Sublime Frequencies: The Construction of Sublime Listening Experiences in the Sonification of Scientific Data." *Social Studies of Science* 44, no. 1 (2014): 34–58.

Toon, Adam. *Models and Make-Believe: Imagination, Fiction and Scientific Representation*. New York: Palgrave Macmillan, 2012.

Turney, Jon. "The Abstract Sublime: Life as Information Waiting to Be Rewritten." *Science as Culture* 13, no. 1 (2004): 89–103.

Weingart, Peter, and Petra Pansegrau. "Introduction: Perception and Representation of Science in Literature and Fiction Film." *Public Understanding of Science* 12 (2003): 227–28.

Winterhalter, Benjamin. "The Morbid Fascination with the Death of the Humanities." *The Atlantic*, Jun. 6, 2014. Accessed Nov. 9, 2019. https://www.theatlantic.com/education/archive/2014/06/the-morbid-fascination-with-the-death-of-the-humanities/372216/.

Index

academic dishonesty, 69

Adams, Dr. Ruth (film chr.), 40

A.I. *See* artificial intelligence

Airtight Case: A Lindsay Chamberlain Novel , 207

alchemy. *See* chemistry

alien, 36, 37, 44, 52, 53, 57, 212, 220, 222

analogy, 82, 130, 201, 204. *See also* science, explanation of

anatomy, 17, 83, 84, 85

androgyny, 39. *See also* gender

The Andromeda Strain: film, 33, 34, 36, 37, 38, 39, 40, 41, 42, 44, 245; miniseries, 43; novel, 32, 33, 34, 36, 43, 56, 57, 245

Anson, Karen (film chr.), 36, 42

anthropology, 17, 100, 215; forensic, 198, 200; physical, 198

apparatus, 7, 8, 35, 83, 92, 93, 94, 126, 178, 204, 205, 221, 234, 247–248

archaeology, 198, 206, 207

artificial intelligence, 36

Asimov, Isaac, 14, 53–55

Bacon, Roger, 205

Banks, Dr. Louise (film chr.), 44

Barton, Dr. Charlene (film chr.), 43

Bates, Harry, 33

Baxter, John, 35

Benford, Gregory, 2–3, 55–56

Benson, Helen (film chr.), 37

biochemistry, 212, 241

biology, 22, 32, 40, 79, 85, 87, 88, 125, 127, 162, 177, 179, 211, 225, 246

The Black Hole , 43

Black Panther, 44

Bohr, Niels, 64

The Boric Acid Murder , 198, 204

Branton, Dr. Stephanie (film chr.), 40

Breaking the Code, 6

Brin, David, 6

Bryson, Bill, 65, 70, 71

Burroughs, Edgar Rice, 53

Byron, George Gordon , 13, 189

Byron, Ovid (chr.), 124, 125–126, 128, 130, 132

chaos, 19, 35, 93

chaos theory, 69

Chapel, Prof. Mabel (film chr.), 39

characterization, 7, 52, 56, 63, 66, 67, 68, 86, 90, 101, 178

chemistry, 83, 83–84, 85, 87, 198, 199, 241; alchemy, 20, 81, 83, 84, 85, 86, 205, 216

The Child in Time, 3

Christianity, 19, 105, 122, 200, 201, 203

cinema, 14, 30, 31, 33, 34, 35, 36, 37, 38, 39, 39–40, 41, 42, 43, 44, 216

Clarke, Arthur C., 53

climate change, 87, 113–114, 117, 122–125, 127–128, 132, 133, 216

A Clockwork Orange (film), 37
cofferdam, 206, 207
Cold War, 40
Colossus: The Forbin Project, 41
Coma : film, 43; novel, 43
Conan Doyle, Arthur, 30
Connor, Beverly, 55, 100
conversation, 23, 24, 25, 64, 65, 66, 67, 74,
    101, 152, 161, 178, 185, 198, 199, 234.
    See also dialogue
Crichton, Michael, 32, 34, 35, 36, 37, 38,
    42, 43, 57–58
crime, 17, 99, 101, 102, 103, 104, 105,
    105–106, 107, 108, 109, 202, 205, 206,
    244

The Day the Earth Stood Still , 33, 37. *See
    also* "Farewell to the Master"
*Dead Hunt: A Diane Fallon Forensic
    Investigation* , 200, 204
*Dead Secret: A Diane Fallon Forensic
    Investigation* , 205
Destination Moon, 31, 33
detective, 101, 104, 106, 198, 199, 213
deus ex machina , 35
dialogue, 63, 64, 65, 117, 187, 189, 197,
    199, 204, 207, 217. *See also*
    conversation
Djerassi, Carl, 2, 6, 7, 212, 213
DNA, 58, 179, 189, 200, 201, 202, 204,
    205, 245

Eco, Umberto, 205
ecocriticism, 114, 116, 117
ecofeminism, 114, 115, 117, 131, 132
ecological disaster, 55. *See also* climate
    change, environmental crisis
Einstein, Albert, 2, 52, 147, 155, 189, 229,
    241
electricity, 17, 18–19, 164
emotionality, 63, 156
environmental crisis (also index
    environmental apocalypse,
    apocalyptic), 2, 113–115. *See also* risk
epigenetics, 200

familiar science, 6
"Farewell to the Master", 33
Faust. *See* Faustus

Faust, Johann Georg, 20
Faustus, 20, 21, 23, 241
femininity, 40, 43, 105
feminism, vii, 37, 117, 151
fiction, vii, viii, 1, 1–2, 3, 4, 6, 7, 9, 10, 29,
    32, 42, 64, 67, 68, 71, 79–95, 80, 127,
    141–166, 177, 185, 197, 211, 213, 214,
    215, 217, 218, 218–238, 238, 241, 243,
    245; climate change fiction, 114;
    climate fiction, 114; historical, 51, 71,
    79, 80, 141, 143, 149, 165, 214. *See
    also* science fiction
fictionality, 9, 10, 67. *See also* thought
    experiment
fictionalization, 2, 213
film. *See* cinema
Fludernik, Monika, 9, 10, 67
forensics, 31, 32, 35, 99–111, 198, 200,
    205, 206, 244
Frankenstein Complex, 14
*Frankenstein; or, The Modern
    Prometheus*, 3, 4, 13, 14–16, 17, 18, 19,
    20, 21, 22, 23, 23–25, 30, 33, 34, 53,
    56, 79, 85, 87, 100, 115, 241, 245. *See
    also* Shelley, Mary
Frankenstein, Victor, 4, 13, 16, 16–17, 19,
    20, 20–21, 21, 23, 84–85, 86, 241
Frankenstein's monster, 13, 14, 16, 17, 19,
    23, 24, 24–25, 54, 79
fraud, 7, 69, 128; See also academic
    dishonesty

Gaines, Susan, 4, 8, 247
Galvani, Luigi, 18
gender, vii, 37, 38, 40, 41, 42, 70, 105,
    113, 117, 120, 121, 122, 132, 151, 185,
    186, 187, 187–188, 192, 193, 216, 242,
    244. *See also* femininity; feminism;
    male fantasy; scientist
genetically modified organisms, 24, 127
genius, 5, 44, 70, 71, 73
geology, 242
Gidding, Nelson, 33, 36, 37, 39, 42
Goodman, Allegra, 6–7, 64, 65, 69, 214,
    247, 248
graphic novel, 246
Greene, Brian, 7, 52

Harkup, Kathryn, 16, 17, 18

Hawking, Stephen, 52, 241, 246
Hendron, Joyce (film chr.), 39
Higgs, Peter, 64
Hollywood, 33, 41, 216, 217, 242
Holmes, Sherlock, 30, 32
Honest Look, The , 4, 8, 69, 71, 175–183, 203, 204, 245, 247, 248
Horner, Jack, 58
The Hound of the Baskervilles , 30
human error, 69. *See also* fraud
humor (as characterization device), 10, 65
Huxley, T.H., 5–6, 87, 88, 147

iDream , 185–193
Individual Differences Theory of Gender and IT, 186
information technology, 189, 190, 193
innovation, 23, 36, 51, 83, 99, 143, 148
interdisciplinary programs, 243–244, 244, 246
invention, 36, 55, 84, 85
The IPCRESS File ,: film, 34; novel, 32, 34

Jameson, Frederic, 87–88, 93, 94
jeopardy, 34, 35, 36
Joyce, Prof. Lesley (film chr.), 40
Jurassic Park , 57–59, 245

Kaku, Michio, 52, 68, 73
Kepler, Johannes, 31
Kipling, Elsie, 29, 44
Kipling, Rudyard, 29
knowledge, 4, 5–6, 10, 16, 17, 22, 38, 41, 58, 67, 68, 70, 73, 74, 80, 84, 90, 91, 92, 102, 114, 117, 126, 128, 129, 131, 132, 159, 165, 175, 182, 192, 197, 198, 199, 204, 214, 216, 217, 218, 224, 234, 242, 245, 249
Kohler, Robert, 88–89

laboratory activities, 4, 7, 16, 33, 66, 81, 88, 92, 93, 125, 144, 157, 179, 181, 216, 217, 225, 235, 242, 247. *See also* apparatus, laboratory animals
laboratory animals, 7, 8, 33, 36, 66, 68, 238, 246–248
Latour, Bruno, 22, 80, 89, 92–93
law and literature movement, 246; and lab lit, 246

Le Guin, Ursula K., 51

Leavitt, Dr. Ruth (film chr.), 37–38, 39, 40, 41, 42, 44
Leavitt, Prof. Peter (film chr.), 37, 38, 39
Lenoir, Timothy, 93
life sciences, 40, 85, 87
Lightman, Alan, 2, 5
literary studies, vii
literature, vii, viii, 1, 4, 5, 9, 14, 15, 16, 31, 33, 35, 39, 41, 43, 52, 68, 72, 73, 80, 84, 88, 91, 93, 95, 114, 177, 211, 212, 241, 243, 244, 245, 249, 249–250. *See also* law and literature movement, science and literature
logic, 4–5, 10, 35, 36, 43, 80, 103, 179, 182, 205
Lohr, Steve, 200

mad scientist, 14, 23, 69, 70
male fantasy, 37
Markham, Dr. Cleo (film chr.), 41
Marvell, Andrew, 51
mass media, 123, 124, 129
McCrae, Dr. Kate (film chr.), 43
McEwan, Ian, 3, 4, 6, 214, 249
metaphysics. *See* physics
methodology, 9, 18, 19, 22, 29, 30–31, 31, 32, 36, 40, 43, 44, 56, 58, 67, 69, 93, 99, 100, 104, 105–106, 110, 115, 126, 148, 156, 197, 205, 206, 218, 220, 228, 234, 245; The Bertillon method, 100, 107
military-industrial complex, 40
Minichino, Camille, 198
monster. *See* Frankenstein's monster
mystery (literary genre), 52, 197–208. *See also* fiction

The Name of the Rose, 205
narrative, 3, 15, 17, 22, 23, 24, 32, 34, 37, 40, 63, 68, 69, 87, 114–115, 115–119, 123, 125, 126, 127, 130, 132, 142, 143, 178, 199, 201, 204, 212, 214–215, 218, 220, 237, 241, 246
New Scientist , 63
The New York Times , 2, 58, 200, 214
Newton, Isaac, 51–52, 70
Nicholson, Nikki (film chr.), 41

Nobel Prize, 38, 83
Noyce, Dr. Angela (film chr.), 43

Oak Ridge National Laboratory (ORNL), 199
Oberth, Herman, 31
optography, 107

paganism, 19
paleobotany, 57
paleontology, 57, 58, 152, 165
pathogen, 32, 34, 35, 36, 42, 44, 238
pathology, 38, 85; psychopathology, 106
physics, 3–4, 40, 52, 55, 68, 73, 84, 85, 89, 243; metaphysics, 83, 91, 156
plot, 6, 33, 36, 43, 187, 189, 197, 200, 204, 206, 207, 212, 245; plot point, 197, 198
Pope, Alexander, 51
presented discourse, 63; presentation of speech, 63, 63–64, 65, 66; presentation of thought, 67, 199, 203
process porn, 36, 43, 44
Prometheus, 20–21
Proust, Marcel, 73
psychology, 30, 31, 40, 44, 86, 99, 100, 102–103, 106, 116, 158, 244, 249

Ripley, Lt. Ellen (film chr.), 43
risk, 25, 216, 227; environmental risk, 113–115, 116–117, 124
robot, 14, 54–55, 188, 189, 190, 218, 234
Rohn, Jennifer L., vii, viii, 2, 3, 4–5, 6, 8, 32, 52, 66, 69, 70, 71, 73, 175–183, 203, 204

Science: access to, 241, 242–245, 249; communication of, 6, 9, 14, 15–16, 18, 22–23, 24, 25, 35, 39, 51, 52, 56, 69, 73–74, 85, 114, 115, 116, 119, 123–124, 128, 129–130, 132, 192, 214–215, 217, 238; economics of, 175, 176, 249; explanation of, 3, 4, 6, 7, 18, 32, 54, 58, 68, 99, 100, 115, 125, 128, 175, 189, 190, 198, 198–199, 201, 202, 203–204, 207; and literature, vii, viii, 1, 1–2, 3, 4, 5, 9, 10, 15, 16, 20, 30, 35, 43, 51, 58, 71, 72, 72–73, 80, 85, 91, 94, 114, 141, 178, 181, 193, 197, 204, 212, 213, 241; philosophy of, 9, 10, 83,
88, 92; popular, viii, 1, 6, 7, 8, 19, 31, 52, 63–74, 131, 153, 156, 217, 241, 242; professional, 5, 6, 9, 15, 19, 20, 21, 30, 51, 53, 58, 69, 70, 79, 82, 83, 85, 88, 116, 125, 126, 143; promotion of, 10, 68, 69, 73; sociology of, 142, 145, 146, 148, 165–166, 241; studies, 93. *See also* science, communication of; science, economics of; science and literature; science, philosophy of
science fiction, vii, 1, 2–3, 3, 4, 5, 6, 9, 14, 15, 18, 24, 29, 30, 31, 33, 34, 35, 36, 37, 38, 39, 40, 42, 43, 44, 51–59, 197, 198, 212, 213, 214, 216, 245, 246, 249; definition of, 1; hard science fiction, 2
Science Fiction and Futurism: Their Terms and Ideas, 3, 54
Scientific American, 63
scientific career, 39, 143–146, 147, 151, 154, 155, 158, 160, 186, 187, 190, 191, 192, 193, 215, 218, 227, 235, 242, 246
scientific community, 3, 6, 8, 52, 63, 65, 66, 68, 69, 71, 73, 74, 116, 143, 145, 147, 149, 151, 156, 175, 179, 180, 191, 192
scientific equipment. *See* apparatus
scientific experiments. *See* laboratory activity
scientific method. *See* methodology
scientific realism, 15, 115, 116. *See also* process porn
scientific research. *See* biology; chemistry; forensics; innovation; invention; life sciences; methodology; pathology; physics; process porn; psychology; scientific career; scientist
scientific writing, 74, 92, 185
scientism, 22, 23, 25
scientist: female, 29, 36, 37, 39, 40, 41, 42–43, 44, 151, 153, 154, 177, 180, 186, 189, 191, 192; male, 32, 179, 216
The Screaming Shadow , 41
setting, 2, 3, 70, 82, 86, 104, 119, 122, 141, 145, 149, 175, 197, 205, 206, 207, 214, 245
Sheffield, Charles, 1, 3, 5, 52, 53
Shelley, Mary, 3, 4, 13, 14, 14–16, 17, 18, 19, 20, 21–23, 23, 24, 25, 30, 31, 34, 79, 80, 84, 85, 86, 90, 100, 245. *See*

also Frankenstein's monster.
*Frankenstein; or, the Modern
Prometheus*. Frankenstein, Victor
Sherlock, 30
Shuri (film chr.), 44
*Skeleton Crew: A Lindsay Chamberlain
Novel* , 206
social media, 114, 116, 124, 130
social sciences, vii, 89
social systems, 91, 101, 105, 110
Somnium, Sive Astronomia Lunaris , 31
STEM, 185–186, 188, 189, 192, 242
Stevenson, Robert Louis, 40
Stone, Dr. Ryan (film chr.), 44
story, viii, 1, 4, 6, 13, 17, 30, 31, 32, 33,
    34, 36, 38, 40, 44, 53, 55, 56, 58, 67,
    68, 73, 79, 108, 114, 115, 116, 117,
    123, 124, 125, 128, 130–131, 132, 141,
    145, 146, 147–148, 149, 151, 152, 154,
    155, 156, 157, 158, 159, 160–161, 161,
    185, 189, 190, 192, 193, 197, 198, 199,
    201, 204, 205, 207, 211, 215, 217, 218,
    238, 243, 245, 249; storyworld, 249
*The Strange Case of Dr. Jekyll and Mr.
Hyde* , 40

technothriller, 34, 56–57, 58, 59, 245
terminology, 3, 5, 14, 22, 32, 56, 66, 81,
    99, 103, 156, 197, 213
theatre, 185–186, 187, 189–192, 192–193

thought experiment, 241, 247. *See also*
    fictionality
time, theories of, 3–4
Tolstoy, Lev, 72, 73
Turnbow, Dellarobia (chr.), 119–126, 127,
    130–132
Tuttle, Lisa, 39
Tyson, Neil deGrasse, 52

utopia, 87–88, 90, 91, 93, 94, 95. *See also*
    Jameson, Frederic
urbanism, 99, 110, 121, 122

Vaihinger, Hans, 9
van Horn, Dr. Lisa (film chr.), 39
vitalism, 19, 85
Voltaire, 51

War of the Worlds, 35
Wells, H.G., 3, 15, 31, 35, 87, 90
Whale, James, 30, 31, 40, 79
Wheeler, Dr. Susan (film chr.), 43
Whitemore, Hugh, 6
Wise, Robert, 33, 42

Zira, Dr. (film chr.), 37, 40
zoology, 40, 127

About the Contributors

Stephanie Chidester is a nursing PhD student at the University of Missouri-St. Louis. She has undergraduate degrees in English, biology, and nursing. She worked as a laboratory technician and specialist in a cancer research laboratory for seven years before pursuing a career in nursing.

Beverly Connor is the author of the Diane Fallon Forensic Investigation series and the Lindsay Chamberlain Archaeology Mystery series, and with her husband Charles, the Frank Hayes Mysteries. Before she began her writing career, Beverly Connor worked in the Southeastern United States as an archaeologist doing both fieldwork and analyzing artifacts, particularly lithic debitage, pollen analysis, and analysis of animal bones. She specialized in Southeastern Indians of the Mississippian period: AD 900–1700. She holds degrees in anthropology, sociology, geology, and archaeology.

Dean Conrad is an English writer, producer, and teacher. He was first published in 1996 with a book on *Star Wars*, which made some contribution to his 1998 PhD thesis on the representation of women in science fiction film. Since then, Dean has lectured, presented, and published on many aspects of the performing arts, including guest-editing two issues of the Texas A&M University journal *Post Script*, exploring cinema exhibition, and distribution. His latest book, *Space Sirens, Scientists and Princesses*—a history of female roles through thirteen decades of science fiction cinema—was published in 2018. He is now working with American and British production companies on drama and documentary projects for large and small screens.

Matt Hadley is lecturer at the University of Minnesota in the department of Cultural Studies and Comparative Literature, where he teaches classes on literature, gender and sexuality, and popular culture. His dissertation, "Laboratory Literature: Science and Fiction in the Place of Production," dealt with the representation of the scientific laboratory in literature as a unique occasion to question the processes and implications of both literary and scientific labor.

Kimberley H. Idol, PhD, is a writer and instructor. Her short stories have been published in *Danse Macabre*, *Portland Review*, *Toasted Cheese*, *Dead Neon*, and *Helen: A Literary Journal*. She has published articles on interdisciplinary topics, on engineering and systems theory and comparative literature and epic text analyses. She is currently at work on a collection of essays on Chaos Theory and Detective Fiction and on a detective novel.

Lynne Magowan is originally from Glasgow, Scotland. She has taught theory and practice across a range of cultural studies, film, and media subjects, in schools, colleges and universities in the United Kingdom and overseas. She is a moderator and assessment writer for British A-Level examination boards and is also involved in the development of new textbooks. Her most recent published collaboration with Dean Conrad was their chapter on *Planet of the Apes* in *The Fantastic Made Visible: Essays on the Adaptation of Science Fiction and Fantasy from Page to Screen*. Lynne is currently working with Dean Conrad to develop television projects with a focus on women in science fiction cinema.

Elaine Pearce is an educator who attended Oxford University, where she studied Shakespeare. She has an M.Ed. from Utah State University and an MA in literature from Middlebury College in Vermont. She is a regular contributor to *Midsummer Magazine* and bard.org—the official publications of the Utah Shakespeare Festival.

Jennifer L. Rohn received a BA in biology from Oberlin College and a PhD in microbiology from the University of Washington, Seattle. She currently leads a research team in the Division of Medicine at University College London, studying the subversive behavior of bacterial infections. She is a part-time science writer and journalist, broadcaster, and sci-lit-art pundit. Her writing has appeared in many places, including the *Guardian*, the *Telegraph*, the *Times*, BBC News, *Nature*, and *The Scientist*, and she also appears frequently on TV, radio, in podcasts, and as an expert in science films. Her short fiction has been published in *Nature*, The Human Genre Project, and in the Springer anthology entitled *Science Fiction by Scientists*. She blogs about the scientific life at Mind The Gap and at Occam's Corner on the *Guardian*. She is also founder of Science Is Vital and a Visiting Fellow at the University of Oxford.

Amanda Scott holds a PhD from University of Nevada, Las Vegas, where she studied nineteenth-century women's literature. Her research interests include the Brontë sisters, visual theory, and pedagogy. She is a visiting assistant professor of English at Dixie State University.

Eileen Trauth is professor of information sciences and technology, and women's, gender, and sexuality studies at the Pennsylvania State University. Her focus is on the intersectionality of gender and ethnicity, class, sexuality, nationality, and disability status. She has served in numerous editorial roles, including editor-in-chief of *Information Systems Journal* and editor of the *Encyclopedia of Gender and Information Technology*. She is the recipient of two Fulbright Awards and has served on the advisory boards for European Union gender projects. With funding from the National Science Foundation, she has written a play, *iDream*, based on over two-hundred life history interviews with women working in the information technology field, in order to increase awareness about gender barriers in the scientific and technological professions.

Suzanne Trauth is a playwright, novelist, and screenwriter. Her plays include *Françoise*, *Midwives, Rehearsing Desire*, *iDream*, and *Katrina: The K Word*. Her screenplays *Solitaire* and *Boomer Broads* have won awards at the Austin Film Festival, among other contests, and she wrote and directed the short film *Jigsaw*. She is a member of Writers Theatre of New Jersey Emerging Women Playwrights program. Ms. Trauth has coauthored *Sonia Moore and American Acting Training* and coedited *Katrina on Stage: Five Plays*. Her novels include *Show Time* and *Time Out*. She is a member of the Dramatists Guild and Mystery Writers of America.

Theda Wrede is professor of English at Dixie State University in Utah. Her books include *Myth and Environment in Recent Southwestern Literature: Healing Narratives*, published in 2014, and *The Way We Read James Dickey*, published in 2009. In 2015, she served as the guest editor of a special-topics issue on space and gender of the *Rocky Mountain Review*. Her essays and reviews have appeared in *Feminist Ecocriticism, Color, Hair and Bone, Journal of Contemporary Thought, Rocky Mountain Review*, and *South Atlantic Review*.

About the Editors

Olga A. Pilkington holds a PhD in applied linguistics from the University of Birmingham, United Kingdom. She is assistant professor of English at Dixie State University and is the author of *Presented Discourse in Popular Science: Professional Voices in Books for Lay Audiences* (Brill, 2017) and *The Language of Popular Science* (McFarland, 2019). With her late husband, Ace, she is coeditor and cotranslator of *Fairy Tales of the Russians and Other Slavs*.

The late **Ace G. Pilkington** published over one hundred poems, articles, reviews, and short stories in five countries. He is the author of *Screening Shakespeare from Richard II to Henry V* (2017) and, more recently, *Science Fiction and Futurism: Their Terms and Ideas* and *Our Lady Guenevere* (2017). He is coeditor of *The Fantastic Made Visible* and *The Kelvin Timeline of* Star Trek. A member of the SFWA, he was a professor of English and history at Dixie State University and Literary Seminar director at the Utah Shakespeare Festival. He had a PhD in Shakespeare, history, and film from Oxford University.